CW01303706

'This is a sophisticated overview of urbanity in the southern Low Countries from the central Middle Ages into the early modern period, a time of extraordinary economic, political and cultural achievements. Written by experts and supported by up-to-date bibliographies, the chapters explain the creativity of these cities and describe their legacy in Europe thereafter.'

Martha Howell, *Columbia University*

'This is a multi-faceted, *longue durée* account of the rise of the urban system of the Low Countries up to the Dutch Revolt, which demonstrates how distinctive it was in European terms – decentralised, dominated not by urban elites but by middle-rank groups and institutions. Written by an all-star team of Belgian scholars, drawing on massive recent research, this book will be essential reading for urban historians and medievalists.'

Peter Clark, *University of Helsinki*

'The Low Countries developed the most dynamic urban network in medieval northern Europe. This comprehensive and lively volume, itself the product of collaborative research undertaken at universities in the Low Countries, provides a fine introduction to this age of achievement and conflict in economic, social, political, intellectual, artistic and religious affairs.'

Derek Keene, *Institute for Historical Research, University of London*

'These essays show how Europe's most densely populated region developed its most dynamically networked urban societies. Leading experts present the urban spaces of the Low Countries as living and lived in, emphasising social groups, material culture, and the complex unfolding of vibrant languages of rituals, spaces and senses over time.'

Nicholas Terpstra, *University of Toronto*

'*City and Society in the Low Countries, 1100–1600* is the product of planning, knowledge and cooperation, just like the urban communities it so effectively explores. It offers an integrated historical analysis of urban life in its many forms, from migration to town planning, social relations to religious lives. In a region where transport was easy, and the drive towards dynamic innovation strong, the foundations for northwest Europe's hegemony – in the Golden Age, but also in contemporary European life – were laid.'

Miri Rubin, *Queen Mary University of London*

'This excellent book combines results from the latest research into a convincing picture of the urban societies in the Low Countries, at a time when these were the northern counterpart of Renaissance Italy. A must-read survey for everyone interested in medieval and early modern European history.'

Maarten Prak, *Utrecht University*

City and Society in the Low Countries, 1100–1600

The Low Countries were collectively one of the earliest and most heavily urbanised societies in European history. Present-day Belgium and the Netherlands still share important common features, such as comparatively low income inequalities, high levels of per capita income, a balanced political structure and a strong 'civil society'. This book traces the origins of this specific social model in medieval patterns of urbanisation, while also searching for explanations for the historical reproduction of social inequalities. Access to cheap inland river navigation and to the sea generated a 'river delta' urbanisation that explains the persistence of a decentralised urban economic network, marked by intensive cooperation and competition and by the absence of real metropolises. Internally as well, powerful checks and balances prevented money and power from being concentrated. Ultimately, however, the most defining characteristic of the Low Countries' urban cultures was located in their resilient middle classes.

BRUNO BLONDÉ is affiliated to the Centre for Urban History and the Urban Studies Institute at the University of Antwerp. He publishes on the history of urban networks in the Low Countries, pre-industrial transport, the history of consumption and material culture, retail trade, urban growth and social inequality.

MARC BOONE teaches medieval history at Ghent University. At the moment, his research is oriented primarily towards financial urban history, the social and political history of towns in the late medieval Low Countries and Burgundian history.

ANNE-LAURE VAN BRUAENE teaches cultural history of the early modern era at Ghent University. Her research is oriented towards urban culture in the late medieval and early modern Low Countries, especially the Reformation and the Dutch Revolt, guilds and confraternities, as well as the social context of art, literature and religion.

City and Society in the Low Countries, 1100–1600

Edited by

Bruno Blondé
University of Antwerp

Marc Boone
Ghent University

Anne-Laure Van Bruaene
Ghent University

CAMBRIDGE
UNIVERSITY PRESS

CAMBRIDGE
UNIVERSITY PRESS

University Printing House, Cambridge CB2 8BS, United Kingdom

One Liberty Plaza, 20th Floor, New York, NY 10006, USA

477 Williamstown Road, Port Melbourne, VIC 3207, Australia

314–321, 3rd Floor, Plot 3, Splendor Forum, Jasola District Centre, New Delhi – 110025, India

79 Anson Road, #06-04/06, Singapore 079906

Cambridge University Press is part of the University of Cambridge.

It furthers the University's mission by disseminating knowledge in the pursuit of education, learning and research at the highest international levels of excellence.

www.cambridge.org
Information on this title: www.cambridge.org/9781108474689
DOI: 10.1017/9781108645454

Originally published in Dutch by Academia Press 2016
as *Gouden eeuwen: Stad en samenleving in de Lage Landen, 1100–1600*

This publication is in copyright. Subject to statutory exception and to the provisions of relevant collective licensing agreements, no reproduction of any part may take place without the written permission of Cambridge University Press.

First published in English by Cambridge University Press 2018
as *City and Society in the Low Countries, 1100–1600*

English translation © Cambridge University Press 2018

Printed in the United Kingdom by TJ International Ltd. Padstow Cornwall

A catalogue record for this publication is available from the British Library.

ISBN 978-1-108-47468-9 Hardback

Cambridge University Press has no responsibility for the persistence or accuracy of URLs for external or third-party internet websites referred to in this publication and does not guarantee that any content on such websites is, or will remain, accurate or appropriate.

In honour of Walter Prevenier and
Raymond Van Uytven, inspiring urban historians

Contents

List of Figures		*page* xi
List of Contributors		xiii
Acknowledgements		xvii

1 City and Society in the Low Countries: Urbanisation and Urban Historiography   1
BRUNO BLONDÉ, MARC BOONE AND
ANNE-LAURE VAN BRUAENE

2 Economic Vitality: Urbanisation, Regional Complementarity and European Interaction   22
WIM BLOCKMANS, BERT DE MUNCK AND
PETER STABEL

3 Living Together in the City: Social Relationships Between Norm and Practice   59
BRUNO BLONDÉ, FREDERIK BUYLAERT,
JAN DUMOLYN, JORD HANUS AND PETER STABEL

4 'The Common Good': Governance, Discipline and Political Culture   93
MARC BOONE AND JELLE HAEMERS

5 Civic Religion: Community, Identity and Religious Transformation   128
GUIDO MARNEF AND ANNE-LAURE VAN BRUAENE

6 Urban Space: Infrastructure, Technology and Power   162
CLAIRE BILLEN AND CHLOÉ DELIGNE

7 At Home in the City: The Dynamics of Material Culture   192
INNEKE BAATSEN, BRUNO BLONDÉ,
JULIE DE GROOT AND ISIS STURTEWAGEN

8	Education and Knowledge: Theory and Practice in an Urban Context BERT DE MUNCK AND HILDE DE RIDDER-SYMOENS	220
9	Epilogue: The Legacy of the Medieval City in the Low Countries BRUNO BLONDÉ, MARC BOONE AND ANNE-LAURE VAN BRUAENE	255
	Select Bibliography	265
	Index	285

Figures

1.1 Printed map of the Low Countries, 1557.
© Royal Library of Belgium, Maps and Plans *page* 2
1.2 Principalities in the Low Countries. Map by I. Jongepier.
© GIStorical Antwerp – University of Antwerp/
Herculesstichting, redrawn by Hans Blomme,
Ghent University 8
2.1 *The Cloth Market of 's-Hertogenbosch, c. 1525*.
© Noordbrabants Museum, 's-Hertogenbosch 23
2.2 Urban centres in the fifteenth century. Data collected
by Peter Stabel, redrawn by Hans Blomme 25
3.1 Pieter van der Heyden, *Big Fish Eat Little Fish*,
print after a design by Pieter Bruegel the Elder, 1556.
© Rijksmuseum, Amsterdam 60
4.1 Miniature from Jean Mansel, *La Fleur des histoires*,
Tournai/Arras/Saint-Omer, *c.* 1455. © Royal Library
of Belgium, Manuscripts 94
4.2 Introduction of the annual renewal of magistrates.
Based on Raymond Van Uytven, 'Het stedelijke leven,
12de–14de eeuw', *Algemene Geschiedenis der Nederlanden,
Deel II* (Haarlem: Fibula-Van Dishoeck, 1982), pp. 227–8,
redrawn by Hans Blomme and supplemented by
Jelle Haemers 108
5.1 *Spinola Hours*, Ghent/Bruges, *c.* 1510–1520. © Digital
image courtesy of the Getty's Open Content Program 129
5.2 Dioceses before 1559. Based on *Het Aartsbisdom
Mechelen-Brussel: 450 Jaar Geschiedenis*, Deel I: 'Het
aartsbisdom Mechelen van de katholieke herleving
tot de revolutietijd 1559–1802' (Antwerp: Halewijn,
2009), p. 16, redrawn by Hans Blomme 133
5.3 Dioceses after 1559. Based on *Het Aartsbisdom
Mechelen-Brussel: 450 Jaar Geschiedenis*, Deel I: 'Het
aartsbisdom Mechelen van de katholieke herleving tot

	de revolutietijd 1559–1802' (Antwerp: Halewijn, 2009), p. 66, redrawn by Hans Blomme	134
6.1	Central portion of a map of the river Scheldt in Tournai, 1622. © State Archives of Belgium	163
7.1	Workshop of Robert Campin, *Annunciation Triptych*, c. 1427–1437 (central panel). © The Met Cloisters, New York/Creative Commons	193
8.1	Woodcut from the Antwerp guild of Saint Luke, first half of the sixteenth century. © Rijksmuseum, Amsterdam	221
8.2	Printing centres in the fifteenth century. Data collected by Hilde de Ridder-Symoens on the basis of available printers' catalogues, redrawn by Hans Blomme	235
8.3	Printing centres in the sixteenth century. Data collected by Hilde de Ridder-Symoens on the basis of available printers' catalogues, redrawn by Hans Blomme	236
9.1	Dirck Jacobsz, *Group Portrait of the Guild of the 'Kloveniers'*, 1529/1559. © Rijksmuseum, Amsterdam	256

Contributors

INNEKE BAATSEN is currently a research coordinator at the Urban Studies Institute of the University of Antwerp. She started as a researcher, funded by the FWO/Research Foundation-Flanders. She has written a dissertation on food culture in Bruges during the long sixteenth century.

CLAIRE BILLEN is emeritus professor of medieval history at the Université Libre de Bruxelles. She focuses on the layout of towns and their spatial development in connection with their political and social history.

WIM BLOCKMANS is emeritus professor of medieval history at Leiden University. He publishes on the legal rights of burghers and the relationship between towns and states, both in the Low Countries and from an international perspective.

BRUNO BLONDÉ teaches early modern social and economic history at the University of Antwerp. He publishes on urban networks, pre-industrial transport, the history of material culture, retail trade and consumption, urban growth and social inequality.

MARC BOONE teaches medieval history at Ghent University. His research is oriented towards financial urban history, the social and political history of towns in the late medieval Low Countries and Burgundian history.

FREDERIK BUYLAERT teaches medieval and early modern urban history at Ghent University. His research is oriented towards the study of elite formation, the interactions between town and country and the impact of state formation.

JULIE DE GROOT was a researcher at the University of Antwerp, funded by the FWO/Research Foundation-Flanders. She finished a dissertation on the meaning and use of private domestic space in towns in the southern Netherlands during the long sixteenth century.

CHLOÉ DELIGNE teaches medieval history, urban history and environmental history at the Université Libre de Bruxelles. Her research is oriented towards the interaction between urbanisation and environmental conditions, on the one hand, and towards the social and symbolic aspects of urban spaces, on the other hand.

BERT DE MUNCK teaches early modern social and economic history at the University of Antwerp. His research is oriented towards the history of labour, poor relief and migration, the circulation of technical knowledge, citizenship and municipal governance, and conceptual approaches to urban history.

HILDE DE RIDDER-SYMOENS is emeritus professor of medieval history at the Vrije Universiteit (VU) Amsterdam and of early modern history at Ghent University. She publishes on the history of education and of universities, student mobility and the professionalisation of society in the late Middle Ages and early modern era.

JAN DUMOLYN teaches medieval history at Ghent University. He publishes on the social, political and cultural history of late medieval urban society, in particular on revolts and social protest.

JELLE HAEMERS teaches medieval political and social history at KU Leuven. His research is oriented towards the history of the Burgundian Netherlands and, in particular, political conflicts and social oppositions in the late medieval town.

JORD HANUS is a research administrator at the University of Antwerp. He has written a dissertation on economic growth and inequality in the early modern Low Countries, in particular in the Brabantine town of 's-Hertogenbosch.

GUIDO MARNEF teaches early modern cultural and religious history at the University of Antwerp. His research focuses on the Protestant Reformation, the Dutch Revolt, the Catholic Reformation and the role of cultural agents like the printing press, rhetoricians and education.

PETER STABEL teaches medieval history at the University of Antwerp. He publishes on market organisation, artisans' guilds, labour markets, gender, migration and standards of living both in Western Europe and in the Islamic world.

ISIS STURTEWAGEN was a researcher at the University of Antwerp. She has written a dissertation on the consumption of fashion and clothing in the Low Countries during the fifteenth and sixteenth centuries.

ANNE-LAURE VAN BRUAENE teaches early modern cultural history at Ghent University. Her research is oriented towards urban culture in the Low Countries, in particular the social and political contexts of art, literature and religion.

Acknowledgements

The editors wish to thank Sabine Van Sprang (Koninklijke Musea voor Schone Kunsten van België) and Ann Kelders (Koninklijke Bibliotheek van België) for their contributions to editing the images; Tim De Doncker (Ghent University) for his assistance in editing the text; Hans Blomme (Ghent University) for drawing the charts and maps; and Wieland Claes and Charris De Smet for making the index. John Eyck and Kate Elliott took care of the translation and language editing of the original Dutch manuscript.

1 City and Society in the Low Countries: Urbanisation and Urban Historiography

Bruno Blondé, Marc Boone and Anne-Laure Van Bruaene

Ever since the eleventh century, no other characteristic has been as typical of the Low Countries as the size of their urban network. Around the middle of the fifteenth century, the first point at which more or less consistent statistics became available, approximately one in three inhabitants of the Low Countries reportedly lived somewhere in a (small) town. Impressive as it is for an agricultural economy, this urbanisation gains even more in significance when regional differences are taken into account. In the county of Flanders well-nigh 36 per cent of the inhabitants lived in an urban environment. In Holland, Overijssel and even Guelders to a lesser degree, that figure was higher than 40 per cent, amounting to almost half the population. Conversely, in heavily wooded Luxembourg only 15 per cent of the population lived somewhere within town walls. After northern and central Italy, the Low Countries – even the least urbanised regions in them – ranked at the top of urban Europe, according to European standards. The Low Countries, therefore, can rightly be called a country of cities and towns. Unlike in the twentieth century, when European historical towns had to battle the centrifugal forces of suburbanisation and urban decline, the town in the late medieval and early modern Low Countries was still the most dynamic, if not the ultimate, force in society.

It is not surprising, then, that successive generations of historians have been fascinated by the phenomenon of the city in this region. In addition to purely academic work on this topic, countless books have been dedicated to the more general public. Narrating the history of one specific town, the genre of the 'town biography' was and remains very popular. Frequently it is a town with which writers and readers can immediately identify, and the publication itself contributes somehow towards enhancing that town's urban identity. For many the ties with their own town and its many *lieux de mémoire* were and are more concrete than those with any principality, province or country. The urban world experienced from day to day is, after all, more tangible than that of more abstract and distant territorial connections. The walls that enclosed urban society,

Figure 1.1 This recently discovered fragment is the earliest known printed topographical map of the Low Countries. The south-east is at the top. The map extends from approximately Calais to Trier in the south and from Vlieland to Marburg in the north. The towns are depicted as densely built-up areas in the landscape. The major rivers (Rhine, Maas, Scheldt) are quite prominent, forming a delta that empties into the North Sea at the bottom. The map was printed by Herman van Borculo in Utrecht in 1557. Its cartouche is in Latin to give the map scholarly cachet, but the names of the towns are all in Dutch.

its gates that drew a clear boundary between citizens and outsiders, the towers that made its self-awareness visible from a great distance – all these structures set in stone the differences in the *modi vivendi* between burghers and rural inhabitants. In addition, cities also do much today to highlight what is special about their own identity. Cultural strategies of 'city marketing' and 'city branding' serve as economic levers for municipal authorities in their attempts to put their towns on the map and on the market. Much can be said for the idea that the recent narrative summaries of the history of individual towns also contribute to that urban identity, even when they harbour the express intention of critically dealing with the past.

Whatever the case may be, histories of towns and paeans to specific towns were already being written in the Middle Ages, as well as during the early modern era. When history subsequently became a discipline with more pronounced scholarly ambitions over the course of the nineteenth century, this development had consequences for the way in which a town's past was seen. In the aftermath of the French Revolution and the Napoleonic Wars, new states came into being, each of which felt the need to legitimise its existence historically with source editions and 'national' histories. Dusting off and polishing up their own pasts also implied that, along with the past of their own nation, region or principality, the history of the town was rediscovered. In the southern part of the United Kingdom of the Netherlands (1815–30) – which became the Kingdom of Belgium from 1830 – the illustrious medieval past was put into service as the subject of novels, paeans, stage plays and operas, but also of more sober historiography. All this writing was also strongly influenced by a Romantic look at the pasts of principalities, such as the county of Flanders, the duchy of Brabant, the prince-bishopric of Liège and so forth, as well as of the cities that were the obvious nuclei of those principalities. Over the course of the nineteenth century the first historical societies came into being in many towns. The task of these organisations was to unlock and publish sources for urban history, as well as to dig up new insights concerning the pasts of their own towns. The earliest among these associations was the 'Société d'émulation', established in 1838 in Bruges.

Towards the end of the nineteenth century the development of a more scholarly practice of history owed much to influences from both Germany – at that time the pre-eminent country guiding the practice of scholarship – and France. The central figure in this development was the historian Henri Pirenne (1862–1935), who was educated in Liège and taught at the University of Ghent between 1886 and 1930. Pirenne was heavily influenced by his studies in Germany and France at the beginning of his career. These influences drove him forcefully in the direction of urban history. In the introduction to his doctoral dissertation of 1883 concerning the constitutional history of Dinant on the river Maas, he reveals this inspiration: 'I have sought to do for a Belgian town that which has been done for so many German and French towns in recent years.'[1] Pirenne's influence on urban history in Belgium cannot easily be overestimated. To a more general public he is probably better known as the celebrated author of the seven-volume *Histoire de Belgique* or of a challenging posthumous work, *Mahomet et Charlemagne*. Yet one of the most incisive (and early) analyses of the figure of Pirenne and of his work, from the pen of Jan Dhondt, rightly presents him as 'historien des institutions urbaines'.[2]

Influential ideas have a chance of making a permanent impact only when they are formulated at the right moment and land in a fertile medium. At the end of the nineteenth century historians sought and found harbingers of the appearance of a successful bourgeoisie in medieval and early modern towns, who took the first steps in a long process of modernisation. First of all, as an apparent precursor to subsequent industrial revolutions, there were economic innovations in sectors that had been emancipated from agriculture. Additionally, there were political manifestations: the creation of their institutions, constituted from below, and an autonomous right to decision-making, based directly on properly understood collective and individual concerns of the townspeople. In the history of the towns of Liège and the medieval county of Flanders, Pirenne – the son of a successful textile entrepreneur from Verviers – saw a foreshadowing of what made a liberal Belgium at the end of the nineteenth century into one of the most progressive and prosperous countries in the West, even if that applied only to those who made up part of the economic and political elites. Max Weber (1864–1920), Pirenne's coeval, would come to very similar findings in his observations concerning the medieval town, whereby he considered above all the towns of northern and central Italy as well as the Low Countries. This ensemble of views was in line with what in pretty much all late nineteenth-century historical traditions was 'bon ton', typified by

---

[1] 'J'ai cherché à faire, pour une ville belge, ce qui a été fait, pendant les dernières années, pour tant de villes allemandes et françaises.' Henri Pirenne, *Histoire de la constitution de la ville de Dinant au Moyen Age* (Ghent: Clemm, 1889).

[2] Jan Dhondt, Henri Pirenne: historien des institutions urbaines, *Annali della fondazione italiana per la storia amministrativa*, 3 (1966), 81–129 (re-edited and expanded with a critical introduction by Wim Blockmans in the collection of Dhondt's essays: *Hommes et pouvoirs. Les principales études de Jan Dhondt sur l'histoire du 19e et 20e siècles* (Ghent: Fondation Jan Dhondt, 1976), pp. 59–119).

Peter Clark as 'town history with a boosterism quality', whereby towns were the physical sites in which modern society acquired its 'Gestalt'.[3] Until the cataclysm of World War I, the aura of modernity remained elevated above any doubt.

The direct students and successors of Pirenne – Hans van Werveke and François-Louis Ganshof in Ghent, Guillaume Des Marez in Brussels, Ferdinand Vercauteren in Liège – have treated the urban-historical topics of their teacher with much respect for his views. In so doing, that treatment has revolved, respectively, around the workings of the urban middle class, the importance of the textile industry and financial history (in the case of van Werveke); around the earliest history of the towns and their territorial development (Ganshof); around municipal institutions and property rights within towns (Des Marez); and around the workings of municipal institutions and repeated uprisings (Vercauteren). Above all in Brussels, too – where Pirenne, out of displeasure at the University of Ghent being turned into a Dutch-language institution, went to teach at the Université Libre for the last five years of his life – attention was focussed on the topic of urban history by Pirenne's first student, Guillaume Des Marez, and the latter's successor, Félicien Favresse. In the following generation analogous topics came up for discussion among historians at Leuven as well. Taking centre stage there were two works that have had an impact as models for their genre: Raymond Van Uytven's dissertation about finance and economy in Leuven, published in 1961; and Herman Van der Wee's three-part study that came out two years later, concerning the Antwerp market as an anchorage in the stormy evolution that the European economy experienced in the long sixteenth century. In that same decade Belgium's Gemeentekrediet bank – the banking institution set up precisely a century beforehand as a bank for municipal governments – set up a historical commission called 'Pro Civitate', which would develop this tradition very actively. At the instigation of its first president, Fernand Vercauteren (from 1960 to 1977), this committee gave direction to comparative research in urban history by way of prizes, the organisation of colloquia, focussed source editions and exhibitions. In 1996 the Gemeentekrediet bank was absorbed into the larger Dexiabank. The same year the last 'Pro Civitate' colloquium was organised, concerning, ironically enough, the topic of urban demolition.

In the Netherlands all this went on in a strikingly similar way: there, too, interest in urban history had already been aroused early on, albeit

---

[3] Peter Clark, 'The city' in Peter Burke (ed.), *History and Historians in the Twentieth Century* (Oxford: Oxford University Press, 2002), p. 38.

with the chronological emphasis falling not on the Middle Ages but rather on the Golden Age (*Gouden Eeuw*) of the United Provinces, dominated as they were by the representatives of the regent class in the major towns, with Amsterdam in first place. Just as in Belgium, the danger of a teleological reading of urban history was real: the town, the workings of its institutions and the activity of its elites were seen as precursors to the triumphant society of burghers in the nineteenth and early twentieth centuries. In this particular conceptualisation, the values and norms of the modern bourgeoisie found their origin in the political, cultural and moral actions of urban elites from the past. Ideas of this sort continue to survive in current debates about the 'Dutch Miracle' or about the so-called 'polder model', in which the separate trajectory of the Netherlands is presupposed, frequently without critically questioning its path-dependency upon the legacy from the southern Low Countries. In the Netherlands today, however, the approach of the city has been generally opened up by injecting historical research across time periods with innovative studies on architecture and urban planning, as well as insights from the social sciences. Beginning in 2006, the research programme entitled 'Urbanisation and Urban culture' ('Urbanisatie en Stadscultuur') ran under the direction of the Groningen professor Ed Taverne, subsidised by the NWO (Netherlands Organisation for Scientific Research), and resulting in the collection of essays entitled *Nederland Stedenland* (*The Netherlands: A Land of Towns*, 2012). Another recent publication on urban history, in which the accent lies on developments in the northern Low Countries, is the collection *Living in the City: Urban Institutions in the Low Countries, 1200–2010* (New York and London: Routledge, 2012), edited by Leo Lucassen and Wim Willems.

Parallel to these developments in Belgium and the Netherlands, practitioners of urban history from the Low Countries met up with each other more and more often in international committees, such as the Commission Internationale d'Histoire des Villes, set up in 1955, and the especially rapidly growing European Association for Urban History, active since 1989. In the latter the input of historians from the Low Countries has always been quite important – and it remains so, as the biennial conventions of the organisation demonstrate (in 1992 in Amsterdam, in 2010 in Ghent). It is not an exaggeration to state that urban history is firmly anchored in the university world of Belgium, above all. Since 1986, therefore, the field has been a topic central to incentive programmes launched by the federal administration of the sciences in Belgium, which creates consortia of excellence under the designation of the Interuniversity Attraction Poles (IAP).[4] In 2002, within the framework of the long-term programme dedicated to urban history, Claire Billen put forward the idea of jointly writing a broadly accessible summary. The book in your hands is the long-sought-after result, after much consideration and adaptation, of that bold ambition.

Geographical and Chronological Markers

The historical territory of the Low Countries coincides approximately with what are today the Netherlands and Belgium, with the addition of Luxembourg and a large chunk of northern France. In the Middle Ages it revolved around a patchwork quilt of large and small principalities and seigneuries, the names of which survive with more or less accuracy in current provinces, sometimes even in a region (Flanders) or country (Luxembourg). There was no genuine political unity among these areas, although the unification of most of the principalities under the Burgundian-Habsburg dynasty, beginning in the late fourteenth century and lasting until the middle of the sixteenth century, comes fairly close. The development of towns was strongly influenced by the political context, to be sure, though it was never entirely defined by it. For example, except for a few years (1468–77) the prince-bishopric of Liège never belonged to the Burgundian-Habsburg complex, though contacts with the towns of Liège on the river Maas were close.

The territory was also characterised by major regional differences and developments. The contrast between, on the one hand, Namur and Luxembourg and, on the other hand, Holland and Zeeland could hardly be any greater. With their rugged terrain and expansive forests, the first two regions still contained large chunks of unspoilt nature. Towns there remained few in number and of modest proportions. In the other two principalities, because of the imminent threat from water, inhabitants found themselves obliged first of all to drain the majority of the territory, and then to protect it by means of increasingly complicated systems of water management. Since around 1300 there has been barely a patch of land here that has not been shaped by human hands. The low productivity from agriculture provided a genuine ecological challenge, which led

---

[4] The programme IAP P7/26, 'City and Society in the Low Countries (ca. 1200–ca. 1850). The condition urbaine: between resilience and vulnerability', brought together the following partners: Universiteit Gent (co-ordinator), Universiteit Antwerpen, Université Libre de Bruxelles, Katholieke Universiteit Leuven, Vrije Universiteit Brussel, Université de Namur, Royal Library of Belgium, Royal Museums of Fine Arts of Belgium, Universiteit Leiden and Universiteit Utrecht.

Figure 1.2 Principalities in the Low Countries.

to nearly half the people migrating to the numerous towns and triggered creative economic responses.

This book starts with the first strong wave of urbanisation, which got underway in the eleventh century, albeit in different phases depending on the region. It was this round of urbanisation that transformed the natural landscape in the Low Countries into one that was (re)arranged primarily as a function of the needs of an urban market economy. Sketched schematically, one can speak of a slow geographic shift in this case: the towns in Artois and Flanders took the lead, but in the fifteenth century were superseded by urban nuclei in Brabant, whereas over the course of the sixteenth century the main focus shifted towards Holland and Zeeland. At the end of the sixteenth century, the political division between the northern and southern provinces as a consequence of the Dutch Revolt (1568–1648) added a new twist to the diversity of the regions. In the south it initially led to mass emigration and demographic stagnation, although the resilience of the urban system in the centuries that followed is striking. The fact is, however, that the relative focus of urbanisation, economy and military power shifted to the north in the seventeenth century. Having been frequently described already, this divergence, as well as the impressive further urbanisation of Holland in the seventeenth century, gave sufficient occasion for the authors of this book to place the end of their analysis around 1600. Even so, it will not escape the attentive reader that – in spite of the mantra of a 'Dutch miracle' – much can be said for the proposition that there is first and foremost a great continuity hiding behind this geographic shift.

The fact that the river Rhine has its delta in the Low Countries contributes to a considerable degree to the strategic position of the entire region. Its very expansive hinterland is connected along this trajectory to the North Sea and England, a route that has remained of enormous importance throughout the ages. An entire series of towns owe their flourishing to the land route from Cologne to Bruges, which goes back to Roman highways for the most part, specifically to river crossings, namely, Sint-Truiden, Zoutleeuw, Tienen and Leuven. In the north the role of Nijmegen, Arnhem and above all Dordrecht was closely connected with their importance in river trade, which to a large degree included the exchange of products from the central Rhine region with those from the Low Countries and from overseas. Towards the north this situation also applied to a lesser degree to towns along the river IJssel, such as Zutphen, Deventer and Kampen, where contact could be established with north German trade routes. Thus, much more than political boundaries, this network of rivers was strategic for the definition of a certain degree of unity in the Low Countries. Moreover, the linguistic boundary ran across the region in the south: Flanders, Hainaut, Brabant, Liège and Luxembourg had both Germanic and Romance linguistic communities. In regular dealings, however, that caused no problems worth mentioning: familiarity with, and in many cases even command of, multiple languages constituted an important trump card that burghers could play in their business dealings.

In the Low Countries the geography exhibits a multiplicity of large rivers (Rhine, Maas, Scheldt) and small ones which, as a consequence of the minor fall in topography, run a diffuse course over an expansive territory. This pattern is entirely different from that of one dominant, very long waterway like the Rhône or the Danube: those have delineated valleys that sometimes formed a narrow corridor of towns but frequently penetrated less deeply or broadly into the hinterland. Formulated in political terms: though it was still possible to control shipping along the valleys from a few strategic points because there was no other way through, in the Low Countries many options to evade such controls existed; controlling people and levying tolls on shipping – or practising outright extortion – were a lot more difficult. Moreover, the rivers did not form any outer boundaries of the Low Countries, and only on certain trajectories did they function as boundaries between principalities. Thanks to the lower cost of river transport, large groups of people were able to take part directly or indirectly in movement and exchange between towns. The rivers were thus an important factor in the economic, social and cultural openness of the Low Countries.

Probably for the same reasons there was no one specific capital in the leading provinces. The medieval princes were almost continually travelling from one of their residences to another, so as to reinforce their authority through their presence. Brabant had four chief towns – Leuven, Brussels, Antwerp and 's-Hertogenbosch – each of which was the largest town and the judicial capital of one of the districts into which the duchy had been subdivided. In twelfth-century Flanders the seven largest towns dominated, of which Arras and Saint-Omer were absorbed in stages by the county of Artois formed at the end of that century. At the beginning of the fourteenth century, Walloon Flanders was placed directly under the French crown, as a result of which Douai and Lille were also separated from the three remaining chief towns of Dutch-speaking Flanders, namely, Ghent, Bruges and Ypres. They, too, exercised diverse forms of administrative and judicial dominance within their districts. When Walloon Flanders reverted as a dowry to the counts of Flanders from the Burgundian dynasty in 1384, it nevertheless retained its separate administrative status, in which Lille was the capital. In the county of Holland, Dordrecht was indeed the oldest town, but it still did not enjoy the position of a capital, in part on account of its location outside the centre of the county; yet for that chief position Leiden and Haarlem stood too much on an equal footing in size and significance, above all from the fourteenth century onwards. In practice Amsterdam, Delft and Gouda also proved to be frequently consulted in government affairs, such that there were de facto six relatively major towns.

Around 1500 the practice of having one central princely residence developed; it came about as a consequence of the consolidation of the Burgundian-Habsburg dynasty, which exercised authority over a complex of principalities, pretty much connected from Holland to Luxembourg. That capital was Mechelen, selected in 1473 as the seat for central institutions, in particular a supreme court. In addition to its central position, Mechelen offered the advantage of being a small seigneurie in between Flanders and Brabant, so that the sensitivities of the two largest principalities could be circumvented. Further consolidation of power under Emperor Charles V led to the relocating of the capital of the Low Countries to Brussels in 1531. The conquest of expansive territories in the north, from Utrecht to Groningen, had also modified political relationships at that moment. Mechelen remained the seat of the supreme court, called the Great Council (*Grote Raad*), and also became the see of the archbishop from 1559 onwards.

In spite of ongoing centralisation of the government, the various provinces as well as the separate towns nevertheless still retained many of their traditional privileges and prerogatives, and therefore Brussels never acquired the dominance that Paris and London, for example, had enjoyed well beyond all other towns in their kingdoms ever since the twelfth century. In this light the spectacular ascent of Antwerp is that much more remarkable, as it grew from a large town into a metropolis in scarcely three generations. To explain this expansion, a combination of economic and political factors will need to be addressed. Yet, loyal to princely authority, Antwerp never became an important political centre.

The close co-existence of numerous smaller political units hindered the formation of one capital centre, one which in that process demographically depleted any expansive hinterland, as was the case in England and France. Dependence upon and interventions by these powerful English and French neighbours – as well as the Holy Roman emperor in his capacity as the liege lord over the vast majority of the principalities in the Low Countries – certainly contributed to the fact that there would be long-term hindrances to the consolidation of larger power blocks in this region. The towns were able to throw substantial weight into the balance, moreover, as became spectacularly obvious for the first time with the revolt of the major Flemish towns against their count, William of Normandy, in 1128. In Liège, Brabant and Holland the collective political resistance of the towns was not made manifest at the level of the principality until one or two centuries later, but even in those provinces it resulted in princes only provisionally being able to count on the support of their subjects. Those burghers did not shrink in any sense, either, from putting the authority of their prince up for debate, or even eliminating it temporarily, in coalition with powerful noble lords or foreign princes (the English king, for example). Thus, the power of the prince in the Low Countries was fettered both by surrounding kings and by the demands of burghers in matters of proper governance. For the towns these conditions meant that they continually had degrees of freedom for negotiation, so as to protect and improve their own position.

Thematic Axes

There are good reasons for narrating the account of urbanity from the perspective of the events of one specific city. Of the many connections among the various social, political, economic and cultural forces at work in and on one town and its population, micro-level study provides no better alternative for bringing these interconnections to the surface. And yet each time the question remains of how typical any one town is for a broader region. Frequently we are also better informed about the larger towns than about the smaller ones. The multiplicity of extant studies concerning individual towns has led us instead to another approach, one that is synthesising, thematically oriented and completely comparative. In this book it is not just one town or principality that takes centre stage but rather the entire urban network of the Low Countries. The bias of the preliminary research and of the types of expertise of the individual authors cannot be entirely excluded, of course, and for that reason the relative weight of Flanders and Brabant is significantly greater in this present analysis. It was there, however, that the main focus of the urban network was located for the period in question. Yet we also look more to the south, east and north, above all to the most urbanised provinces: Artois, Liège, Holland and Zeeland. Some chapters follow more or less chronological developments, but it is precisely the complexity of the city as a phenomenon that has necessitated frequent deviation from any doctrinal perspective of development.

In its own way, this book formulates and supplements the classic thematic axes of economy, society, politics and culture. Thus, for example, Chapter 4 (entitled 'The Common Good'), which foregrounds the political activity of townspeople, is less oriented towards the formation of institutions and more towards the discourse that those townspeople developed – even without having any direct political say. In addition, we have opted for significantly broadening our subject thematically. In terms of content and methodology, spatial aspects as well as urban identity also receive their proper due, in accordance with innovations in the field of urban history. That urban history is not only time but also space is one of our guiding maxims. The experience of space in public rituals, for example, has proven to be strongly defining for the formation of the identity (and identities) of townspeople. At this point the concepts of spatiality and identity have become well integrated into urban-historical research, but two newer topics – at least in this field of research – are also treated in detail. In the first instance, we are talking here about material culture, inextricably connected to the economic narrative as well as the spatial dimension of the city, yet also to the inception of an identity politics at the micro-level. In the second place, we are conducting research into the role of knowledge, in its economic, political and cultural dimensions. In this light the town can be observed as both a laboratory and a conduit. All topics impinge upon one another, and we indicate that impact by way of many cross-references in the chapters themselves. Those who so desire may read by jumping from one topic to the next and, in the process, may well come even closer to the heartbeat of urban society.

The primacy of the economy in the geographical space of the Low Countries cannot easily be denied. Chapter 2 delineates the urban network as it developed between 1100 and 1600. Its point of departure is the paradox of 'the great durability of a system in constant change', as the authors call it on p. 31. For half a millennium the main geographical centres were shifting and new industries were developing, but the nature of the urban network itself remained unchanged. A constant was the strong rural basis for the urban economy, in terms of supplying foodstuffs and raw materials but above all in terms of human capital. Continual immigration was literally a vital necessity for the town, even though preference was given to 'useful' new arrivals who were able to strengthen the local economy with their skilled labour. The sturdy ramparts that so intensely defined the image of the medieval town thus mask the reality of a community with large groups of newcomers.

In a market economy it is desirable to direct not only the flow of people but also the flow of commodities as efficiently and effectively as possible. Towns were formed at the junctions of traffic routes, and until railways were laid out waterways remained the best routes for the transport of bulk goods such as grain. These waterways were indispensable for all kinds of urban life. In the pre-industrial economy transport by river was as a rule four times cheaper than transport by land. Being located on a navigable river was a significant advantage above all for foodstuffs – which sometimes had to be brought in from far away – and for firewood and peat, but for building materials as well; and having a good maritime connection was an absolute trump card. For that reason transport is one of the rationales used in structuring this book. The development of the *gateway* town, which served as a central link between the hinterland and regions located farther away, is telling. The successive roles as centres played by Bruges in the fourteenth and fifteenth centuries, Antwerp in the sixteenth century and Amsterdam in the seventeenth century are well known. The gateway town had important economic as well as cultural functions, above all after the conversion from (primarily) cloth manufacture to luxury industries.

This conversion happened in the fourteenth century and coincided with the breakthrough of the middling groups in society that will play a central role throughout this entire book. In this case it concerned small manufacturers and shopkeepers, organised into craft guilds, who strove to regulate and control the marketplace and, in that way, provided a counterweight to mercantile entrepreneurs. These corporative pressures did not impact upon innovation and growth, as the early historiography would sometimes have it. Whether we are dealing with the 'golden age of the manual labourer' is another question. First of all, the craft guilds were not as strong all over, and they were often divided internally, with a small elite of master artisans at the top calling the shots. Secondly, the 'skill premium' – the extra that skilled labour provided – was relatively low, precisely because knowledge and training were so easily accessible. Raymond Van Uytven has demonstrated convincingly that most of the artists who gave shape to Burgundian prosperity in all manner of eye-pleasing artistic objects earned little more than skilled construction workers.

The social dimension receives full attention in Chapter 3. Central are the emergence and development of different social groups: the merchants and landowners who dominated urban communities in the eleventh and twelfth centuries, the corporately organised middling groups who came to the fore more and more strongly in the thirteenth and fourteenth centuries, the nobility who in part exchanged demesne for urban life in the fifteenth century. In this chapter attention is paid to real social relations as well as changing discourses. At first glance we are able to discern a kind of evolution from a harmonious 'commune' in the high Middle Ages to an intensely polarised society with a concomitantly repressive discourse concerning 'deserving' and 'underserving' poor in the sixteenth century. Yet this chapter offers a crystal-clear demonstration that we have to be on our guard against these kinds of linear views of history. Social conflict is inherent in urban society, and politics, religion and morality continually provide new means of dealing with these clashes. Views concerning the family and the position of women also fluctuated as a function of economic necessities, as a result of which it is not always easy – and certainly not for the earliest time period – to separate reality and discourse from each other.

And yet the towns experienced relative stability and an extremely tough but also resilient social fabric thanks to the countless corporations, from artisans' guilds to confraternities, military guilds and chambers of rhetoric. The culture of the urban middling groups is the leitmotif in the social history of the city in the Low Countries. The master artisans, marketplace peddlers and shopkeepers played a key role in the economy. In a reaction to the wealth and concentration of power at the top, they put their stamp on the political dialogue, even though they would ultimately pay for their great ambitions in the sixteenth century with a considerable loss of power. Nevertheless they acquired and retained considerable social and economic positions. They took part quite actively in social and cultural life, which moreover offered occasions for contacts with the urban elites and even the nobility. Indeed, the model of the (urban) nobility and its attractiveness were too great for one to be able to speak of a genuine bourgeois society at any moment whatsoever in this period.

If we typify relations between urban elites and middling groups via a colourful and alternating mixture of coalitions and conflicts, via upward as well as downward social mobility, the fact is that the middling groups themselves contributed to the continual reproduction of social inequalities. How powerful the processes of inclusion and exclusion can be is evident from this chapter, which explicates how urban middling groups knew to create an ideology of their own that was hard-hearted towards people without the requisite economic, social and cultural capital. Those who were unable to appropriate the increasingly complex and demanding codes of conduct among burghers could forget about making it in urban society. In short, the middling groups themselves were an important factor in the inherent social polarisation of the city in the Low Countries. The towns in the Low Countries teach us, therefore, that much more than economic growth is needed to make social problems disappear.

These Janus-faced middling groups are also the subject of Chapter 4, which emphasises how an urban society is constructed. The de facto rules of living together take centre stage in this case, but also the continuing struggle surrounding who is allowed to (co-)determine those rules. The *bien commun* or common good of the town was an ideological construction that everyone could support, but one that different social groups (and individual power players, too) framed in very different ways. The fundamental tension between town and prince – so characteristic of the Low Countries – also comes up for discussion here. The towns in the Low Countries were not city-states as were their counterparts in north Italy. Although the larger centres aspired to a strong form of autonomy, they remained bound to princely authority in their minds as well as in fact, first under the various counts and dukes and, from the fifteenth century onwards, under the Burgundians and later Habsburgs in power. Republicanism did not acquire any practical application until around 1600 in the northern Low Countries, albeit as an unforeseen consequence of the Dutch Revolt (1568–1648).

Rather than any clear ideology, a repertoire had been developed in the preceding 500 years which townspeople of differing rank and status could put to work. In this process literacy played a key role. Historians tend to overestimate the role of writing, because they are rather helpless without written sources. The breakthrough of writing (and the vernacular) in institutional administration from the thirteenth century onwards – consider, for example, the thousands of chirographs – is so overwhelming, however, that it can be taken as a barometer of urbanity. Literary texts, too, followed nearly in tandem, with Jacob van Maerlant being an early example from the thirteenth century of an urban author. For a long time there was a fair amount of condescension concerning the artistic level of late medieval poetry, but that is entirely beside the point: it was precisely the functionality of these moralising texts in verse that determined their success. This chapter demonstrates that these texts could be expressly political, with the understanding that many poets and rhetoricians had a profile resembling the middling groups, which allowed them to lecture to the social groups above and below them at the same time, without themselves ever preaching revolution.

That situation can help to put the revolutionary potential of the towns in the Low Countries into perspective. There were frequently plenty of revolts, uprisings and riots, yet seldom was it their intention to overthrow the social order or princely authority. Violence had a purpose and was a last resort in a much larger repertoire of actions. It was a complaint against bad governance and a call for more autonomy. That broader political say-so came about initially in the south; once again the fourteenth century can be seen as a key period. In this way we can also put the 'Dutch Miracle' into perspective: formal political participation was considerably broader in the late medieval towns of Flanders and Brabant than in the seventeenth-century Dutch Republic.

In Chapter 5 the function of religion in creating identity is explored. The Church has been ignored as a power broker in urban-historical research for too long. In the medieval ideology of the estates – clergy, nobles, burghers – the first and last estates seem to have little to do with each other. And yet the Church as an institution played a role that cannot be disregarded in urbanisation, most visibly in the case of episcopal cities. Conversely, from the thirteenth century onwards there was a very important influence on the part of towns upon the development of religious orders and movements, such as the mendicant orders and the beguines and also, from the late fourteenth century onwards, the *Devotio Moderna* as a phenomenon specific to the Low Countries. It was literally a question of give and take: the town provided the religious with alms, work and an audience and, in exchange for these, the clergy brought God to the town, stretching a spiritual baldacchino over the urban community.

The institutionalisation of the urban corporate system served spiritual purposes as well. Guilds of merchants and manual labourers, confraternities and later military guilds and chambers of rhetoric, too, were essentially religious organisations, with a strong emphasis on praying for the dead. In this way the care for the urban community was lifted across the boundary between life and death, and an illusion of continuity was created in a heavily fragmented society. From the late thirteenth century onwards the corporate notion also took shape in the form of grand town processions, which served the pretence of visualising the urban community's unity in its diversity. Most of these *ommegangen* (processions) disappeared for political, religious or economic reasons over the course of the early modern era, yet it is intriguing to ascertain that a number of them – such as the Procession of the Holy Blood in Bruges – have had an almost uninterrupted history to this very day. 'Invented traditions', certainly, but precisely that plasticity of urban ideology can be seen as a constant.

Once again what is striking is how strongly the corporately organised retailers and manufacturers defined the delineation of an urban religious culture that was typical of the Low Countries. Confraternities and processions were not unique, of course, but the way in which they functioned within the broader urban network was indeed peculiar. The creative treatment of religious matter, which led to the ascent of the chambers of rhetoric, was also special. This cultural attitude contributed to an early yet critical reception of the Reformation. Townspeople preferred to mark out their own spiritual path, which could vary from tepidly to fervently Catholic or Protestant. This was not what the central authorities had in mind, and the loss of the northern provinces was the price they had to pay for their stiff-necked attempts to keep the hereditary lands of the Burgundian-Habsburg dynasty orthodox. As a result of the different pace of urbanisation and the stronger profile created by middling groups in the south, there were already manifest differences in the religious cultures of north and south in the Middle Ages, yet those did not in any sense predict the ultimate outcome of a Calvinist north and a Catholic south around 1600.

The urban ideology took shape not only in written rules and verbal agreements, in weekly sermons and annual religious festivals, but also, and expressly, in the built space. In Chapter 6, the city is dissected as a spatial object. Under the influence of the 'spatial turn', not only is the practical functionality of buildings, squares and bridges examined but also how these structures came into being as a consequence of local political power struggles or changing social relationships. Instruments of economic infrastructure, military fortifications, town halls and belfries, houses of prayer and almshouses: all of these are the result not of a rational decision-making process but rather of continual negotiation and even 'bricolage'. In this way, the topics from the previous chapters come together, if not materialise, in concrete, tangible cases.

Cities are recognisable by the concentrated development of their built environments. In the earliest phase, though, that building frequently revolved around a loose collection of small settlements. A town had to be literally fitted together by building bridges, laying out large marketplaces, constructing market halls and, in a subsequent phase, erecting monumental buildings such as belfries, town halls, municipal weigh houses and additional structures like these. In this way meeting places were created where the townspeople – or at least a portion of them – were able to experience their communal identity, whether that revolved around market transactions or political negotiations and various rituals. At first glance town walls constituted the final component, yet these ramparts frequently turned out to be too encompassing or, on the contrary, could erect (un)intended boundaries in the town, by closing off neighbourhood districts, for example. For as much as architectural structures in the town were able to unite, they were just as able to divide. We do well to remember that imposing Gothic churches were frequently connected to parishes that divided the town into well-delineated spiritual units. Even more striking is how almshouses were frequently reserved for one specific group in town, a specific artisans' guild, for example. That peculiarity proves again the remark made earlier that society's middling groups often shamelessly put their own corporate interests first.

To this very day, the patrimony of medieval building provides one of the most important touristic trump cards played in the Low Countries and is the object of contemporary urban pride as well. The consternation in 2012 concerning the construction of a modern hall in Ghent between the belfry and the Gothic Church of Saint Nicholas speaks volumes. Yet we cannot forget that what we now see as medieval is frequently only that to a limited extent. The building and restoration campaigns inspired by the nineteenth-century Romantic 'rediscovery of the Middle Ages' are well known – and infamous. Still, even before that time representative buildings like belfries, town halls and churches were continually rebuilt and adapted to meet new needs. A spatial approach to urban history thus also challenges us to bring our broader conceptual frameworks up to date.

Except for a number of stone residences for the patriciate and town palaces for the nobility, barely anything remains of the thousands of houses in the frequently narrow streets and alleyways that defined the look of the town. A large proportion of them were built in wood and replaced bit by bit with stone and especially brick structures over the centuries. These houses, frequently with open workplaces or shops, were nevertheless the sites where in the main the social and economic lives of many people played out. Some townspeople were owners (of the house and/or the land), but many had to manoeuvre around on a fluctuating real estate market as renters. Yet inhabitants of both spacious premises and cramped little rooms tried to make homes of their houses, as Chapter 7 richly documents.

With that documentation this chapter positions itself explicitly within the debates concerning the 'consumer revolution'. In the towns of the Low Countries during the late Middle Ages, an increasing demand for and supply of consumer goods came about. Furniture, clothing, tableware and other objects of this type became more diversified in size and shape, materials used and workmanship executed. That process seems to have come to a head above all in urban centres like Bruges and Antwerp. What is striking, however, is the broad degree to which the material culture was above all socially embedded in the late medieval Low Countries. As a function of an individual's purse, variations on more luxurious objects came onto the marketplace, up to and including inexpensive paintings. In the Low Countries restrictive sumptuary laws on clothing also did not apply (or attempts at such failed), which indicates that society was less strictly regulated socially and was literally more colourful than in the surrounding regions. That relative lack of restrictions led to the increasing importance of *savoir vivre*. If there are no formal rules, and if lines of social division can be easily transgressed, it is proper conduct that becomes the bar by which an individual's position and prestige in the town are measured.

Continually changing fashions, as well as the ever-increasing importance of interior design, also offered an answer from the demand side to the economic challenges that the traditional textile towns in Flanders, Brabant and Holland had to deal with during the late Middle Ages. They provided for an ever-diversifying economy in which a broad array of consumer goods was developed. A considerable portion of these commodities were consumed in the domestic market – that is, within the urban network itself. Moreover, the towns of the Low Countries were prominent exporters of (semi-)luxury goods for nearly 500 years. Sales of these goods reached all of Europe, and later even the New World.

At the foundation of the urban economy in the Low Countries was a strong school system serving broad strata of the population. Chapter 8 therefore examines the role of education and knowledge. Elementary education was accessible to many, even girls. The Church remained an important actor in such schooling, though municipalities also provided incentives for other, frequently private initiatives. As a function of economic opportunities and parental expectations, elementary education could be followed with training either in trade schools or in so-called Latin (i.e. humanities-oriented) schools, and even possibly be topped off with a university education. However, an apprenticeship spent in artisans' trades was more often the rule. It became increasingly highly regulated as a result of the introduction of testing artisans to produce a 'master's piece'.

In so doing, a rapprochement between theory and praxis can also be ascertained. Though the scientific revolution was still some time off, it is striking how a proportion of trade artisans redefined themselves as practitioners of the 'liberal arts' along the way towards the sixteenth century. Here we mean master artisans highly specialised in luxury industries, who coupled the reception of the Renaissance and humanism to a strong sense of self-awareness. Many were also active as rhetoricians and thus were very present in the public sphere by way of both their artisanal and their literary products. The printing press, too, played an important role in the circulation of knowledge. And, in addition to the printing/publishing house, the princely court cannot be forgotten as a physical locus. In the Low Countries, this centre of decision-making, and of the arts and sciences, too, was an essentially urban phenomenon.

All this can be read as an economic success story. A genuine knowledge economy developed in the Low Countries, with a large share of skilled labour in industry and trade, as well as in institutional administration. This development lies at the foundation of the many economic, political, cultural and material innovations that are treated in the various chapters in this volume. A number of qualifying remarks, such as about the limited 'skill premium', have already been made above. Whoever takes the measure of wages in the Low Countries in the middle of the sixteenth century cannot help but ascertain that they were among the highest in Europe. Yet in comparison to cloth manufacture in Flanders and Brabant during its heyday, it is not likely that per capita incomes at that moment were truly much higher. In more fundamental terms, however, the question is whether training and education also had an emancipatory effect. The relatively large quantitative size of the middling groups in society was certainly due in part to the vast spread of knowledge and the great accessibility of schooling. The effect was also tangible in a much more direct sense for a portion of the male population, such as those masters who developed famous enterprises or those jurists who made their careers in the princely administration. For most people, however, social mobility – both upward and downward – was most likely limited. In the end, we have to be aware of the fact that education can also work as a way to discipline. This disciplinary role is most obvious in the case of schools for the poor, which were supposed to boost the productivity of the poor population – with moderate success, as it turned out – though without much concern for the well-being of the individual.

It should be clear, then, that this book is first of all a social history of towns in the Low Countries. That history is the outcome of the inherent oppositions peculiar to this region. In an area with strong towns and strong lords, there was never any talk of city-states. Moreover, the major industrial and trading towns were woven into a dense fabric of smaller towns. With the exception of the brief ascent of Antwerp, any genuine metropolitan dynamic remains absent. Instead there was much more a gradual shifting of the main centres, from south to north, roughly speaking. In the first major growth phase between the eleventh and thirteenth centuries, the merchant class was able to amass great power and wealth. In the long fourteenth century, in contrast, the artisans' trades made their move and the foundation was laid for the remarkable role of society's middling groups in the economy, politics and culture (see Chapter 9). As a result, however, poverty and social oppositions would never disappear, and they would become even more acute as a consequence of the demographic recovery in the sixteenth century, at the moment when the middling groups most intensely made themselves manifest. Yet that is of course far too strong a simplification of the narrative that will unfold in the pages to follow.

2 Economic Vitality: Urbanisation, Regional Complementarity and European Interaction

Wim Blockmans, Bert De Munck and Peter Stabel

Durability and Change: The Specific Development of Urban Networks in the Low Countries

From the eleventh century onwards, towns and cities became a tangible component of economic development in the Low Countries. Until well into the seventeenth century the degree of urbanisation was considerably higher than in the rest of Europe, with the exception of north and central Italy. How can this exceptional and long-lasting urban density be explained? The size and the growth of towns depended, first of all, on the production capacity of the countryside. In the initial phase, sheep farming on the coastal plains offered the opportunity to bring into play an export-oriented textile industry, which remained an important component of the Flemish economy until as late as the 1960s. This one factor of domestic wool production – which in fact lost its importance quite early – is not enough, however, to explain the lasting strength of the urban economy. In addition, the geographic situation in the delta regions of the rivers Scheldt, Meuse and Rhine made it possible to supplement the provisioning of towns by importing basic foodstuffs and raw materials from areas located further away, which could then be exchanged for their own high-quality products and services. It is remarkable how dynamically the urban economies in the Low Countries thus adapted to changing circumstances. From the twelfth century to the seventeenth they constituted, in complementarity with Italy, a core region of the European economy. Not only was the population density exceptionally high, but so too was the concentration of capital and human expertise. The towns were able to play this role thanks to their mutual networks with one another, and their intense interchange with their rural surroundings and with more distant markets.

For the earliest periods, the simplest method of coming to grips with the process of urbanisation consists of charting those places that acquired specific urban privileges. This approach offers the advantage of clarity, and it allows for determining differences in rates of urbanisation, as well as emancipation of burghers vis-à-vis feudal lords, in various parts of

Figure 2.1 *The Cloth Market of 's-Hertogenbosch, c.* 1525. This altarpiece of the cloth-sellers of 's-Hertogenbosch shows how Saint Francis gave away his possessions to the poor, here in the context of the town's cloth market. The part of the market with the rows of stalls was allocated to guild members. Order and peace here contrast with the more chaotic organisation outside. The altarpiece's message conveys that the cloth-sellers' guild brings the town prosperity and, in the long term, salvation as well. This message is bolstered by the imperial eagle on the town fountain.

the region. Around the year 1100 numerous Flemish towns had already achieved some form of self-governance. In the county of Holland, in contrast, the earliest texts on municipal rights handed down date from 1220 for Haarlem (based on those of Leuven, by way of the 1195 charter for 's-Hertogenbosch), 1254 for Dordrecht and 1266 for Leiden. These places had already been developing as towns for quite some time, however. Around 1300, twenty or so places in Holland enjoyed formal urban privileges.

Even so, substantial differences among these earliest privileges argue against a method that takes the granting of such municipal rights as the point of departure for urbanisation. In all of Europe, the oldest municipal privilege is that of Huy – located on the river Meuse in the prince-bishopric of Liège – which in 1066 curtailed the rights of seigneurial lords over those serfs who fled from them into the town. Even in the twelfth century, when the rights of the town of Namur were granted to a number of other places, their rural nature still resounded strongly, as, for example, in the regulation that a farmer with a plough would have to pay a per capita tax of two patards. Moreover, many of the earliest urban privileges were not put down in writing and remained customary law that was not recorded until a much later stage. As a result of these conditions, there is sometimes a considerable discrepancy between historical documentation and the rights as they were actually in effect during the preceding period. Another, even more important gap is that between text and reality: not every town with privileges did indeed grow into an important concentration of population with complex urban functions.

For that reason it is necessary, when possible, to take population numbers into consideration. Much more than communal rights, they offer a reflection of the viability and vitality of a town. For the Middle Ages, however, statistical data are extremely rare and fragmentary. Estimating the population more or less reliably is not possible before the end of the fifteenth century – in some regions not even before the end of the sixteenth century. Of the approximately 2.6 million people living in the Low Countries in this period, approximately one in three lived in a town. This average concurs well with the situation in the most populated principalities of Flanders, Brabant, Hainaut and Liège. The county of Holland – where in 1514 no less than 44 per cent of the 254,000 inhabitants were townspeople – constitutes an outlier at the higher end of this range. Much lower was the degree of urbanisation in the county of Artois and the duchy of Luxembourg, with 20 and 12 per cent of townspeople respectively. The population density varied considerably in its intensity as well: it was by far the highest in Flanders, where there were

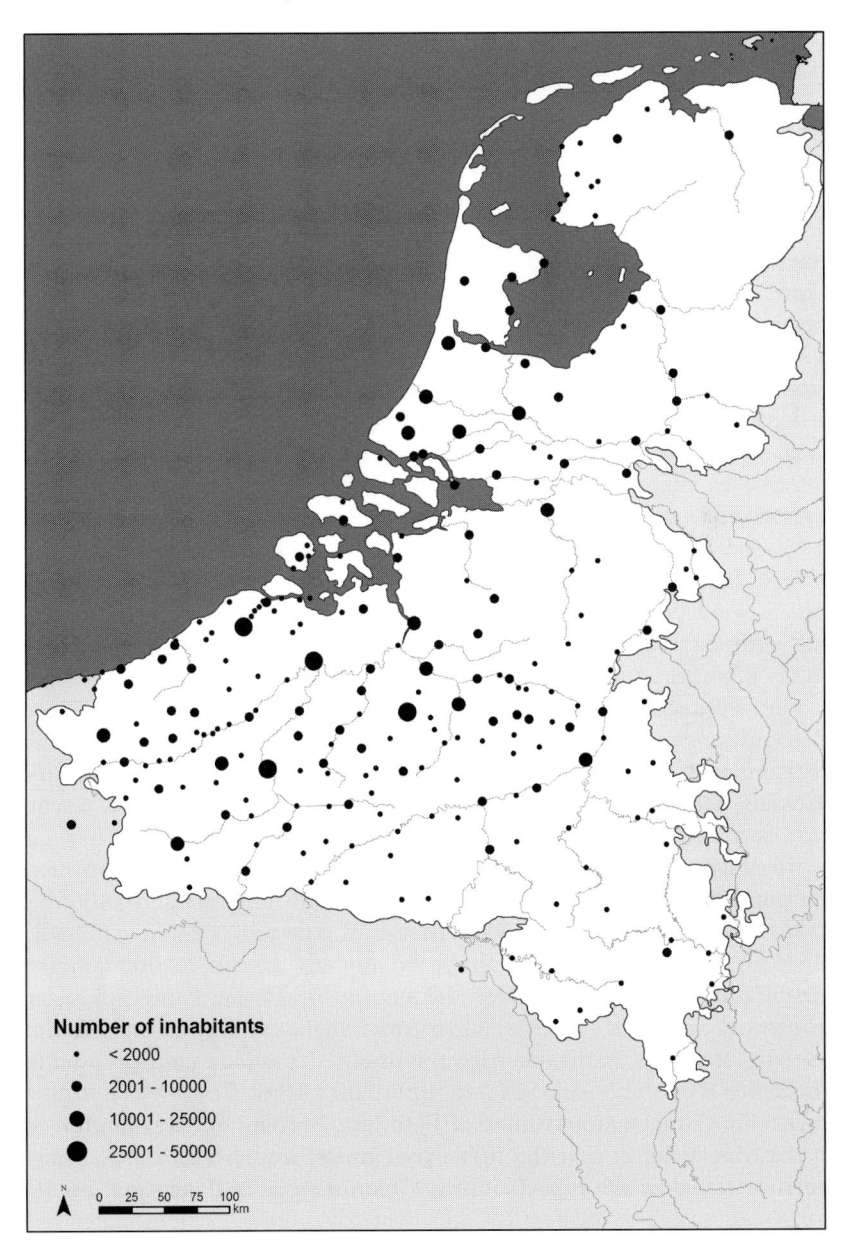

Figure 2.2 Urban centres in the fifteenth century.

72 people per square kilometre; in Holland it was 63, in Hainaut 40 and in Brabant 39, with lower densities in the Campine area in particular.[1]

A clear connection existed between population density and degree of urbanisation. In most cases, high urban density brought about a large number of inhabitants per square kilometre in the countryside, too. The logic for this correlation is twofold: on the one hand, the urban population grows in the first instance through immigration from the immediate environment, that is, a radius of less than 50 kilometres; on the other hand, it goes without saying that townspeople strove to ensure that their vital necessities were available in the immediate vicinity. As a result, urban markets generated the cultivation of high-quality rural and horticultural products, which frequently required much labour and thus brought with it dense habitation. Moreover, in the hinterland of towns diverse artisanal activities took hold in order to cater for the (urban) marketplace. In some cases, these activities happened because lower wages in the countryside made it more profitable for entrepreneurs to outsource low-level work, such as the spinning and weaving of simple textile products. For other activities, such as making bricks, burning shells for lime, extracting salt, digging peat, bleaching linen, weaving reed and making rope, the link with the countryside was more obvious, just because of the availability of required raw materials.

The presence of many towns, as well as a great number of large or medium-sized towns, in combination with high population density was pre-eminently prominent in Flanders and in Brabant along the Leuven–Brussels–Mechelen–Antwerp axis, where relatively significant towns were at a distance of approximately 20 kilometres from one another – a proverbial stone's throw apart. In the province of Holland, in contrast, the population density was very high as well, but until around 1500 the towns remained relatively modest in size: the largest of them – Leiden, Haarlem, Delft and Amsterdam – did not yet exceed 12,000–14,000 inhabitants. The population of the county of Holland did gradually rise from the 1530s onwards, when Amsterdam came to constitute the nucleus of a new maritime network oriented towards connecting the Baltic Sea with the North Sea and the Atlantic Rim.

Despite the later importance of Flanders, Brabant and Holland, it is in the Meuse valley that the first major breakthrough of an urban network occurred in the Low Countries. Commercial and artisanal nuclei

---

[1] For purposes of comparison, the current figures for the corresponding contemporary Dutch and Belgian provinces are: South Holland 1,265, North Holland 1,018, Antwerp 598, Flemish Brabant 503, East Flanders 472, West Flanders 366, Hainaut 343, Walloon Brabant 342 and Luxembourg 59.

developed along the course of the river like a string of pearls: Namur, Huy, Dinant, Liège and Maastricht. Along the other river transport artery, too – the Rhine and its delta – the urban fabric grew to the rhythm of the waterborne trade from Dordrecht and Nijmegen to Cologne. Another cluster of urban commercial nuclei arose along the river IJssel and the Zuiderzee and included Kampen, Zwolle and Deventer as its most important centres. From the fifteenth century onwards, however, the Rhine and IJssel towns were clearly overtaken by the growth of urban networks in Brabant and Holland.

The largest towns were located in the county of Flanders. At its demographic highpoint around 1300, the size of Ghent – the largest industrial town in the region – is estimated at more than 65,000 inhabitants, while that of the more trade-oriented town of Bruges was above 45,000, and the population of textile towns like Ypres, Lille and Douai came in at or near 30,000.[2] In their immediate environment, there were during that period yet other towns that can be called major on a European scale, with approximately 20,000 inhabitants, namely Saint-Omer and Arras in Artois, Valenciennes in Hainaut and the episcopal city of Tournai. As a result of their location on the river Scheldt and its tributaries and their connection with the North Sea, these centres belonged very much to the economic sphere of Flanders. Somewhat later the towns of Brabant reached a similar size, and from the thirteenth century onwards Leuven, Brussels, Antwerp, Mechelen and 's-Hertogenbosch were growing into nuclei with 25,000 to 30,000 inhabitants. After 1480 Antwerp started to surpass all other towns of north-west Europe, and around 1560, as second only to Paris, it exceeded the symbolic mark of 100,000 inhabitants, a scale that at that point had been attained by only five towns in Europe, including Paris, the others all being Mediterranean.

Jan de Vries calculated a measure for expressing urban density on a European scale, independently of political boundaries, which he called 'urban potential'. In doing so, he took as his point of departure only towns with at least 10,000 inhabitants, for which he combined the population figure and the distance from other major towns in a formula that yields a measurement of the global urban interaction potential in a specific region. For the period around 1500 he concluded that the southern Low Countries attained a density amounting to 80 per cent of the highest density in that era, namely that of Venice and its hinterland. This kind of value was otherwise reached only in the basin of the river Po in northern

---

[2] These estimates are mainly based on data from the middle of the fourteenth century, when famine, war, epizooty, economic crises, revolts and the plague had already severely reduced numbers.

Italy, and in the immediate environs of Naples. The Paris region attained more than 50 per cent, while everywhere else the urban potential was significantly lower. According to this method, the southern Low Countries, from the river Meuse to the sea, were, therefore, the most urbanised area outside Italy.

The peripheral areas were significantly less urbanised. In the rural county of Hainaut a number of central places, such as Mons and Valenciennes, were still to develop, with a certain level of industrial activity in textiles and the processing of stone and metal. In principalities such as Luxembourg, Loon (more or less the present-day provinces of Limburg in Belgium and the Netherlands) and large parts of Guelders, Drenthe, Overijssel and Groningen, however, urbanisation remained limited. Having long been oriented towards trade and shipping with the German Hanse, only the Frisian towns on the Zuiderzee such as Harderwijk, Elburg and Stavoren also attracted commerce. Still, such dynamics remained limited in comparison with the soaring heights reached by the harbour and herring towns in Holland and Western Frisia (which corresponds to parts of the modern province of Noord-Holland north of Amsterdam) in the late Middle Ages.

Taking the work of various researchers together, we find approximately 150 towns with a population of 10,000 inhabitants or more for the late Middle Ages in Europe. Of these, at least twenty-five around 1500 were situated in the relatively limited area of the Low Countries. Moreover, the unique nature of the urbanisation process in the Low Countries consisted precisely of the fact that a very large number of small and medium-sized urban nuclei developed, with inhabitants numbering between 2,000 and 10,000. As early as the late Middle Ages, the Dutch-speaking part of the county of Flanders alone had fifty or so smaller towns, in addition to the three main cities of Ghent, Bruges and Ypres.

Thus, the urbanisation model in the Low Countries came to develop very differently from elsewhere in Europe. The sorts of political equilibrium that had to be sought between city and princely state prevented the flourishing of a city-state model comparable to Florence, Venice or other cities in central and northern Italy. Similarly, it kept a dominant political capital from being able to emerge as head of any hierarchy, as happened with Paris and London, and later with Naples, Madrid and Berlin. The allocation of economic activity also did not lead to the concentration of all functions in one dominant town. Although the commercial metropolises of fourteenth- and fifteenth-century Bruges, sixteenth-century Antwerp and seventeenth-century Amsterdam were in many respects dominant in their regions and, in their heyday, even far beyond them, other towns remained important as economic nodes or as centres of production. It is essential, then, to pursue the development of these types of equilibrium and frequently complementary urban functions.

That the urban system in the Low Countries was constantly characterised by the existence of different dominant nuclei alongside one another is undoubtedly also connected with the problems of provisioning and the limitations of agriculture. After all, the largest population concentrations did *not* develop in the most productive agricultural areas, as was the case for Paris and the Ile-de-France, for example. Ghent and Antwerp were surrounded by sandy soils; Amsterdam was in the middle of shovelled-up peat bogs. This paradox points to the primacy of the transport economy over the agricultural economy: the optimal connections for shipping enabled the exceptionally strong growth of towns, which created sufficient surplus value to have their foodstuffs and raw materials supplied. While the major rising states of the late Middle Ages and the early modern era imposed the provisioning of major population concentrations in their capitals by way of far-reaching, non-economic constraints, no individual princely power succeeded in permanently controlling the autonomous growth of towns in the Low Countries.

This did not mean, however, that the first urban nuclei in the southern Low Countries did not initially grow in close association with the agricultural economy and the regional trade along the rivers. But in the eleventh and twelfth centuries the development of large-scale textile industries destabilised this pattern. Smaller commercial settlements were overtaken by the industrial expansion in a number of towns in the counties of Artois and Flanders. The attractiveness of early centres of growth such as Arras, Lille, Ghent, Saint-Omer, Douai, Bruges and Ypres quite rapidly spread beyond the borders of the region. These towns continued to dominate the urban hierarchy for a long time, but from the thirteenth century onwards a second wave of industrialisation already provided competition. In Flanders, smaller market towns like Oudenaarde, Aalst, Diksmuide, Armentières and Poperinge developed industrial activities as well, and in that way emerged as formidable competitors for the entrepreneurs in the larger towns. In addition, regional market towns such as Bergues (Sint-Winoksbergen) and Veurne, as well as specialised smaller towns (consider the fishing and harbour towns like Dunkirk, Nieuwpoort and Sluis, and salt-processing towns like Hulst and Biervliet), increasingly developed.

In the other regions similar developments occurred, albeit with some delay. The early urban network along the river Meuse gained a sequel upstream in the north, and at the same time a counterpart along the rivers Rhine, IJssel and Waal. The systems of towns that began to develop in the duchy of Brabant, and later in the county of Holland, were also already characterised by a multiplicity of towns of approximately the same size until well into the fifteenth century. They were economically dependent on one another and gradually became connected to interregional and international trade networks. The densest concentration was perhaps along the Antwerp–Brussels axis (even today still the most urbanised zone in Belgium). Although in the thirteenth and fourteenth centuries Mechelen, Brussels and Leuven were still clearly smaller than the large Flemish and Artesian towns, they grew quite quickly into important centres of textile production. In their wake smaller towns began to develop as well, especially in the western parts of Brabant, and, just as had happened in Flanders, these became a patchwork of economically often very complementary market and industrial towns. A century later, the same development occurred in the county of Holland, first around the commercial town of Dordrecht in southern Holland, and subsequently also in the north around Leiden, Haarlem, Delft and Amsterdam.

Thus, urbanisation materialised along clear chronological and geographical lines, with the Meuse region, Artois and Flanders as the pathfinders and Brabant, Holland/Zeeland and the river IJssel area as their successors. Once established, the internal relationships remained remarkably stable, and they have to a certain extent remained so until this very day. The one fundamental alteration to this urban network did not come until the second major wave of urbanisation during the industrial revolution of the nineteenth century and the rise of urban nuclei in the coal and textile belt of northern France and the industrial regions of Belgium and the southern Netherlands, with their coal-mining, textile and steel industries. In addition to obvious path-dependent components such as the presence of urban infrastructure and housing stock, this remarkable durability can in large part be explained by the geographical advantages connected to being situated in the delta region of major rivers. Time and again, that location stimulated the network's function as a hub for flows of commodities and capital in Europe.

This role did not, of course, keep individual towns from having to struggle with economic decline, or even from facing total collapse. In the early modern period Ypres became only a shadow of the proud medieval industry town it had been in the twelfth and thirteenth centuries, with the largest cloth hall in all of Europe. Leuven met with a similar fate. The former capital of Brabant was only able to preserve a certain degree of importance thanks to its university, founded in 1425. The major commercial towns of Dordrecht and Bruges (after 1500) and Antwerp (after 1585) lost much of their most important international trading function, whereas the capitals of Brussels and

The Hague came to play an increasingly significant role. Yet these shifts, however striking they may be, ultimately changed very little in the nature of the urban system, decentralised and geared towards complementarity as it was. It is this paradox, this great durability of a system in constant change, that has continued to characterise the essence of the urban system in the Low Countries. In order to interpret and to explain this paradox, what follows in this chapter will gauge three processes that have given shape to the economic development of towns in the Low Countries: the degree of urbanisation and the regional dimension; interregional relations; and finally the organisation of the urban economy itself.

First of all, the intense urbanisation has to be seen in the context of the pre-industrial economy in general. Second, the intense urbanisation process would not have been possible without a very strong interregional dimension. The strategic location on the lower reaches of the rivers Rhine and Meuse – two of Europe's most important transport axes at this period – as well as on the rivers IJssel, Scheldt and Leie (Lys), directed regional trade flows and shaped the structure of the urban network in a definitive way. Third, this chapter will go into the way in which groups of producers and merchants gave shape to the 'urban economy' via institutions such as guilds for merchants and artisans or via their control of municipal policy itself. Central to this aspect is the hypothesis that a transition took place from a relatively 'free market' dominated by the so-called merchant-entrepreneurs to a market largely regulated and controlled by the artisans' guilds from the fourteenth century onwards (above all in Flanders and other southern principalities).

Regional Dynamics: Town and Country

From the twelfth century onwards, the degree of urbanisation in the central regions of the Low Countries was far above that which was considered to be the ceiling elsewhere in Europe. This situation, of course, presupposes a specific relationship with the surrounding countryside. As already stated, towns were dependent on their rural hinterland for their continued existence. Not only did the rural surroundings have to be capable of guaranteeing the supply of food, raw material and immigrants, but industrial and commercial developments also made it necessary for the hinterland to be engaged in trade and production. Additionally, the question needs to be asked whether this integration generated growth over the long term or whether the countryside was instead slowed down in its development as a result of forms of exploitation based on unequal power relations.

Townspeople had to be provisioned with foodstuffs (grain – the basic foodstuff – in the first instance, as well as vegetables, dairy products, fish and meat), yet also with all manner of raw materials. Wood, stone, brick, peat, flax, wool, leather and so forth allowed for the building and heating of houses, and for provisioning industries. Economic relations of this sort between town and country were crucial right from the beginning of the urbanisation process. Certainly, quite a few of the earliest urban centres had come to develop as small trading settlements on the banks of the rivers Meuse, Scheldt, Dender, Zenne and Leie (Lys). Yet what is as striking is that a fortress, seigneurial centre or major ecclesiastical institution was never far away either. The earliest towns in the southern Low Countries had probably grown from nuclei that were responsible for the provisioning of those traditional feudal domains and abbeys with their concentration of artisans, small traders and transporters. Urban settlements were in the first instance marketplaces and providers of all manner of commodities and services for their hinterlands. They created markets for commodities that otherwise could not have been as easily distributed.

Yet it was not only commodity flows that gave shape to the relations between towns and their hinterlands. At least as important were the people who moved back and forth between the town and the countryside. Demographically speaking, towns in the pre-modern era were typified by a surplus mortality rate. Owing to a relatively high number of single people and a low average number of children per household, more people died in towns than were born there. Therefore, in order to remain stable, let alone grow, towns were dependent on immigration. Sadly enough, little is known concerning the size of the continual influx of newcomers who tried to find their safety in town, and, above all, hope for a better future. Scant tax rolls or population censuses, such as the one conducted in Ypres during the early fifteenth century, already show large numbers of single persons and servants. Girls, in particular, seem to have found their way into the service of better-off urban households. Frequently they were young women who came for a short period of time from the surrounding countryside, subsequently to return and settle in the district of their birth, the so-called 'life-cycle migration'. Yet many immigrants also stayed around, got married in town and found other work there. In the early modern era, frequently more than half the urban population came from elsewhere, and that was probably the case for the medieval town as well.

There is better information concerning one specific type of migration, namely the immigration of skilled workers, who frequently had aspirations of breaking through to the urban middling groups as master artisans. Newcomers who wanted to become members of one of the artisans' guilds in the late Middle Ages also needed to become *poorters* or 'citizens' of the town, and for that purpose were obliged to pay a financial contribution (see Chapter 4). Thanks to the registration of entry fees in the *poorter* ledgers or the municipal accounts, there is evidence today for the immigration of these skilled workers. This migration also shows the enormous potential of towns as training centres for skilled labour and professional expertise.

The largest groups of newcomers came from the immediate environs of the town: the vast majority of the immigrant bricklayers and carpenters, tanners and rope-makers, coopers and cabinet-makers, weavers and fullers, and all manner of retailers as well, were recruited in villages less than 20 kilometres from the town. In many cases, therefore, the town was not seen by the migrant upon arrival as an alien environment. The area for recruiting newcomers increased with the size of the town, though. Towns at the top of the urban hierarchy – such as fourteenth- and fifteenth-century Bruges and sixteenth-century Antwerp – attracted many more immigrants from other towns and principalities. Large flows of temporary migrants and permanent immigrants encountered one another in town, although they frequently maintained close ties with their place of origin. It is perhaps no coincidence that in the textile towns of Oudenaarde and Kortrijk even fairly poor inhabitants had property in the surroundings of the city at the time of their death, probably as part of the (inherited) patrimony of their own families.

The close ties between town and country were mutual. How else could it possibly be in areas with urbanisation coefficients that frequently exceeded 25 per cent? Farmers were dependent on urban markets in an economy that was steadily more commercialised. Even the so-called 'peasants' of the interior of Flanders – small-scale farmers who, owing to egalitarian inheritance laws (as a rule, the inheritance was divided equally among all children), had to survive on increasingly small farms – were obliged to think commercially and bring portions of their agricultural production to the marketplace. Where this practice no longer sufficed for survival, they tried to boost the scant income of their household by means of so-called cottage industries. From the fifteenth century on, this increasingly implied weaving linen or, in the coastal areas, combining fishing with intensive husbandry. Moreover, in the countryside there were a number of possibilities for carrying out seasonal work as a paid labourer, such as digging peat, weaving baskets and hunting waterfowl – not to mention the vital water management works on larger and smaller canals, sluices and dykes. Finally, in many coastal places in Holland, Zeeland, Flanders and Frisia, shipbuilding was an important activity that also attracted a large number of other industrial activities related to it.

From the twelfth and thirteenth centuries onwards, an increasing number of specialisations started to emerge in the rural economy. Fodder crops had to facilitate the growth of livestock so as to meet the rising urban demand for meat. At times this specialisation was also dictated by ecological circumstances. As a result of the exploitation of peat bogs (peat was, along with wood, the most important supplier of energy) and of the subsidence of aqueous soil, this ground condensed and sank after dyking and draining. Above all in the counties of Holland and Zeeland, much of the agricultural land that had been reclaimed fairly rapidly became unusable for growing crops, and people were forced to switch over to livestock and dairy production. At the same time, the urban markets ensured reliable sales of foodstuffs of increasingly high quality. In this way, the great demand for agricultural commodities in this urbanised region provided incentives for a process of specialisation and regional complementarity. Whereas textile production continued to dominate in the south, the north was more oriented towards shipping and food products. Moreover, a considerable portion of the production of peat, beer, dairy products, meat and processed herring was shipped to the major towns in Flanders and Brabant. Heavy raw materials and the necessary basic foodstuffs were imported and supplemented from outside the core region. Wool came from the British Isles and later Spain, wood from the forested areas south of the river Meuse and from the Baltic, grain from northern France and, from the sixteenth century, also from the Baltic region, natural stone and metals from the areas along the rivers Meuse and Rhine, and wine largely from the Rhine valley and western France. After the towns, trade also held the countryside in its grip.

And yet this process of regional complementarity was not always dictated by maximising profit or free choice. In the interior of Flanders many farmers had little choice other than to migrate to town or cobble together a supplementary income by weaving linen or woollen cloth during the quiet periods of the farming season. Moreover, their wives and daughters were often engaged in spinning for the urban wool industry. Nowhere is this process better illustrated than in the county of Holland. The poor agricultural land in Holland was never able to produce sufficient foodstuffs, especially cereals, to feed more than 100,000 townspeople. From as early as the fourteenth century their survival had depended on the import of grain, preferably from a region located as close as possible to the waterways (which were much less expensive for transport). Grain was first brought from Zeeland and initially also from the north of Brabant; subsequently it came from further upstream on the river Rhine and from Westphalia. The densely populated principalities of Flanders and Brabant had to import grain for their very large cities from neighbouring regions as well, especially from Hainaut, Artois and Picardy. From there it could be easily shipped downstream. That meant that there was little left for those in Holland, where there was also poorer accessibility. For that reason, it became necessary to look even farther afield in the fifteenth and sixteenth centuries: to Picardy and, in years with high prices, even further southward. In the sixteenth century, rye for the Amsterdam market was supplied to an ever-increasing extent from the region of Prussia flanking the Baltic Sea.

Grain was the basic foodstuff from which beer was produced, in addition to bread. Any scarcity in this strategic product brought an entire chain of trading relations between neighbouring regions into play, and gradually with districts farther away as well. This interrelatedness also involved mutual dependency, for disruptions in one area automatically produced effects in another. Only as a result of compensatory interchange between the provinces could the high degree of urbanisation be maintained in the most populated provinces.

Market dependency, complementarity of economic activity and in many areas the combination of agriculture and manufacture ensured that for most rural inhabitants in the Low Countries the town was always nearby. For many of them it was also a constant factor in the search for income and commodities. Moreover, migration flows saw to it that there was always a member of the family living and working in a town nearby. It need not come as a surprise, then, that this close tie was also given shape institutionally. As a result of the so-called *hoofdvaart* – the transfer of legal cases to aldermen of a larger town – municipal law courts functioned as centres of knowledge for those institutions in smaller seigneuries and villages. By becoming a *buitenpoorter* (an 'outburgher', a well-to-do villager buying citizen status), many rural inhabitants acquired protection from the municipal courts. The status of *buitenpoorter* provided a quasi-municipal legal status in their own village or part of the country and enabled them to escape all manner of seigneurial obligations (see Chapter 4). In inner Flanders, characterised by a significant presence of cottage industries, this status was enormously successful. Ghent was able to recruit considerable numbers of *buitenpoorters* from both inside and outside its own quarter, but it was the medium-sized industry towns of Kortrijk, Oudenaarde, Aalst and Geraardsbergen that had the largest numbers of this special sort of citizen in their own hinterlands in the late Middle Ages. In the villages in the immediate vicinity of Kortrijk and Oudenaarde nearly everyone was a *buitenpoorter*, and even farther from town the more well-to-do farmers certainly acquired this legal status. Towns in this region frequently competed with one another for the largest numbers of 'outburghers'. Even in small market towns like Deinze and Tielt there were, in addition to the town's own *poorters*, a large number of Ghent and Kortrijk *buitenpoorters*.

In effect, towns exercised power over the countryside as well. Financially strong townspeople invested in peat extraction and forestry; they financed the production of construction materials; and they owned property to a large extent outside town. Above all, they participated in the financial markets by purchasing annuities (a kind of long-term mortgage loan on land) on agricultural businesses. Whereas many farmers lost their property as a result of accumulating debt in this way, townspeople frequently opted for the safe economic return of income from rents, as well as for the status of being a property owner, instead of having to engage in risk-bearing investments. As a result they undoubtedly played a role in the transformations that led, for example, to larger lease-holding farms in coastal Flanders.

This change was not a purely economic process. The major Flemish towns supposedly developed all sorts of market constraints, whereby commercial developments in the countryside were hindered and surplus extraction was stimulated. Burgeoning industrial developments in the countryside were sometimes even stopped *manu militari* – with raids on industrial villages or small towns where competing activities in the textile industry emerged. Concerning the impact of these measures, however, there is little unanimity. The incidents in which municipal militia members destroyed looms in villages and smaller towns in order to defend their broadcloth monopolies took place only in short periods. In addition, they happened during the transitional periods when urban entrepreneurs had to go through a difficult switch to luxury textiles in the early fourteenth century (see below, pp. 47–9). What is certain is that, even in the southern Low Countries, the towns have never been able to block industrial development in the countryside and in the smaller towns. When the export markets for cheap textiles grew again from the fifteenth century onwards, the greatest vitality came precisely from the countryside in western Flanders (where woollen cloth was manufactured). Meanwhile, in southern Flanders and in parts of Hainaut and Brabant, the linen industry in the countryside was assuming greater proportions.

An important institutional instrument seems to have been the staple rights, that is, the obligation to transport commodities via a specific town as well as to store them and offer them for sale there. Without exception the successful staple privileges were oriented towards interregional or even international trade and concerned commodities such as wine (Dordrecht, Damme) and herring (Damme and quite a few harbour towns along the coast). Yet the influence of these privileges was not necessarily negative for other places. The fact that a number of smaller fishing villages and towns (such as Blankenberge, as well as the recently excavated Walraversijde) were abandoned in the late Middle Ages to the benefit of larger fishing towns with a better harbour infrastructure (Dunkirk, Nieuwpoort, Ostend) had little to do with these storage rights. Even forms of institutional market constraints for cereals, for example, were anything but common and usually barely effective. Time and again the so-called 'Members of Flanders' (*Leden van Vlaanderen*, the three major towns of Ghent, Bruges and Ypres) had to go to great efforts to restrict the free trade of grain and to forbid exports in periods of scarcity. Those pains already bear testimony to the difficulties of imposing institutional constraints effectively. In areas where, on account of belated growth, no towns had grown up in the Middle Ages (for example, the territory known as the *Land van Waas* between Ghent and Antwerp, or the centre of the similarly designated *Land van Aalst* in Imperial Flanders), rural market activity did develop (Lokeren, Sint-Niklaas, Zottegem) without urban market rights being able to exercise any influence over them.

The best-known staple privilege was undoubtedly that of Ghent for the trade in grain via the rivers Leie (Lys) and Scheldt. This privilege concerned above all the import of wheat from Picardy, Artois and southern Flanders (the lifeline for the urban network until the arrival of Prussian rye), rather than control over Ghent's own hinterland. The most urbanised areas in the Low Countries were dependent on this import. The Ghent lobby of grain traders and guild-organised river shippers nevertheless succeeded for the most part in monopolising the transport of and trade in grain, thanks to the strong political position of Ghent in the county. That policy was so successful that the curve of grain prices in Ghent during periods of crisis proceeded much less unevenly than elsewhere in the region.

When the import of grain from northern France was compromised and Baltic grain became more important in the late fifteenth century, the focal point for the provision of grain shifted to Amsterdam. Yet, despite being less tied to the institutional constraints of staple rights, here, too, the trade in grain gradually fell into the hands of a specific group of traders and carriers, who also did not hesitate to eliminate possible competitors – even by force of arms at times. The German Hanse merchants, who had controlled trade between the Baltic and the North Sea until the late Middle Ages, would experience new competition from Holland shippers rather rapidly. The impact of the influx of (relatively cheap) grain on the rural economy must have been significant and must have strongly influenced the choices available to agricultural holdings in the Low Countries. Whether this impact came about as a result of formal staple and transport privileges or as a result of the workings of the market, the effects (and the power positions that resulted from them) were for the most part very similar.

Crossroads of Northern Europe? Trade and Transport in the Late Middle Ages and the Long Sixteenth Century

The soaring heights reached by the process of urbanisation in the Low Countries are above all connected with the development of a trade network that allowed for the industrial goods in the Low Countries to find a way out towards customers across all of Europe (and from the sixteenth century the New World as well). Transport by water was generally slower than by land, but it was much cheaper – as a rule only a quarter of the price of land transport. As a result of the easy and relatively cheap supply routes along the rivers and coastline, then, not only luxury products but also essential bulk goods could be shipped at relatively low cost. In addition, soil conditions in certain regions forced agriculture to specialise and to commercialise, making economic actors even more dependent on interaction, far beyond the boundaries of the Low Countries. The core provinces exported artisanal products like their famous textiles, beer and specialised luxury goods. Since the emergence of the urban network, the merchants involved had acquired a dominant position in the political and economic system and, for the most part, they would keep that status until the end of the eighteenth century, despite the social emancipation of independent craftsmen in the thirteenth- and fourteenth-century artisans' guilds.

Central to the development of trade in the Low Countries was the gateway town, which functioned as a link for the export of products from the hinterland and for the supply of products for which there was a shortage in the network itself. From the thirteenth century, Bruges and to a lesser extent Dordrecht developed as such economic nodes; Antwerp served as such from the late fifteenth century onwards; and from the late sixteenth century Amsterdam gradually carried out these functions too. As portals to the outside world, gateway towns stood at the top of the commercial hierarchy. Bruges became the marketplace for textiles from the Low Countries and in that way determined the internal industrial and urban networks extending into Artois, Hainaut, Brabant and Holland. Gateway cities grew into nodes that concentrated capital, demand (from foreign merchants as well as the important domestic market), distribution of finished products and raw materials and, last but not least, know-how and knowledge (see Chapter 8). In view of the increasingly high-quality nature of the export industries, know-how became steadily more important, causing hierarchical heads of the urban network like Bruges, Antwerp and Amsterdam to become frontrunners at the same time in the development of industries for luxury goods and refinement processes.

As a commercial town, Bruges had become a node for maritime trade for the German Hanse and for Italian and Iberian merchants from the fourteenth century onwards. These merchants congregated in Bruges to avoid the risky transcontinental routes through France and Germany. As genuine network-makers they accounted for the majority of the trade in the town. Insecurity and political conflict – and, therefore, more expensive transport systems by land – made the sea routes during this period relatively advantageous despite their considerably greater length. Bruges, which had already had a prominent presence earlier at the annual fairs of Champagne, was in a position to alter its financial and commercial infrastructure to fit these new circumstances. The town was in the vanguard in north-west Europe when it came to the introduction of new trading techniques and commercial institutions.

These dominant gateways were connected to the urban network, in which other towns also constituted nodes for specific trade flows, industrial goods and services. This was undoubtedly the case for Lille and Ghent, given their hinterlands of production centres for broadcloth made from imported wool and linen made from regionally grown flax. Some of the subordinate nodes were located in more agricultural regions, such as the commercial towns on the rivers Meuse and Rhine, Deventer on the river IJssel and 's-Hertogenbosch in northern Brabant, which was connected with the river Meuse. Late medieval Bruges is a typical example of how a gateway was closely connected with hierarchically subordinate networks for consumption and supply. Paradoxically, this interaction was stimulated by the fact that the major industrial towns, including Bruges itself, experienced more and more competition from smaller industrial centres in Flanders, Brabant and Holland. Nodal towns developed a complex market infrastructure, whereby access to capital, product markets and raw materials became more efficient and less expensive. As a consequence, the fact that more and more towns, even small ones, were oriented towards the export of cloth, for example, correlated with the possibilities for distribution via new trading systems in Europe.

Over the course of the fifteenth century a significant turn of events occurred. Bigger and more easily controllable state structures made the transcontinental routes across Europe more predictable and less expensive. Additionally, just as had happened in the Champagne region in the twelfth and thirteenth centuries, annual fairs were able to profit from this change, particularly in central Germany, with Frankfurt-am-Main becoming the most important one. Lower population densities and the great distance to the seaports made the annual concentration of supply and demand at fairs there profitable for much longer than in the West. In the Low Countries the major annual fairs of Brabant were organised in Bergen-op-Zoom and Antwerp. During Antwerp's 'Pentecost Fair' (*Sinksenmarkt*), Italian traders left Bruges en masse in order to do business in Antwerp with other partners.

The wider range of connections and the more flexible opportunities offered by the Brabant fairs contributed greatly to the focal point gradually shifting from Bruges to Antwerp. The political difficulties under the regime of Maximilian of Austria (1477–93), the rebellion and the concomitant blockade of Flemish towns ultimately tied the noose around Bruges's role as a gateway, though the transition from Bruges to Antwerp was the consequence of a multiplicity of factors. Traditionally, the shift is explained by the silting up of the Zwin channel, whereby Bruges's access to the sea became more difficult. In the same period, storm surges in 1375 and 1404 'dredged' the western branch of the river Scheldt, which then made Antwerp more accessible to larger sea-going ships. Antwerp was able to play several additional trump cards. The town was relatively far inland, for instance, and opened up the German hinterland, which was more difficult to reach via Bruges.

The end of the galley voyages organised by the Venetian state to Flanders shortly after 1500 symbolised the reversal of fortune. Whereas Italians and especially north German Hanse merchants were losing more and more ground on the north European markets, south German traders in wine, metals and textiles, English merchant adventurers and Portuguese spice merchants – groups that had never been very important in Bruges – were now coming to Antwerp. Trade in finished commodities intended for export also shifted irrevocably to the river Scheldt and the Brabant fairs: tapestries from Brussels and Oudenaarde, damasked table linen from Kortrijk, light woollens (the so-called says) from Hondschoote, black luxury cloth from Menen and Armentières, and Italian silks also relocated from Bruges and joined new commodities, such as English broadcloth, which were finished in Antwerp, south German fustians and metals, Portuguese spices and now, too, locally manufactured silk fabrics.

In this way, over a short time Antwerp perhaps became a genuine primary city in the Low Countries – much more than Bruges had been a century earlier – a city that through the concentration of urban functions and its population size dominated other towns in the network and caused a constant drain of skilled labour from those secondary towns.

Yet even Antwerp was provisioned by other urban subsystems for certain products: for example, grain from the Baltic was traded through Amsterdam and Rhine wine through Dordrecht; until the 1570s, however, these two ports remained limited in the range of their products and services, and dependent on Antwerp's primacy, especially as the leading financial centre. In the sixteenth century Ghent, Lille and Bruges remained important transit markets for textiles, now manufactured most extensively in western Flanders (Armentières, Heuvelland (southwest Flanders) and so forth). Yet, in contrast to Bruges, Antwerp exhibited a tendency towards extinguishing economic activity in the smaller towns in its hinterland.

In the past decades, under the influence of 'new institutional economics', the economic success of the Low Country towns has been connected to the presence of effective and efficient institutions. Indeed, inside these towns all manner of institutions and legal structures developed. Itinerant international traders were organised into merchants' guilds, which developed legal functions in addition to their functions of stimulating social relations and economic power. The requirement in late medieval Bruges to engage local brokers and hostellers for all transactions between foreigners promoted conditions for trade as well as allowing for keeping control of transaction costs. Moneychangers like Collard de Marke in the fourteenth century and brokers like Wouter Ameide in the fifteenth century were important actors with an eye towards smooth commercial transactions in Bruges. The aldermen's benches were responsible for the rapid resolution of trade disputes and they guaranteed the legal security of merchants in foreign countries via bilateral agreements. Aldermen's benches did everything to make sure that merchants had everything to their liking. They provided various vital legal services, while conflicts with and in the community of traders were left as much as possible for the merchants to resolve amicably on their own. Should tempers still run high, the traders be arrested and their assets confiscated, then the 'Members of Flanders' (see above) made every effort during the fourteenth and fifteenth centuries to come to settlements with their foreign partners and authorities. It was not for nothing that in Bruges the *Beursplein* (the little square, named after the hosteller's family Van der Beurze, which would give its name to financial markets everywhere) and the adjacent *Wisselbrug* ('Exchange Bridge') served as a meeting place for regional and international financial transactions.

Amsterdam had even more effective institutions, and as a result of that the city would succeed in drumming out Antwerp from the second half of the sixteenth century. Although this institutionalist explanation tends towards a teleological narrative of a triumphant modernity, it is certainly true that the institutional underpinnings were of crucial importance for stimulating trade and entrepreneurship. Institutions, however, often adapt to markets rather than shaping them. By definition, a dynamic economic setting changes capital relations in society; it also generates new social groups and aspirations and changes the existing balances of power. In Antwerp virtually the same institutions were developed as in Bruges. But in sixteenth-century Europe, commercial companies working with agents became more permanent and larger. Hence the need for institutions like merchants' guilds and broker-hostellers to act as intermediaries diminished. In seventeenth-century Amsterdam, such merchant guilds were, in fact, completely absent. In other words, the institutions deemed to be effective in hindsight were in practice deployed in a process of trial and error in order to guarantee successful economic performance as much as possible. And the economic development produced the institutions that the groups concerned deemed necessary, rather than the other way round.

The consequences of the growing Antwerp market in the sixteenth century were not simply an exact copy of the effect that Bruges had had a century earlier, however. The success and the attractiveness of the metropolis were so great that the Antwerp trading system developed from an annual fair system to a permanent marketplace. As a result it became more difficult for entrepreneurs from elsewhere to sell their goods on the Antwerp market, which caused difficulties for the towns in the hinterland of Brabant, among other places. Initially Leuven and the towns around it in the Hageland region paid the price, but in a second phase 's-Hertogenbosch and even Mechelen began to suffer from Antwerp's growth.

In contrast, Bruges – and by extension the textile towns in the network of Flanders and Artois – did not entirely dissolve as a result of the relocation of the gateway. From the middle of the fifteenth century on, Flemish textile entrepreneurs were oriented increasingly and very successfully towards Antwerp. But until well into the sixteenth century there was also a functional and complementary co-existence between Bruges and Antwerp: Bruges remained the most important hub for commodities like French wine, (Venetian) spices, tropical fruits and oil. By maintaining the Spanish trade (the Castilian merchants' guild kept its wool staple in Bruges), the city also continued to keep a substantial share in the trade with the Iberian peninsula for wool and sugar, among other things.

Moreover, European growth in the sixteenth century, stimulated in part by increasing demand from the New World, prompted a further expansion of rural (textile) industries. Linen from Flanders, Hainaut and the Campine region, cheap and mixed fabrics from the districts around Weert and Ronse, high-quality broadcloth from western Flanders (Heuvelland)

and the region of Lille, light woollens in Tournai, Valenciennes and above all Hondschoote, and tapestries from Oudenaarde and its region all profited from the opportunities created by the Antwerp gateway. Whereas urban heavy cloth production almost completely disappeared in the county of Flanders, success was achieved here with a radical switch to lighter fabrics, such as bays in Dendermonde, says in Hondschoote, and table and bed linen and linen damasks in Kortrijk. In the duchy of Brabant the focal point shifted to the north from the last quarter of the fifteenth century, particularly to the present-day province of Noord-Brabant in the Netherlands (Breda and 's-Hertogenbosch), to the disadvantage of older textile centres like Leuven, Mechelen and Herentals. Here, too, rural industries became especially successful: in Duffel, Maaseik and Weert inexpensive woollens were manufactured; and the villages around 's-Hertogenbosch and in the Campine area produced linens, the so-called tick fabrics, which became popular in England.

By this time the economy in the county of Holland was running at full speed, too. The late medieval 'jump start' generated results, and Holland was on the way to becoming the most densely populated province in the Low Countries. The interwoven nature of the urban and rural economies contributed to that development, in addition to countless other advantages of the Holland economy: experience with shipping, fishing and trade; numerous accessible seaports; inventive shipbuilding techniques, cheap labour in a proto-industrialised countryside; and specialisation of the agricultural economy, including the rise of not purely agricultural activities in the countryside and the success of the brewing and dairy industries. The complementarity with the southern principalities in the Low Countries is striking. In the south the economy was geared towards textile production and, although textiles were far from absent in towns like Amsterdam, Haarlem and particularly Leiden, the north also offered possibilities for providing the southern towns with beer, dairy products and peat. All these factors were strongly influenced by developments in the rural economy itself. One of them was the growth of a relatively efficient, effective capital market. Mobilising risk-bearing capital for shipping in Amsterdam, for example, seems to have had a lower threshold than in Flanders or Brabant. In Amsterdam's share-holding shipping companies (*partenrederij*), the ownership of ships was distributed across less financially powerful brewers, millers, grain merchants and many others. Macro-economic shifts like the increasing importance of central and northern European markets, as well as major internal stability, also played a role in the development of what has subsequently been called the first 'modern' economy. Moreover, from the 1580s onwards the influx of capital and know-how of hundreds of thousands of immigrants from the south, as a consequence of the Spanish repression of the Dutch Revolt, had a large impact.

When the political boundary between the Habsburg Netherlands and the Dutch Republic gradually came to be established around 1600, the Amsterdam network became independent of its Antwerp bias. The transition was also made from the 'mother trade' (grain) to the so-called 'rich trades' (the very profitable trade routes between the Far East, the Levant and the New World). The towns more oriented towards industry in and around the county of Holland (Haarlem, Leiden, Delft, Gouda, Utrecht) also joined in that growth. In so doing, specialisation in niche products – such as broadcloth and other textile commodities in Haarlem and Leiden, beer in Gouda and so forth – took place, much more emphatically so than in the late Middle Ages. Yet, even in this case, Amsterdam did not become the 'depot of the world', as it was held to be for a long time. Just like Bruges and Antwerp before it, the new gateway continued to function within specialised and differentiated networks. Hierarchies continued to differ from product to product, and they were neither stable nor unchanging. Secondary centres remained nodes in complementary networks and sometimes directly maintained contacts with far-away areas in Europe, Asia or the Americas. Rotterdam, Hoorn, Enkhuizen and Medemblik, for example, remained active in 'the mother of all trades' in the Baltic.

What is clear, though, is that the revival of international trade and the demand for transport capacity and for agricultural products brought into play important structural modifications to the urban system very early on in the northern parts of the Low Countries as well. The medieval river towns of Dordrecht, Nijmegen, Deventer and Zwolle lost ground, while the seaports in Holland and Zeeland were able to profit from the capitalistically organised cargo trade and from the crucial role that Baltic rye had acquired in provisioning the urbanised Low Countries. During the seventeenth century, the textile centre of Leiden still stood out as the second city of the Dutch Republic, having around 65,000 inhabitants in 1675. Thereafter its population declined, and the gap with Amsterdam and its more than 200,000 inhabitants increased significantly. Rotterdam, the third largest town at that point, did not grow beyond 50,000 until around 1795. Again, a tendency towards primacy of the leading city seems to be apparent.

It can thus be stated that, generally over the long term, the focal point shifted geographically from the south to the north, while fundamental changes were occurring within the urban network itself. As a result of functional changes and a new equilibrium between town and countryside, a process of de-urbanisation set in in the southern provinces (certainly in relative terms: from 35 per cent to 25 per cent). In the county of Flanders, the dominance of the three major towns was replaced by a much more uniform pattern of large, medium-sized and small towns. In the duchy of Brabant, in contrast, an opposite pattern seems to have developed: polarisation between the largest towns on the one hand and much smaller towns on the other. From the early sixteenth century onwards, Brussels and above all Antwerp dominated, whereas the remaining urban centres fell far behind. In the northern provinces the process of urbanisation continued to persist: in the Dutch Republic, the urban population, living in towns of at least 25,000 inhabitants, grew substantially in absolute numbers – from approximately 300,000 around 1525 to 815,000 around 1675 and 781,000 in 1795 – as well as in relation to the total population – from 27 per cent to 42 per cent to 37 per cent respectively. At its high point around 1675, 61 per cent of the people in the county of Holland were living in towns with at least 25,000 inhabitants. In the other provinces of the northern Low Countries this figure was only 27 per cent, which shows the exceptional concentration that took lasting shape at that time. Of the nine towns with at least 20,000 inhabitants, seven were located in Holland. Only Middelburg in Zeeland (approximately 27,000) and Utrecht (approximately 25,000) were in the same league, being capitals of provinces without other major towns. These shifts illustrate how, from the Middle Ages, the core position in the international economy was situated in the most urbanised regions because the highest concentration of human and material capital settled there.

From Unfettered Capitalism to Regulated Labour Market? Changes in the Supply Sector and the Development of Artisans' Guilds

By now it should be clear that industrial development was also an enduring factor in urbanisation, the proviso being that the nature of urban manufacture was changing throughout the era. In the Middle Ages the cloth industry gained strong predominance, whereby advantages of scale as well as efficient and effective division of labour, specialisation and concentration of knowledge and capital could be achieved. Yet the 'monoculture' of woollen broadcloth also made the urbanisation process vulnerable to changes in the economic cycle and to changing demand. At the time when the cloth industry was confronted with shrinking markets in the fourteenth century, more than half of the urban population was directly employed in a sector related to textile production in the leading industrial towns (Ghent, Douai and Ypres, and perhaps Saint-Omer, Mechelen, Leuven and Brussels as well). Even in the smaller industrial towns – such as Kortrijk, Eeklo or Oudenaarde, which would threaten the market position of the larger towns from the fourteenth century onwards – more than half of the population was active in textile manufacture until well into the sixteenth century.

The towns along the river Meuse (Liège, Maastricht, Huy, Namur) experienced an entirely different evolution. Here it was not so much textiles as specialised industrial commodities related to the rich resources above and below ground (charcoal, natural stone, coal, copper and iron) which paved the way for export-oriented industrial organisation. Even in Flanders the chief activity was not limited to the industrial monoculture of woollen cloth alone. Among other places, Bruges – the 'second city' in the county of Flanders in terms of population – had a more varied profile: in the fourteenth century when only a quarter of the population worked in the textile industry, nearly 40 per cent worked in artisanal trades on the local market and 20 per cent were active in trading and banking. Moreover, to the extent that the cloth industry was retrenched over the course of the fourteenth century, the relative share of luxury and service industries grew (fashion, processes of refinement of textiles and leather industries, artistic production like painting). After the Black Death in 1348–9, increasing purchasing power must have stimulated the demand for refined consumer goods. The breakthrough of artisanal middling groups and the so-called 'golden age for the manual labourer' in the same period strengthened this phenomenon. Fashion became an important economic sector. The number of tailors, shoemakers, leather workers, furriers and hat-makers steadily grew, and Bruges certainly led this movement. Changes in residential culture also provided new opportunities for work for cabinet-makers and construction workers.

In the county of Holland, where the towns at that time were much smaller, a few important textile centres developed as well, above all Leiden and Haarlem. This development took place at a later stage, however, from around 1350, and it never reached the same level of dominance (except in the case of Leiden) as it had in the major southern industrial towns. In the northern provinces industrial growth was also much more divided between town and country. Capital-intensive sectors, such as shipbuilding, brick-making, brewing beer, extracting peat and refining salt, went hand in hand with non-agricultural activities, such as herring fishing in the coastal towns of Zierikzee, Veere, Rotterdam, Hoorn and Enkhuizen, in Zeeland and northern Holland, as well as peat extraction and cheese and hemp production in the smaller centres of the interior and in the countryside. With their strikingly regular parcels of land and canals, the morphology of most towns in Holland points to a past as centres for clearing land and extracting peat. The only large-scale industrial export activity in Holland towns, in addition to the textile industry, was undoubtedly brewing beer. The brewers' towns of Haarlem, Delft and Gouda not only provided for local needs but also succeeded in exporting to urban markets in the southern Low Countries from the fourteenth century. The export of peat from north-west Brabant and from Holland to major towns in the south reached a capacity of 6,000–7,000 shiploads per year in the middle of the sixteenth century. At that time in Flanders and Brabant, prices for fuel were higher than in Holland by approximately 50 per cent, so that exports paid off despite high transport and transaction costs. Nevertheless, demand rose in Holland as well, specifically for the growing beer industry and for brick-making. In this way the markets became connected, whereby Holland in its turn had to import peat from Utrecht, Overijssel and Guelders – with Gouda as the central node for transit traffic.

Of course these processes were not straightforward or linear. For the relationship between industrial cycles and the urbanisation process, the Leuven historian Herman Van der Wee has put forward the model of the so-called 'product life cycle'. This model assumes that the chronological and geographical shifts of economic centres correlated with overall transformations of the urban network. The shift of the commercial centre of gravity from Bruges to Antwerp in the 1480s is typical. But a much earlier initial shift has been identified from the twelfth century to the first half of the fourteenth. This period was dominated by the export-oriented wool industry and by cloth merchants who organised production networks and markets for raw materials and finished products. They profited from a far-ranging division of labour and the deployment of much unskilled labour. In this period the textile industry was nigh on synonymous with the cloth industry. Originally, the supply of wool was organised regionally, thanks to the significant sheep farming in the coastal areas of Flanders. Yet international supply networks gradually became necessary, in the first place for high-quality wool from England. Flemish merchants from the major towns, organised into the 'Flemish Hanse of London' (*Vlaamse Hanze van Londen*), were especially active in the British Isles. At the international annual fairs in Champagne, Flemish textiles reached customers from Mediterranean Europe as well.

Initially even cloth of lesser quality was exported, while being woven with domestic, Scottish, Irish, French or German yarn instead of English wool. At the end of the thirteenth century and in the early fourteenth, however, a radical shift towards manufacturing luxurious high-quality cloth occurred, woven exclusively with the best English wool. As a result of chronic warfare, among other things, transportation costs along the continental routes in Europe had become too high, and even the larger, less expensive capacity of ships was not enough to be able to compete successfully with less exclusive woollens manufactured in other regions. International competition became increasingly fierce. The English moreover used their wool exports as a political and fiscal weapon, taxing them ever more highly, which made this basic raw material even more expensive for Low Countries entrepreneurs. To make things worse, from the fourteenth century on, the English developed an increasingly vigorous cloth industry oriented towards export of their own – for which even skilled labour from the Low Countries was recruited.

These industrial transformations went hand in hand with social and political shifts in the manufacturing towns. The key figures of industrial expansion in the long twelfth century had been the merchants: they supplied the raw materials and marketed the finished products. These traders did not always intervene directly in the production process, though they did hold the strings in their hands. Via intermediaries and agents they controlled the activities of hundreds of textile workers; and via their cloth guilds or the municipal authorities they imposed their norms and standards on manufacturers (see Chapter 4). The classic independent artisan at work under his own roof with a few journeymen and apprentices (including his own sons) is a mere fiction in such circumstances. Frequently the weavers did not even possess their own looms and they were bound to the merchant by credit arrangements or lived in houses owned by them. But the switch to high-quality luxury cloth changed this situation fundamentally, putting the master craftsmen rather than the merchants at centre stage.

Simultaneously, the population crisis of the fourteenth century, in the wake of the Great Famine (1315–17) and the Black Death (1348–9), made skilled artisans scarcer, so that they were able to demand higher wages. The purchasing power of urban middling groups rose across the continent, resulting in a greater demand for artisanal products. Moreover, the increasingly exclusive woollens manufactured from the latter part of the thirteenth century required much more elaborate quality control, and it was the artisans' guilds – instead of the merchants' guilds – that succeeded in monopolising this function. Only a few important towns in the counties of Flanders and Holland, such as Douai and Leiden, constituted an exception to this development. The artisans' guilds gained political clout in a number of violent revolts before and after 1300. Especially in the towns of Flanders those conflicts led to far-reaching and lasting political and institutional shifts (see Chapters 3 and 4). The masses of proletarianised textile workers of the twelfth and thirteenth centuries were supplanted by a smaller group of corporately organised 'small commodity producers'. A portion of these artisans were capable of working their way up to become clothiers (*drapiers*) who succeeded both in expanding their control over the manufacturing processes – primarily via subcontracting – and in accessing local politics.

A hundred years later, at the end of the fourteenth century, the smaller production centres in inner Flanders followed suit, and here, too, they chose to manufacture more expensive cloth. Initially their efforts met with great success, the more so because they could switch more radically to processing the newly imported Spanish merino wool than could the more traditionalist larger textile cities. Inevitably, however, here, too, cloth manufacture met with increasing difficulties in the late fifteenth century and the production of less expensive textiles shifted once again. A few smaller urban centres in south-west Flanders (Poperinge, Menen, Roeselare, Armentières) were able to hold on to their industrial infrastructure for a while, but most lower- and middle-quality woollens made from lower-quality wool shifted to the countryside for good, especially in western Flanders (Nieuwkerke) and central Brabant (Duffel). In addition, from the second half of the fifteenth century other market segments came to the forefront. The so-called 'light drapery' or 'dry drapery' (worsteds and semi-worsteds) had been given up in most towns around 1300, but from the fifteenth century onwards a few new centres specialised fully in the production of says and other lighter fabrics, which required less complex processing than the traditional urban 'greased drapery' (*draperie ointe*) with its luxury cloth. Some larger semi-rural and semi-urban production centres in particular achieved great success, for example Ronse and above all Hondschoote. Towns that were unable to pursue this switch fell irrevocably into decline. In the fifteenth century, the impoverished town of Diksmuide was but a shadow of the proud textile town that it had been around 1300. What is striking is that smaller towns proved to be particularly vulnerable.

In spite of these sometimes radical changes, the urban network in Flanders, Artois and Brabant remained very much intact, while room for growth was apparent in the province of Holland. The reason for this relative stability in the urban system and for the growth in the north lay not so much in holding on to the industrial monoculture – as historians have mimicked Henri Pirenne (1862–1935) in declaring for a century now – but in the switch to other industries and functions. This was not limited to the textile sector, of course. Over time, textile industries were supplanted in large part by other sectors, primarily in the area of specialised art and fashion industries. During the fifteenth century, the towns of Bruges, Tournai, Brussels and Antwerp – and by extension the urban networks in Flanders, Brabant, Hainaut and Zeeland – were known for the flourishing of painting, book production, sculpture and woodcarving (Bruges, Brussels, Ghent, Mechelen and Antwerp), the tapestry industry (first Tournai and Arras, later Brussels and Oudenaarde), silk weaving (Antwerp), silver and goldsmiths (Antwerp, Lille), furniture making, Cordoba or Spanish leather (Leuven and Mechelen), embroidery (Antwerp, Mechelen, Lier, Brussels), ironwork (Liège), hats, gloves and other specialised ready-made clothing (Bruges, Brussels), weapons (Valenciennes, Bruges, Mons) and so forth. In each instance these are sectors in which virtuosity, inventiveness, flexibility and artistic design played a major role. At the same time these were industries in which specialisation and division of labour persisted. Master artisans specialised in certain products and developed niches of their own, such as the miniaturists and scribes for books of hours and other devotional books, printers, landscape painters, wall tapestries from Oudenaarde characterised as 'green-pieces' or *verdures*, images of Our Lady from Mechelen, cupboards from Antwerp, earthenware and carved altarpieces – the list goes on.

Product innovation was necessary to counter the changing circumstances of the market. In view of the fact that competition had become more difficult inside and outside the Low Countries, 'traditional' production centres started competing instead on the basis of quality and inventiveness. In economic terms this can be described as progress towards 'monopolistic competition', that is, competition with relatively 'unique' products. This had been the case for the luxury woollens of the big cities from the thirteenth century onwards; now similar processes took place with the new luxury goods that were increasingly manufactured from the fifteenth century. As a result of their specific identity and their particular niche markets, such commodities are less sensitive to competition from comparable products. The process involved products with a high added value (expensive textiles, artistic and luxury goods, etc.), in which the price of raw materials played a major role, in addition to the highly qualified labour. In this way, specialised urban entrepreneurs succeeded in evolving from price-takers into price-makers and from trend-followers into trend-setters. This transformation had also occurred in Italy and England, but the incentives in the southern Low Countries were greater as a result of their high level of urbanisation, the growing domestic market and the central location in European trade routes. The process was helped because the traditional export markets for textiles were thoroughly redefined as a result of increased transportation costs and import substitutions (the process whereby – in the sales regions, in this case – imported goods are replaced by production of one's own).

In order to better understand this development, the labour relations between merchants and producers, as well as the institutional underpinnings of the production process, have to be looked at over the long term. The fact that the turn towards products with high added value took place in the older centres was undoubtedly connected to the extant infrastructure and the human capital present. The strong tradition of economic regulation (of large-scale textile production) was also of importance. Above all, the artisans' guilds that had formed in the thirteenth century played a central role in the process (see Chapter 3). Chronologically, the breakthrough of the previously rather embryonic artisans' corporations that had come to develop coincided with the beginning of the conversion to production of high-quality textiles. New rules – such as an obligatory apprenticeship term and a master's trial – came about at approximately the same time as the high-quality art and luxury industries were developing. The current state of research cannot indicate to what extent a causal relationship existed between the two phenomena, yet in theory the technical qualities of journeymen and master artisans could be encouraged by regulating training. Via quality control, production requirements, market segmentation and the development of hallmarks, standardisation and supervision of product quality became more easily enforceable. Nevertheless, although in most towns the development of these guilds correlated with the ever greater political and institutional power of master artisans, these regulations were possible without the artisans' guilds too – witness in that regard the success of towns like Leiden and Douai, where artisans could not impose regulations through guilds themselves. Moreover, in the northern provinces the connection between economic development and the growth of artisans' guilds was less pronounced. Export-oriented industries such as woollen cloth and silk weaving in Amsterdam, linen bleaching in Haarlem, silk and fustian weaving in Gouda and cloth weaving in Leiden, Haarlem and Delft were able to grow without or with only weak craft guilds.

The causes for the establishment and the success of craft guilds are traditionally sought in social and political contexts, specifically in the struggle for emancipation on the part of proletarianised manufacturers versus major merchants (see Chapters 3 and 4). In Belgium the ideas of Henri Pirenne strongly influenced the debates for a long time. Given his liberal orientation, this historian saw the corporate regimes that had risen as a result of the 'democratic revolutions' of the fourteenth century as distant predecessors of the nineteenth-century Belgian state, praised for its liberal freedoms. From an economic point of view, however, according to Pirenne, the establishment of craft guilds supposedly also had disastrous consequences. Guilds, after all, obstructed the emergence of a free market and of the free competition upon which that market ought to be founded. They provided for high wages and higher production costs and, therefore, for increasing handicaps in an export-oriented economy. The guilds themselves partly played into this image of strong protectionism. The raids organised by artisans to destroy looms in the surrounding countryside may well have been a phenomenon limited in time and space, yet they had other means at their disposal for eliminating competition too. Thus they took legal steps against the production of certain fabrics in smaller towns which they called 'imitations', as the conflicts between Ghent and Dendermonde and between Ypres and Poperinge testify. Urban authorities influenced by artisans sometimes also imposed protectionist measures: in the county of Flanders as well as a few towns in Brabant, the import of English cloth, among other items, was forbidden.

During recent decades, however, the establishment and consequences of guilds have been understood in a different way. The emergence of craft guilds ushered in a struggle for control over regulations, yet, from the perspective of the so-called 'new institutional economics', regulation is not opposed to economic effectiveness. According to this research tradition, craft guilds fostered market transparency, product quality and the production of human capital. As the durability of monopolistic competition required the imposition of strict product standards and a high level of quality from the entire group of producers concerned, the conversion to high-quality textiles or the development of art industries could benefit from strict corporate rules and regulations oriented towards standardising the product and monitoring its 'value'. The trust of buyers in the product was guaranteed by mechanisms for controlling and sanctioning, whereby either products needed to be presented systematically to examiners from the guild or guild deans were authorised to visit workshops and to confiscate 'bad' products. Good quality was also made visible to the client by means of a collective hallmark, which served as a kind of 'label' or 'brand' in the modern sense of the word. Where necessary, new techniques that threatened to cause harm to quality were forbidden, as happened in the case of the fulling mill. Although this engine had been introduced relatively rapidly into the production process for cloth, it proved to be unusable in the turn towards quality that urban cloth entrepreneurs were making from the late thirteenth century onwards, and its use was restricted as a consequence.

From the same perspective the corporate apprenticeship system supposedly provided both masters and apprentices with incentives to invest in human capital through the exclusion of free-riders and contract enforcement mechanisms. Masters were assured of a return on their investment in a training programme by means of an obligatory term of apprenticeship and registration fees (which prevented an apprentice from absconding once he could earn a wage elsewhere). The apprentice was guaranteed good training (by way of a limit on the number of apprentices per master and the objectification of the acquired skills by means of the master's trial). According to the economic historian Stephan R. Epstein, such incentives allowed decisive (technological) innovations in corporately organised industries in the long run.

Without a doubt, the emergence and development of guilds also had a social and political dimension. By the establishment of craft guilds, tensions arose between merchants and the corporately organised producers. Before the switch in the thirteenth century, merchants had all production cycles under their guard, in addition to the commercial circuits. In so doing they themselves vouchsafed the standardisation of products. As a result of the establishment of the craft guilds, this was no longer self-evident. In the county of Flanders, new rules and regulations frequently prevented traders from still being involved with actual production. In fifteenth-century Nieuwkerke, for example, merchants were forbidden from weaving, dyeing, fulling or shearing cloth. In Kortrijk and Menen, wool merchants and cloth retailers were not allowed to order woollens to be woven, whereas masters generally were still allowed to conduct trade via the Bruges or Antwerp gateway. In Leuven and Namur, too, the major masters (the so-called *drapiers*) reserved certain production steps for their own workshops (or for their subcontractors). In the northern Low Countries the situation was fundamentally different, however. There, traders were indeed still frequently admitted to the craft guilds or allowed to take up specific production activities in export industries, and it was generally more difficult for producers to accumulate capital and to develop industrial networks than it was in the south. Frequently, producers were not even allowed to be involved with certain trading activities. In the southern regions, in contrast, even the mechanisms for entry into the guild seem to have had the main purpose of preventing merchants from being involved with manufacture, by the guilds directly recruiting apprentices, journeymen or junior masters for themselves. Among other things, the master's trial was targeted to prevent that kind of intrusion into the guild sphere.

There was, therefore, both a socio-political and an economic rationale behind the fact that 'free-masters' (*vrijmeesters*, that is, producers who were members of the guild after they had finished an apprenticeship and had paid the admission fees) guarded the division between production and trade. Craft guilds saw to it that products were manufactured by or under the supervision of a master – that is, someone who had an apprenticeship and later also a master's trial behind him – regardless of whoever sold those products on the marketplace. By the same token, masters protected their own status, since the division between trade and production via the master's status prevented them from degenerating into wage or piece labourers in the service of major merchant-entrepreneurs. Thus the classic image of the artisan who worked with a few journeymen and apprentices in his own shop and for his own account remained intact to the outside world. In practice, this model was undermined by less visible dependencies and forms of subcontracting, but that did not prevent master artisans from holding on to their privileged status.

The guilds in the southern regions owed their economic impact in large part to their political and religious prestige, which they showed by building guild houses, usually located in the centre of town, and by administering religious and social institutions like almshouses, chapels and altars, among other things (see Chapter 6). It is no coincidence that 'free-masters' were obliged to be *poorters* ('burghers') of the town, and they insisted on working in the front halves of their workshops, in sight of guild administrators and examiners as well as the public. Until well into the eighteenth century, master artisans continued to cultivate the interwoven nature of economic privilege and the town as a political body by means of the great visibility of their prestigious guild houses, chapels and altars and their participation in processions and pageants (*ommegangen*), among other things. Nevertheless, 'urban' is not necessarily synonymous with 'corporate', nor did the town have a monopoly on 'regulation'. Before the establishment of craft guilds, and even in towns where the craft guilds were never truly established or powerful, like Douai and Leiden, certain crucial economic activities, such as cloth manufacture and food supply, were also intensely regulated. Moreover, even rural industries could be thoroughly regulated, with an eye on certain product standards and quality requirements, as the examples of Hondschoote says or Nieuwkerke woollens clearly demonstrate.

In general, however, the turn towards autonomous artisans' guilds was not taken in the countryside or in many of the smaller centres of production. In that case merchants still stood at the head of hierarchical commercial networks, oriented towards the commercial gateways and/ or finishing centres. Moreover, the existence of craft guilds did not prevent guild-organised *drapiers* from themselves going to markets less and less often over the course of the sixteenth century. In textiles, the export trade often ran via foreign merchants who themselves stayed in the major commercial cities and who seldom entered into direct contact with the production process. That interaction occurred through the intervention of financiers, brokers and traders, as the preserved trading ledgers of the Bruges broker Wouter Ameide clearly demonstrate. Above all, in the new textile industries (light woollens, linen, tapestries), the scale of manufacture changed and small commodity producers were supplanted by traders, intermediaries and major entrepreneurs. Sales came to be concentrated in the hands of local agents of important Antwerp firms such as Van der Molen or Cordes, or local or regional traders who conducted trade with these firms gained prominence. Some of these middlemen were genuine 'putting-out merchants' (*Verleger*) – for instance, traders from Antwerp, Calais, Lille and Hondschoote who allowed small local *drapiers* to concentrate production. Only in the more traditional cloth industries (Menen, Nieuwkerke) did entrepreneurs work like medieval urban *drapiers*, by being responsible themselves for marketing and for contacts with international merchants.

What also remains as yet unclear is what evolution corporate regulations underwent in the long sixteenth century. Economic growth went hand in hand, after all, with industrial conversion and a shift of the gateway function to Antwerp, a city that was seen as 'freer' than Bruges, although that 'freedom' is more often than not vaguely defined by historians. Up to a certain point the craft guilds adapted to the change and innovation, and even steered them. When necessary, maximum limits on the numbers of journeymen and apprentices per master were relaxed, as happened, for instance, in the important craft guild of Antwerp cloth dressers, who finished the processing of English cloth in particular. Occasionally a craft guild was even temporarily abolished, as happened with the Antwerp bricklayers and dyers in the sixteenth century and the beginning of the seventeenth century respectively.

A great deal depended on the power relations between merchants and major master artisans, as well as on the position taken by the local authorities in the process. This can be illustrated with conflicts about the maximum size of workshops. The opposing interests of merchants and major master craftsmen in sixteenth-century Antwerp have been investigated in this respect. Whereas the masters strove for deregulation and the admission of larger businesses (and, therefore, concentration), the merchants benefitted from keeping businesses small (and from a large number of minor master artisans). For them, the presence of many smaller masters meant cheap skilled labour and a strong bargaining position, whereas the position of masters with large workshops was much stronger. As far as entry into the craft guild was concerned, the interests of the two groups were perhaps less divergent. Neither in Bruges nor in Antwerp were excessively high financial barriers thrown up (at least before the seventeenth century): major master artisans could expand their activities by subcontracting other masters, and they, like the merchants, must therefore have been in favour of relatively low thresholds for entry into the guild, which inevitably also lowered the price of skilled labour.

Whatever the case, in the northern provinces the craft guilds never had such an influence over municipal economic policy, except in some of the older centres like Dordrecht or Utrecht. In contrast to the craft guilds in Flanders, Brabant, Hainaut, Namur and the prince-bishopric of Liège, the craft guilds in the core regions of the north never acquired access to municipal power (or only indirectly, by participation in election committees). In the county of Holland, the guilds did not emerge until the political momentum they had achieved in other regions had already long gone. Moreover, the craft guilds in the north lost their religious function and a large part of their status during the Dutch Revolt. In the seventeenth century they were first and foremost social organisations, which collected entry fees and charges with an eye towards mutual assistance. Economic regulation came about under the impetus of the merchant-regents and therefore also with the interests of trade in mind, rather than those of the producers.

Conclusions

Until the thirteenth century the most prominent international trade nodes were located outside the Low Countries. Merchants from Flanders, Artois and Brabant sold their textiles at the fairs of Champagne, or they expanded trade networks themselves in Italy, England or central Europe. By 1300 this situation had changed dramatically. The Flemings lost ground in the international trade circuit, whereas their industrial commodities remained very much desired. For two centuries, foreign traders – Italian and Hanseatic merchants the first among them – congregated in Bruges. From the 1460s onwards most commercial activity relocated to Antwerp, as a consequence of macro-economic changes and political events. After Antwerp was conquered by the troops of Governor-General Alexander Farnese in 1585, it was Amsterdam's turn to develop into the most important commercial centre in the Low Countries.

Throughout the centuries, however, structural changes had occurred, both in the towns and within the urban network. The continuing tension between European commerce (and gradually also commercial links with the Americas and beyond) on the one hand, and regional commercial and industrial developments on the other, turned the densely urbanised Low Countries into an exceptionally dynamic economic region. The economic vitality made persistent growth possible, but at the same time it was a process of continuing the restructuring and relocation of activities. In the towns of Flanders, Brabant, Hainaut, Holland and the river region of Guelders and the river IJssel, an entrepreneurial climate prevailed whereby nodal cities could grow into prominent centres of interregional trade, oriented towards export and towards provisioning the urban network itself. This entrepreneurial climate was based upon age-old commercial and manufacturing expertise that was institutionalised in structures oriented towards protecting trade interests and safeguarding value (the quality of products), but at the same time allowed for sometimes dramatic phases of adaptation and innovation. In the dense network of small and medium-sized towns, moreover, the relatively numerous, financially strong and productive middling groups constituted an active and flexible factor. In the larger industrial and trade cities, very diverse and highly specialised economic activities were concentrated, yet ultimately it was the interplay of small and large towns and rural industries that created a very varied supply of artisanal commodities for which there was demand across all of Europe and far beyond.

In an initial phase the towns owed their specific importance to a long period of economic growth in north-west Europe from the twelfth century to the end of the thirteenth. The development of artisanal production of textiles oriented towards export – initially in Artois and Flanders, though from the thirteenth century onwards also in Brabant, Hainaut and Holland – played a crucial role in that process. In the Meuse valley (metals) as well as in the county of Holland (shipbuilding, brewing, fishing, peat extraction), it was other industries that provided the vitality. This industrial expansion laid the foundation for the entire process of urbanisation and made possible the great density of urban life over a relatively limited land area. Moreover, this industrial fabric proved to be especially flexible in the long run, despite the difficult periods of transition and regional change.

In a second phase – from the fourteenth century until the beginning of the seventeenth – it was precisely this regional diversity that lay at the foundation of economic conversion and new growth in regions that were urbanised at a later date. The interaction between neighbouring regions that developed in different ways generated complementarity, competition and relocation. The demand in the large towns of Brabant and Flanders stimulated export-oriented production in the county of Holland. The structural shortage of cereals in Holland forced a search for massive imports from Artois and Picardy first and from Prussia thereafter, whereby cargo trade and shipbuilding in Holland and Zeeland pushed the German Hanse aside. In the process, the position of the Hanse, one of the pillars of the export trade in neighbouring Flanders, was jeopardised. Amsterdam thus developed from a transit harbour for Hamburg beer to a seaport with more favourable possibilities for growth than even Antwerp for bulk trade. The shift of migration flows and the transfer of knowledge and capital provided late bloomers in Holland with opportunities for further expansion, sometimes even against a more general European trend. Thanks to innovation and the relocation of industrial production within the urban network itself, between the various provinces and between town and countryside, the urban economies succeeded, albeit with considerable difficulty, in once again being the engine for remarkable growth during the long sixteenth century and well into the seventeenth.

3   Living Together in the City: Social Relationships Between Norm and Practice

Bruno Blondé, Frederik Buylaert, Jan Dumolyn, Jord Hanus and Peter Stabel

Introduction

In 1556, Pieter Bruegel the Elder (1520/25–1569) made a drawing commonly called *Big Fish Eat Little Fish*. It is no coincidence that the skyline of Antwerp's harbour adorns the background. With that image, Bruegel depicted an idea that was prevalent in mid-sixteenth-century Antwerp: that of a hard, merciless world in which the rich pursued happiness at the expense of the poor. Antwerp was, of course, a commercial metropolis, yet the success story also had its dark side. Not everyone profited in the same way or to the same extent from global trade and the ensuing economic growth. Undoubtedly hundreds of merchants, artisans and entrepreneurs made a fortune. At the same time, however, great numbers of master artisans were degraded to virtual wage-labourers in the service of merchant capitalists. The actual wage-labourers themselves saw their wages eroded as a result of rising house rents and food prices. For beggars and vagabonds – the undesired immigrants – the towns of the Low Countries, and the metropolis of Antwerp first among them, were anything but hospitable.

In the very same town in 1566, a neighbourhood committee from around the Eiermarkt turned to the municipal government with a special request. It asked for a patch of common land that could be used by local militiamen as training grounds and a place for assembly. With nostalgia the petitioners referred to earlier times. Back then the neighbourhood residents had gathered 'once a year for love of neighbours and out of friendship' (*uyt gebueren liefde ende vrientschappe alle jaeren eens*). On these occasions they had enjoyed each other's company and had a meal while a jaybird was shot. With regret, however, they stated that, from around 1530, all this had fallen into disuse and 'gone to nothing' (*te nyeten gegaen*), all as a result of war and the 'costly times' (*dueren tijt*). That the inhabitants of the Eiermarkt referred to the years after 1530, above all, as the period in which neighbourhood life had lost its conviviality is not without significance. Antwerp experienced an explosive increase in

Figure 3.1 Pieter van der Heyden, *Big Fish Eat Little Fish*, print after a design by Pieter Bruegel the Elder, 1556. Pieter Bruegel the Elder first worked as a print designer for the prolific Antwerp publisher Hieronymus Cock. The engraving bears the title 'Oppression of the poor: the rich are oppressing you through violence' ('Verdruckinghe der armen. De rijcke lieden verdrucken u door gewelt'), thus making reference to the apocryphal Gospel of James. This print has a clear social message, but it was also repeatedly used as a caricature during periods of political conflict, as in the campaign of Maurice of Nassau against Johan van Oldenbarnevelt in 1619.

population in those years, and the town kept on growing to the top of the European urban hierarchy. The petitioners understood that 'prosperity' (*prospersiteyt*) did not necessarily lead to 'unity' (*eendrachtigheiyt*).[1]

Such sighs and lamentation were undoubtedly loudest in cosmopolitan Antwerp because here social change had come most rapidly, though they were unmistakably shared across the entire urban network of the

---

[1] City Archives Antwerp, Privilegekamer, 629, fol. 63r; An M. Kint, 'The community of commerce: social relations in sixteenth-century Antwerp', unpublished PhD dissertation, Columbia University (1996), p. 127.

Low Countries. In this part of north-west Europe, representations of society from the late Middle Ages to the end of the sixteenth century changed drastically. Besides the traditional image of society comprising three complementary estates – the clergy, the nobility and the third estate – more and more new conceptualisations were developed. In the process, there were laments about those who were unfairly becoming rich at the expense of their honest fellow citizens, about quarrelsome women not knowing their place, or about the undeserving poor who allegedly disturbed the public order. Social change, or concern with social change, was reflected in Netherlandish culture. Between the eleventh and the sixteenth centuries, the social fabric had become not only much more complex but also, in many aspects, less 'stable'.

This chapter describes the trajectory from the first articulation of an ideal of urban community in the central Middle Ages to the sixteenth century, when social divisions became deeper. Which social forces and tensions characterised the medieval town in the Low Countries and how did these develop under the influence of economic growth, adversity, war, state-building, disease and occasionally also dearth and famine? From the contemporary claims discussed in the chapter's introduction, it immediately becomes clear that sketching an entire set of social relationships is a delicate operation. In many cases the sources are so scarce that a creative reading of the few remaining traces is necessary. Where sources are available, discourse on social tensions must be approached with a critical eye. In the following pages it will become clear that the 'good old times', to which the collectivity of neighbours from the Eiermarkt referred, had actually never genuinely existed. What is more, despite decades of active commitment to social history, research is not as thorough for every period of time, or for every social group or form of social relationship. Even though much is known about friendship, pub-crawling, church attendance, poor relief, charity, prostitution, crime, housing conditions and work, a number of social relationships have yet to give up their secrets. This chapter thus provides a social narrative with many lacunae.

The Ideal of the Commune

The eleventh and early twelfth centuries constitute a watershed in the self-image and social organisation of new towns. From that time on, written evidence makes extensive mention of diverse groups with an unmistakably 'urban' social, economic and cultural profile. Moreover, from then on the available evidence suggests that town dwellers were developing their own view of the world, in which their social, legal and political identity and autonomy were emphasised in relation, sometimes even in opposition, to traditional rural society. The earliest urban communities were composed of diverse groups, either with an earlier urban background or coming from outside an urban milieu. The perception that town dwellers were very different from the countryfolk and the concomitant feeling of their belonging together, however, developed only gradually. It seems unlikely that monks, knights and stewards in the abbey demesnes and castles around which settlements had formed in the earliest phases of urbanisation will have experienced these concentrations of artisans and traders as essentially urban. Even later, ecclesiastical and feudal demesne institutions and enclaves – small pieces of territory with their own jurisdictions – continued to exist. They constituted a kind of 'foreign body' inside the town (see Chapter 6). But they could not prevent the urban community itself from being economically and spatially dominant. Yet this was clearly still not the case in the ninth, tenth or early eleventh centuries, when in many towns it was abbots, bishops and secular feudal lords who dominated what would later become almost autonomous towns. For all sorts of reasons, urban growth rapidly went hand in hand with the rise of greater personal freedom. This freedom applied both to the merchants, who used their know-how to trade on their own account, and to previously unfree or semi-free peasants, who settled in the emerging towns as craftsmen.

After the eleventh century, urban population increased quickly, a fact which was mirrored, among other things, in the expansion of urban territory and the increase in the number of parishes (see Chapter 5). Urban infrastructure expanded considerably and the social and professional diversity of the urban population broadened. Towns became the stage for the rise of more complex systems of division of labour, as well as new social relations, in addition to the traditional family structures and networks of patronage that had characterised feudal society. This expansion phase peaked at the end of the thirteenth century. The dominant socio-economic, legal, political and symbolic form of organisation that framed this process of growth was the 'commune', a sworn community of free men who wanted to establish a rule of law with the protection of property rights as a necessary precondition to engaging unmolested in trade and industry.

This so-called 'communal movement' came of age in Western Europe between the end of the tenth century and the beginning of the thirteenth. It was a process of political and legal emancipation with important social dimensions. Although historians have traditionally hesitated to consider most towns in the southern Netherlands as communes, recent research has pointed to specific forms of commune that can be identified in the episcopal cities of Cambrai (1077) and Tournai (1147), and in Valenciennes in the county of Hainaut (1114). In Flanders the term *communio* was used explicitly in Saint-Omer, while in Aire-sur-la-Lys and Lille there was talk of an *amicitia* (a 'friendship'). In essence, however, it seems to have been a very similar phenomenon in each of these cases, albeit with legal and institutional differences. Nevertheless, we should have no illusions about the social harmony in such urban communes. Although town seals or bell towers deliberately and symbolically express such unity and social cohesion, whereby the commune presented itself invariably as an indivisible political collectivity until the middle of the thirteenth century, the commune's internal harmony was more an ideal image than a daily reality. Even the earliest urban settlements experienced fierce social clashes. Opposition between poor and rich or rivalries among town residents with different social and professional status, for example, can be traced back in Galbert of Bruges's narrative on the murder of Count Charles the Good in 1127 and the subsequent crisis in the county of Flanders. So in Bruges, for instance, an elite – literally a group of 'wise men' (*prudentes viri*) – assumed the judicial and political prerogatives within the communal order. Furthermore, twelfth-century sources make distinctions between a number of typical elite groups, such as the *milites*, *scabini*, *iudices*, *meliores* and *potentes*, as well as the middling groups of artisans that are increasingly mentioned in written sources. Unfortunately, those sources remain silent about the poorer strata of society and about women.

Merchants and Landowners: The Powers That Be

When the available written sources become more numerous from the twelfth and the thirteenth centuries on, more details become available about social inequality in the towns of the Low Countries. The urban upper class left the earliest, or at least the clearest, traces of group identities in the sources. One constituent of the urban elite was the mercantile capital that was earned, probably in long-distance trade. At the beginning of the eleventh century, merchant guilds appear in the sources as institutions that are usually linked to communal organisation (e.g. Tiel in 1020, Valenciennes in 1051–70 and Saint-Omer in 1100). From the middle of the twelfth century these guilds seem to have been gradually replaced in some towns by Hanse-like societies, which included members from multiple towns. Both the one-city-based merchant guild and the multi-city hanse provided mutual protection for merchants, not least through the organisation of armed convoys. Yet clearly the notion of 'charity' (*caritas*) was important as well. Guild members attended the funerals of their deceased confrères. They shared a common devotion and they gave alms to the poor on feast days. These organisations also organised joint guild meals and drinking parties (see Chapter 8). Merchant guilds often managed the halls that served as the infrastructure for trade. In eleventh-century Saint-Omer, there was talk of a guildhall (*gild'halla*). The merchant guilds even participated in the town government. Certainly in the leading commercial towns, the merchant guilds began to overlap with the economic and political elites. In thirteenth-century Bruges, for instance, it was stipulated that anyone who wanted to be a member of the bench of aldermen had to have been a member of the 'Flemish Hanse of London' – the leading merchants' guild – for at least a year and a day.

The twelfth-century town was, therefore, a fluctuating and dynamic society dominated by a very small (usually) mercantile elite. The elites presented themselves as the *sapientes, meliores, maiores, discretissimi, fortiores, prudentiores* or *magisfideles*, claiming that, in one form or another, their political authority was rooted in moral superiority. Although commercial wealth and the possession of land were fundamental criteria for access to the elite, the social self-fashioning of these terms also indicates the importance of experience and social status. In the largest centres of growth, the increasing accumulation of capital in export-oriented trade and industry gradually undermined the social balance. The medieval growth phase between approximately 1050 and 1270 was characterised by great concentration of wealth and power in the hands of the merchant class. In the thirteenth century, the segment of the urban elite that dominated the town government and public finances assumed a profile that was increasingly distinct from that of other urban groups.

Apart from revenues from trade, ownership of land in towns was important for claiming social superiority. This was most strongly felt in Ghent, where the political elite went by the name of *viri hereditarii*, or *erfachtige lieden*, that is, people who were to inherit land. In Douai and Saint-Omer, too, ownership of urban land was an important matter, and in a similar way the elites in the episcopal city of Tournai and in Arras in Artois derived their status from the possession of land with hereditary rents. During the same period, the lands that the earliest city dwellers had acquired at fixed customary rents were further subdivided (or the customary rent on them was sometimes completely abrogated).

Landownership was, however, often closely entwined with trade. The increasingly large revenues from property in expanding towns were often re-invested in commercial enterprises, and property deeds could also serve as pledges for business contracts or credit arrangements. From the late thirteenth century onwards, these same considerations encouraged the urban elites to buy land outside the towns as well. Investments in agricultural land have long been understood as a sign that urban elites had abandoned the urban economy, fraught as it was with risk, for the security of large-scale landownership (the so-called 'betrayal of the bourgeoisie'). But landownership is now understood as a necessary buffer against the risks that came with money-changing, market speculation or trade in raw materials. It is revealing that around 1400 the middling groups of Ghent also began investing in land possession outside the towns, much as the elite had done earlier, and that around 1500 even less well-off families of craftsmen often acquired a patch of land outside the town walls. This not only provided a welcome supplement to their income but it also helped to protect them against recurrent crises in the markets for cereals and other foodstuffs.

Many of the investments in land outside the towns were not aimed at income stability, however. They were sometimes also highly speculative investments, linked to the progressive urbanisation of society. Many families from Ghent, for example, invested in the purchase of peat-rich land to meet the insatiable urban demand for fuel. In the town of Leiden in Holland, prominent families built brick and lime kilns to exploit the clay and lime deposits that were abundant in the town's hinterland. In this way they attempted to profit from the increasing preference for bricks to construct urban dwellings. In light of the precocious urbanisation of the Low Countries and the growing reliance on the import of subsistence cereals from abroad (see Chapter 2), town dwellers increasingly invested in building dykes round land for food production in regions where the risk of flooding was never far away, speculating that the revenues would be greater than the initial outlay. Quite a few polders on islands in contemporary Zeeland are named after prominent urban families that financed the dyke works. The combination of speculative investments and a constant risk-spreading diversification of revenues explains the sometimes remarkable durability of urban elites. The Borluut family, for example, participated in Ghent's political arena from the twelfth century until after the French Revolution. That is not to say that downward social mobility was unknown. At the same time, as elite families often failed to produce male heirs, the ranks of urban elites were often reinforced with much-needed new blood recruited from middling groups.

Traditionally, historians proceeded from a dichotomy between a 'capitalist' urban economy fraught with risk and a more 'traditional' agrarian society. In reality, urbanisation reshaped both urban and rural society. The rise of towns was, after all, dependent on surpluses of the rural economy (see Chapter 2). This was also true for political power. In most towns in the Low Countries – the large towns of Flanders and Brabant constituting an important exception – the administration of justice became the prerogative of a small elite over the course of the Middle Ages. Building on the influential views of the Belgian historian Henri Pirenne (1862–1935), historians often insisted that the commercial town differed fundamentally from its 'feudal' hinterland. In the towns there was no place for forced labour, such as the lords demanded from their peasants, and residents in the countryside could free themselves from manorial obligations by moving to the towns (*Stadtluft macht frei*: 'urban air liberates'). In a similar vein, the difference was stressed between the exercise of power in the countryside, where, as a rule, seigneurial prerogatives were hereditary, and in the town, where hereditary claims to a seat on the bench of aldermen were not accepted or were contested. Caution is, however, in order. As the Borluut case shows, urban political dynasties did exist, and urban politicians expressly defined themselves as members of the seigneurial system. After all, the town council was the legal representation of the prince in the Low Countries.

This is not to deny that, as soon as someone walked through a town gate, he must immediately have recognised the distinct nature of urban identity. Yet, recent research also suggests that contemporaries framed the fundamentally new world that was the town within an aristocratic, or even 'feudal', world view. Thus, for instance, Jelle De Rock has shown that patrons of religious paintings and portraits in the fifteenth-century Low Countries developed a taste for backgrounds in which the lifeblood of the 'urban'– the hustle and bustle of trade and industry – was brushed away in favour of rural backgrounds or architectural skylines with aristocratic towers. These fifteenth-century elites were probably no less rooted in the urban economy than their predecessors, yet they came to cherish pastoral or feudal tropes to counterbalance the experiences of everyday life in the town. The habit of many early modern urban elites of spending the summer on their country estates and the winter in their urban mansions has medieval roots.

A last element of urban elite formation in the Low Countries that deserves consideration is the historiographical trend of describing urban elites of the southern Low Countries as a 'patriciate'. The term is derived from Ancient Rome and suggests that the elite consisted of a cluster of powerful families. The Roman patriciate consisted of a well-defined group of 'lineages' with a distinct legal status. This image is undoubtedly fitting for thirteenth-century Ghent, where the elite was uncommonly cut and dried. Yet, this was not the case for most other towns in the Low Countries. In neighbouring Bruges, for example, the town council consisted of a core of well-known political families that held an exorbitantly large number of the available seats in the bench of aldermen: between 1350 and 1500, the most powerful families constantly claimed approximately half of the available mandates. This cluster of political dynasties was embedded in a broad, and volatile, periphery of individuals who became aldermen only once or twice. This suggests that moneyed, talented and ambitious individuals also had the chance to participate in urban government, even if they did not belong to an elite lineage. In spite of a high degree of endogamy, the urban elite – moving between the nobility and the elite of the craft guilds – only rarely constituted a hermetically sealed caste. Thirteenth-century Ghent was clearly the exception.

A similar observation has been made for the well-documented elite in Leiden, the leading textile centre in the county of Holland. Here, the political elite, called the *vroedschap*, was dominated by a clique of powerful families who derived their incomes from multiple activities. Yet they were unable, or unwilling, to keep *homines novi* out of the town council. Urban politics in the medieval Low Countries was the prerogative not only of the family but also of the individual. For important issues, the political elite was often inclined to involve other social groups of good standing. Over the course of the fifteenth century, for example, the *vroedschap* of Leiden increasingly consulted with the economic elite, called the 'wealthy' (*rycdom*). This was the moneyed upper stratum of the town not directly involved in politics, but which clearly expected to have a voice in the decision-making process nonetheless.

While the urban elite based its power and status primarily on the systematic accumulation of capital from land, finance and trade, the dominant families also used their power and networks to enrich themselves. They did so through mechanisms that today would be described as corrupt and fraudulent, although they were not yet necessarily perceived as such by contemporaries. A typical example is that, well into the thirteenth century, urban finances were managed by the leading political dynasties as a private matter, not subject to any form of monitoring by other urban groups. In the late Middle Ages, when middling groups in the town had, as a rule, successfully demanded control over the town accounts, it was still normal for a substantial portion of the revenues to be used for doling out prestigious gifts – in the case of Ghent, this is estimated as approximately 15 per cent of annual revenues. Those gifts ended up with people whose support for the establishment was considered important (e.g. members of elite families, well-to-do master craftsmen, surgeons). Dominant networks also reserved the most lucrative aspects of tax collection for themselves by means of informal pressure; or they simply bought off the prince's commissioners, who annually re-appointed the town council. As new groups in society aspired to gain access to political power, this behaviour gradually came to be considered inappropriate.

The different subgroups of the elite in the twelfth- and thirteenth-century town – knights, stewards, high clergy, merchants and urban landowners – found a common goal in safeguarding their position of power against the growing group of immigrant artisans. Until the late thirteenth century, craftsmen in the large Flemish textile towns were closer to a proletariat than to the small commodity producers they would become in later centuries. In the process, the elites frequently received support from the princely authorities and from the secular and regular clergy. Generally their interests ran parallel to those of the new entrepreneurs and the more well-to-do artisans. The latter, too, had every interest in securing property rights to land and to the means of production, and in keeping the transaction costs on urban markets as low as possible. Conflicts were possible, of course, between towns and neighbouring noblemen, who often levied tolls on the access routes to the towns, or who resorted to outright extortion of merchants.

In spite of these and other frictions, the urban elites of the late twelfth and thirteenth centuries were bent on controlling urban space, commerce, finances and the workforce. The social tensions within the commune were increasingly reflected in the town's spatial organisation. Labourers often lived in the outskirts of the expanding towns. Because of the higher prices for land and housing, the centre often became the preserve of elites and increasingly also of ambitious middling groups.

The Rise of Corporate Middling Groups

Over the course of the thirteenth century a remarkable semantic shift took place in the large Flemish towns. The concept of commons (*commun* and its variously related forms in Middle Dutch: *ghemeen*, *meente*, *meentucht*) no longer indicated the urban population in its entirety: in the connotation of 'commoner', it was now placed beside the term *poorterie* ('bourgeoisie' or 'citizenry') and referred only to the lower social strata. In large towns like Ghent and Bruges, the term *poorter* ('burgher') acquired the meaning of belonging to the urban 'upper class' or even someone who did not belong to the craft guilds but rather to the group of merchants and landowners. The discursive change was by no means absolute. In a broader sense, *poorter* still signified a 'burgher with legal rights'. Yet around 1300, the shift occurred in many places, reflecting the growing social and political oppositions, or at least a growing awareness of them. In 1245 the earliest known labour strike in the Low Countries broke out in the textile town of Douai. Although little is known of this event, it is clear that, between *c.* 1250 and *c.* 1280, social issues were claiming centre stage in the towns oriented towards textile manufacture in Artois, Flanders and Brabant. The original idea of harmony and mutual aid behind the term 'commune' now had to be framed another way, ideologically as well as legally, and it was corporatism that provided the answer.

The growth of fraternities and craft guilds – which in the towns of the Low Countries certainly constituted one of the fundamental elements of the social fabric – is frequently associated with the need for new social networks for the many immigrants in the booming towns (see Chapter 5). After all, immigrants were uprooted, as it were, from their villages and family communities. The earliest craft guilds may well have arisen spontaneously from the proximity between individuals who shared an occupational niche in a town. In Arras, for instance, an early confraternity of craftsmen can already be found at the turn of the twelfth century. Over the course of the thirteenth century these associations emerged in most of the larger towns, and by the fourteenth century even the smaller towns were touched by the trend. This process could be strengthened by various factors, ranging from shared devotional activities over occupational and social reciprocity and charity to the organisation of municipal militias.

Another important stimulus was that merchants had a vested interest in controlling artisanal production. For this, corporate structures proved very useful. They provided an effective framework to implement much-needed regulation, especially from the twelfth century onwards, when Flemish woollen textiles would conquer European markets. In the thirteenth century, the manufacture of woollens in the duchy of Brabant and the county of Holland followed similar trajectories. This strategy contained risks for elites nonetheless. The craft guilds were able to become powerful and, sooner or later, they would inevitably demand self-governance as well as their share of the power in the municipal government. This process gained strength at the end of the thirteenth century and it soon culminated in a wave of revolts around 1302 in Flanders, Brabant, Mechelen and Liège. In the large towns the craft guilds claimed representation on the town council; more generally, in many towns these power struggles resulted in a fragile social and political balance by around the 1360s. But it proved a short-lived and uneasy balance. Corporate participation in urban government went hand in hand with constant social and political conflict well into the early modern era.

This politicisation of craft guilds in the southern principalities of the Low Countries contrasts sharply with the situation in the northern principalities, where urban economic development did not really take off until the first half of the fourteenth century. In the county of Holland there was no talk at all of the political emancipation of guilds (see Chapter 2). It is striking that, in the fourteenth century, the craft guilds acquired sizable political power only in Utrecht, an episcopal city, and in Dordrecht, a commercial town economically oriented towards the Rhineland and the southern Low Countries. In most towns of Holland, the governance of the town remained the privilege of a wealthy elite – the so-called *vroedschappen* discussed earlier. Even in Leiden – where a well-oiled organisation of labour was necessary for cloth manufacture – the formation of real craft guilds was successfully stopped by the town council. This was achieved with comital support. When Duchess Mary of Burgundy was forced into granting far-reaching concessions to her subjects in 1477, one important demand from the elite in Holland was that she would allow no new guilds in the county. This did not put an end to new guilds, however. As the economy in Holland's towns expanded, greater numbers of craft guilds were organised, but their access to municipal power remained limited. Yet, despite the absence of strong political guilds, it seems that urban elites – at least in Leiden – took measures to cap the increasing concentration of capital and the means of production in a small group of merchant-drapers, and thereby protected the livelihood and independence of many small drapers and their families. For that matter, comparable social injustice was present within occupational groups in the southern Netherlands, in spite of the much more strongly developed corporate solidarity.

Even within the craft guilds a trend towards oligarchy manifested itself. First, there was the inequality between the independent master artisans vis-à-vis the journeymen, who worked for time or piece wages for a master, and the apprentices. Second, the differences in status among master artisans could be important. This was particularly true for towns where representatives from corporate organisations held office on the bench of aldermen. Very often, a political elite emerged within the craft guild, whereby a group of politically influential masters monopolised power in the guild as well. Sometimes richer citizens even joined a guild, not to take up that particular occupation, but to use it as a tool for political leverage. Even more frequently, progressive commercialisation pushed for socio-economic polarisation within the trade. Increasing conflicts – among the larger towns with one another, between the large towns and the smaller towns, or between a town and the surrounding countryside – often forced corporate groups to align their interests with those of the elites. It would thus be wrong to assume that the political eruptions in the 1280s and a second, much stronger wave of revolts shortly after 1300 were caused by a completely polarised society. The social oppositions sketched above were continually filtered through various forms of vertical solidarity. It is precisely the tensions between horizontal and vertical ties which would shape the social history of the late medieval town.

By 1300, the progressive division of labour and the concentration of capital had given birth to a complex and multi-layered urban society. Urban space was also increasingly divided between various social groups (see Chapter 6). In the case of Bruges it seems that the earliest *poorters* ('burghers') were those who lived within the town wall of the original *portus* (*poert* (harbour) in the vernacular). As early as 1280, the inhabitants of the poorer outer districts, which had been incorporated into the municipal territory five years earlier, asked for rights equal to those of the original inhabitants of the town centre. At the same time, house prices and rents inside the first town walls were much higher than outside them, and it is undoubtedly that economic logic of 'gentrification' that provided the aggregate group of *poorters* with greater social coherence. Even in more industrially oriented towns like Ypres and Saint-Omer, social and economic differences were reflected in the urban landscape. Until the thirteenth century it was common for members of one occupational group to cluster in a particular district, which often left a toponymical palimpsest. In a few towns, such as in Antwerp before its fifteenth-century growth, neighbourhoods were dominated not only by occupational concentrations but also by elite families. Some leading families, some of them noble, possessed real estate in clearly recognisable blocks. Over the course of the late Middle Ages the urban landscape seems to have become more diverse. Clustering was henceforth limited to a few crafts with specific ecological demands (e.g. the danger of pollution or logistic requirements for supply of resources or waste disposal).

An Urban Nobility?

The progressive urbanisation of Netherlandish society gave birth to broad middling groups that constructed their collective identities primarily around occupational activity. Yet, the social consequences of urbanisation did not stop at the town gates. As discussed earlier, the craft guilds in the major towns of the southern Netherlands were able to force access to the municipal government in the fourteenth century. In the fifteenth century, however, a seemingly contradictory development took place, namely, the increasing presence of nobles in the large and medium-sized towns.

For the noble lords in the countryside, the rise of towns could not be ignored, ambiguous as the consequences were for them. First, towns constituted a threat to the power of the rural nobility. For their part, the towns cast themselves as political actors of the first rank, projecting their economic and political ambitions onto the surrounding countryside. In this process, not only were rival rural industries in the hinterlands challenged, but local lords were also expected to respect the rights of individuals who in one way or another enjoyed the protection of the municipal government. This could lead to fierce confrontations, as in the case of the fourteenth-century nobleman Eulard de Mortaigne. In response to Eulard's maltreatment of an outburgher (*buitenpoorter*) – in this case an individual granted citizen's rights from Kortrijk in Flanders – the urban militia of Kortrijk burned his castle to the ground.

From an economic perspective, however, there was often a rapprochement between towns and the nobility. Numerous members of the nobility responded to the process of urbanisation by themselves granting urban charters. Although towns of this sort were seldom successful – the rise of towns in the Low Countries was chiefly an economic development that was not easily manipulated – they show that nobles understood that fortunes could be made by levying tolls and taxes on trade and industry and that, as a consequence, they also had much to gain from flourishing towns. The most prominent noble family from the county of Zeeland – Van Borssele – derived a large part of its wealth from tolls in the county's harbour towns of Veere, Vlissingen, Westkapelle and Brouwershaven. The family went as far as to lure merchants away from the neighbouring town of Middelburg by granting them advantageous privileges. The urban network early on also became the pre-eminent market for the fruits of the nobility's rural estates; as a consequence, the incomes of the lords became entwined with fluctuations in urban demand.

The town also became a locus for consumption for the nobility, ranging from tools via luxury products to services such as education and medical care. Even the benchmarks of the nobility's material culture – armour and the tombstones in the parish church of their village seigneurie – were not fabricated by villagers but commissioned from specialised urban workshops. Little wonder then that some nobles themselves settled in towns. They had a mansion built in the town, or they participated actively in the urban economy. The Zeeland noble Van Borssele family, with its own merchant fleet, was an extreme example, but lower-ranking nobles also engaged in these kinds of activities. In Bruges around 1480, for example, Nicolas de Montigny, a nobleman from Hainaut and Flanders, was not only involved in the trade of products from the Orient but for a time was also the dean of the hat-makers' guild. In Leiden, scions of the Van Boschuysen family, a prominent lineage of knights, were active as wool merchants and clothiers. For noblemen, manual labour was shameful and forbidden, and the same is perhaps true for retail trade. Yet nothing suggests that in the late medieval Low Countries one's noble status was endangered by wholesale trade, as was the case in neighbouring France.

The most far-reaching step in nobles' integration into the towns was the assumption of public office. In the core regions of Flanders, Brabant and Holland, noble involvement in urban government became increasingly common, even if there was some regional differentiation. While scarcely 12 per cent of the documented Flemish noble lineages had an alderman in their ranks shortly after 1350, this share had increased to at least 44 per cent by 1500. Similar data are lacking for Brabant, but many case studies suggest an analogous development. So, for instance, around 1400, the Cruppelants, a family of knights, had representatives on the bench of aldermen in Brussels, while the Van Immerseel family was regularly represented in the Antwerp magistracy. For the towns in the northern Netherlands, the picture is still unclear because research has remained limited to members of the so-called knighthood (*ridderschap*), the institutionalised hard core of the nobility. In Holland, knights and their family members were only rarely inclined to take on the positions of *schout* (town sheriff) or *schepen* (alderman), and in the sixteenth century their numbers fell even further. Yet, in Leiden, a number of the most powerful political dynasties belonged to a knightly milieu (Van Zwieten, Van Poelgeest, Van Boschuysen), and different urban families in the *vroedschap* did acquire seigneuries in the countryside. Moreover, at least 54 per cent of Leiden's magistracy belonged to the *welgeborenen* (that is, the 'well-born'), which implied a lower noble or semi-noble status. In the towns of Zeeland, too, noble presence in towns became increasingly common. Some small towns had a highborn lord as their protector or patron, whereas lower nobles sat increasingly often on town councils. One outlier was Middelburg in Zeeland, where a third of the burgomasters were of noble status from 1400 onwards.

Outside the core principalities, however, this pattern was barely present, if at all. In the somewhat less urbanised county of Hainaut, the urbanisation of the nobility was less pronounced, although it must be noted that more nobles gradually settled even in Mons and Valenciennes. Inversely, members of the urban elite often acquired seigneuries or knightly titles, and in this way also achieved noble status, as they did in the core principalities. That the most prominent families from the urban elites had a realistic hope of becoming noble was largely facilitated by the preceding integration of nobles into the upper stratum of urban society.

The fortunes of the nobility illustrate how progressive urbanisation pushed for social change among groups and individuals in the countryside. Inside the town walls the middling groups became in a certain sense victims of the 'success of the town'. Over the course of the late Middle Ages into the sixteenth century, the representation of craft guilds in town councils of the southern Netherlands often had to give way to a fusion of the urban elite with the elite from the countryside. The end result was the town of the *ancien régime*, in which the names on the aldermen's lists were usually preceded by noble and academic titles, something that was still exceptional around 1300. But, in spite of this loss of political status for the urban middling groups, the late medieval era cannot be presented as a period of doom and gloom for them; on the contrary, it proved to be their heyday.

Guild, Clan and Nuclear Family

It was precisely during the late Middle Ages that numerous corporate organisations came to full flower, and throughout the early modern era they would continue to shape urban life. They gave substance to social aspirations, economic activity, social interaction and religious devotion: craft guilds, religious fraternities, military guilds and chambers of rhetoricians were instrumental in the articulation of a specific set of social identities for urban middling groups. Up to a certain point, they complemented the existing frameworks of family and kin, of neighbourhood and street, and of other, more informal forms of solidarity (see Chapter 5). For too long now these corporations have been studied from a one-sided point of view, be that political, economic or religious. Although they were, of course, active in each of these spheres, it is precisely the combination of diverse functions that constituted their considerable impact on society.

Because of the multifaceted character of the corporate system, the differentiated forms of social access, and the overlaps in membership and function of each of the guilds, a platform of constant social negotiation was developed. Some organisations, like the shopkeepers' or mercers' guilds and certain fraternities, were quite inclusive. Others were very exclusive: that was the case with very specialised occupational associations such as the guilds of the precious metalworkers (jewellers, gold- and silversmiths) and the brokers, for instance, or with the higher ranks of the military guilds' civic militias (crossbowmen and others). Town dwellers were not necessarily limited to one corporate circuit, as they often combined the membership of multiple associations. Together with the strong economic connections between craft guilds, those social cross-overs contributed to the striking social stability that was to be found in many towns in the Low Countries from the late Middle Ages onwards. Admittedly, social frictions could be intense, but they were generally short-lived. Nevertheless, it is important not to entertain a rosy image of these middling groups. It was precisely their corporate framework that contributed to the reproduction of social inequality in the town. The popular trope of the harmonious, organic urban community masks a much more complex narrative of confrontation, tension and inequalities.

Sometimes the flowering of urban corporate organisations is expressly connected with the almost simultaneous proliferation of the nuclear family. The late Middle Ages are presented as a crucial tipping point in this respect. Demographic catastrophes like pestilence, war and famine (see below, pp. 79–82) supposedly broke up older connections of family and kin. The nuclear family, it is often assumed, became the new bedrock of society. Many historians have argued that, before the outbreak of the Black Death in the middle of the fourteenth century, it was the clan and the extended family that were dominant, with all the concomitant implications for vertical and horizontal ties of kinship and solidarity permeating every level of society. Tenacious social phenomena such as feuding have been explained as a corollary of those familial structures. After the Black Death and the ensuing demographic collapse had undermined the role of the clan and extended family, the nuclear family – the cohabitation of a companionate married couple and their children or dependants in one household – came to dominate. Older familial forms of solidarity supposedly cleared the way for the external, horizontal connections of the fraternity, the craft guild and other associations.

With the nuclear family, a new ideological construction of partnership in the family emerged that intensified the love of parents for children: as a reaction to massive child mortality in the recurrent epidemics of the late Middle Ages, even the deceased children began to live on symbolically in the naming of descendants born later. Tine De Moor and Jan Luiten van Zanden went so far as to connect the so-called 'Western European Marriage Pattern' – which was closely related to the rise of the nuclear family and was characterised by a later age at marriage on the one hand and an extensive permanent celibacy on the other – expressly to long-term economic growth. In their view, a later age at marriage unlocked the labour potential of young women, who began to take up a stronger and, above all, more independent position in the labour market. A later age at marriage also contributed to lower fertility and thus decreased population pressure. This phenomenon was supposedly strongest in the towns of the Low Countries. In consequence the 'Malthusian' pressure was the smallest, and in Netherlandish towns economic growth was less rapidly consumed by the Malthusian cycle of increasing population and positive checks of recurrent population crisis.

The presumed connection between the fourteenth-century demographic crisis, the rise of the nuclear family and the reduced role of the extended family is, however, far from certain. Extended familial structures still existed in the fifteenth century among well-to-do middling groups and among the elite. Around 1400, for example, the leading Antwerp dynasties were still conforming to notions of 'old-fashioned' clan behaviour. In addition to political power, real estate inside and outside the town was an important component of the strategy of an extended family. Analysis of property deeds shows that (semi-)noble Antwerp families such as Bode, Van Wesele, Van der Elst and Van Hoboken acquired and maintained their houses and land in certain streets and neighbourhoods. In that way, they demarcated their territory in the town – a strategy that resembled that of the *Alberghi* in Genoa. Yet it was not only elites that continued to hold the extended family dear; other groups in the town, too, invested in their relationships with *vrienden en maghen* ('kith and kin'). In short, the extended family remained important, even when associations, corporations or other collective organisations offered an alternative. Thus, for example, from the sixteenth century, beguines in Mechelen preferred to leave their property in their wills to even distant family members, rather than bequeathing it to the community of women of which they were part. Until well into the early modern era, in some circles the extended family maintained a central role in all manner of social strategies, not least of which were those of marriage and inheritance.

Additional nuancing is required. The increasing dominance of nuclear families does not exclude extended ties of kinship that could exist between various nuclear households. Such an approach risks a linear, homogeneous and teleological vision, in which the 'modern' nuclear family supposedly wrested itself from 'archaic' clan connections. It is certainly true that over time property law tended to restrict the opportunities for interference by extended kin. That is well attested to for the county of Holland, for example. Yet caution is still urged. Specific social niches, like the nobility and the urban elites, expressly shielded themselves from these kinds of trends while favouring ideas of lineage. Well into the sixteenth century, for example, the top stratum of society in Holland was still regularly torn apart by factional conflicts between the so-called Hook and Cod leagues (*Hoeken en Kabeljauwen*), in which extended family connections and traditions continued to play a major role.

In addition, and even more importantly, the general chronology of increasing individuality is not always convincing. Recent research shows that, in the case of the nobility, 'thinking about the extended family' was not always the continuation of an old situation but, on the contrary, sometimes a new phenomenon. The nobility in the twelfth century were presumably much more autonomous vis-à-vis their own circle of kin than were their successors in the late Middle Ages or early modern period. The striking role of 'clans' and factional conflict in urban elites in the late Middle Ages must, therefore, be reconsidered. It has been repeatedly suggested that the top stratum in the town copied the older value patterns set by the rural nobility – among them, a strong awareness of family and lineage. Yet it is quite possible that in reality this was all about 'invented tradition', which saw its roots and was propagated in the towns themselves.

At the same time, there are indications that the nuclear family and the accompanying European marriage pattern were possibly already the norm in the towns of the Low Countries before the successive plague epidemics from the middle of the fourteenth century onwards. In late thirteenth-century regulations on cloth manufacture in some of the textile towns like Douai and Ypres in Flanders, it is clear that the nuclear family stood in the foreground as an economic unit as early as the late thirteenth century. This was a new phenomenon, though. In the earliest charters for cloth manufacture, the industrial workers were seen as individuals in the first instance. In remarkably gender-equal terms, different textile occupations are listed, since even crucial occupations such as weaving could apparently be carried out by men and women alike. The stages of processing wool (where women were active as spinners) and of finishing woollen cloth (only men seem to have been active as fullers) were exceptions. Other occupations in these genuine industrial towns were carried out by women as well as men, without the nuclear family appearing to matter at all as the economic unit.

In the second half of the thirteenth century and the early fourteenth century – that is, more than half a century before the demographic blow of the Black Death – change enters into this picture. Occupations became increasingly 'gendered', and, in particular, the core jobs in cloth production became exclusively male. That is the case, for example, with weaving, dyeing and shearing. The reverse of this masculinisation was the further feminisation of the less well-paid activities in wool processing, such as spinning and combing. At the same time, increasing numbers of stipulations integrated women's labour in the nuclear household. The catalyst for this masculinisation may well have been the arrival of the new ideology of the craft guild. The values that crafts began attaching to their products were linked to personal status, and, therefore, to the dominant patriarchal tendencies in European society. It was no coincidence either that it was in exactly this period that Flemish textile towns became increasingly dependent on the export of more expensive kinds of broadcloth, for which quality control and regulation gained importance. Women were systematically kept out of the training circuit in most craft guilds. As a result, independent women's labour was marginalised and limited to low-paid jobs or to domestic service. The cliché of the life-cycle servant girl may well have come into being in this period. The demographic crisis of the late Middle Ages, allegedly the catalyst for this change, seems to have changed little in this situation.

This does not mean that women in the urban society of the Low Countries did not enjoy relatively great legal capacity and freedom of action in their daily affairs. It has been shown for late medieval Ghent and Douai in Flanders that women were able to become legally and economically active. The status of 'merchant woman' allowed them to carry out trade with a great degree of independence from the supervision of their husbands or fathers. Hence it was no coincidence that quite a lot of women were active in all manner of commercial occupations. In the guild of the linen weavers in medieval Bruges, apprenticeship and independent entrepreneurial activity were reserved for men, as in most other craft guilds in the town. The market stalls for linen sales in the Old Hall, however, were almost all run by women. Women were crucial in most retail trades, as the spouses or daughters of master artisans. But in numerous shopkeepers' or mercers' guilds, in the dairy trade and in petty retailing outside the guild framework, they were active independently. The increasingly stringent gender stipulations in cloth manufacture regulation in many industrial towns of Flanders, Artois and Brabant from the thirteenth and fourteenth centuries onwards did not prevent women from being commercially active in the cloth trade. Until well into the fourteenth century they could typically be clothiers or drapers – entrepreneurs organising the manufacturing stages in cloth manufacture – without problem, whereas it was no longer possible for them to take on the role of weaver, fuller, dyer or cloth finisher.

How the position of women evolved in the fifteenth and sixteenth centuries is the subject of debate. Armed with arguments based on laws of succession, marriage practices, literacy and wage relationships, some scholars observe a 'return of patriarchy' and a pronounced socio-economic weakening of the social position of women in the towns of the Low Countries. Frequently on the basis of the same material, others point conversely towards increasing female independence. The precise chronology (and geography) of the position of women is difficult to reconstruct. Gender differences constitute just one dimension of the multiplicity of social and economic, cultural, religious and age-related fault lines. The fact is that a foreign visitor such as Lodovico Guicciardini (1521–89) could express his amazement at the great freedom of movement that women enjoyed in his Florentine eyes. Research confirms that the quality of girls' education in sixteenth-century Antwerp, among other places, was at a very high level. As 'business partners' of their husbands, not only were they taught different foreign languages, but arithmetic and bookkeeping were on the agenda as well (see Chapter 8). To be able to grasp the background for this situation better, however, a deeper insight into the economic and demographic structures and cycles of the late medieval urban economy is of vital importance.

The Horsemen of the Apocalypse Gallop from Crisis to Crisis

Returning to the urban landscape in the southern Netherlands of 1400, it is striking that the urban network was dominated by a few great centres. Towns like Saint-Omer in Artois, Ypres in Flanders and Leuven in Brabant had fallen behind, while Ghent, Bruges, Lille, Tournai, Arras, Douai and Brussels held the lead at the top of the urban hierarchy. This list was gradually supplemented by growing medium-sized towns such as Antwerp and 's-Hertogenbosch. Even the smaller towns still displayed great vitality: in Flanders the harbour towns (like Ostend and Dunkirk) and the industrial towns in the basin of the rivers Scheldt and Leie (Lys) did especially well; in Brabant the smaller towns like Lier and Diest grew into important regional service centres. The same is true for the towns in the county of Holland, where the process of urbanisation really did not get under way until the fourteenth century, and where the main focus in the urban system shifted from Dordrecht in southern Holland to the harbour and textile towns in northern Holland (Amsterdam, Haarlem, Leiden).

All in all, the vitality of the urban network was scarcely affected, and that is remarkable. The fourteenth century is reputed in scholarly literature as one of the most difficult periods of crisis that Europe ever went through. 'A bello, fame, et peste libera nos Domine' ('Deliver us, Lord, from war, famine and pestilence') was a frequently heard supplication. War, famine and pestilence were the three Apocalyptic Horsemen that affected demographic and social resilience throughout Europe. In Italy the major cities lost more than half of their population, and even in England and France the demographic impact of recurrent periods of crisis was enormous. Seen from this perspective, the stability and resilience of the urban network in the Low Countries is striking. To be sure, strong growth was capped, but there was no demographic or social collapse.

Even so, the fact that demographic disaster did not spare the towns of the Low Countries, albeit with varying intensity, has been established in the past decades. The infamous outbreak in the middle of the fourteenth century was a virulent version of the bubonic and pneumonic plague that was brought into Europe from the Mongolian steppes via international trade routes. In the Low Countries, as in other regions, it wrought horrible havoc. That was the case not only in a few isolated agrarian areas in Hainaut and southern Brabant but also in the urbanised areas of Artois, Flanders and central Brabant. Moreover, the subsequent outbreaks of plague in the second half of the fourteenth century and the first half of the fifteenth smothered any permanent recovery from the start. In later years the plague became endemic in Western Europe, although the extent of the damage substantially differed with each outbreak. In sixteenth-century Antwerp, for example, at least twenty plague years were recorded and another thirty-two years with more limited plague flare-ups, albeit without lasting impact for population growth.

The coming of a second, black horseman, famine, was at least as dramatic. During the food shortage of 1315–17, in particular, the major towns were heavily hit. Flanders, which was dependent on grain imports from northern France for its food supply, proved to be extremely vulnerable in this period. In the worst months of famine, so the urban accounts of Bruges tell us, municipal functionaries counted more than 150 casualties per month, and in the somewhat smaller industrial town of Ypres there were more than 190 casualties in the worst of the famine. Bruges lost 5 per cent of its population to grain shortage; in Ypres the figure rose to more than 10 per cent. However, it is the only period of acute food shortage with that kind of high direct death toll in the history of the towns in the Low Countries. In the late fifteenth and late sixteenth centuries, too, bad harvests and the disruption of regional or international grain trade made for numerous victims of famine, yet never quite on the scale of the 'Great Hunger' of 1315–17. Certainly in the regions on the front lines of the Dutch Revolt (1568–1648) – the north of the duchy of Brabant in the first instance – any guarantee of food was completely lost in the Revolt. In contrast to the initial outbreak of the plague in the middle of the fourteenth century, when all were vulnerable, rich and poor, grain shortages immediately caused exorbitant price rises in basic foodstuffs and did not strike indiscriminately. The less well-off were direct victims of such rising grain prices as wages were not adjusted to the changing costs of living, or only with a serious time delay. But larger towns were generally better equipped to secure grain supplies, at least for the greater part of the town dwellers. They did not hesitate to use their coercive power to guarantee supply and counter speculation, often at the expense of the surrounding hinterland.

The third horseman was the red horseman, the symbol of war. In the fourteenth century, war, itinerant gangs of soldiers, plunder and rising tax burdens (because of rising war expenditures) were endemic in the Low Countries. Frequently, armed conflict also triggered the spread of pestilence as well as famine: the Great Hunger of 1315–17, which hit Flanders particularly hard, fell in the middle of a prolonged Franco-Flemish conflict, which did not help the authorities to take countermeasures. The conflicts that time and again put towns in opposition to their prince flared up as regularly as clockwork. The heights of sorrow were reached in the late fifteenth century, during the divisive conflict with Archduke Maximilian of Austria, and again in the late sixteenth century in the initial phase of the Dutch Revolt in the 1570s and early 1580s. The countryside, in particular, paid an especially heavy price at that time, but towns were the stage for plunder by the badly paid military (the so-called 'Spanish furies') and siege warfare. Antwerp and Mechelen would experience this first-hand, but so would Zutphen and Naarden in the northern Low Countries.

The Apocalyptic Horsemen did not, therefore, spare either the large or the small towns. For that reason the resilience of the towns – or, rather, the absence of collapse in the fourteenth century as in Italy, France or England – is that much more remarkable. The same is true for the crisis of the late fifteenth century. Tienen, for instance, was besieged and plundered in both 1498 and 1507, but by 1526 its population had recovered to a higher level than a century before. And once the gun smoke from the war years of the late sixteenth century had cleared, demographic, economic and social recovery ensued as well. This process of recovery was swifter than has long been assumed by scholars, albeit with important regional differences. Different structural elements are responsible for this striking resilience.

Thus, for example, the towns succeeded in remaining attractive to large groups of immigrants. As such they were able to compensate for the heavy demographic deficit resulting from the higher death and lower birth rates. There is very little precise information concerning urban migration patterns: the only proxy available is the influx of new citizens (burghers or *poorters*), by definition a more or less limited and specific segment of the urban population (see Chapter 4). Rights of citizenship (*poorterrecht*) – acquired at birth by town dwellers but also for sale to immigrants – provided access to economic and political networks. Yet they do not seem to have been an absolute necessity for being able to function in urban society outside the guild framework. Newcomers interested in becoming citizens were mostly those apprenticed craftsmen or retailers wanting to gain access to the town's guilds. They indeed constituted those groups which in the late Middle Ages would see to the successful economic conversion of the towns. For those in search of skill as well as integration into the corporate fabric, acquiring citizenship was, after all, still a *conditio sine qua non*. Although the overall majority of new citizens came from the immediate vicinity of the town, the larger towns also attracted significant groups of promising newcomers who were often willing to travel hundreds of miles in search of a place within the advanced commodity and service economies of the Burgundian and Habsburg Low Countries. Thanks to sometimes remarkably economic adaptations, the towns in Flanders, Brabant and Holland, specifically, were able to maintain their attractiveness, and they remained in a position to reallocate labour, commercial activity and industrial production among the large towns, the small towns and the countryside (see Chapter 2).

Economic Conversion and the Triumph of the Urban Middling Groups

During the late thirteenth and early fourteenth centuries, the Flemish textile towns, driven by growing international competition, made the transition to the production and sale of high-quality textiles. Over the course of the late fourteenth and fifteenth centuries, a fundamental process of diversification can help to explain the Low Countries' urban resilience in the late Middle Ages. Bruges and Lille in Flanders and the leading towns in the Duchy of Brabant in particular devoted themselves to the supply of a broad swathe of luxury goods and services (see Chapter 2). The quality of tapestries from Brussels became proverbial, yet even in smaller towns such as Lier and Herentals highly specialised production like embroidery flourished. Diversification of the export trade was essential in this process, although another fundamental pillar of urban economies also needs to be addressed. Urban economies not only acted as entrepôts in transit trade; they also had a fundamental role as central places in providing services for the urban and rural hinterlands. This dynamic combination financially benefitted the middling groups in the town.

It is precisely these roles that constitute an important explanation for the economic resilience of the towns in the Low Countries. In the thirteenth and fourteenth centuries the towns had been able perceptibly to bolster their role as regional marketplaces. Local and regional demand contributed to strengthening specialisation in urban production and commerce. Even when export and transit trade were suffering from cyclical and incidental setbacks caused by epidemic disease and war, the towns were always able to fall back on a 'domestic market'. And even at the height of growth in the sixteenth century, only one third of non-agricultural production was exported abroad, according to some estimates. In other words, the domestic market was a substantial economic factor (see Chapter 7). The economic diversification that ensued from both domestic and export markets stimulated the urban middling groups and accelerated the complexity of the urban social fabric. Both in numbers and in social status, small guild-organised manufacturers and traders clearly gained in importance. They left an unmistakable imprint – as demonstrated in all chapters of this book – on the history of the towns in the Low Countries.

The late medieval crisis was first and foremost a period in which a new social balance was sought after. Old elites saw their source of income drying up and their status contested. The Flemish merchants – in an earlier period actively involved in purchasing raw materials for the textile industry and selling finished materials all over Europe – were obliged now to switch to more regional trade flows. Large groups of proletarianised textile labourers – wool workers, weavers and fullers, above all – were faced with chronic unemployment and social disruption as a result of decreasing demand for cheaper fabrics. However, there were also winners. Old and new elites succeeded in making the transition to 'passive' trade and were well practised in skimming off the added value in the major trade towns of the Low Countries. The latter had now become nexuses for important communities of international merchants. Brokerage between these merchants or between them and Low Countries entrepreneurs was institutionally framed in well-developed brokerage legislation (which served not only the interests of the urban elites but also those of the international traders themselves), as well as in the strict division between international trade flows and the regional trade that was still very much controlled by local mercantile elites.

Yet, regardless of how important and politically influential these elites were, the most important social development in this period was undoubtedly the economic triumph of the middling groups. This collective term is understood to cover the many small traders and independent producers who were oriented, above all, to providing commodities and services for the local and regional markets. For the most part they were organised corporately into craft guilds. At present, it is not entirely clear how these middling groups became so influential. But, in any case, if they were not in a position to rule the political, cultural and social life of the town, they did indeed expressly give shape to that life. Of course, there have always been groups in the middle, yet in the late Middle Ages their numbers increased significantly in the large towns, and in the smaller towns they were, relatively speaking, stronger still.

Economic development seems to have played an important role in establishing this new social equilibrium. In the textile towns of the southern Netherlands, the forced transition to high-quality textiles in the major manufacturing centres turned labour relationships on their head. Instead of a dichotomy between capitalist traders and entrepreneurs on the one hand and proletarianised labourers on the other, a third group arose in the production process, namely, the clothiers or *drapiers* – relatively small-scale entrepreneurs who began to dominate the production chain for woollens from the second half of the thirteenth century onwards. The process resulted in more complex social hierarchies. In particular, successful weavers were able to carve out this pivotal role for themselves. The advantages of being a *drapier* were of such a nature that in no time all manner of thresholds were built in, which were supposed to prevent other groups, such as the dyers, fullers or cloth finishers, from making any inroads. Thanks to the higher quality of the manufactured cloth, the *drapiers* – who had the central position in the production chain – landed in a favourable position and a great number of them used this opportunity to accumulate capital.

Much seems to indicate that these social processes prevailed around 1300. The remarkably high consumption of meat in Flanders stands out in this period, and the demand for clothing increased in the first quarter of the fourteenth century as well, even before the major changes in purchasing power after the Black Death were felt. After 1350, the tide had turned for good in favour of the middling groups. Military draft lists for Bruges, which were organised along the social fault lines in the town, show how economic specialisation and higher purchasing power caused a genuine expansion of the specialised craft guilds that were involved in manufacturing and marketing durable consumer goods and items of fashion. Elsewhere, too, this trend seems to have persisted: over the course of the fifteenth and sixteenth centuries the craft guilds gained additional ground in the urban economies of the Low Countries. Their share in sixteenth-century Ghent was estimated at approximately 50 per cent of the urban population. In other places in the Low Countries, master artisans and their households easily represented between one and two thirds of the urban population.

At the same time, those profiting from accelerating merchant capitalism were also found in the large towns. The high added value that came from the production of high-quality textiles and other luxury products landed much more frequently in the coffers of rich traders than in the purses of the small producers. Thus, for instance, in the sixteenth century, the Antwerp merchant Gerard Timback controlled a relatively extensive network of production and trade in which needles produced in 's-Hertogenbosch were marketed to England. Without any doubt, the highest profits were for Timback himself. The actual producers in 's-Hertogenbosch, who were dependent on him, tended to be poor. Certainly, scores of the commercial 'wealthy' clustered in sixteenth-century Antwerp, but the social results of expanding mercantile capitalism there were mixed. While some master artisans were degraded into barely more than wage-labourers in the service of commercial capitalists, others saw excellent opportunities for making themselves considerably wealthier in the spectacular growth of the domestic market and of the export industries (see Chapter 2).

A 'Golden Age' for the Wage-Labourer ... or for the Urban Middling Groups?

It is not easy to reconstruct how things went for the common man in this period. Traditionally, economic historians rely on prices and wages to form an image of the development of purchasing power and the standards of living. Seen in this way, under the influence of structural population decline, per capita income during the late Middle Ages supposedly grew to a record height, one which was not equalled until the nineteenth century. Employers had to pay increasingly high wages for labour that was growing scarce. When the population began to grow again in the latter part of the fifteenth century, an opposite trend supposedly set in. Substantial rises in production were not followed by equally significant rises in productivity, whereby per capita income only moderately increased. In the expansion of the sixteenth century, the discovery of silver in central Europe and later in the New World provided for a genuine price revolution. In the process, the nominal prices of basic goods such as grain increased fourteen-fold between 1500 and 1630. Even for meat and textiles, prices rapidly shot sky-high. Although nominal wages limped behind for a long time, they did in a sense connect partly with this general rise in prices, but with a serious delay.

In the meantime the cycle of real wages, apparent in studies concerning Bruges or Antwerp, shows – after a breakdown in the first post-plague years – a slight rise from the last quarter of the fourteenth century onwards. Yet the main characteristic is feverish cyclicity, with an upward trend at the end of the fourteenth century and around the middle of the fifteenth. In the interim period, though, and once more at the end of the fifteenth century, the purchasing power of craftsmen's wages came under great pressure. In the sixteenth century, doom and gloom was the wage-labourer's portion: in the well-documented town of 's-Hertogenbosch in northern Brabant, real wages were halved between 1500 and 1550. In the metropolis of Antwerp, the strong guilds in construction provided for a more rapid adjustment of nominal wages to the general price rises. Yet there, too, wage-labourers seem to have paid the social costs of economic growth, as Hugo Soly has argued.

And yet for all sorts of reasons it is not simple to draw major conclusions from this kind of statistical material. There is reasonably good information concerning the prices of food and house rents; frequently not taken into account, however, are all manner of smaller products and services. Changes of consumer preferences are even harder to integrate into the analysis: in times of crisis, people often switched to cheaper beer and bread. On the income side, as well, the results of earlier studies need to be put into perspective. The family wage was determined by a multiplicity of frequently unknown factors: the effective number of days worked by the breadwinner is one such factor; the contribution to the work by women and children is another, not to mention the contribution of other sources of income in the household, such as earnings from annuities and real estate. New data concerning thirteenth-century wage formation in the region of Bruges are already casting a different light on the preceding period. It is important to note that the purchasing power of skilled labourers prior to 1300 was barely less than their purchasing power in the period after the Black Death, in the years from 1390 to 1460! And yet, around 1300, at the end of a long period of Malthusian growth, the economies of Flanders and Brabant were encountering the limits of their possibilities. There seems, therefore, not to have been a genuine collapse of the labour supply during the demographic catastrophe of the late Middle Ages. What, then, were the employment opportunities for the labourers, who in principle were or should be earning decent wages? And what were the job opportunities for those with less training in an economy that was increasingly characterised by a switch to more specialised and capital-intensive industries and luxury commodities?

Labourers dependent on time wages (those who were paid by the day, as in construction) constituted a quantitatively small proportion of the active urban population in the Low Countries. Estimates of 5–7 per cent could be made for this segment in Leuven and 's-Hertogenbosch during the sixteenth century. Their experience, too, was not necessarily representative of the prosperity and incomes in other social groups. A recent analysis of tax rolls confirmed this phenomenon: wage-earners in the construction industry, upon which most studies dealing with standards of living are primarily based, are invariably found in the poorer groups of urban society. Detailed research for 's-Hertogenbosch in the sixteenth century – in addition to a more impressionistic analysis of tax records in Bruges, Kortrijk and Eeklo shortly before and after 1400 – indicates how entrepreneurs in construction (the organisers of so-called *taswerken*, which included control of the markets for both labour and raw materials) could be especially prosperous. They even had a significant presence among the richest strata of the population, whereas their fellow craftsmen, who lacked capital to take on such works and were completely dependent on wage-labour, frequently commissioned by those same wealthy entrepreneurs, barely made their way out of the very lowest groups in urban society. The same is true for the much more numerous textile workers who – whether or not they were journeymen or subcontracted master artisans – had become de facto wage-labourers in the service of the more capitalised entrepreneurial *drapiers*. Occupational groups like dressmakers and tailors, who frequently worked with materials from their clients and, as a result, who themselves barely had any floating capital at their disposal, can also be considered as coming into this category.

However, most craftsmen who were active as small independent masters or as retail traders were more likely to belong to the middle strata of society. A taxation list in 's-Hertogenbosch of 1552, called the *gemene zetting* or 'general levy' (a kind of per capita, direct-income tax), allows for a fascinating look into the socio-professional hierarchy of the urban population. Around this time, 's-Hertogenbosch was a satellite of the Antwerp economy. The major merchants, who were engaged in the most important export sectors, can be considered without a doubt to be among the 'winners' of sixteenth-century growth. Linen merchants grace the top of the social ladder. The contrast with the weavers, entirely at the opposite end of the social ranking, can hardly be more conspicuous. The image of a society polarised by international trade is further reinforced by the low social ranking of needle-makers and knife-makers, two vanguards of the export industries in 's-Hertogenbosch at the time. What is particularly revealing is the fairly low position of bricklayers, who, with a median tax of 20 *stuiver*, are one third lower than the median for the town as a whole. The relative position of the bricklayers with regard to other craftsmen is not positive either: the farther down the socio-professional ladder, the greater the portion of occupations in which wage-labour was important. At the top of the middle strata are those capital-intensive trades in which investments in floating capital (for raw materials, cash advances, tools and infrastructure) were important. The wealthy merchants at the top of the fiscal hierarchy are joined by a rich pawnbroker, as well as by members of the town's political and governing elite, who (certainly after 1525) were recruited on an increasingly plutocratic basis.

In contrast to traditional historiography, which has looked well-nigh exclusively at the top and bottom of the social ladder, recent research indicates the preponderance of the social middling sort for urban civil society in the Low Countries. By definition, middling groups are a vague and heterogeneous social category. But craftsmen who combined labour or retail with entrepreneurship made up most of this category in the late medieval and sixteenth-century towns of the Low Countries. It was the guild-organised coopers, cabinet-makers, wheelwrights, goldsmiths and copper-founders who found themselves in the 'wealthier half' of the population. And for quite a few of these occupations, this meant that the average guildsman earned a whole lot more than the average inhabitant of the town. Among them retailers figure prominently, and not just in 's-Hertogenbosch. Even traders in second-hand goods, peddlers as well as small-scale grocers, were often able to earn a substantial income. On account of their less evocative place as suppliers for the local market and the surrounding countryside, this midfield has been neglected for much too long in historiography – and wrongly so, for the social position of the middling groups in the towns was much more favourable than has always been thought based on the older price and wage studies. Even for the strongly polarised situation in the by then leading commercial metropolis of Antwerp, Ludovico Guicciardini spoke in superlatives about the scope of the retailers' guild. Around 1560 the Antwerp mercers' guild registered some 200 new members annually, of whom market stallholders constituted by far the largest group. In a town like Ghent, the preponderance of these middling groups would have been even greater.

However solid the position of the middling groups in the late Middle Ages and sixteenth century, it cannot make one of the essential characteristics of urban society disappear. Social inequality remained important throughout the entire period. The 1552 tax list in 's-Hertogenbosch reveals that the poorest 20 per cent of the population received less than 0.5 per cent of the total income, whereas the wealthiest fifth of the population had nearly 77 per cent at its disposal. These kinds of ratios were recorded in all the other towns documented, whereby the size of the town seems to have been in direct relationship to the scope of the inequality in income. Thus, for example, in the county of Holland the wealthiest 10 per cent of households in the small town of Edam (1462) contributed 35 per cent of the total wealth tax, in Alkmaar (1534) 58 per cent and in the much more significant town of Haarlem (1498) at least 68 per cent. It is high time, therefore, to shift the spotlight away from the urban elite and the substantial middling groups and in the direction of the people without power and means.

Slipping Through the Net? Poverty and Discipline

In addition to the groups of winners (wealthy merchants and the middling groups) – which were nevertheless far from stable – there were numerous losers at the bottom of the social hierarchy in the sixteenth century. From the fifteenth century onwards, partly under the influence of an emerging bourgeois ideology, poverty – in spite of its structural character – was presented for the first time as a social and moral problem, instead of as an opportunity for the wealthy to earn a place in heaven by demonstrating charity. Real figures are missing and therefore there can only be speculation about the precise trends of poverty in this period. Yet, poverty certainly becomes more visible to the historian. The fiscal censuses that late medieval princes had drawn up show that the group of fiscal poor – those who were exempted from a contribution in direct taxes on account of their poverty – was especially extensive, even in those towns where the middling groups held strong. Although information for the large towns is not readily available, in economically dynamic, smaller and medium-sized towns of Flanders like Eeklo and Tielt on average between 10 per cent and 25 per cent of the households were classified as too poor to contribute to the municipal tax system. Towns that had to abandon their industrial output in the period of fundamental economic change in the fourteenth century fared much worse. At its low point in the fifteenth century, a textile town in decline (like Diksmuide in Flanders) counted up to 40 per cent of its households as poor. In 1584–5, when a monthly tax was levied on Antwerp's population, it turned out that only 24 per cent were 'wealthy' enough to contribute to any effect. The largest portion of the population was simply exempted. An important question with such figures is whether absolute poverty (defined by a poverty threshold expressed in quantities of calories) or relative poverty (defined as households with an income below a certain percentage of the median income) increased, or whether urban societies simply grew more sensitive to poverty, independently of actual poverty levels.

The infrastructure of and access to poor relief were very much a layered phenomenon. The vulnerable groups in society may well have experienced the consequences of gradually unravelling extended family ties. Poorer groups in the population and those earning wages migrated more frequently than the middling groups and the elites. For that reason they could not always count on family ties of solidarity. In any case, the initiative for acute support shifted more and more towards semi-private institutions: parochial charities for the so-called 'house poor' (*armendissen*), religious almshouses or residential courtyards (*godshuizen* and *hofjes*) sometimes organised by the craft guilds, and municipal poorhouses. In the late twelfth and thirteenth centuries this layered infrastructure had increased in number and scope, and generally they would constitute the pre-eminent area of action for the (usually female) third mendicant orders. From the late twelfth century onwards, the parochial charities or tables of the Holy Spirit (*tafels van de Heilige Geest*) became much more numerous in the larger towns of the southern Low Countries. They were organised by wealthy laypeople, first at the level of the entire town, and later, over the course of the thirteenth century, frequently at the lower level of the parish. The earliest documented are those in Tournai, Liège, Mechelen, Mons, Ghent and Bruges, yet they also appear in smaller towns like Comines, Zoutleeuw, Lier and Dinant. It is no coincidence that their origin is connected to the explosive urban expansion in the last phase of medieval growth. The industrial towns that were dependent on the export of textile products repeatedly had to struggle with cyclical fluctuations, which sometimes caused high unemployment in the short term. Parochial charities were ideally suited for absorbing at least a part of the social consequences of these periods of crisis.

The greater number of these institutions from the last quarter of the thirteenth century onwards, and the stronger connection to the parish may well, therefore, be no coincidence. In the large textile towns the cloth industry, as the largest employer, began to switch to the production of more expensive fabrics. This specialisation towards high quality went hand in hand with a fall in total output and thus with the unemployment of less-skilled occupational groups in textile manufacture.

The poor tables provided spiritual care and they distributed so-called *provenen*, packages that mostly consisted of staple foods like bread, butter and peas, and now and then meat, fish or cheese. On occasion they were responsible for housing, medical care, shoes and basic clothing, including linen breeches and shirts. We can only speculate about the efficiency of this support. Given the composition and the scope of the alms, support for the poor was only intended to supplement a real and regular household income. In Ghent, with more than 50,000 inhabitants in the fifteenth century, a total of approximately 600 beneficiaries was, in that sense, not much more than a drop in the ocean. Elsewhere, somewhat more than 15 per cent of households received support from the poor tables. This aid was insufficient to provide fully for the large groups of poor, but it may well have been just enough to relieve the poor from a worse fate. In the meantime, however, another dichotomy was gradually put in place: a distinction was made between, on the one hand, the group of town dwellers who received and deserved support and, on the other, the undesired and undeserving poor, who were not allowed to benefit from the system.

Poor relief followed more or less the same trend all over the Low Countries. From a relatively open-door policy with regard to various categories of those needing aid, access was made increasingly selective. Being a member of a certain defined community became a basic requirement. That community might be the town proper, but frequently it was also the smaller groups that had a role within the town. For the larger urban craft guilds or other associations, poor boxes were an instrument for supporting their own members or those members' families. They can rightly be called a system of social security for an in-crowd. It was the poorer transients, the itinerant labourers and beggars, who paid the price of the gradual inclusion of particular groups in the poor relief system. They were the outsiders, hence excluded. Moreover, in the fifteenth century it seems that the quality of the support extended by the parishes decreased. Food packages became more monotonous and they were gradually limited to only basic needs. Distributions of clothing decreased both in scope and in importance. At the same time, this process of exclusion was coined in moral terms. Aid recipients had to conform to desired behaviour. In Ghent the municipal authorities, by way of alms, annually gave overgarments in the heraldic colours of the town to a very select group of the poor. Elsewhere, as in Bruges, a small token with the town's arms was attached to the clothing of the poor. The recognisability of the poor receiving aid suddenly came high on the agenda. With such connotation, the aid recipients were symbolically linked to the ranks of the marginal groups who had to wear specific dress, such as the lepers, the plague-stricken and the prostitutes.

A document that demonstrates the spirit of the sixteenth century well with regard to the poor and the weak is *De subventione pauperum*, published in 1526 by the Spanish humanist Juan Luis Vives (1493–1540), who lived in Bruges. In his treatise Vives wrote beggars off as treacherous tramps, who refused to work, while employers, in contrast, were in desperate need of a workforce. In the sixteenth century, beggars and other 'work-shy riff-raff' were marginalised, criminalised and increasingly held responsible for their personal failings. Only the 'deserving poor' – women, the disabled, widows, the aged – might still come knocking for support. Whoever was healthy, however, could no longer count on compassion. In 1531, when Charles V proclaimed a new ordinance on poor relief, in a period of utter economic crisis and famine, he was inspired by this urban ideology. A few years earlier, in 1525, towns like Ypres in Flanders and Mons in Hainaut had taken initiatives to coordinate poor relief. The policy was aimed at 'activating' the poor: a prohibition on begging was coupled with labour discipline as a requirement for support from an integrated fund for the poor. The emperor adapted these initiatives and tried to provide a framework in which poor relief could be centralised. There was a requirement for healthy poor people to work and in different towns the willingness to work was strictly monitored. Emperor Charles also forbade begging and vagrancy. Although the actual implementation of the ordinance took decades to realise, the ink on his imperial ordinance was barely dry when the number of those persecuted for these offences soared, for example, in Antwerp. Some authorities immediately used the occasion to discipline the poor even further, starting to consider alcohol abuse, for example, as an excluding factor for poor support – a strategy that would be applied more and more systematically in subsequent centuries.

And with that turn of events, the circle is as good as complete. The towns of the Low Countries were indeed characterised by the strength of their middling groups, despite a general social inequality which was already present in the central Middle Ages. Above all, it was economic processes that fed the importance of the urban middling groups. Diversification from a broad range of textiles to (semi-)luxury fabrics and the supply of a wide range of goods and services for the local and regional economy supported the typical social architecture of the towns in the Low Countries, especially in Flanders and Brabant. The developments in the sixteenth century tellingly illustrate, moreover, that economic growth in and of itself did not suffice to make problems at the bottom of the social ladder disappear – on the contrary. The steadily burgeoning bourgeois mentality surfed on the economic success of merchants and entrepreneurs, but it also provided extra thresholds for those without possessions. That bourgeois mentality – with its great emphasis on work ethic, frugality and civility – strengthened the reproduction of social inequality to a great extent, and was partly responsible for the social frictions with which we started this account of five centuries of social urban history.

4 'The Common Good': Governance, Discipline and Political Culture

Marc Boone and Jelle Haemers

The Question of Discipline: Paradigms and Propositions

With large population groups living together in cities and the need to integrate newcomers into them, it became necessary to develop rules for managing disputes and finding peaceful settlements to them or, even better, preventing them altogether. Such disputes can occur in the (semi-)public domains of property, labour, political power and financial management, but also within the private sphere, such as, for example, in marriage, sexuality and the protection of children, widows and the mentally ill. Several attempts to synthesise these aspects of urban life have been undertaken in the past. In 1939, Norbert Elias (1897–1990) published his magnum opus about the 'civilising process', which has had a profound influence, even today. Elias posited that interdependence among individuals has increased over the course of history, and that this interweaving of separate human intentions and actions has led to permanent changes in codes of conduct. According to Elias, as a result of societal pressure people adopt behavioural codes directed at making society peaceful. His thesis has important consequences for urban history because it allows for the linking of the development of a political process (the confrontation between the city and the state and the struggle for power within both the city and the state) to the imposition of values and beliefs that are subsequently adopted and interiorised by individuals. In other words, those who have power are able to sanction and thus influence the beliefs and actions of others, both individually and collectively, consciously and unconsciously.

The French historian Robert Muchembled is an advocate of Elias. He views the city as a 'machine à produire du consensus social'. As his research into behaviour labelled as criminal in the towns of Artois and adjoining regions concludes, living together compels people to draw up rules of conduct. Herman Pleij also tracks down a 'civilising process' in the towns of the Low Countries. For both authors, the city, the

Figure 4.1 Miniature from Jean Mansel, *La Fleur des histoires*, Tournai/Arras/Saint-Omer, *c.* 1455. Inhabitants of a town execute an individual while the prince is counselled in his palace. The image narrates the biblical story of Esther, but also represents a fifteenth-century imagination of town justice.

workings of its institutions and the collective actions of its burghers take centre stage. When Muchembled analyses how the repressive arsenal of the city ultimately had to bow to the coercive as well as communicative force of princely repression, he even talks about 'l'impossible république urbaine'. Slowly but surely, the city had to cede the initiative for sanctioning conduct to central government. In contrast, Pleij decodes the urban literature of rhetoricians, composers of occasional poetry and versifiers of all stripes as tell-tale signs of tensions in society, as well as of the zeal of burghers in obtaining control of the lives and conduct of their fellow burghers. Within the city, according to Pleij, a civilising campaign plays out. By proclaiming all manner of rules, demonstrating 'civilised' codes of conduct and making literary propaganda for them, well-to-do and powerful groups in the city would sanction their fellow citizens when they over-indulged in 'misconduct'.

In present historiography these findings are becoming somewhat more nuanced. A new generation of historians is instead localising the 'agency' for disciplinary measures in the hands of middling groups, which had an important voice in governance 'from below' and, as a consequence, also in urban 'discipline'. On the one hand, Anne-Laure Van Bruaene demonstrated how urban middling groups were the engine for one of the pre-eminent 'disciplinary instruments' touched on by Herman Pleij, namely, the rhetoricians' chambers (see Chapter 5). On the other hand, it has been proven repeatedly that these groups were also the driving force behind numerous political changes. New government structures arose in towns during the fourteenth century, specifically under the pressure of craft guilds and middling groups. Afterwards, too, they took up numerous initiatives to make complaints against administrators and to punish them for corruption and misconduct, for example. Thus, disciplinary action and the governmental organisation of the city also came about without initiatives from above. Burghers themselves took measures to rein in conduct and to sanction transgressions against agreed-upon rules. In short, an urban community would not be disciplined procedurally via a civilising campaign from those in power, but would continually discipline itself by regulating labour, social life and market activity (see Chapter 2).

There is also, of course, the tradition stemming from the history of law, which discerns in this disciplinary process effects descending from Roman as well as canon law. These legal traditions were taught at universities from the twelfth century onwards, mixed with locally developed customary law, and resulting in an ensemble of normative stipulations. Traditional reception history of this sort has already been brought up to date by authoritative legal historians themselves. So, for example, Philippe Godding argued that municipal law constituted a source of inspiration for the 'constitutional law' that princes promulgated for a larger territory. In view of the fact that municipal law goes back to problems that city administrators faced daily, city ordinances are usually a generalisation of a concrete solution given to a specific problem, and not the result of legislation *in abstracto*.

For a long time these kinds of rules were also passed on through oral tradition from generation to generation. The earliest formal records to stipulate norms therefore carry traces of a preceding oral phase. Many cases concern formal ratification by a prince who, even so, can seldom be seen as an 'author' and, even then, only as the material but not the intellectual author. A typical example is the early town charter, the *charte de la paix*, for Valenciennes, dating from 1114 – which served to bring 'peace' to the town – or the even earlier 'peace' of Huy from 1066. In the latter charter, for example, Theoduinus, the prince-bishop of Liège, granted the *burgenses* of Huy a number of freedoms (*libertates*) in exchange for financial support. In concrete terms, then, this charter affirmed their growing independence from feudal lords (see Chapter 3). The document also legalised locally developed customs, such as calling witnesses in trials instead of settling disputes by means of duels.

Yet, even when the law was codified and recorded, communication was characterised by an oral procedure. The stricture to 'Oyés et faites pais' ('Listen and make peace'), for example, preceded the municipal decrees of fourteenth-century Mons.[1] Obviously, the concrete site of the declaration was not arbitrary: at the marketplace, in front of the town hall, on the balcony (or *bretèche*) of the town hall, or at the *perron* (a column erected to symbolise civic freedom in, for example, Nivelles, Verviers and Liège). In large towns, municipal decrees were repeated in front of the various parish churches or at the most important marketplaces, preceded by bell-ringing or by the shouting of an established cry (see Chapter 6). In short, customs and rules that developed orally and performatively gave shape to municipal legislation.

In the second half of the twelfth century and the first half of the thirteenth, many towns in the Low Countries would, like Valenciennes and Huy, set up what were called *communes*, which were themselves responsible for the proclamation of laws, as well as for ensuring compliance with them and punishment for breach (see Chapter 3). This community of burghers called itself a *communio* (as in Brussels in 1229) or a *communitas* or *universitas* (as in Namur in 1265). Sometimes towns also used the appellation *conjuratio* ('conspiracy') to describe themselves. In doing so they referred to the oath of joint allegiance to a legal text put together of their own accord, written down in a charter (or *keure*). In Genappe (1211), Zoutleeuw (1213), Antwerp (1221) and Leuven (1234), it was the duke of Brabant who promulgated this charter. Yet it explicitly mentioned that the burghers had taken the initiative, or at least had acted as advisors.

In the northern Low Countries, texts of this type did not come into being in large numbers until the beginning of the thirteenth century (the exceptions being Staveren around 1068, and Utrecht and Deventer around 1120). In the north and the south alike, they first reined in misconduct. As a comparison, John Najemy likes to describe the eleventh-century

---

[1] Léopold Devillers, *Ban de polices de la ville de Mons du XIIe au XVe siècle* (Mons: Duquesne-Masquillier et fils, 1897), p. 190.

Italian communes as 'laboratories of self-discipline'. Murder, intentional bodily harm, thievery and other criminal offences were severely punished by the community and those they elected; the perpetrators were removed from the *conjuratio*. They were exiled and their goods were confiscated and sold for the benefit of the entire community. Or, even more drastically, their houses were destroyed so that nothing would ever remind one of their existence. The texts generally gave effect to oral proscriptions that had already applied previously, and punished smaller offences as well. In Zinnik and Diest, for example, inhabitants who insulted one another or got into fights had to follow a specific route through the town carrying 'stones of justice' (stones depicting scandalmongers). A similar sanction existed in Mechelen, Hasselt and Eijsden (now in the Dutch province of Limburg), where the local 'book of freedom' (*vrijheidsboek*) called for this punishment only for women who insulted one another by calling each other 'whores'. The proclamation of these kinds of punishments shows how, from their beginning, urban communities aspired to bring their fellow urbanites to repentance in cases where they had disturbed the peace and disrupted order.

The terminology of the *commune* would be used by the inhabitants of towns long after their establishment to account for the promulgation of laws, or to justify their resistance to them. It is striking to note that, in the coming centuries, both those with authority and their political challengers would use similar wording to provide grounds for the promulgation of laws to justify revolt or to legitimate the suppression of precisely those uprisings. Accounting for legislative action is exceptional in earlier centuries, yet in thirteenth- and early fourteenth-century texts administrators were already repeatedly referring to the *bien commun*, the 'common good' or the general welfare of the town: 'for the town's best' (*Pour le miols de le ville*), as it was called in the case of the promulgation of a decree in Tournai at the end of the thirteenth century.[2]

Even the groups that lived in the towns used the same discourse. In 1378, for example, the craft guilds in Leuven demanded that the municipal government allow them thenceforth to meet together 'for the common prosperity' (*omme 't gemein orbor*) of the town.[3] In the 1280s, when, during a wave of revolts, the inhabitants of many towns demanded that the regime at the time prosecute criminal misdeeds, the insurgents called themselves the *ghemeente* or the *meentucht*; these and various related forms in Middle Dutch referred to the 'commons' or the

---

[2] Léo Verriest, *Coutumes de la ville de Tournai* (Brussels: J. Goemaere, 1923), vol. I, p. 461.
[3] Antonin Schayes, *Analectes archéologiques, historiques, géographiques et statistiques concernant principalement la Belgique* (Antwerp: Buschmann, 1857, p. 359).

'commonalty' – as was the case in Damme in 1280. Or they used the French term *le coumun* – as in Ghent in 1275.[4] Those in revolt – an amalgam of manual labourers and rich merchants excluded from governance – presented themselves in their pamphlets as the 'true' successors of the commune, the foundational principles of which they had, by their own account, seen watered down. Artisans wanted self-government and they no longer accepted being ruled by administrators who, as they saw it, continually transgressed municipal legislation and managed municipal finances badly or levied taxes felt to be unjust. In the case of internal conflicts, townspeople thus used the argument that they, and not their opponents, were the best protectors of the public good.

Taxation and its visibly unjust aspects for contemporaries were considered to be the pre-eminent, tell-tale sign of social tensions. For organisational, political and economic reasons, towns in the Middle Ages and early modern era preferred indirect taxes, which affected production and above all consumption in a way that touched everyone. Complaints by townspeople concerning the tax burden prove not only how sensitive the matter was but also to what degree the perception of contributing to the municipal tax system was a defining factor in the individual's identification with his or her town. Paying taxes was equal to contributing to the 'general interest' and was included among duties, yet it also conferred rights.

The use – or abuse – of the notion of the 'common good' should not contradict the fundamental observation that it was a generally accepted concept. Gradually the idea of the general interest influenced and set up a framework for many diverse actions in the administration of justice and practical governance. From the central Middle Ages onwards, political thinkers debated the essence of this discourse. In his *Cura Reipublicae*, Philips van Leyden (*c.* 1320/8–1382), a jurist from the Low Countries educated at the law faculty in Orleans, explicitly posed questions concerning whether or not princely legislation was dominant over municipal legislation. He made fundamental observations about the fact that the pursuit of private interests was required to be subordinate to the *bien commun* of the town. It is intriguing to see how intellectuals like Philips van Leyden and the wealthy upper strata in towns, as well as middling groups, artisans and manual labourers, made use of a similar ideology to account for their political deeds. Presumably they were influenced

---

[4] See, respectively, Antoine De Smet, 'De klacht van de "Ghemeente" van Damme in 1280', *Handelingen van de Koninklijke Commissie voor Geschiedenis*, 115 (1950), p. 9; Georges Espinas and Henri Pirenne, *Recueil de documents relatifs à l'histoire de l'industrie drapière en Flandre* (Brussels: Kiessling et Imbreghts, 1909), vol. II, p. 382.

by the ideology of the mendicant orders (see Chapter 5). Each group contended that its actions were in the (general) interest of the commonalty, but the debate about in exactly whose interest the town was being governed would drag on for all of the late Middle Ages and into the early modern era, and lead to serious conflicts.

Textualisation and Urban Identity

The way in which townspeople deal with their institutional memory is crucial for normative actions in the city. Putting rules down permanently in written form is naturally a first step: pragmatically speaking, textualisation of this type is dictated by the need to repeat or adapt certain rules and regulations regularly. In this case, at first glance such regulation frequently revolves around banal worries such as the need to keep streets clean or to store grain. Nevertheless, these regulations are essential applications of the shared care for the 'commonweal'. In the Low Countries, the earliest attestations date from the late thirteenth century: more than 800 policing orders (or *bans*) in the registry of Saint-Omer (1280) and the rolls containing the municipal regulations of Mons in Hainaut. From the fourteenth century onwards, almost every town conceived regulations of its own, since, from the last quarter of the thirteenth century, most towns had a chancellery. Earlier evidence of regulating urban society can be found once again in the border region between Flanders and Artois, as well as around the linguistic boundary at that time. Douai, for example, has a collection dating from 1204 of approximately 35,000 chirographs in the vernacular, namely, a variation of the French spoken in Picardy. This archive provides early evidence of one of the most valued functions of the town aldermen: so-called 'voluntary judicial jurisdiction' (*jurisdiction gracieuse*), understood as providing for legally valid documents (such as marriage certificates and wills) as well as registering them. The nearby town of Arras has an aldermen's document in French from 1238, supplemented by a fragment of the town accounts from 1241 to 1242, in addition to chirographs dating from 1246 onwards.

The development of a municipal secretariat and the introduction of the vernacular spread chronologically in a north-easterly direction. Of the major cities in Flanders, Ypres stayed with the chirograph as a text type for preserving municipal documents until the beginning of the fifteenth century. From the fourteenth century onwards, Ghent and Bruges employed the book format for their registries, which in fact did not prevent small islands of tradition from persisting: thus, for example, the craft guilds in Ghent employed the chirograph as a form of documentation until the fifteenth century. Over the course of the thirteenth century, the trend of drawing up voluntary legal documents in the vernacular reached the counties of Holland and Zeeland: in the latter, Middelburg was using the vernacular in 1217; in Holland, it took until 1267 for Delft and 1277 for Dordrecht to do so. It is telling that the transition to an administration in the vernacular was a genuinely urban trend: the comital chancellery waited until 1285 to make the same move. Even on this level, though, variety and conservatism occurred: in northern Brabant it took until the middle of the fourteenth century before the vernacular genuinely prevailed at the expense of Latin. For 'voluntary legal' transactions in 's-Hertogenbosch this did not happen until the sixteenth century.

In general, these early municipal collections of documents and archival material made urban *memoria* and identity incarnate to such a degree that they became the object of repressive measures. On 23 September 1408, John the Fearless (duke of Burgundy) and his brother-in-law William IV of Bavaria (count of Hainaut as well as of Holland and Zeeland) beat the militias of Liège and neighbouring towns on the battlefield of Othée, having come to the aid of their relative John of Bavaria (the prince-bishop elect of Liège). As punishment they confiscated all the charters of the rebellious towns in the prince-bishopric. The documents were taken to the Burgundian Chamber of Account in Lille and for the most part destroyed. Almost the entire archives of the craft guilds in Liège before 1408, along with hundreds of ceremonial documents (among them, the charter for Huy's freedom from 1066), were wilfully lost in this way. The effects can be guessed at: for decades some of the towns in question existed in a state of legal vacuum, in search of a new equilibrium. In 1540 Charles V repeated these actions when he punished his birthplace, Ghent, destroying the archival material of his most fervent opponents, the craft guilds and thus extinguishing their living memory.

Conversely, rebellious movements in the Low Countries during the sixteenth century emphatically dusted off important documentary markers of urban resistance against the central authorities. The best-known example is Mary of Burgundy's 'Great Privilege' (*Groot Privilegie*) of 1477, which granted a general privilege to the entire Low Countries for the first time. The text specifically justified the Dutch Revolt (1568–1648) with arguments. In this way, the urban collective memory – based upon privileges and regulations of its own and preserved in an intrinsic context in the charter chests of many belfries and town halls – was an essential component of urban identity. It therefore comes as no surprise that municipal governments invested large sums in the buildings in which such charters, accounting documents and municipal archives were preserved (see Chapter 6).

Middling groups played an important role in this textualisation of the municipal administration. Not only were they acquisitive collectors of voluntary legal transactions, but they also obliged the urban elite to account for its acts of governance as well as its management of municipal money. In its turn, this explicit demand for such an accounting was the consequence of the growth of the towns of the Low Countries and the result of increasing social polarisation in the densely populated urban centres at the end of the thirteenth century. From the 1280s onwards, craft guilds, middling groups and other townspeople fought – by means of revolts, among other things – to make the administrators literally put their expenditures in the books. And they did so successfully. Ever since – once again, the precise chronology differs from town to town – accounts have been presented annually in a written version for audit to representatives of the people. In the preceding period, established wealthy families governed the towns in mutual (oral) agreement with one another. The late thirteenth- and fourteenth-century revolts led not only to the admission of larger groups to municipal government, but in so doing also to a greater textualisation of that government (see Chapter 3). Numerous other administrative documents, such as judgments of the aldermen's bench and town ordinances, were thenceforth drawn up in the vernacular.

Norms and Rules: The City as a Regulatory Body

Legislative practice accounted for various needs: providing inhabitants with the administration of justice, safeguarding and further elaborating existing legislation, and ultimately also affirming urban identity. After all, belonging to a town implied subjecting oneself to, yet also knowing oneself to be protected by, municipal law. Educated jurists like Bartolus of Sassoferrato (1313/14–1357) broadcast the principle that 'to every people that has jurisdiction, it is permitted in matters of civil law to determine legal rules as well'.[5] With those principles they took up an idea that had originally been put into words by canonists in the twelfth century, namely, that a community of common law, such as a city (*civitas*), is able to act legislatively in being able to issue judgments without needing to have the consent of a higher, princely or ecclesiastical authority. But it

---

[5] Cited in Claudia Storti Storchi, 'Betrachtungen zum Thema "Potestas condendi statute"', in Giorgio Chittolini and Dietmar Willoweit (eds.), *Statuten, Städte und Territorien zwischen Mittelalter und Neuzeit in Italien und Deutschland* (Berlin: Speyers and Peters, 1992), p. 257: 'Omni populo jurisdictionem habenti, statuere permittitur quod jus civile vocatur'.

was not only in the major centres that one caught echoes of legal claims of this sort. A judgment that came from the modest town of Thuin (which made up part of the prince-bishopric of Liège) stated in 1347 that 'the aforementioned burghers are able to have the council of [burgo]masters and the sworn town council make regulations and ordinances'.[6]

In more significant towns, from which laws radiated out over the surrounding countryside, any prerogative of this type almost automatically came into conflict with the ambitions of the territorial lord. It depended, then, on what the actual power relations were whether the town was or was not able to continue making legislation unhindered. The town charters for Ghent from Queen Matilda and for Flanders and Hainaut from Count Baldwin VIII in 1191 bound the legislative actions of prince and townspeople to mutual consent with each other: in that way neither party got the upper hand in this essential area for the exercise of power.

Tactically, it was a convenient point of departure. In 1401, for instance, Ghent's aldermen got on the wrong side of their duke, Philip the Bold of Burgundy, concerning the ban they had pronounced on Jacob van Lichtervelde, the sovereign bailiff of Flanders. The twelfth-century documents were then ceremoniously shown and used to argue their case. Conversely, when the prince was in a strong position in his confrontation with self-willed towns, municipal legislative actions came under pressure. The regime of Charles the Bold was one such period. In Mechelen, for example, there were riots at the start of his reign. In a pardon dated 16 October 1467, the duke stipulated that thenceforth he would be able to revoke the charters of the city at his discretion. There were precedents for such action. In 1407 Duke John the Fearless had imposed a similar series of financial reforms, among other things by means of the so-called 'calf's skin' (*calfvel*) of Bruges. And in 1469 Charles the Bold would intervene similarly in Leiden in the county of Holland. At this level, the equilibrium between prince and town was thus continually subject to change.

Municipal governments and higher authorities were not always on a collision course, however, for both had an interest in keeping the peace and order in society. For the town of Ath in Hainaut, for example, Philip the Good promulgated a prohibition in 1445 against the organisation of gambling. The ordinance explicitly mentions that 'our well-loved burgomaster and aldermen' (*noz bien amez les maire et eschevins*) had asked

---

[6] Cited in Léopold Génicot and Rose Allard (eds.), *Sources du droit rural du quartier d'Entre-Sambre-et-Meuse* (Brussels: Ministerie van Justitie, 1981), vol. II, p. 791: 'puelent ly dis bourgoys faire statutz et ordonnances par le conseillz des maistrez et dou conseillz jureit de le ville'.

for this promulgation, for gambling had brought about many 'things that were bad and inappropriate' (*maulx et inconveniens*). For that reason, the aldermen had addressed the duke with a 'humble request' ('umble supplicacion') asking him to place restrictions on this activity.[7] More often, however, the bench of aldermen acted alone in these kinds of cases, or customary law regulated the resolution of disputes. In sixteenth-century Borgloon, for example, 'female persons who resist combatively with their fists' were fined seven shillings.[8] The aldermen strictly supervised compliance with these kinds of customs, and supplemented them with prohibitive stipulations if necessary. In 1424, for example, the town council in neighbouring Sint-Truiden took action against prostitution within the town ramparts by requiring every 'prostitute' (*ledich wuf*) to leave the town immediately. They, too, were coerced by a fine, as well as by being branded with a red-hot staff if they did not conform to municipal legislation.[9] In short, the pre-eminent body that was to monitor the town and its inhabitants was the aldermen's bench.

It was not just the municipal government (whether in collaboration with the prince or not) but also the subordinate municipal bodies that could require rules to be applied. Administrations of craft guilds had the requisite technical competences, of course, to set out their complex production processes in provisions of their own, and above all to demarcate the possible domains where their prerogatives overlapped with those of other craft guilds. In towns like Ghent where artisans' associations had enforced a great tradition of political participation, administrators of craft guilds – convened under the presidency of an arch-dean (*overdeken*) – sat on tribunals of their own to adjudicate on and punish transgressions against their rules and regulations. Research by Myriam Carlier and Peter Stabel has drawn attention to the moral facets of legislative and judicial actions of the craft guilds: bastardy, prostitution, adultery and other conduct deemed to be dishonourable were objects of concern. Among these topics the notion of the 'honour of the town', for which every artisan was responsible, played a central role. In some associations, such as that of the rosary-makers in Bruges, exemplary conduct was essential to their reputation, and the actions of widows, for example, were followed more strictly than in other craft guilds. Ecclesiastical authorities, too,

---

[7] Jean-Marie Cauchies, *Ordonnances de Philippe le Bon pour le comté de Hainaut, 1425–1467* (Brussels: FOD Justitie, 2010), p. 220.
[8] Cited in Louis Crahay, *Coutumes du comté de Looz, de la seigneurie de Saint-Trond et du comté impérial de Reckheim* (Brussels: J. Goemaere, 1897), vol. III, p. 278: 'vrouwenpersoenen die strijtachtig weren met vuysten'.
[9] François Straven, *Inventaire analytique et chronologique des archives de la ville de Saint-Trond* (Sint-Truiden: Moreau-Schouberechts, 1886), vol. I, p. 257.

attempted to direct the way that townspeople conducted themselves, though research on Bruges has demonstrated that they suffered enormously from the unbridled conduct of some clergy, which could not be considered particularly exemplary of their own rules (see Chapter 5).

The prerogatives of aldermen were vast, and also concerned affairs that at first glance were ecclesiastical matters, such as marriage. In view of the fact that a union between husband and wife had far-reaching consequences for society, it may perhaps be logical that local authorities concerned themselves with the consequences of that contract. In Leuven in 1406, for example, the municipal government promulgated an ordinance that prohibited its inhabitants from entering into clandestine marriages. Wedding parties of this sort consisted of couples exchanging valid marital vows in a secret location (generally outside the bishopric concerned). This practice allowed women of standing – whether with their consent, or not – to marry the offspring of families beneath them in society. That any municipal government desired to take action against this kind of practice demonstrates first of all that established families used their power to counteract what in their eyes were socially destabilising practices. Moreover, this example indicates that disciplining inhabitants often proceeded from specific political concerns. The authors of this 1406 Leuven ordinance were not in the first instance possessed by moral concerns. Rather, they were designing a legal instrument for maintaining and expanding social networks. Research on Douai, Ghent and other towns has shown that townspeople generally married within their own social group, even within their own profession ('trade endogamy', as Martha Howell described this practice in Douai). Controlling the proper conduct of marriages was therefore an important matter for well-to-do groups such as nobles, patricians and established middling groups. Social networks were not only of great political importance but were just as much a kind of economic insurance and a social safety net. In such a case, the punishment of uncontrolled conduct was not a moral initiative for inciting other townspeople to religiously inspired self-control, but rather a means of maintaining social and economic prosperity. Regulatory activity illustrates, with regard to the nuclear family, how much the so-called reduction of the influence of the extended family was not an unequivocal process (see Chapter 3).

Discipline in Practice: Conflict Management and Criminalisation

The medieval and early modern town seems to be the pre-eminent setting for criminal activity. Many examples, such as that of Leuven, confirm the image of a 'den of iniquity' that pops up in much literature, having germinated earlier in the imagination of clerical authors. As a result of the role of many towns as centres, criminals found favourable conditions there for activities such as dealing in stolen goods, yet also an easy connection to other crime-inducing activities, such as prostitution. The town also provided anonymity, and as a result of the concentration of a number of economic and social practices the likelihood of both property crimes and violent crimes rose considerably. Interpreting criminality in late medieval and early modern towns is difficult as there is a dearth of tools for measurement, but historians assume that an average of two murders were committed annually in a town of approximately 10,000 inhabitants. The nature of these sorts of crimes was continually changing. At the start of the fourteenth century the old, pseudo-noble law of vengeance was gradually superseded. From then on, a typical urban approach aimed at peaceful settlement acquired the upper hand. In this phase, reconciliation and reversible punishments like banishment or punitive pilgrimages replaced corporal punishments such as execution or mutilation on the scaffold. These sentences belonged to the legal essence of what Robert Muchembled has described as the 'city republic'. As the control of the central authorities increased over the course of the late Middle Ages – in the case of the towns of Arras and Saint-Omer studied by Muchembled, such monitoring involved the French king – once again the number of executions and maimings increased. The scaffolds became the venue at which state power put itself on display and demonstrated its supremacy over municipal jurisdiction.

Maarten Van Dijck has demonstrated for early modern Antwerp that, nevertheless, the influence of state formation upon reining in violence has to be relativised. Just as Frederik Buylaert concluded for the vendettas carried out in Leiden and Ghent, it is striking that groups of urban elites had their own particular mechanisms for making peace, such as forms of amicable settlement and arbitrage. The image of a pre-eminently violent town, therefore, has to be readjusted. The pronounced urban preference for conciliatory procedures did not, of course, rule out executions or corporal punishment for serious criminal offences such as murder during robbery or rape. Where possible, however, a peaceful settlement was striven for. Such 'pacification' was primarily accomplished by temporarily banishing the criminal or by sentencing him to a punitive pilgrimage, as a result of which he disappeared from the town as well. In this way the perpetrator was literally taken out of the sight of the victim and his or her family, which reduced the urge to take revenge, and also immediately provided time and space for making amends for the harm suffered by way of deliberation. Moreover, the formula of the punitive pilgrimage was inherently religious, with the intention of moving the transgressor to repentance and purification. Whereas municipal law in Leuven in the twelfth century still employed the principle of 'an eye for an eye, and a tooth for a tooth', in the fourteenth century perpetrators of mayhem were punished by a pilgrimage to Rocamadour. For that matter, punitive pilgrimages were a characteristically urban phenomenon, though over the years the practice was eroded: pilgrimages could be bought off. In the Liège region they went even further, with pilgrimages being reduced to accounting units that expressed monetary fines. Antwerp, in contrast, preferred to impose pilgrimages as sentences. Between 1414 and 1445, the heyday of the practice, the great majority of cases recorded letters of proof that the pilgrim brought back from the pilgrimage site.

It is tempting, once again, to label punishments of this sort as a kind of moral reining in of mores. Yet there is more going on here. It is striking that time and again exemplary punishments such as pilgrimages, carrying stones around or piercing the tongue with a red-hot staff (for punishing defamation) were public occasions that served in the first place to emphasise the authority of the one doing the punishing. Casting slurs and calling names were in the main fined if they were expressed in the public arena, and retribution was very considerably increased if the honour of figures of public authority or men of standing was impugned. Thus, there was an extra level of punishment for putting the political hierarchy of the town into question. In Ypres in 1320, at the house of an alderman, Hannin Mont cried out that that alderman was a 'bad, false alderman' (*mal fauls eschevin*) and not worthy of sitting on the aldermen's bench. Though understandable from the point of view of the municipal government, the punishment was severe: the man was banished from the town.[10] In craft guilds, too, authority figures were to be treated with respect. When in 1527 Thomas Hagebaert yelled at the governing board of the Bruges fishmongers, 'I shit on you Sirs and on you aldermen, and on all those who might do me harm', the board of the craft guild, in collaboration with the aldermen's bench, sentenced him to banishment.[11]

The promulgation of numerous ordinances reining in similar conduct demonstrates that administrators reacted vigilantly to slander and libel. In that way they most likely wanted to prevent such denunciations

---

[10] Prosper De Pelsmaeker, *Coutumes des pays et comté de Flandre. Quartier d'Ypres. Registres aux sentences des échevins d'Ypres* (Brussels: Ministerie van Justitie, 1914), p. 255.

[11] Cited in Albert Schouteet, 'Jurisdictie over ambachtslieden te Brugge in de 16de eeuw', *Bulletin de la Commission Royale pour la publication des anciennes lois et ordonnances de la Belgique*, 20 (1962), p. 420: 'Ic schyte in ulieden ende in scepenen, ende in al deghonne die my deeren moghen'.

developing into large-scale political resistance. All of this points not so much to a deficient level of civilisation among townspeople as to the fact that authority was fragile, in addition to what was continually at stake in the struggle.

The Struggle for Power in the City

The stakes in the struggle were high. In view of the fact that towns in the Low Countries had a far-reaching form of autonomy, a concentration of considerable economic, political and legal power lay in the hands of town administrators. The emergence of communes in the Low Countries (see above) was, as it were, a form of 'urban emancipation' at the expense of higher authorities (count, duke, bishop, etc.) who granted the towns extensive rights of self-governance. In the 1120s, for instance, Bruges became the scene of a serious succession crisis. In the days following the murder of Count Charles the Good in 1127, the town rebelled against William Clito, the successor imposed by the French king. The unique report of these events by Galbert of Bruges demonstrates that the Flemish count was successful only in part in his attempts to take into his hands the administrative autonomy of the urban communities. In 1128, the people of Ghent even called Count Clito a 'reneger' because he had broken his oath and trampled upon their municipal rights. During this crisis, Flemish towns underwent their variation of the communal movement that had exploded in all its intensity around the same time in the Picardy region, but which also spread elsewhere in urbanised Europe.

In Brabant the power of the central authorities was initially less strong in view of the fact that the count of Leuven – who became duke of Lower Lorraine in 1106, later assuming the title 'duke of Brabant' – only gradually expanded the boundaries of his power and his territory. Towns rebelled against this expansion many times, such as in 1194 when Antwerp, Brussels, Leuven, Tienen, Zoutleeuw, Lier, Nivelles, Gembloux and Jodoigne agreed to refuse all service to their duke if he ignored concluded treaties. From the very beginning, therefore, municipal independence in the southern Low Countries was an acquired right, and that right, along with the duties accompanying it, was laid down in and formulated as a mutual contract. That regulatory bodies existed for the central authorities was in and of itself seldom questioned by subjects. However, there was widespread rebellion against their deficient workings, their expansion of prerogatives felt to be unlawful, and the transgression of existing customary law.

In view of the fact that aldermen were the most prominent drafters of municipal law – and at the same time enforced compliance with it as

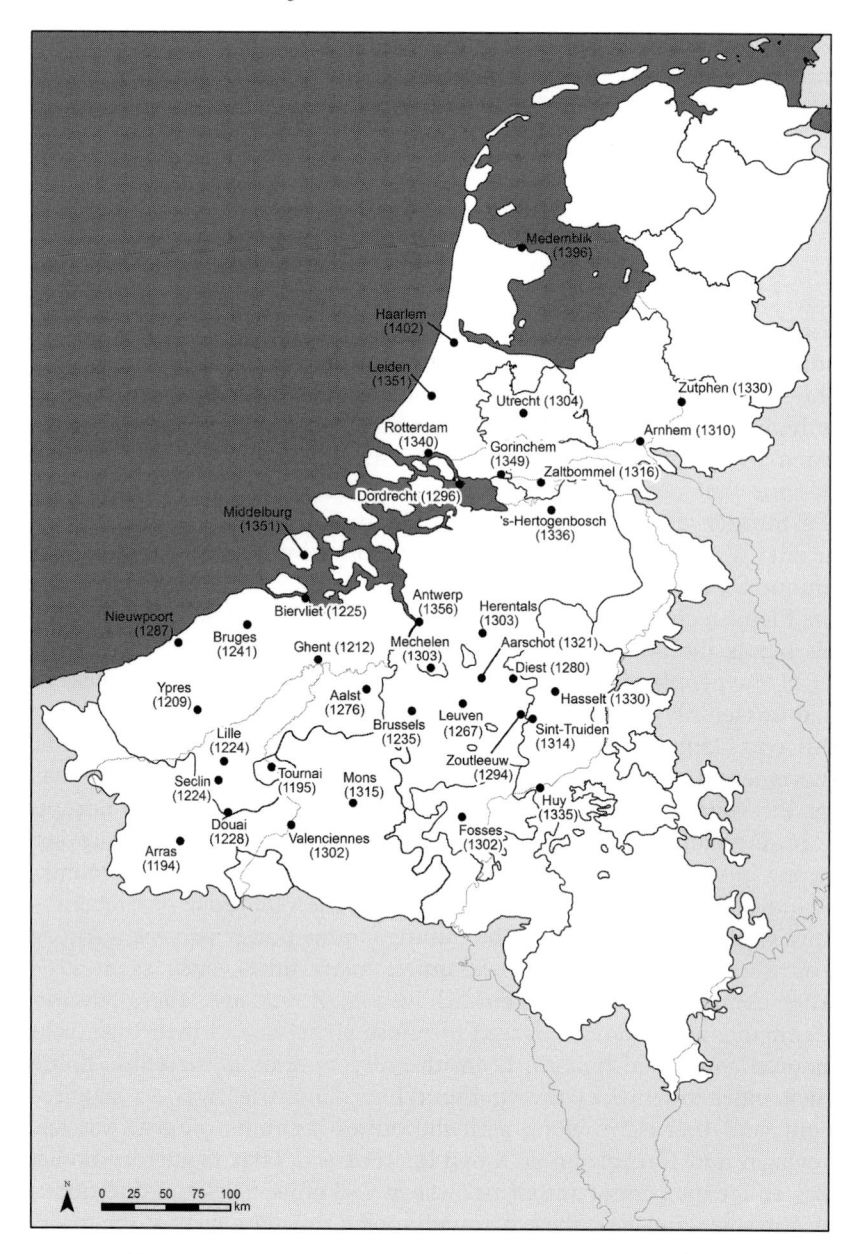

Figure 4.2 Introduction of the annual renewal of magistrates.

well as punishing transgressions against it – fighting to be admitted to the government of a town was frequent and intense. This struggle played out on various fronts. On the one hand, the balance between prince and town was continually fluctuating; on the other hand, unrest welled up many times in groups that were excluded from power. In an initial phase after the emergence of communes, different urban groups demanded that the appointment of aldermen for life should be stopped. In the beginning aldermen were representatives of the prince who were to ensure justice in the town. The position became, however, a de facto monopoly of important families, like the *viri heriditarii* or *erfachtige lieden* ('hereditary men') in Ghent and Saint-Omer, the so-called 'men of Saint Peter's' (*Sint-Pietermannen*) in Leuven, the 'lineages' in Liège, and so forth. In order to break their exclusive hold on power, their opponents, sometimes allied strategically with the prince, introduced the so-called 'annuality rule' (*annaliteitsregeling*), legislating for the annual appointment of administrators. The earliest trace of an annual renewal of the aldermen's bench can be found in Arras in 1194, at a point when the French king Philip II Augustus was relying on the communes to weaken his most important political opponent of that moment, the count of Flanders. Tournai followed this route in 1195, Ypres in 1209, Ghent in 1212, Lille in 1224 and Douai in 1228 (see Figure 4.2).

Bruges's annuality model was different in the sense that it did not come into being until 1241 and provided greater comital intervention. It served as a model for the smaller towns in western Flanders, as well as for Aalst and Geraardsbergen. In Brabant, annuality seems to have been acquired after 1235 by pretty much all towns. From that time too, *jurati* (or *gezworenen*, i.e. sworn judges of the commune) pop up in the sources. These representatives of the urban community generally governed the town together with the aldermen. In Liège, the earliest mention of them dates from 1185: jointly with the burgomasters, the *veri jurati* made up rules and regulations for the almshouse of Cornillon. It is difficult to check precisely who selected those sworn in, but in view of the fact that first mentions of them coincide with the first annuality rules, it can be assumed as likely that the same group must have fought for their admission. Presumably it was families who did not have the power base that the traditional factions in the town had (namely, large-scale landownership inside and outside the town). Thus they hoped to break the power of these factions, or at least to rein it in, by appointing new people to the town government every year.

From the middle of the thirteenth century, and even more so from the last quarter, a new group of townspeople claimed a political voice, namely, skilled manual labourers (see Chapter 3). What is remarkable is that their protest was widespread over the entire south of the Low Countries (Mechelen in 1242, Douai in 1245, Zoutleeuw in 1248, Ghent in 1252, Dinant in 1254, Leuven in 1265) and that, not coincidentally, the weavers and/or fullers constituted the engine of this protest. Some rebels even concluded agreements between towns, while in 1249 the aldermen of Mechelen and Antwerp promised one another support to prevent these kinds of alliances. Those who rebelled were day labourers and workers in cloth manufacture, the most prominent branch of industry in the Low Countries. Being self-aware, they wanted to influence the municipal decision-making process in various places. Self-governance was the most prominent demand of these artisans. In that way, the 'poor people who earn their grub with their hands and feet' (as they put it in Damme in 1280) hoped for a fair distribution of taxes, proper administration of justice and 'to have some men from the community as aldermen'.[12]

Once again, it is striking how taxation functioned as a catalyst for these complaints: felt to be socially unjust, indirect taxes – which weighed just as heavily on consumption (of beer, cereals, peat and so forth), irrespective of wealth – were a bone of contention. Indeed, these kinds of taxes accounted on average for more than 80 per cent of the municipal income. Excise duties also provided the financial basis on which the town met its fiscal obligations to the prince. This system implied a direct connection between an increased form of princely appeal (a tax) and a greater kind of internal fiscal pressure in the town. As a result, displeasure concerning the tax system transcended municipal politics. The ideas of the artisans and the citizens (*poorters*) sympathetic to them were not new. Ideologically speaking, one recognises in them an application of the principle 'that which concerns everyone ought to be approved by everyone after consideration' (*quod omnes tangit a omnibus tractari et approbari debet*). This tenet comes from Roman law but acquired broad influence by way of the mendicant orders. Though a small and wealthy group of townspeople already selected the municipal governments, around 1300 that base was evidently too small to be recognised still as a credible authority. What is more, those in revolt demanded that support for the private interests of aldermen and related factions should be a thing of the past: 'it falls to them that the general interest takes priority and is better than the interest of an individual person' (*comme il leur samble, uns communs pourfis doet alier et miex valoer de une singuliere personne*), as was said in Nieuwpoort in 1295.[13] This protest

---

[12] Cited in De Smet, 'De klacht', pp. 9 and 12 respectively: 'arme lieden die 't winnen met haren leden' and 'menighen man te hebbene van der ghemeente alse scepenen'.

[13] Roger Degryse, ''s Graven domein te Nieuwpoort', *Annales de la Société d'Emulation de Bruges*, 85 (1948), p. 111.

breathed new life into the ideology of the commune, and pointed the town administrators towards their duty of supporting the general interest of the townspeople.

The result of the protest movement looks impressive: control mechanisms were introduced for the municipal budget; craft guilds acquired the right to exist and to govern; and a kind of 'democratic' expansion took place. In the wake of the victory over the French king Philip the Fair by town armies from Flanders in 1302, craft guilds in Bruges and Ghent even acquired the right to elect aldermen. In addition, in Brussels, Leuven, Mechelen, 's-Hertogenbosch and towns in the prince-bishopric of Liège (such as Liège, Huy and Hasselt), as well as in Utrecht, other groups came to power after the revolts, albeit sometimes only temporarily. Whatever the case may be, then, it ushered in a so-called corporate era, in which different corporations (such as craft guilds) enjoyed far-reaching autonomy and a political voice.

For that reason, Henri Pirenne (1862–1935) described late medieval towns as 'démocraties de privilégiés'.[14] It is a concept with two meanings. On the one hand, it refers to the greater political voice from below that was present in the towns. On the other hand, Pirenne recognises that political decision-making in these towns remained the field of action for well-off groups in society. Research into the social composition of fourteenth-century municipal governments in the Low Countries shows that primarily wealthy, privileged groups remained in play, even if thenceforth well-to-do middling groups also participated. While following Pirenne's proposition that politics was a playground for men of esteem, some nuance may nevertheless be applied. Informal influence via networks, as well as clientelism, deliberations in meetings at the level of the craft guilds, and the submission of demands by means of petitions (i.e. *rekesten*, these being texts drawn up by subjects which were sometimes promulgated as municipal legislation): all these methods were strategies frequently utilised by burghers to weigh in on the decision-making process. At the same time, however, artisans literally fought for higher wages, the acquisition and maintenance of privileges, and the punishment of corruption on the part of town administrators. The history of the towns between 1100 and 1600, then, is one of an internal struggle for privileges and power between elites ('patricians'), middling groups and manual labourers.

Apart from all the details colouring the narrative about conflicts over aldermen's seats in every town, it is striking that time and again

---

[14] Henri Pirenne, *Les Anciennes Démocraties* (Paris: E. Flammarion, 1910), p. 197.

the general pattern is one of changing coalitions. The traditional image that the prince displayed of himself as a 'neutral' peacemaker hardly ever agreed with reality. Often he incited administrative conflicts in the towns by explicitly supporting a local party. At the start of the fifteenth century, for example, the De Scutelaere family acquired privileges from John the Fearless, the Burgundian duke, with the intention of deposing the Honin faction in Bruges. The revolt that resulted, and which ended in violence between the two families and their sympathisers, shows that intervention from above can cause rivalry between local factions to escalate. Another telling example is the factional struggle between 'Hooks' and 'Cods' (*Hoeken en Kabeljauwen*) in late medieval Holland, in which the Burgundian dukes supported the former faction, and in doing so increased violence. The dukes' opponents generally sought support from the craft guilds, although other coalitions were possible, too. When the sheriff (*meier*) Pieter Couthereel tried to seize power at the expense of the most important families in Leuven in 1360, he was initially able to count on the support not only of Duke Wenceslas but also of the weavers' guild. In exchange, the latter demanded a voice in the government – successfully, at that. Similarly, Prince-Bishop Hugo of Chalon supported the craft guilds of Huy in 1297 so as to drive the traditional elite from power.

At least as frequently, however, the craft guilds and the central government faced each other with daggers drawn. When Daneel Sersanders got the artisans on his side to request an important administrative function in Ghent in 1447, Duke Philip the Good convened his supporters to achieve a stalemate in the aldermen's elections. It would become the umpteenth conflict between the duke and his subjects. They experienced first-hand how much the central authorities wanted to eliminate the political voice of the craft guilds, which was considered uncontrollable. The duke had already suppressed revolts in Antwerp (1435), 's-Hertogenbosch (1437), Bruges (1438) and the small town of Limburg (1446). Above all in Bruges he had subjected the aldermen's elections to substantial control. After a long struggle, the people of Ghent, too, were obliged to literally kneel before the duke. In 1453 Philip decided that thenceforth 'notable and virtuous persons' (*personnes notables et souffisans*) were to be elected as aldermen 'without consideration for the weavers and other artisans' (*sans avoir regard aux tisserans et aux autres mestiers*).[15] Revolts at the end of the fifteenth century reversed many of these measures, but during the reign of Charles V the influence of the craft guilds on the election of aldermen once again became extremely limited. At Ghent, Oudenaarde

---

[15] Louis Prosper Gachard, *Collection des documents inédits concernant l'histoire de la Belgique* (Brussels: L. Hauman), 1834, vol. II, p. 159.

and Kortrijk in 1540, the emperor promulgated a *Concessio Carolina*, a charter that took political influence away from the craft guilds. In subsequent years in Antwerp, 's-Hertogenbosch and Utrecht, the craft guilds would be similarly 'removed' from the political scene, as would also be the case in many towns in the Rhineland. Though their independence blossomed again in the 1580s, it still could not prevent the craft guilds from losing the political argument all over the Low Countries in the long run.

The prince did not always draw the longest straw. When towns forged a strategic alliance against central authority, princes were frequently obliged to restrain themselves and sometimes permit far-reaching privileges. Leagues of towns were particularly prominent in Brabant. These towns were in any case smaller in size than their large Flemish counterparts of Ghent, Bruges and Ypres. If they wanted to stand up to the duke and the nobility, they were dependent upon mutual alliances with one another. Each time that ducal authority went through a temporary bout of weakness – generally as a consequence of succession issues – the towns set up an alternative form of government. In 1312, for example, the Council of Kortenberg came into being as an assembly of nobles and representatives of seven towns in Brabant, which (at least in theory) was supposed to hold the policy of their duke up for scrutiny. In Liège and Luxembourg, too, similar councils with representatives from the town, the clergy and the nobility were set up in the fourteenth century. In the prince-bishopric of Liège, after the Peace of Fexhe in 1316, the bishop promised to allow himself to be assisted by representatives of his subjects, who would check whether or not the rights of inhabitants had been violated by him. In order to counteract transgressions against their privileges, towns in Brabant even imposed a kind of constitution in 1356, the so-called 'Joyous Entry' (*Blijde Inkomst*), which every duke was obliged to swear to uphold thereafter, until the French invasion at the end of the eighteenth century. The text stipulated that towns had 'nevermore [to provide to their prince] any service' (*nemmermeer neghenen dienst*), if he or she trampled upon their privileges.[16]

Alliances between towns could at that time rapidly transcend territorial boundaries. In 1339 Ghent – with Jacob van Artevelde (*c.* 1290–1345) as its leader – concluded a treaty with towns in Flanders and Brabant, in which they promised one another mutual support if the prince did not keep to the job description laid down for him in the privileges and 'Joyous Entries'. Taking such a position was remarkable; it was dusted off again

---

[16] Ria Van Bragt, *De Blijde Inkomst van de hertogen van Brabant, Johanna en Wenceslas. Een inleidende studie en tekstuitgave* (Leuven: E. Nauwelaerts, 1956), p. 106.

in the sixteenth century during the Dutch Revolt, when it experienced a second life as the source of inspiration for the 'Act of Abjuration' (*Plakkaat van Verlatinghe*, 1581), whereby Philip II of Spain was given his final warning as the sovereign lord of the Low Countries. In 1477, all the towns and provinces of the Low Countries would receive support from one another to force Mary of Burgundy to accept a new set of privileges on the central, provincial and municipal levels. At the time they explicitly chose to preserve the unity of the Low Countries and to support the 'natural' Burgundian princely house in its struggle against France. This shows that, in exchange for recognition of customary law and their autonomy, the towns desired to preserve some central institutions, albeit cleaned of corruption. When, after her death in 1482, however, Mary's spouse, Maximilian of Austria, wanted to refuse the privileges in his capacity as regent, a new alliance between the towns came into being. In 1488 Ghent, Bruges, Brussels, Leuven, Nivelles, Namur and Luxembourg took up arms against the son of the Habsburg emperor. The support of Antwerp, Lier, Mechelen and Vilvoorde for Maximilian, however, as well as the deployment of German mercenaries, proved to be crucial. In exchange for advantageous economic privileges, the latter towns would ultimately help the prince achieve a military victory.

As mentioned above, Emperor Charles V and King Philip II of Spain would once again have to deal with the tradition of rebellious towns in the sixteenth century. At that time, the insurgency was entangled with unrest over the methods of the religious reformation movement (see Chapter 5) and reached its climax in the establishment of 'city republics' after the proclamation of the Pacification of Ghent in 1576. It was a new collaborative association among subjects to eliminate the repressive politics of the higher authorities. At Ghent, Bruges, Antwerp, Mechelen and Brussels, craft guilds made a grab for power in collaboration with a faction of the urban elite. The idea of the *bien commun* – or, as translated according to the taste of that day, the *res publicae* – was revived when the new town administrators proposed that, in the name of the general interest, they would once again confer legal power on the old privileges abolished by Charles V. In Antwerp from 1577 onwards, for example, the *Brede Raad* – the 'broad (or general) council', which included representation from the craft guilds – would once again govern the town. Before then it had been assembled only in order to provide the prince with taxes. Thenceforth, however, the *Brede Raad* would take binding decisions concerning all essential government matters. But the advance of Habsburg troops in 1584, and the conquest of the town the following year, stuffed Antwerp into an oligarchic straitjacket again. That had happened in other towns in the southern Low Countries, too.

In contrast, the north stood firm. There the united towns succeeded in delivering a military riposte to Philip II, and ultimately in wresting themselves from the Habsburg political order. As a result of a less strong tradition of participation in municipal government, however, the oligarchic tendencies were strong in the Dutch Republic as well, and the wealthy merchant families kept a good hold on the reins of power. 'Republican', therefore, is certainly not synonymous with 'democratic'.

Sword, Flag and Pen: Resistance in the City

The numerous revolts in the Low Countries caused Victor Fris (1877–1925), the municipal archivist of Ghent and a student of Henri Pirenne, to conclude that the townspeople there were 'restive'. In his eyes, artisans constituted an undisciplined pack of dogs that used violence tempestuously and almost instinctively, because it was simply impossible for them to live together peacefully.[17] Current historians think differently about social life because they have learned to listen to the voice of the 'common man and woman'. They have concluded that violence was an integral part of revolts but that, all in all, it remained limited. Frequently it was directed only towards authority figures whom those in revolt considered to be responsible for maladministration, purported or not. Aggression, therefore, was more a means to a specific political end than an expression of the people's nature as restive. Official chroniclers nevertheless depicted those in revolt as such, and they highlighted above all the violent aspects of political resistance. In view of the fact that such narratives were commissioned and read by those who were often the victims of violent acts (the municipal or clerical elite, as well as the authority figures at court), they were obliged in the first instance to justify the repression of revolts and the dominion of the victors who ultimately triumphed in these conflicts. When in 1303 artisans flung the burgomaster of Ypres through a window of the cloth hall and lynched nine aldermen because they were found guilty of transgressing corporate rights, chroniclers reported these 'misdeeds' in detail. An annual mass was even established to condemn the injustice and to preserve the memory of this misdeed for the future – a tradition that was maintained until the end of the *ancien régime*. And yet this kind of audacious laundering of past events is the exception rather than the rule; historians are able to recognise more regularity discipline and a strategic repertoire in resistance than they initially thought were present. Along these lines, an almost anthropological reading of

---

[17] Victor Fris, *Histoire de Gand* (Brussels: Van Oest, 1913), p. 115.

urban resistance teaches us that those in revolt employed not only the sword but more often their flags and the pen to carry out acts of political resistance against transgressions of their rights and for the maintenance of privileges. There were hotheads in every conflict, and sometimes actions took place 'in hot blood' (*in hitte van bloede*), as was said in the medieval town. Yet the leading factions within the craft guilds – generally belonging to the well-off middling groups – employed rituals instead and used violence sporadically in order to reach the ultimate goal of the revolt: to be heard.

An important phase that preceded these revolts was that of deliberations. The submission of petitions or letters of request – a customary type of communication between the municipal authorities and angered townspeople in the Low Countries – redressed many complaints. In 1374, for example, the tanners in Ghent informed the municipal government that 'they had gathered together'. They asked the town to promulgate an ordinance 'to have their wages improved'. The aldermen consented and allowed that they would thenceforth earn three groats per day instead of two.[18] In 1539 the tapestry weavers in Oudenaarde even proposed a new administrative structure for the town via a petition. As a remedy for some financial fooling around on the part of the aldermen, they opted thenceforth to appoint six 'masters of the commune' (*communmeesters*) to manage the monies from taxation.[19]

Via official or semi-official channels inhabitants were thus able to have items placed on the agenda of a major town council. The decisions were taken in principle, 'after thorough deliberation by the council, by joint agreement and will', as they said in Namur in 1293.[20] Much local legislation probably came into being in this way, though scarcely any petitions to and reports from the meetings of government bodies for this period remain. The reports from the town council of Maastricht are preserved, though, and show that, by this point, decisions were taken many times after representatives from the craft guilds had brought items up for discussion. In 1392, for example, their governors put forward a proposal for

---

[18] Cited in Espinas and Pirenne, *Recueil de documents*, vol. II, pp. 539–540: 'zij hebben te gadere gheweest' and 'omme haren loen ghebetert te hebbene'.

[19] Jelle Haemers and Lars De Jaegher, '"In den tijt dat de stede van Audenarde beleit was": de politieke en militaire geschiedenis van Oudenaarde op de kentering van middeleeuwen en nieuwe tijden', *Handelingen van de Geschied- en Oudheidkundige Kring van Oudenaarde*, 46 (2009), p. 113.

[20] Cited in Isabelle Paquay, *Gouverner la ville au bas Moyen Age. Les élites dirigeantes de la ville de Namur au XVe siècle* (Turnhout: Brepols Publishers, 2008), p. 38: 'par meure deliberacion de conseil … d'un commun accord et volonté'.

a vote 'that the common craft guild recommended'.[21] Whatever the case may be, deliberations and petitions were frequently the last stage before a violent urban conflict. If the municipal authorities dismissed a packet of complaints, the only thing left to those in revolt was ritual or, after that, physical violence to push through their demands. Town administrators were frequently warned beforehand.

Rituals and symbols were weighty instruments for the leaders of a rebel movement. They also helped keep artisans in line for the purpose of jointly sending an important signal to the higher authorities. Artisans first convened in their own guild house with a staff, before occupying a central square together, carrying the guild flag (banner) as the bells were ringing. In Tournai in 1307, insurgents marched to the house of the political leaders to seize the town flag, which they subsequently planted in the market square. With the town banner in their hands, the insurgents demonstrated that they spoke in the name of the entire town and desired to be heard. For those who rebelled, noise was also an important weapon for demanding attention. Revolting citizens screamed their slogans in the marketplace, or crashed cymbals in the streets, as in Aardenburg in 1311. In 1349, for example, 'shouting and taking up arms' (*roupe ende wapenninghen*) took place at Dendermonde. In this way, shouting and running about during a revolt could label the movement, as in Ghent in 1332, when the weavers 'went on the run' (*den loop maecten*) through the town.[22] So as to reinforce their demands, these kinds of demonstrations frequently used rituals and symbols that those in power also employed in justifying their policies. The earliest traces of these rallies are found in Sint-Truiden. There, in 1135, the weavers held a demonstration that took the form of a religious procession. To argue for an improvement of their position in society they compared themselves to the first Christians, who were also manual labourers. On a parade float shaped like a ship they had come down from Aachen via Tongeren and Borgloon to Sint-Truiden, but their protest was ultimately nipped in the bud.

At other times, craft guilds employed their right to strike; now and then they left the town if they disagreed with a decision of the municipal government. In Mechelen in 1524 the fullers and weavers undertook a protest march of this sort, which was called an *uutganc* (in the sense of both 'way out' and 'walk-out'). Remarkably, artisans themselves

---

[21] Cited in Marie Antoinette Van der Eerden-Vonk, *Raadsverdragen van Maastricht, 1367–1428* (The Hague: Instituut voor Nederlandse Geschiedenis, 1992), p. 183: 'dat hon van honnen gemeynen ambachte bevolen es'.

[22] Citations from Raf Verbruggen, *Geweld in Vlaanderen. Macht en onderdrukking in de Vlaamse steden tijdens de veertiende eeuw* (Bruges: Van de Wiele, 2005), pp. 105, 110 and 111.

used words like *ghaderinghe* (literally 'gathering') in denominating their resistance, as in Leuven in 1360.[23] These meetings often assembled at a symbolic place. In 's-Hertogenbosch in 1525, the weavers debated in the burial grounds of the Order of Preachers (the Dominicans) whether to complain – ultimately in vain – against the tax-exempt status of mendicant orders. These kinds of assemblies were often strictly staged, as shown in a Ghent ordinance dating from 1451. During the revolt there against Duke Philip the Good, the deans of the craft guilds stipulated that anyone who wanted to say something needed to tell them first. They would then decide whether the matter would be raised as an issue before the entire craft guild. In Sint-Truiden and Herk-de-Stad in 1417, artisans were even forbidden to assemble 'and to carry banners on the marketplace' without the consent of the municipal government.[24] What is remarkable is that this new measure was proclaimed in collaboration with the governors of the craft guilds. It demonstrates all the more clearly that the guilds wanted to control their members' behaviour through the use of rituals and the proclamation of rules and regulations.

In the event that such repression did not succeed, or the path of compromise did not lead to results, then aggression and frustration frequently sought a way out in the adjudication of administrators of the regime, or in a targeted act of audacity. In 1467 the people of Mechelen plundered the house of the sheriff because the duke had allowed the transgression of municipal storage privileges. The protest against the transport of grain on the river Rupel in order to provision ducal troops thus degenerated into violence against the possessions of the representative of the central authority. The seizure, imprisonment or, even worse, execution of political opponents during revolts was quite purposive for the most part. The exemplary punishment of municipal officers who had publicly violated rights served to prevent their colleagues and successors from committing similar misdeeds in the future. For that reason, aldermen, burgomasters and men of esteem frequently functioned as carefully selected scapegoats. In Brussels in 1532, a crowd of poor men and women plundered the houses of grain merchants because – according to those in revolt – they had driven up grain prices. The deans of the craft guilds, backed by the municipal military guilds, made use of the occasion to formulate more of a political voice for their demands, but the revolt ultimately turned out to be a failure. Even the plunder of the supply cellars of various monasteries

---

[23] Jelle Haemers, 'Bloed en inkt: een nieuwe blik op opstand en geweld te Leuven, 1360–1383', *Stadsgeschiedenis*, 7 (2012), p. 23.

[24] Cited in Stanislas Bormans, *Recueil des ordonnances de la principauté de Liège* (Brussels: Gobbaerts, 1878), vol. I, p. 510: 'noch banire te dragen op die merckt'.

during the 's-Hertogenbosch revolt in 1525 can be interpreted as a targeted act of retribution. By consuming the beer and wine there, upon which no municipal taxes had been paid, the rebels demonstrated that they disagreed with the tax-exempt status of the clergy.

Sometimes retribution affected the prince directly. In 1325 the people of Bruges imprisoned Count Louis of Nevers at Kortrijk after his troops had burned down part of the town, and then had him taken to Bruges on a little horse. But the princely aura, fear of reprisals and above all the desire not to definitively blow up the bridge of deliberations kept those who rebelled in the Low Countries from attacking princes themselves. Protest leaders did take concrete measures, though, to subject the policy of a prince or municipal administrators to their control. Such control by insurgents took place in Ghent in the context of the rebel movement of 1477, when the chancellor, Guillaume Hugonet, and the lord of Humbercourt, a senior advisor for Charles the Bold, climbed the scaffold together with a representative of their own governmental elite, Lord Jan Van Melle. With Humbercourt's demise, the architect of the cruel punishment of the city of Liège also disappeared from the political scene. In this regard, a Liège source noted that the world had breathed a sigh of relief. The vacuum that arose at that time at the top of the state apparatus created an exquisite opportunity for many towns to utter a few audible sighs. In Luxembourg, for example, the aldermen once again demanded and received approval to use their town hall (*raethus*) for their sessions – a right that had been taken from them after a revolt in 1452. The craft guilds of Zoutleeuw obtained by coercion the privilege of thenceforth selecting one of the two burgomasters annually. In Tienen, corrupt aldermen were imprisoned. And so on. In short, by means of targeted retribution and specific measures, subjects tried at certain points to direct policy in the towns, to hold urban governors and representatives of the prince to their duties and, in the event, to punish them.

The repression by town administrators of those who rebelled – frequently supported in that subjugation by the prince – was relative. On the one hand, the victors in the conflicts repealed the measures taken by those in revolt. The craft guilds in Tienen – which in the spring of 1477 had been able to expand their power – lost the right to meet together without approval from the town magistracy in the autumn of the same year. In Antwerp in 1486, in consultation with wealthy merchant families, the duke forbade the craft guilds from being included any longer in the aldermen's elections. Yet, on the other hand, repression often degenerated into violence, sometimes even against established families. Willem de Deken, the burgomaster of Bruges, who had shown open resistance to the limitation of municipal autonomy by Count Louis of Nevers, was executed in Paris in 1328 in an exceptionally gruesome manner. Similar punishments for 'crimes of religion' (*godsdienstdelicten*) in the sixteenth century demonstrate that not only adherence to Protestant religious doctrine but also the subversive political nature that was inevitably connected with that creed became a major bone of contention. One of many illustrations of the severity of that offence is the execution in 1568 of the instigators of the Iconoclastic Fury in Ghent (1566). At that time Jan de Jonghe, an ex-alderman of Mesen, died on the scaffold because, as a member of the Calvinist consistory, he had been a pivotal figure in getting troops together; other Calvinists from Mesen were given more lenient punishments. This type of flouting authority and inciting to military resistance deserved – from the point of view of that authority – nothing less than the death penalty (see Chapter 5).

An extreme form of punishment was the destruction of a city. After his authority had been undermined for the umpteenth time in the recently subjugated towns of Dinant and Liège, Charles the Bold had both towns burned to the ground in 1466 and 1468, respectively. Thereafter came the systematic dismantling of the ramparts and forts in smaller towns, such as Tongeren, Verviers, Thuin and Visé. In 1533 Charles V meted out the same punishment to a revolt by the city of Thérouanne. At a lesser level than destroying a town, symbolically intervening in the urban space remained an option, too (see Chapter 6). Thus, for instance, a gate which those in revolt had removed to fight against the prince could be bricked up for a time, or a fortified stronghold could be erected. During the fifteenth century in Italy, these kinds of structures had developed into a weapon in the princely arsenal of repressive measures, as with the castle of the Sforzas in Milan, for example. In the Low Countries for the time being such actions remained merely as plans (e.g. Liège and Ghent under Charles the Bold), which were not put into practice until Charles V and Philip II did so. Larger towns, which, not coincidentally, were symbols of urban resistance, generally had their citadels planted on the site of a religious institution, making such an assault on their urban identity – as at Utrecht (1528), Ghent (1540), Antwerp (1567–71) and Brussels (1579) – even stronger. During the Dutch Revolt these citadels would become targets for those who rebelled, and would be rebuilt into places of support for their revolts. In addition to such spatial interventions for punishing a revolt, there was often an act of penance that followed. By means of a so-called *amende honorable*, representatives of the towns were obliged to beg the duke for forgiveness; the aldermen fell on their knees in their undershirts and the craft guilds were obliged to give up their flags. The *amende prouffitable* accompanying this penalty generally concerned a limitation of privileges and a stiff monetary fine. The Burgundian dukes and Habsburg rulers, in particular, imposed large reparations payments on the towns.

Despite the foregoing focus on the violent nature of revolts, it should not be forgotten that the pen was also a mighty weapon for those in revolt *and* for those in authority. Whereas the latter rewrote history to their advantage in the chronicles, their political challengers sought adherents by distributing texts in the towns. Pamphlets and flyers were hung at symbolic sites, such as belfries, the town hall or on church doors. Not only did those places have many passers-by; the inflammatory language there also immediately affected town administrators. In 1488 a pamphlet at the Church of Saint Nicholas in Brussels warned that all inhabitants were obliged to support the revolt of the nobleman Philip of Cleves against the regent Maximilian of Austria, because aldermen who had previously fled were threatening to reach an accord with the prince. 'There are many traitors here', the pamphlet started out.[25] It was no coincidence that this church housed the warning bell that was rung during times of military threat to mobilise the inhabitants (see Chapter 6). Such broadsides were a foreshadowing of the major pamphlet war in the Low Countries during the sixteenth century. In 1539 in Mechelen, for example, a couple from Hasselt were publicly pilloried because they had insulted authority figures in defamatory writings. Whereas his spouse had sung protest songs at Mechelen and Dendermonde, Lenaert Janssens had had them published, distributed in the marketplace and publicly read aloud these '[in]famous libels' ('fameuse libellen').[26]

These examples from Brussels and Mechelen demonstrate that agitators strategically appropriated public buildings and communications channels for themselves, so as to increase the impact of the criticism they were delivering to the town administrators. They illustrate, too, that the pen or printing press could serve those in revolt in composing texts about aldermen, in inciting fellow supporters to resist, and in spreading subversive ideas. Repression by authorities and self-censorship caused many documents to disappear, yet an important amount of politically inspired poetry and prose is still preserved. It gives historians a unique insight into the conceptual world of those who rebelled and the political discourse of urban middling groups.

---

[25] Cited in Valerie Vrancken, 'Papieren munitie: een pamflet over verraad uit de Brusselse opstand tegen Maximiliaan van Oostenrijk (1488–1489)', *Handelingen van de Koninklijke Zuid-Nederlandse Maatschappij voor Taal-, Letterkunde en Geschiedenis*, 65 (2012), p. 62: i.e. 'Hier zijn vele verraders'.

[26] Robert Foncke, 'Verboden liedjes en paskwillen', *Mechlinia. Maandschrift voor Oudheidkunde-Geschiedenis*, 7 (1928), p. 82.

Political Morality as a Weapon and an Ideology

By means of poetry and prose that indicted vice and denounced undisciplined conduct as heretical, rhetoricians in the fifteenth and sixteenth centuries tried to rein in the passions and immoral excesses of their fellow burghers (see Chapter 5). The study of poems and manuscripts in which rhetoricians condemn the misconduct of administrators demonstrates that their moralistic finger-pointing had not only a religious but also a political purpose: reminding administrators of their duties. Delivering complaints concerning corruption, abuse of power and sexual malfeasance to regime leaders undermined the authority of those groups who were responsible precisely for promulgating and observing rules for urban living, and who governed the town in the name of the general interest. In one and the same move, rhetoricians also accused the 'common man and woman on the street' of all manner of impolite practices, such as slandering others, having fights, staging strikes and conducting revolts. According to the poems, manual labourers and artisans were obliged, just like town administrators, to respect legislation, to carry out their work properly and to preserve public order. In this way, the urban middling groups – the milieu that rhetoricians came from – jolted the consciences of all their fellow townspeople. While authority figures were reproached for infringing the rights that townspeople had acquired, the less-advantaged groups who disturbed the public order were equally repudiated. Accordingly, disciplinary action served a specific purpose: the maintenance of privileges that formed the basis of the social prosperity and the well-being of the middling groups. That was the general interest they were fighting for, armed with the pen and with political morality as their ammunition.

Thus, Jacob van Maerlant (who lived in the second half of the thirteenth century) can be seen not only as the inception of literature in the Low Countries but also as a predecessor on this political terrain. In his oeuvre at the end of the thirteenth century, he indicted the avarice of humanity in general and among administrators in particular. The fact that he lived in Damme – a harbour town where, as we have seen, the 'common folk' were screaming for political rights at that time – probably contributed to this perspective. In his verse he wrote, 'There are two words in the world; those are just "mine" and "thine". Could one but drive those two away, the peace and rest remaining would be fine.'[27] The

---

[27] 'Twee woorde in die werelt sijn, dats allene "mijn" ende "dijn". Mocht men die verdriven, pais ende vrede bleve fijn.' Cited in Eelco Verwijs, *Jacob van Maerlant's strophische gedichten* (Groningen: Wolters, 1879), p. 26.

fact that Maerlant himself belonged to the urban elite evidently did not deter him from taking up a sharp pen to condemn the rapacious culture of moneyed groups at that time and to argue for a town where grain and wine would be available to everyone.

With those who followed in the fourteenth century – such as Jan van Leeuwen in Brussels, Jan de Weert in Ypres and Jan van Boendale in Antwerp (*c.* 1285–*c.* 1351) – this type of argument is more refined. Their literature had adapted, after all, to a modified context. The socio-political changes in towns had turned governing them into a complex balancing act. Privileges recently acquired by craft guilds constituted the final component in maintaining that equilibrium. In the *Brabantse Yeesten* (*The Deeds of Brabant*) – the history of the dukes of Brabant by Jan van Boendale – or in the treatise *Hoe men een stat regieren sal* (*How a city shall be ruled*) – various versions of which circulated in Dutch- and German-speaking territories, one of which Boendale put into a book around 1330 – one thus reads a plea for 'correct government'. By this concept the authors meant respect for the rights of townspeople and compliance with agreed basic political principles, such as the incorruptibility of town administrators. The care taken to maintain unity and union in the town and the unselfish pursuit of the 'common prosperity' (that is, the *ghemeyn oirbaer* mentioned above) also played a prominent role as a political guideline for aldermen.

That these kinds of principles were widespread and made up part of a popular political mindset is demonstrated by an analysis of the rebukes and invectives directed at the town administrators by those who rebelled. In the invective tirades cited above that were delivered to aldermen by townspeople – and above all in the slogans that craft guilds collectively chanted in the marketplace – elements of a more sophisticated political body of thought can be read. A textbook example is the invective 'liver-eater' (*levereter*), which those in revolt at various times and in various places in the Low Countries slung at the heads of those mandatees considered to be corrupt. Aldermen in Ghent in 1432 as well as functionaries at Dordrecht in 1477, and the sheriff Pieter Lanchals in Bruges in 1488, were all rebuked for having damaged the 'liver' of the town. Using typically medieval symbols, townspeople compared their community with a human body, which was governed by important organs like the liver. Having consumed tax monies for their own gain, greedy authorities in charge were eating up the liver of the town in the eyes of their challengers, and in that way they were damaging the entire community.

This logic justified fitting punishment for those who made the town ill, such as imprisonment, banishment or execution (as happened to

Pieter Lanchals). 'Beat them to death' ('Slaet doot') and similar slogans chanted collectively by those who rebelled were, as a consequence, not so much an expression of indiscriminate brutality but, rather, a cry asking for the trial of persons who were considered responsible for sickening political mores and for concrete types of maladministration – *maulvais gouvernement* or *quaede regheringe* ('bad government').[28] In accordance with this kind of indictment, these 'traitors' no longer deserved to remain in the community, let alone to govern the town. In the oath that they were obliged to take upon their installation, had the aldermen not promised to safeguard the rights of the town? Opponents found a reason in these broken promises, whether purported or not, for electing new aldermen, as well as grounds for accusing their predecessors of reneging on their oath and for punishing them appropriately.

And yet the cries for retribution and the tumult from those in revolt could not count on approval from most writers. This situation might seem to be a contradiction, but it actually points to the balanced position of urban middling groups. Although they desired to punish the corrupt conduct of town administrators, they disdained extreme violence, exorbitant commotion and radical slander. More specifically, middling groups and guild administrations feared that violence from hotheads could derail political resistance. As history had proven, repression by authorities could also turn against the middling groups, ending ultimately in the abrogation of privileges. For them, then, it came down to confining violence against municipal authority to the ritual occupation of a square or to a legally grounded demand for the trial of those purported to be guilty of a specific wrong.

Moreover, too much of a disturbance of the public order benefitted trade – the other fundamental pillar of their prosperity – least of all. As an anonymous poem from the beginning of the sixteenth century put it: 'Each person should continue his trade and just keep quiet'; manual labourers had to obey master artisans, after all.[29] Or, as the town rhetorician Anthonis de Roovere encouraged his fellow inhabitants of Bruges to compromise in the last quarter of the fifteenth century, 'No grumbling

---

[28] As cited, among other examples, in Jan Dumolyn and Jelle Haemers, 'A bad chicken was brooding: subversive speech in late medieval Flanders', *Past and Present*, 214 (2012), p. 77.

[29] 'Elc doe sijn neringhe ende swijch al stille', from the poems collected by Jan van Stijevoort in Frederik Lyna and Willem van Eeghem (eds.), *Jan van Stijevoorts Refereinenbundel anno MDXXIV* (Antwerp: De Sikkel, 1930), vol. II, pp. 134–6.

around, if you want to live reasonably, you get more with love than with violence.'[30] For these reasons, slander, gossip and 'jabber' – that is, *clappeye*, as Antwerp's poetess Anna Bijns described it in the sixteenth century – were rejected as well.[31] As was argued previously, it was feared that backbiting of this sort would harm the good name and reputation of the town, its craft guilds and its inhabitants. 'For more than any sword, you should be clear, it is a bad tongue that one ought to fear', as the author Wein van Cotthem wrote in a couplet, continuing the chronicle written by Jan van Boendale. To illustrate the kind of suffering that excess from 'jabberers' (*clappaerts*) could lead to, he would immediately begin that sequel with the narrative of the revolt in Leuven in 1360.[32]

With their moralistic criticism, urban middling groups thus undertook a selfish attempt at directing the conduct of their fellow townspeople. From this point of view an ideological message can be discovered in their literary compositions, which desired to make propaganda for their group interest much more than for the 'common good'. Yet self-criticism, too, made up part of their oeuvre. Using the characteristic metaphors peculiar to poetry and drama at that time, Cornelis Everaert, the sixteenth-century rhetorician from Bruges, wrote a socially critical poem about 'The daily tattling' ('Den daghelicxschen Snaetere'). It condemned the gossiping of a woman selling hazelnuts in the marketplace, though it spared no-one. On the one hand, the poem accused the master artisan of the pursuit of profit, while also reminding manual labourers of their duties. On the other, it lashed out at those waging war who had incited the master artisan into being miserly. In short, the poem thought ill of all strata of the population for having transgressed prevailing norms and proclaimed laws. It is a message also encountered in the poetry of Rombout De Doppere, a fellow inhabitant of Bruges. In 1490 – in the middle of Bruges's revolt against Maximilian of Austria – this civil-law notary rebuked the 'notable master with the power' that the situation had got out of hand, for 'the wound has thus begun to stink'. Making use of imagery inspired by medicine and the Bible, he wanted to incite all the fighting factions to resolve the dispute. Reason and compromise ought to

---

[30] Cited in Jacobus Mak, *De gedichten van Anthonis de Roovere* (Zwolle: Tjeenk Willink, 1955), p. 250: 'Murmureert niet, wilt nae redene leven, doet meer by minnen dan met ghewelt'.

[31] Jan-Frans Willems, 'Twee refereinen van Anna Byns', *Belgisch museum voor de Nederduitsche tael- en letterkunde en de geschiedenis des vaderlands*, 4 (1840), p. 87.

[32] Cited in Jan-Frans Willems, *De Brabantsche Yeesten* (Brussels: Hayez, 1839), vol. II, pp. 155–6: 'Want een quade tonghe, si u verclert, es meer t' ontsiene dan enich swert'.

predominate, and no longer 'corruption' (*correptie*), or trade would come to a halt.[33] In that case, the poet feared that Bruges and the county of Flanders would go under.

With these kinds of moral finger-pointing, rhetoricians attempted to convince pretty much all strata of the population that privileges and trade had brought prosperity to the Low Countries. After the fact, it can be stated that they proved to be successful for more than a few centuries, as inhabitants of numerous towns in the Low Countries enjoyed fundamental privileges such as exemptions from tolls, storage and property rights, and above all an exceptional legal and political position for a long time. In conclusion, even the princes understood all too well that the way in which industrious townspeople conducted themselves had made the Low Countries into promised lands. Or, as an anonymous poet from Brussels put it at the end of the fifteenth century, 'Poor people, poor land; poor land, poor lord.'[34]

Conclusion

The towns of the late medieval and early modern Low Countries were passionate in experimenting with political power. Their ideological discourse found its inspiration in feudal notions of mutual rights and duties, customary law, principles of Roman law and a Christian world view. Supported by those lines of reasoning, a political culture came into being that can be seen as typical of and yet distinct from what was the norm in many other parts of Europe. The workings of its particular institutions, as well as the financial and fiscal organisation needed for it, included the basic conditions for providing urban society with the chance to develop as a social organisation. Above all, persistent concerns remained for urban middling groups in safeguarding their fundamental economic and social interests. That disquietude was responsible for the fact that a great kind of internal vitality continued to characterise urban society. In this permanent process of negotiating, the creation of a characteristic identity was essential, one constructed upon insights into its particular history and upon a kind of living memory of the urban society. From this critical

---

[33] Cited in Alain Ricour, 'Complaintes et chansons inédites en langue flamande', *Bulletin du comité flamand de France*, 1 (1857–9), pp. 183–5: 'meesters notable en wien de macht es' and 'de wonde beghinne alzoo te stinckene'.

[34] 'Erm volc, erm lant; erm lant, erm here.' Cited in Samuel Mareel, 'Theatre and politics in Brussels from Charles the Bold to Philip the Fair: the Leemans' collection', in Hanno Wijsman (ed.), *Books in Transition: Manuscripts and Printed Books at the Time of Philip the Fair* (Turnhout: Brepols Publishers, 2010), p. 226.

consciousness came, in turn, the impetus for a persistent questioning of the conduct and actions of fellow townspeople and authorities. The result was a rebelliousness that could barely be subdued, which led over time to the short-lived realisation of 'city republics' in the south as well as a fully developed republican form of government in the north. In the period that followed chronologically, those governments developed into a permanent source of amazement and, at times, of admiration.

5 Civic Religion: Community, Identity and Religious Transformation

Guido Marnef and Anne-Laure Van Bruaene

Civic Religion?

Although city dwellers lived together in a clearly defined urban space, they remained a heterogeneous group, making it unclear whether or not they can legitimately be considered 'an urban community'. Many inhabitants had not been born in town but migrated there in search of work or in the hope of being able to benefit from the social services. Mobility between towns was also considerable. Citizenship (*poorterschap*) was not available for everyone, nor was it aspired to by everyone. Social oppositions and political tensions – much as the previous chapters have shown – did not always make integration into urban society easy for either the poor or the rich. Nevertheless, historians frequently present the medieval town as a commune, a community in which collective rituals represented or even effected unity. In that narrative, religion is seen as a binding agent. The Reformation, on the contrary, supposedly functioned as a divisive force. For the Low Countries, this split even seems to be literal: the Dutch Revolt (1568–1648) provided for a de facto partitioning of the Burgundian-Habsburg Netherlands into a Catholic South and a Protestant North.

Few will deny that the Reformation was in essence 'an urban event'.[1] Conceiving of this urban Reformation properly from a medieval perspective is not as obvious, however. A nuanced use of the concept 'civic religion', whereby in effect town and religion are firmly linked to each other, can resolve this matter. In the 1990s André Vauchez defined 'civic religion' as a conscious form of appropriating religious institutions, practices and values on the part of civic authorities, with the intention of giving the urban community a sacral status as well as legitimising civic authority. In this form, the concept is applicable, above all, to the Italian city-states that cultivated local patron saints, organised great

---

[1] Having since taken wing, the expression comes from Arthur Geoffrey Dickens, *The German Nation and Martin Luther* (London: Arnold, 1974), p. 182.

Figure 5.1 *Spinola Hours*, Ghent/Bruges, c. 1510–1520. This miniature visualises a Corpus Christi procession in a Flemish town. The Holy Eucharist, believed to be Christ himself, is transported in a monstrance on a horse and under a baldacchino. Various ecclesiastical and lay groups go forth in a clear order of succession. At the bottom left the onlookers can be seen, ordinary townsmen and women expressing their devotion to the Corpus Christi by kneeling. This miniature is part of an extraordinarily precious book of prayers, which was made in Ghent and Bruges for a rich patron, perhaps for the governor Margaret of Austria (1480–1530).

processions and placed many religious institutions under direct civic authority.[2] Pierre Monnet more recently remarked that this formulation is an entirely different response from that found in German historiography, which – looking ahead towards the early Reformation – has put much more emphasis on urban *Kommunalisierung*, or appropriation from below, of religious values and institutions.[3] The differences between the towns in the Low Countries and those in northern Italy and the Holy Roman Empire are well known, but have perhaps not yet been sufficiently highlighted from a religious perspective. Most towns in the southern and northern Low Countries, for example, were not episcopal cities like the Italian city-states. At the same time, in contrast to the Holy Roman Empire, the Reformation in the Low Countries remained a very divisive underground movement until well into the second half of the sixteenth century.

The following pages will pose the question of which forms religion assumed in the specific urban context of the Low Countries and ask in the process – indeed from a comparative perspective – to what extent there can be talk of a 'civic religion'. Doing so, this chapter emphasises processes of transformation between the twelfth and sixteenth centuries, while attending to regional differences as well. It will try to demonstrate that only to a limited extent can 'civic religion' in the Low Countries be traced back to a conscious project on the part of civic authorities, and that there was also talk only in part of a laicisation of religious practices. In our view, the agents of change in an initial phase were the religious orders and semi-religious communities, and in a second phase (from the last quarter of the fourteenth century onwards) were urban corporations like confraternities and guilds, though still with important input from the clergy. In all of this, the question naturally remains of what precisely ought to be understood by religion. This chapter considers ecclesiastical structures and hierarchies, collective values as well as rituals, individual beliefs as well as practices. In doing so, it resists the trend towards separating the materiality and the spirituality of religious experience from each other, whereby materialistic medieval devotion was supposedly gradually exchanged for a more spiritual and individual early modern faith. Rather, we will argue, it is precisely in an urban environment that form and content are always inextricably connected with each other.

---

[2] André Vauchez (ed.), *La Religion civique à l'époque médiévale et moderne* (Rome: Ecole française de Rome, 1995).
[3] Pierre Monnet, 'Pour en finir avec la religion civique?', *Histoire Urbaine*, 27 (2010), pp. 107–20.

Urbanisation and Ecclesiastical Structures

In general it is assumed that economic factors drove the intense urbanisation process from the twelfth century onwards; yet in a number of cases ecclesiastical structures also unequivocally determined the way in which a city developed and functioned. That was certainly true for cities like Liège and Utrecht, which functioned simultaneously as both centres of bishoprics and ecclesiastical principalities. Petrarch (1304–74) characterised Liège as *insignem clero locum* – that is, a place made famous by the clergy. Other episcopal cities like Tournai and Cambrai also derived their importance in part from their ecclesiastical role. Yet the relationship between episcopal authority and urban identity was complex. The bishops generally had little understanding of the communal ambitions of the cities where their seats were established. In 1195 Bishop Etienne of Tournai (d. 1203) called the communal movement one of the great afflictions of his times, townspeople in his eyes being on a par with insatiate women, pigs and canons regular. Yet the earliest traces of consciously cultivating an urban identity can be found precisely in episcopal cities. Long before an urban historiography originated in other places, the clergy were writing glorious foundational narratives in Latin. These accounts served, of course, to reinforce the claims of their (aspiring) episcopal cities. At the end of the eleventh century, by commission of the chapter of Saint Servatius at Maastricht, a Trojan origin myth was elaborated in the *Vita Servatii* for the city of Tongeren, where the episcopal see was initially established. In the fourteenth century, the same myth was recycled by Jean d'Outremeuse (1338–1400) to glorify his own episcopal city of Liège. Three Latin texts have been transmitted from the twelfth century containing a legendary history of the city of Tournai which were intended to affirm the position of the city as an episcopal residence.

More generally speaking, however, the influence of episcopal structures on urbanisation in the Low Countries was weak. That condition can be blamed for the most part on the location of the episcopal cities. Utrecht, Liège, Cambrai, Tournai, Arras and Thérouanne were all established on the margins of or even outside the regional complex that would eventually constitute the Burgundian-Habsburg Netherlands. In this case there is a striking difference from northern Italy, where most of the urban centres were also sees of bishoprics. In the Low Countries the direct influence of the bishops over the towns in the very expansive bishoprics was limited until their major re-organisation during the second half of the sixteenth century by means of the papal bull *Super universas* (1559). Before 1559, the bishopric of Tournai, for example, was divided up into the three arch-deaneries of Tournai, Ghent and Bruges. These were, in turn, split into deaneries, which resulted in a very decentralised approach. The re-organisation of the bishoprics makes the *terminus ante quem* employed in this book very relevant indeed from an ecclesiastical/institutional perspective. In the seventeenth century the new bishops in the cities in the Catholic southern Netherlands, like Mechelen, Antwerp, Ghent, Bruges, Ypres and Namur, would become a major force.

Until the re-organisation of the bishoprics, quite a few ecclesiastical competences that theoretically fell to the bishop were appropriated by other ecclesiastical institutions. An important role was reserved for the chapters: colleges of secular canons who were connected to a specific church and who performed a choral mass every day. In towns with multiple parishes, these chapters frequently had a supervisory role and, for example, had the right to appoint pastors. The chapters also developed into important centres for culture, with an impressive music scene, for instance, given that many of the canons, frequently of noble origin, did not reside there and that their tasks were carried out by deputies. In the county of Flanders from the tenth century until the first half of the twelfth, there was a wave of newly founded chapters. Frequently, initiatives for these foundations came from the count himself. The earliest of these kinds of 'seigniorial' chapters include Saint Donatian's at Bruges, Our Lady and Saint Walpurga's at Veurne, Saint Martin's at Bergues and Saint Amatus' at Douai. In the duchy of Brabant, the first secular chapters came in the eleventh century, in Antwerp, Brussels, Leuven and Mechelen, among other places. In the expansive bishopric of Utrecht, an entire series of chapters had been founded, beginning as early as in the eighth century, but in Holland and Zeeland the development did not get under way until significantly later, in the fourteenth century.

In the town as well as in the countryside, the parish was regarded as the basic unit for pastoral care, liturgy and poor relief. Some historians emphasise this strong parochial identity and even see a counter-argument in it for the existence of a 'civic religion'. Supposedly, townspeople identified in the first place with their parish church. It was not only the place where most sacraments were administered and the liturgy celebrated, but also one of the most important physical markers of identity in the urban landscape. The stone Romanesque and, above all, Gothic churches literally towered above the town, were surrounded by burial grounds and were generally built near marketplaces (see Chapter 6). The relationship between urban and parochial identity, however, has as yet barely been researched for the Low Countries. What is indeed clear is that, as a result of the complex episcopal situation, the parochial structures were

Civic Religion 133

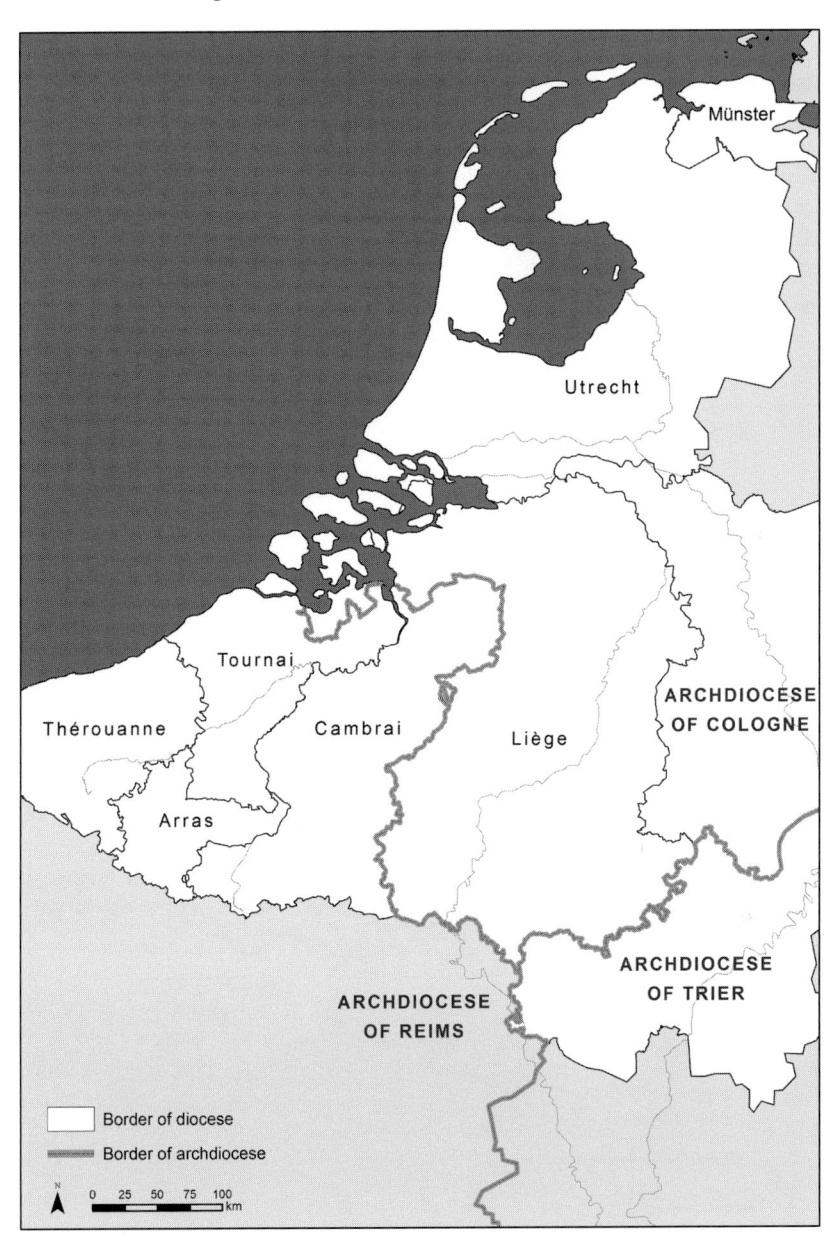

Figure 5.2 Dioceses before 1559.

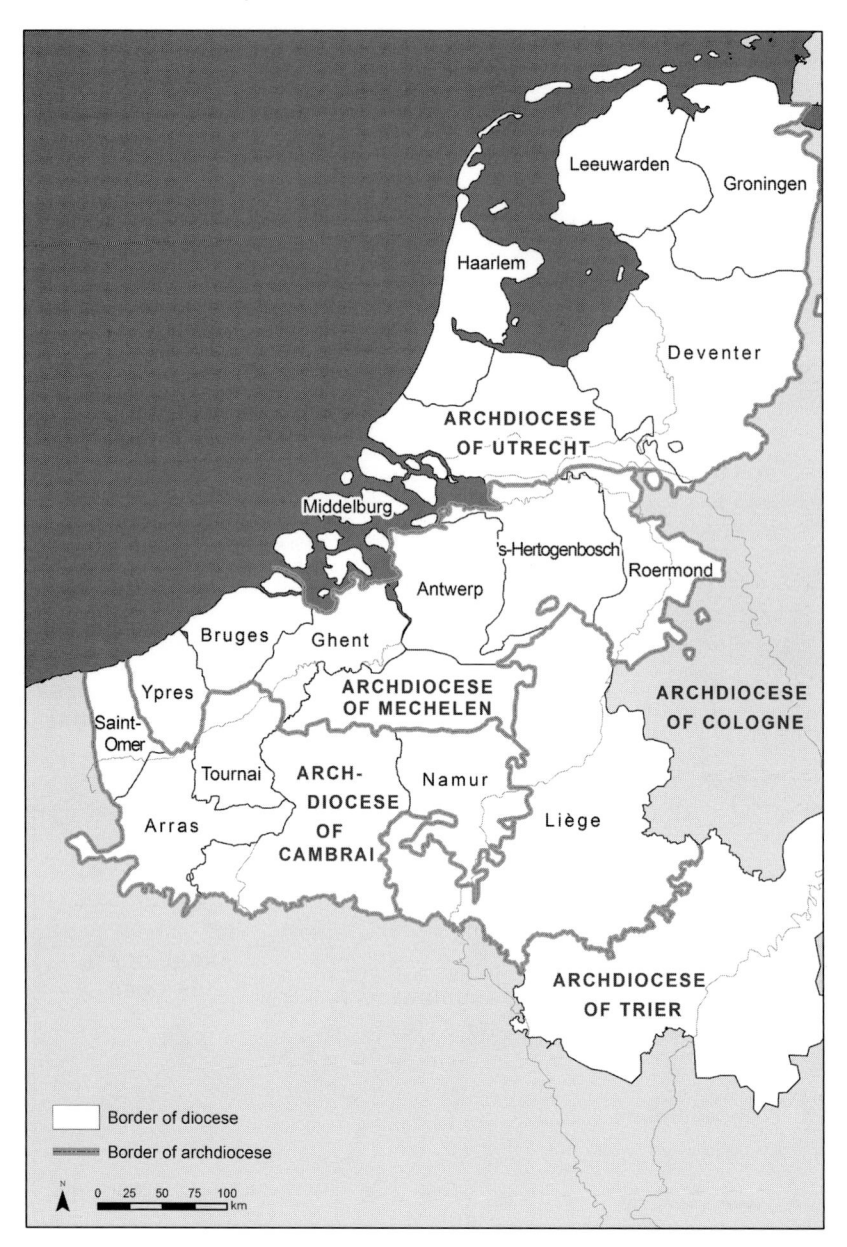

Figure 5.3 Dioceses after 1559.

adapted to the reality of a rapidly growing urban population only bit by bit. At the end of the twelfth century, Liège, as an episcopal city, had twenty-four parishes; yet most of the other towns had to make do with a lot fewer. Certainly in the larger urban centres, in comparison with other European regions, the parishes were especially populous, with a few thousand parishioners on average. Until 1477, Antwerp had only one fully developed parish; even after subsequent partitioning in the sixteenth century, there were still about 20,000 parishioners living in the parish of Saint James. An answer to the challenge of large parishes came in the late Middle Ages through the development of an extensive cadre of secular clergy, sometimes with different pastors per parish and frequently with dozens of chaplains who served the side chapels in the churches.

The 'Monasticisation' of the City

The initially fairly deficient parochial structures for a strongly growing urban society appear to have resulted in a religious vacuum until around 1200. In the twelfth century the towns – primarily the large commercial centres in the southern Low Countries – were faced with all manner of heresy, the adherents to which were labelled 'Cathars' to an increasing extent. From the thirteenth century onwards, however, a turning point came about as a result of the establishment in the towns of monasteries, or religious communities related to them. The first regular orders to see the potential of an urban environment were the mendicant orders. They honoured an intense ideal of poverty and devoted themselves to pastoral care. In their eyes, the public in the major towns were undoubtedly a godsend: they were able to provide the mendicants with the necessary alms and donations and at the same time seemed to benefit from more strongly organised pastoral care and proper religious instruction. In 1225 the Dominicans (or Order of Preachers) and the Franciscans (or Friars Minor) took the lead by founding monasteries in Lille and Ghent, respectively. In subsequent years, foundations were made in various other towns. In addition to the Dominicans and Franciscans, there were other mendicant orders, namely, the Augustinians, the Carmelites, the Saccites (*zakbroeders*) and the Pied Friars (*eksterbroeders*). These last two orders, though, gradually disappeared from the stage after the Second Council of Lyon (1274) had condemned the proliferation of mendicants.

In the second half of the thirteenth century there was a strong concentration of mendicant monasteries in Flanders, Brabant and Hainaut. Towns in Zeeland and Holland – such as Middelburg, Zierikzee and Dordrecht, which accommodated these settlements relatively early on – were clearly connected to the pattern in the southern Low Countries. Farther into the northern Low Countries, the mendicant monasteries were much more thinly spread, with locations in Utrecht, Deventer, Haarlem, Bolsward, Leeuwarden and Groningen. Naturally that difference had to do with the significantly more intense level of urbanisation in the southern regions. Walter Simons' research has shown that there was a positive correlation between the spread of the mendicant orders and the size and wealth of the towns. It was no coincidence that it was the three major towns of Ypres, Ghent and Bruges that attracted most monasteries, having four, five and six foundations respectively. The fact that Bruges scored higher in that regard than Ghent, which was stronger in terms of demographics, indicates that the financial capacity of towns also played a role. The presence of wealthy burghers in Bruges, an active trading centre, apparently exerted greater appeal. The mendicants themselves seem to have come from better-off urban settings, such as the families of landowners, merchants and well-to-do master artisans.

The impact of the mendicant orders on urban identity and urban ideology (see Chapter 4) should not be underestimated. They took on a large part of the pastoral care themselves; until the sixteenth century this resulted in conflicts with the parish clergy over competences, for example, about who had the right to bury (well-to-do) laypeople. The sermons that the mendicants preached in their churches or in public places could count on a large audience. They explained in a language comprehensible to laypeople how, even in town, a Christian way of life was possible. This was done by presenting Christ as a just merchant, for instance. In other ways, too, the mendicant orders showed their intense commitment to the urban community. They opened up their monasteries for meetings of merchants' guilds, craft guilds and confraternities (see Chapter 6). The relationship with the urban authorities was generally close. Thus, the monks said masses every day in the aldermen's chapels, for example, and in times of need the Franciscans in Ghent preserved the municipal archives. Usually they also received donations from the town treasury. In their support of the mendicant orders, the municipal authorities referred more than once to their role as advocates for the town before God. In 1468, when a new Dominican monastery was founded in Zwolle, the monks received the full support of the municipal government. The goal of the mendicants, after all, was that 'God be honoured in our lives, the good town of Zwolle be bettered and the entire community be edified'.[4] The success of the mendicant orders also resulted in the establishment

---

[4] Cited in Folkert Jan Bakker, *Bedelorden en begijnen in de stad Groningen tot 1594* (Assen and Maastricht: Van Gorcum, 1988), p. 78: 'god in onsen leven geeert, die goede stat van Swolle gebetert ende die gantse gemeynte gesticht werde'.

of confraternities affiliated with them, and of the so-called 'second order' monasteries – the female branches of these orders. Not until the fifteenth century did this last movement experience any major spread across the Low Countries. A number of early monasteries were founded, like that of the Poor Clares in Bruges (1255) and that of the Dominican Sisters at Brussels (1262), but these were cloistered monasteries, which barely came into contact with the wider urban society.

From the thirteenth century onwards, the religious commitment of women in town took shape, above all, in the beguine movement. The beguines chose a type of middle path – a *via media* – between the religious and the laity. In so doing, they put emphasis on a simple life in a material sense and a better knowledge of the basic texts of Christianity. The beguines were not a phenomenon exclusive to the Low Countries. It was typical for the Low Countries, though, that the movement became more and more expressly channelled into the formation of beguinages, that is, the courtyard residences of the beguines. The beguines took vows only of chastity and obedience – not of poverty, which enabled them to keep private property. The available data indicate an important influx from the countryside. Within the courtyard walls of the beguinage they lived a relatively secure existence. Quite a number of beguines were engaged in activities in the textile industry, such as spinning, weaving linen, carding wool and later making lace as well. In that way the beguinages provided a cheap female workforce for the important urban textile industry (see Chapter 2). The municipal authorities were frequently not unwilling, then, to support the foundation of a beguinage.

Just as in the case of the mendicant orders, the beguines spread more rapidly and intensely in the southern Low Countries. From the thirteenth century until 1565, Walter Simons counted no fewer than 298 court beguinages and beguine convents for the southern Low Countries, spread across 111 locations. Among the earliest beguinages founded were those in Leuven (1232/4), Cambrai (1233), Ghent (1234), Namur (1235), Vilvoorde (1239), Valenciennes (1239) and Liège (1241). In the initial period, the larger court beguinages predominated, whereas from the late thirteenth century onwards, the small beguine convents spread widely. In the convents, there were a limited number of women under the leadership of a headmistress. For religious services they usually continued to frequent the parish church situated nearby. Court beguinages, in contrast, were larger complexes. Around a garden or courtyard they grouped together various houses, a chapel and service-oriented buildings, such as a bakery, a brewery and an infirmary. Sometimes they grew into a genuine, walled 'city within the city' (see Chapter 6). Their population could vary according to time and place, but even so the majority of the beguinages contained more than a hundred female residents. Three beguinages in the southern Low Countries were exceptionally large: the Great Beguinage at Ghent (between 610 and 730 beguines in the late thirteenth century), Saint Christopher's at Liège (about 1,000 in the middle of the thirteenth century) and the Great Beguinage of Mechelen (no fewer than 1,500–1,900 beguines in the late fifteenth century and first half of the sixteenth).

Though there were already 152 court beguinages and beguine convents in the southern Low Countries around 1300, the movement in the northern Low Countries got under way much more sluggishly. Only one beguinage dates with certainty from before 1250 – not coincidentally that of Middelburg, which was oriented towards Flanders and Brabant. Other older beguinages founded were those of 's-Gravenzande (1255), Haarlem (1255), Dordrecht (1264), Delft, Schiedam and Zierikzee (all 1271) and Groningen (1276). Most beguinages in the north were founded primarily at the end of the fourteenth century and the beginning of the fifteenth.

The beguines were the most striking proponents of a religious *via media* in town. There were variants, too, such as the movement of beghards – the male version of the beguines. It is clear that this male variant never achieved the same scale as the beguine movement. Moreover, the beghard movement had to deal with allegations of heresy and was absorbed by existing and new monastic orders to a considerable extent. Yet the religious landscape was even more multi-coloured, including the Black Sisters (of Saint Augustine) and the Grey Sisters (of Saint Francis), the Alexians and members of the Third Order, among others. What is striking in this case is that a powerful movement to catch up arose in the northern Low Countries. The figures for Holland are telling: in 1380 the county had 22 convents, by 1430 there were 107, and in 1475 there were no fewer than 180; of these last, at least 140 were established in the fifteenth century.

The explosive growth ought to be ascribed in large part to the movement of the *Devotio Moderna*. This 'Modern Devotion' – set in motion from around 1380 in the river IJssel region by Geert Grote (1340–84) from Deventer – put the emphasis on 'inner' devout practice, a rejection of worldly status and a contemplation of the Passion of Christ. This practice resulted ultimately in three distinct religious movements: the Canons Regular of the Congregation of Windesheim, the Brethren and Sisters of the Common Life, and the Tertiaries or religious of the Third Order. In the latter two categories, a process of 'monasticisation' came about during the course of the fifteenth century. What had frequently begun at the end of the fourteenth century and the beginning of the fifteenth as relatively informal groupings gradually became institutionalised. Strikingly enough, such institutionalisation came about elsewhere than in those towns such as Kampen, Zwolle and Deventer that belonged to the core region from where Geert Grote operated. In other municipalities, most of the communities accepted formal rules. In that way they developed into genuine monasteries.

Looking at the spread of the convents of the Third Order of Saint Francis in the bishopric of Utrecht, it becomes evident that the expansion of the number of monasteries in the northern Low Countries cannot be viewed in isolation from patterns of urbanisation. In this regard it almost exclusively revolves around women's convents (those of the so-called Tertiaries), where the sisters frequently shared a social profile comparable to that of the beguines. Of the 166 convents counted by Koen Goudriaan, no less than 58 per cent were located in the county of Holland. The duchy of Guelders and the Oversticht (those territories in the northern Low Countries belonging to the bishopric of Utrecht) trailed a long way behind with 16 per cent and 7 per cent, respectively. The preponderance of Holland certainly ought to be ascribed to the high level of urbanisation in that region. Since the middle of the fourteenth century a rapid process of urbanisation had been under way there. But the relatively intensely urbanised county of Zeeland had only 4 per cent of the Third Order convents established, although that low percentage is certainly explained by the fact that urbanisation in Zeeland had occurred earlier. A respectable number of mendicant monasteries were established there relatively early. In that regard, the region – just like Dordrecht, the earliest developing town in the county of Holland – connected rather to the pattern in the southern Low Countries.

In general, then, the basic rule holds true that the Third Order monasteries and other convents under the banner of the *Devotio Moderna* permeated into the 'younger' towns, where the monastic landscape was relatively weakly developed. The influence of urbanisation on ecclesiastical structures therefore appears indisputable. The lands of numerous churches and monasteries took up a considerable portion of the urban space *intra muros*. The share of male and female religious in the total urban population could rise considerably. In the town of 's-Hertogenbosch in 1526, one in eighteen or nineteen inhabitants was an 'ecclesiastic'. In the episcopal city of Utrecht around 1500, the numbers were even higher, amounting to one in thirteen inhabitants. As a result of their specific attire, the religious were also directly recognisable in the public space. As advocates before God, male and female religious were certainly appreciated by the municipal government and townspeople. Moreover, a respectable number of families had a more personal connection with one of the ecclesiastical institutions because one of their offspring had found shelter there, ancestors lay buried there or foundations had been established for memorial masses.

Yet there was also an anti-clericalism inherent in urban society. That was sustained by two significant concerns. On the one hand, there was frequently dissatisfaction concerning the legal privileges and numerous fiscal exemptions claimed by the religious, such as exemption from beer taxes. The economic activities of beguines and nuns ran into resistance from corporately organised artisans as well. On the other hand, the religious expectations of municipal governments and townspeople increased. Precisely on account of the role of religious as advocates before God, no (perceived) slackening was tolerated regarding compliance with rules, waste of money and unrespectable moral lifestyles. The situation of the mendicant orders in the fourteenth and fifteenth centuries illustrates this pattern well. In providing for stricter discipline in a large number of Franciscan and Dominican monasteries, the movement of the Observant branches had been well received, certainly; yet in the sixteenth century the Dominicans, in particular, provoked quite a lot of controversy. Their furious sermons against the up-and-coming Protestantism could count on a large following from a considerable proportion of the population. At the same time, however, many accused them of abuses and hypocrisy. For that reason it is not a coincidence that the Dominican monastery in Ghent, for example, was repeatedly the target of Calvinist iconoclasts.

Lay Piety in Town

Anti-clericalism was an important trait of lay piety in the late Middle Ages. In most cases, this feature resulted not so much in an antithesis between the clergy and the laity but acted as a stimulus for a strong religious vitality through which many laypeople aspired to a more active religious commitment. A proportion of the clergy responded adroitly to that dynamic by writing religious texts in the vernacular tailored to an urban audience, or by specialising in liturgical activities for guilds and confraternities. To this day, an artificial distinction is made by many historians between the tendencies towards internalising and externalising – or between the more spiritual and the more material experiences of faith – which go hand in hand with this response. That distinction can, on the one hand, be imputed to the power of the 'Protestant paradigm', in which lay spirituality of the late Middle Ages is considered to be a good, since it heralded the Reformation. On the other hand, the materialistic 'comptabilité de l'au-delà' (or 'mathematics of salvation') of that same laity is seen as bad, since the Reformation threw it overboard.

There are no indications that late medieval townspeople saw any fundamental opposition between reading Bibles and devotional books as individuals and celebrating masses for the souls of the deceased as a collective – quite the contrary. It is indeed the case that many more options arose for religious experience. The frequently employed term of 'economy of salvation', however, implies a much too instrumental vision of religion. Within the late medieval experience of religion there was a significant sense of unease concerning the tension between prosperity and piety. Not everything was for sale. Few questioned any form of physical, ritual devotion, yet many well-off townspeople were still apprehensive of being buried with too much pomp or being depicted in attire too richly ornamented on the altarpieces of which they were patrons. In the Van Eycks' famous *Mystic Lamb* (1432), that kind of splendour was reserved for God and his saints, whereas its commissioners Joos Vijd (d. 1439) and Elisabeth Borluut (d. 1443) stand out in distinguished austerity.

Reading texts became very popular as a religious exercise, but here, too, different tendencies can be seen. The majority of religious texts in the vernacular from the late Middle Ages were written by and for a semi-religious setting. The great production of manuscripts by followers of the *Devotio Moderna* is well known. They saw copying texts as a religious exercise in and of itself, an example of the strong connection between a physical and a spiritual experience of religion. There were, however, also numerous texts oriented towards laypeople who remained in the world completely, such as the *Spieghel ofte reghel der kersten ghelove* (*Mirror or rule of the Christian faith*, 1462), which prescribed a number of simple religious rules for living, from frequently attending mass to Christian forbearance to keeping out impure thoughts by repeating the Sweet Name of Jesus. Another genre oriented towards an audience of (well-to-do) laypeople was that of richly illuminated books of prayers and of hours, with rhymed devotions. Johan Oosterman ascertained that this genre was mainly a phenomenon of the southern Low Countries, with Bruges as an important centre of production. It formed, as it were, a counterpart to the manuscript production by followers of the *Devotio Moderna* in the northern Netherlands, which was characterised in contrast by its formal simplicity and functionality.

There were also a large number of Bibles written in the vernacular in circulation. For the period before 1520 there are around 430 manuscripts and at least 200 printed copies in Middle Dutch. A well-known example is the 1360 Bible translation that was written for a male layperson but afterwards copied for and by female religious. Of the total number of manuscripts for which an owner can be identified, approximately one quarter belonged to ordinary laypeople. What is as striking is that manuscripts were given readily as gifts by (semi-)religious to laypeople, or vice versa, which indicates that they all belonged to one and the same urban setting, one in which religious readings played an important role. The great need for devotional texts in the fifteenth century was also an overriding factor in the invention and rapid breakthrough of the printing press. Nearly 70 per cent of the 500 or so Dutch-language incunabula can be considered part of this devotional literature. Printers' centres in Holland, such as Delft, Gouda and Leiden, initially captured an important share of that demand. It was Antwerp, however, that rapidly acquired the major part of the production.

The more externalised, materialistic experience of religion that was characteristic of lay piety has acquired a very bad press as a result of the pioneering study by Jacques Toussaert about *Le Sentiment religieux en Flandre*.[5] Toussaert proved very pessimistic about the religious level of townspeople. The supposedly superficial and calculating nature of late medieval materialistic piety is, however, a construction of historians who were unable to detach themselves from a Protestant or Tridentine vision of what a correct religious experience ought to be. Perhaps even more fundamentally, that view takes as its point of departure the presupposition of a strict division between the material and the spiritual – or between body and spirit. However, a division of this kind is completely alien to the reality of the late medieval town. It is better to think of an 'embodied piety'. Reading devotional books, kneeling before images of saints, burning wax candles and other religious activities are all an externalisation of religious ideas and feelings, just as is a strong belief in the existence of a community of the living and the dead and, from the fifteenth century onwards in particular, an intense identification with the Passion of Christ. This embodied piety also had a strong social dimension because religious activities – certainly in an urban context – were generally inextricably associated with the social groups one belonged to.

Take, for example, the parish church. This was a centre for pastoral care and liturgy, but was also the immediate externalisation of the religious commitment of townspeople. The churchwardens' accounts for a few major town churches, such as the Cathedral (*Dom*) at Utrecht and the Church of Our Lady at Antwerp, show how construction financing was made possible by donations and foundations of individual faithful,

---

[5] Jacques Toussaert, *Le Sentiment religieux en Flandre à la fin du Moyen-âge* (Paris: Librairie Plon, 1963).

confraternities and craft guilds. City magistracies, too, chipped in their two cents' worth. So, for example, Gouda's town fathers permitted part of the revenues from the excise duties on beer and meat to go towards the construction of the Church of Saint John. The governance of the parish church's patrimony was for the most part in the hands of laypeople. These churchwardens mostly belonged to the better-off, politically active families from the parish. In some towns like Kampen the churchwardens were even directly appointed by the city magistracy. The masters of the Holy Ghost or wardens of the poor were similarly laypeople, who in that position were responsible for the poor relief of the parish, including, among other things, distributing bread and other goods, providing basic healthcare and taking care of burials. Only over the course of the sixteenth century would poor relief be placed under broader municipal supervision (see Chapter 3).

The most striking characteristic of the late medieval parish church was the increasing partitioning of the space inside, as found in the Buurkerk in Utrecht, for example. Well-to-do families, as well as urban corporations such as craft guilds, confraternities, shooting guilds and chambers of rhetoric, acquired altars in churches, generally in the side chapels that were frequently added during this period (see Chapter 6). Thus, in Gouda's Church of Saint John around 1539, for instance, there were no fewer than forty-five altars. In addition to the high altar there were sixteen altars founded by craft guilds, thirteen by confraternities and two by shooting guilds; the church also had thirteen benefice altars. At these altars chaplains read masses every day, primarily memorial services for the souls of the departed. The earliest foundations were established by clergy. From the second half of the fourteenth century onwards, however, there was a striking trend of foundations established by individual laypeople as well as (the often recently established) lay corporations. This trend could be interpreted as a splintering of the religious community resulting from a growing emphasis on the status of the family or the corporation. The parish church, though, constituted a sacral microcosm where both the earthly status interests and the heavenly aspirations of members of the urban community (individuals and groups) were interwoven in many sorts of ways. The altars with their altarpieces of often artistically high quality, the polychrome statues of patron saints, and the glass windows decorated with the coats of arms of families or guilds: all these point to distinct social identities. Yet, a flood of prayers filled the entire space of the church, along with accompanying, frequently very sophisticated music, while torches used at funerals and other celebrations lit up the entire building. The imposing, often richly sculpted, sacrament houses in which the Holy Eucharist was kept were a focal point of devotion. The religious material culture cannot, then, be grasped outside this context: in a multimedia microcosm where the living and the dead were connected with each other, relics, statues of saints and religious images invited prayer and physical handling, too, by being decorated with candles, flowers and ex-voto donations.

The growing presence of many corporations in both parish and convent churches – particularly from the late fourteenth century onwards – indicates that much of the religious life of townspeople was mediated by these very groups. Artisans' guilds, whose goals were still primarily economic, as well as purely religious confraternities were both dedicated to a patron saint, maintained an altar – frequently with an associated chaplain – and invested in veneration of the dead. The essentially religious character of late medieval urban corporations was paradigmatically understood by Georges Espinas as being 'sans religion, pas d'association'.[6] As a kind of surrogate family, the corporations put members of the middling groups in particular in a position to appropriate for themselves a share in the religious aura of the town or the parish, a role analogous to that of the noble and patrician families. The religious confraternities constitute the most bona fide example, of course. In Ghent – as studied extensively by Paul Trio – some forty confraternities can be identified in the period from the late twelfth century to the late sixteenth century. In the episcopal city of Utrecht (much smaller than Ghent) there were more than seventy, reaching a peak in the fourteenth and fifteenth centuries. After 1400 the initiative for the establishment and governance of confraternities often lay exclusively in the hands of laypeople. Not until after the Council of Trent (1545–63) would the influence of the clergy strongly increase again.

The charitable initiatives of the religious confraternities in the Low Countries, as opposed to the confraternities in Italy, were mostly limited, with the exception of a number of confraternities that managed hospitals, where travellers, the poor, the needy or the aged were given shelter (see Chapter 6). The core activities for most confraternities were veneration of the patron saint and care of the dead. In this case, too, it is not necessary to make a strict division between a material and a spiritual experience of religion. As the devotion for Our Lady of the Seven Sorrows, for example, shows (see pp. 150–1), part of the religious literature in the vernacular was directly intended for members of confraternities.

---

[6] Georges Espinas, *Les Origines de l'association. I. Les origines du droit d'association dans les villes de l'Artois et de la Flandre Française jusqu'au début du XVIe siècle* (Lille: Raoust, 1941–2), pp. IX–X and 998.

A limited number of confraternities, like *De Droge Boom* ('The Dry Tree') in Bruges, united representatives of the elite including courtiers, nobles and foreign merchants. Others, like the confraternities of the Rosary from the last quarter of the fifteenth century, barely used admission requirements and functioned instead as large communities of prayer. In contrast to the later post-Tridentine confraternities, there seems in general to have been a preponderance of men in late medieval confraternities. All in all, though, a considerable portion of the population – predominantly belonging to the middling groups – had access by way of these corporations to a collective yet at the same time more personalised religious experience.

Collective Religious Repertoires

Thus an urban religious culture developed in the Low Countries initially as a result of the active presence of groups with clerical or semi-religious status, and from the late Middle Ages onwards as a result of initiatives of the laity to an increasing degree, albeit generally in dialogue with the clergy. The involvement and the approval at least of the municipal authorities in founding convents or in establishing confraternities are clear in many cases. Yet that does not necessarily point to a conscious strategy of 'sacralisation' of the urban community or to a religiously inspired communal ideology. In historiography, reference is frequently made to the importance of large civic processions or *ommegangen*, in which ecclesiastical and secular authorities worked together closely. Many of these town processions were instituted in the late thirteenth century. At occasions of this kind, representatives of the secular and regular clergy marched together, as did the city magistracy and later also members of the guilds, crafts and confraternities.

The example of Corpus Christi processions is telling. Dedicated to the Holy Sacrament or body of Christ, they were a direct visualisation of the bodily metaphor that seemed so applicable to urban society: in a body there is a clear hierarchy between the head and the parts, but they still cannot function without one another. Corpus Christi processions were held in large towns like Antwerp, Leuven and Ghent, but their formula seems to have been successful above all in the smaller towns such as Kortrijk, Lo, Diksmuide, Oudenburg and Tielt (all in the county of Flanders). The major regional Corpus Christi processions in Oudenaarde and Nieuwpoort radiated appeal. Processions of Our Lady, in which the Blessed Virgin maternally took the urban community under her protection, were equally popular, having well-known examples in Lille, Tournai, Valenciennes, Ypres, Brussels and Leuven. Another famous example is the Procession of the Holy Blood in Bruges, which expanded over the course of the fourteenth century thanks to increasing municipal investment. In the episcopal city of Utrecht a dozen or so town processions were organised annually.

From the last quarter of the fourteenth century onwards, the major pageants were keenly adopted by the urban community – a phenomenon that has been noted for many other European regions, for that matter. Investments by the municipal government increased substantially, the guilds entered the foreground more markedly and the solemnities and festivities surrounding the actual procession were elaborated. This expansion went hand in hand with the rise of religious drama. In this case it could revolve around scenic representations (e.g. *tableaux vivants*) on wagon stages during the processions, but more extensive plays after the conclusion of the actual pageant were also among the possibilities, or performances on other religious feast days. In the Cathedral of Cambrai in 1376, a resurrection play was performed; in Dendermonde during Easter in 1391/2, priests put on a similar play. In Deventer in 1394 – during Easter as well – the clergy performed a passion play in the presence of the city magistracy. In Bruges in 1396, the municipal treasury financed a presentation including the twelve apostles and the four evangelists in the Procession of the Holy Blood. Via religious drama much more complex messages could be communicated than the static ideology of the body metaphor. The performers drew material from the Old and New Testaments, from the lives of the saints and from miracle stories. The rise of the theatre, as a result of its public and often interactive character, preeminently adapted to an urban context, would also provide entirely new momentum for urban religious culture in the Low Countries.

As these examples clearly show, religious drama was initially still very much the business of the clergy. It would be wrong, then, to assume any strong opposition between clerical and municipal agendas in the late fourteenth and fifteenth centuries. To an increasing degree laymen took on responsibility for the organisation of dramatic performances in the context of processions. In the francophone Low Countries there were *sociétés joyeuses*, transitory or permanent theatre companies adorned with playful names like 'Peu de Sens' and 'Pape des Gingans' (active in the Procession of Our Lady in Lille). In the Corpus Christi Procession in Oudenaarde – studied in detail by Bart Ramakers – neighbourhood districts assigned certain scenes had quite a lot of room for manoeuvre in the fifteenth and sixteenth centuries. The city magistracy did appoint a director, though; in the first half of the sixteenth century that was the priest and rhetorician Matthijs de Castelein (d. 1550). In this way the town hoped to retain some oversight over the eclectic ensemble of presentations. Moreover, it rewarded the neighbourhood districts and companies with gifts of wine for their efforts. Nevertheless, this example from Oudenaarde seems to point more to the community's being strongly embedded in the town processions, than to the municipal governments having any conscious strategy of self-legitimation by way of a sacral ideology. Andrew Brown reached fairly similar conclusions for the Procession of the Holy Blood in Bruges. He also points to the influence of the Burgundian duke on this famous Bruges pageant, which cannot be disregarded, if only for the fact that, according to legend, the precious relic of the Holy Blood was a gift of the count of Flanders, Thierry of Alsace (d. 1168).

The impact of the central authorities on urban religious practices was expressed even more clearly in the so-called general processions, which were supposed to draw together the ties between the townspeople and the ruling dynasty. On special occasions, such as a birth or death in the princely family or a military victory, participation in a general procession was called for by the city magistracy. Certainly in the sixteenth century it was a means frequently tested by the central authorities for warding off many problems of a political, economic and, to an increasing degree, religious nature.

And yet the most striking characteristic of the public religious culture of the Low Countries is the active role of corporately organised middling groups. This part is nicely illustrated in the example of the chambers of rhetoric, which were dedicated to drama and poetry, frequently in a religious context. Many chambers of rhetoric had their roots in drama groups, related to the *sociétés joyeuses*, which performed in the context of *ommegangen* and Carnival celebrations. In a number of cases the example of the francophone corporations called *puys* (derived from the Latin word *podium*) also had an inspirational effect. These *puys* were confraternities that organised poetry contests to honour the Blessed Virgin in the francophone Low Countries (Artois, Hainaut and Walloon Flanders, but also Picardy and Normandy) from the last quarter of the fourteenth century onwards, such as the 'Confrérie de Notre Dame du Puy' in Valenciennes. An early predecessor of these *puys* was the 'carité Nostre Dame des jogleors et des borgois' in Arras, a professional confraternity of minstrels in the first instance, which was established in the second half of the twelfth century. In this case it is possible to make connections to the German *Meistersinger* as well. Yet, the rhetoricians' movement in (the Dutch-speaking part of) the Low Countries is a unique phenomenon on account of the wide spread of chambers of rhetoric, their strong institutionalisation and, above all, their broad social embedding.

The oldest example of a fully developed chamber of rhetoric is *De Heilige Geest* ('The Holy Ghost') in Bruges, a setting of brokers and highly skilled master artisans from the luxury industries. *De Fonteine* ('The Fountain') in Ghent was founded in 1448 by a group of visual artists (see Chapter 8). Before 1450, in addition to these two leading chambers of rhetoric dedicated to both drama and poetry, traces are found of early rhetoricians' guilds oriented towards drama in western Flanders (Ypres, Lo, Nieuwpoort, Oudenburg, Diksmuide) as well as in Leuven. In the last quarter of the fifteenth century, a genuine breakthrough of rhetorician culture came about, including its intense proliferation in Flanders and Brabant, as well as the first chambers of rhetoric in the towns of Zeeland (1480), Holland (1482), Hainaut (1486), Liège (1495) and Overijssel (1497). Utrecht (1501), Gelderland (1506) and Friesland (1572) followed later. The main focus of rhetorician culture always remained in the core regions of Flanders, Brabant, Holland and Zeeland. In these regions in the sixteenth century, one or more chambers of rhetoric were established in just about all the larger and smaller towns – and in Flanders even in a respectable number of villages.

The chambers of rhetoric, organised like confraternities, recruited in the first instance from the urban middling groups, above all among (highly) skilled master artisans, but also among priests and schoolmasters, for example. In this way there was a large group of townspeople participating in urban literary practices. Those practices partly played out inside the chambers – rhetoricians convened convivial gatherings where the emphasis lay on the declamation of refrains – but were nevertheless oriented predominantly towards the public sphere. At all manner of public events rhetoricians presented allegorical morality plays, farces (*esbattementen*) and *tableaux vivants*. The emphasis lay on questions of religion and morality, but frequently local political and social circumstances were defended or derided, too (see Chapter 4). In the second half of the fifteenth century, the municipal authorities forged increasingly close ties with local chambers of rhetoric. They accomplished that by conferring statutes, privileges and subsidies and by installing members of the magistracy as protectors.

One of the roles of the chambers of rhetoric was the spread of local devotions. In this way in 1533, for instance, the rhetoricians of Deinze propagated the relic of the breast milk of the Blessed Virgin with 'a newly composed play about the breast milk of Mary and how that miraculously came here to Deinze'.[7] In a number of cases the chambers of rhetoric themselves were directly responsible for the organisation of local

---

[7] State Archives Brussels, Chambre des Comptes n° 33971, Deinze city accounts, December 1531–November 1533, fol. 51r-v: 'een nyeuwe ghedicht spel van der spunne van Marien ende hoe dat bij miraculen hier quam te Deynse'.

city-wide *ommegangen*, for example, in towns in Brabant like Bergen-op-Zoom, Lier, Diest, Zoutleeuw and Mechelen. In other large towns, responsibility was assigned to a professional 'town rhetorician'. Well-known examples are Anthonis de Roovere (d. 1482) in Bruges and Colijn Cailleu (d. *c.* 1484) and Jan Smeken (d. 1517) in Brussels.

A typical phenomenon for the Low Countries was the emergence of regional procession networks. Thus, for example, Bruges sent messengers out into the county of Flanders and beyond to recruit spectators for the Procession of the Holy Blood. The success of the pageant was measured in part by the number of religious dignitaries participating. From the fourteenth century onwards, Ghent sent a delegation of prominent citizens to the Procession of Our Lady in Tournai in order to put a seal on its good religious and economic relations with that episcopal city. It is apparently no coincidence that the first directors of *De Fonteine* (1448), the leading chamber of rhetoric in Ghent, were the artists responsible for producing a costly baldacchino to protect the Shrine of Our Lady that was carried by the Ghent delegation in the procession at Tournai. Precisely because of the success of chambers of rhetoric, the regional religious networks would be further expanded.

In various towns, chambers of rhetoric were invited to put on plays after the local pageant ended – and frequently in connection with a competition. So, for example, in Flanders' harbour town of Nieuwpoort, from the late fifteenth century until 1560, a competition was held annually in the context of the Corpus Christi procession. In 1527, Bruges's *De Drie Santinnen* ('The Three Female Saints') chamber of rhetoric won second prize in Nieuwpoort with an allegorical morality play composed by the well-known rhetorician Cornelis Everaert (d. 1556), in which the Blessed Virgin was typologically compared to the city of Jerusalem. This kind of custom, which is also attested to in other towns (primarily in the county of Flanders), lays bare another important trait of 'civic religion' in the Low Countries. Rather than emphasising the autonomy of the city-state as in northern Italy – including vertical relationships with the *contado* – it was precisely this ceremonial interaction between large cities, smaller towns and even villages, in which much less emphasis was placed on hierarchy, that was typical. The connection to economic and political interaction within the urban network is significant (see Chapter 2). Competitions between chambers of rhetoric, whether in a devotional context or not (as in the case of the *landjuweel* contests in Brabant, for example) emphasised the importance of that network. In addition, they provided the opportunity to ease inherent tensions – and the increasing hierarchisation – to a symbolic level of brotherly, literary competition.

The devotion of Our Lady of the Seven Sorrows gives a good illustration of the complexity of urban religious practices at the end of the Middle Ages. This particular Marian devotion was strongly patronised by the Burgundian-Habsburg court. It was, however, entirely tailored to the needs of an urban audience. In the 1490s, at the end of the long civil war that had profoundly marked the population of the Low Countries (see Chapter 4), this devotion was spread by means of all available media. As with the confraternities of the Rosary, communities of prayer were established which all laypeople or clergy could become members of. The only proviso was that the member in question meditated a number of times per week on the Passion of Christ and the compassion of his mother, the Virgin Mary. Even the deceased could become members, if a living relative carried out the exercises. As a result of this open model, the Brussels confraternity of the Seven Sorrows was able to recruit no fewer than 6,000 members – half of them women – in the year of its establishment (1499). In order to facilitate the devotional exercises, small books were printed in the vernacular with simple woodcuts as well as texts. At the same time, members were encouraged to attend masses that were set up in religious institutions in various towns. The cult was further propagated by way of sermons and processions. The two most important means of spread of the devotion, however, were theatre and miracles. The rhetoricians pledged themselves to this theatre, with quite a few plays being produced about the Seven Sorrows in Flanders, Brabant and, to a lesser degree, Holland. In the case of Antwerp and Brussels, the chambers of rhetoric were even involved in establishing new confraternities. During the same years, miracle cults developed in Abbenbroek and Haamstede in Zeeland and particularly in Delft in Holland, which grew into a successful pilgrimage site surrounding the miraculous statue (a pietà) of Our Lady.

The case of Our Lady of the Seven Sorrows confirms all qualifying remarks that can be made regarding the overly narrow use of the concept of 'civic religion' for the Low Countries. In the first place, this devotion was thought up by members of the Burgundian-Habsburg court, all of whom were clergy with various religious affiliations. The municipal authorities do not seem to have played any major role in the spread of the devotion. And yet this practice was embraced rapidly and with much success by an urban audience. The involvement of the rhetoricians, among whom a few of the most prominent were in direct contact with the court (such as Jan Smeken, mentioned above), is indisputable.

The case of the Seven Sorrows also points to another phenomenon that has yet to receive sufficient attention in the historiography. Whereas in the southern Low Countries theatre had become the privileged medium for religious communication in an urban context, that proves to have been much less the case in the north. The rhetoricians' movement did break through at the end of the fifteenth century in the counties of Zeeland and Holland, yet, in the process, according to Arjan van Dixhoorn, the accent on public activities became less strong. The delay in urbanisation can no longer be invoked as an explanation in this case: Holland experienced intense urbanisation precisely during the fourteenth and fifteenth centuries. As indicated above, the differences in phases of urbanisation led to divergent patterns in the success of (semi-)monastic movements in the towns. There was a preponderance, on the one hand, of mendicant monasteries and beguinages in the south and, on the other, of convents affiliated with the *Devotio Moderna* in the north. Is there a direct connection between these earlier developments and the different religious cultures in the south and north around 1500? Or can this difference instead be imputed to the stronger corporate structures in the south? In the northern Low Countries, convents, parish churches and the private residences of well-to-do laypeople were the privileged spaces for religious practice in the town. The success of the miracle cults, as in Delft, shows that this need not lead to an anachronistic presupposition of a stronger internalised religion in the north. The Delft case points to a strong belief on the part of many in the magical power of images, as well as to an equally strong perception on the part of a few that there was money to be made from this faith – an entanglement of 'devotion and doing business', as Gerrit Verhoeven put it.

Religious Transformations

Religious culture in the Low Countries was continually in motion, and for that reason it is difficult to discern in the early sixteenth century a genuine break caused by the introduction of the Reformation. There were no major reformers in the Low Countries, with the exception of Erasmus (1466–1536), who did remain within the Catholic Church, even though he formulated clear criticisms of what he took to be abuses by the Church (see Chapter 8). For a long time, historians put 'Erasmianism' forward as an explanation for many of the religious views and practices in the sixteenth-century Low Countries. The problem is that this interpretation revolves around quite a vague concept, and that it can be argued just as well that Erasmus himself was strongly influenced by the religious culture that had developed in the fifteenth century, including the literature of the rhetoricians. Nevertheless, historians have gone in search of moments where breaks occurred in order to make the success of the Reformation in the Low Countries more comprehensible. Shortly after 1520, as a result of the reception of the ideas of Martin Luther (1483–1546), the late medieval 'economy of salvation' supposedly came to an end: the devotional donations made by laypeople decreased, the willingness to participate in processions diminished, entries into monasteries fell, fewer and fewer new chaplaincies and confraternities were established and the number of members in extant confraternities dropped severely. Such circumstances have been ascertained for towns like Antwerp, Ghent, Mechelen, Turnhout, Delft, Utrecht and Zwolle. Provisions for the salvation of souls (i.e. legacy donations to the Church) found in Frisian wills from the period 1400–1580 seem to confirm this trend too. Without questioning the data collected, however, a few qualifying remarks still need to be made. Much of the statistical material suggests just as well that fluctuations continually existed, while some data point, in fact, to a considerable rise in practices of this type in the late fifteenth century, including the success of the devotions of the Rosary and of the Seven Sorrows, among others. Observed over the longer term, the decline was therefore much less dramatic than is frequently supposed.

Once again, the example from rhetorician culture helps us to understand these transformations better. In the establishment of new chambers of rhetoric after 1520 there is no decline at all to be detected. Until 1566, the number of drama and poetry competitions organised annually even showed a strong increase. And yet these chambers of rhetoric were organised like confraternities, and it was precisely for this reason that many members joined them. Until well into the sixteenth century, traces can be found of a material experience of religion, too. At the *landjuweel* contest of 1561 in Antwerp, for example, a prize was handed out to the chamber of rhetoric that undertook the most ceremonial procession to church and arranged for the most ceremonial mass to be sung. Even so, the success of the rhetoricians' movement indicates that around the middle of the fifteenth century religion was already being treated in a different way by townspeople, not necessarily in the sense of more internalised and less materialistic, but in fact in a more creative sense. The intense training of the urban middling groups and the increasing availability of printed books certainly played a major role in this difference (see Chapter 8).

The rhetoricians liked to compare themselves to the Apostles, who through divine inspiration had obtained access to the knowledge of revelation as uneducated men. From their active members they therefore expected an extensive knowledge of religious texts, headed by Bibles in the vernacular. The difference with classic religious confraternities was that rhetoricians treated religious matter in an active, creative way. At drama and poetry contests, first prize did not go to the rhetoricians who demonstrated the greatest adherence to religious tenets, but rather to those who could best lay bare the critical thinking process for arriving at one of those tenets. The consequence was recognition of the pluriformity of religious ideas, even though that did not have to lead to heterodoxy. Thus at a Brussels rhetoricians' contest in 1512, for instance, forty-eight songs of praise in honour of the Immaculate Conception of the Virgin Mary were publicly declaimed before a jury of theologians and passed on afterwards to the Church of Saint George in Antwerp. Each week one of them was displayed there 'for each one whom it shall please to read'[8] – an example that nicely illustrates the role of religious texts in the vernacular in churches both as a means of deepening faith intellectually and also as a devotional object. More generally speaking, debate took priority over dogma in the rhetorician setting. That situation also explains the very divergent religious profiles of the rhetoricians over the course of the sixteenth century – from loyal Catholics to radical Calvinists, with quite a few gradations in between which are difficult to grasp according to confessional lines.

The creative religious habitus of the rhetoricians raises the question whether the religious transformations in the Low Countries ought rather to be seen in a continuum. On the level of content, as well as from the perspective of media, the late fifteenth-century Marian devotions with a strong emphasis on the Passion of Christ may well have been seen by the contemporaneous faithful as new and refreshing, as were the ideas of Luther a few decades later. For that matter, these Marian devotions provoked significant uproar, too, and ran into opposition from sceptics. There is no doubt that Luther's – real or supposed – ideas caused a sensation in the Low Countries in the 1520s. The wardens of Antwerp's Church of Saint James formulated it very clearly, sighing in their accounts that incomes had fallen since 'that rumour and opinion from Luther has been reigning'.[9] The beloved Antwerp poetess Anna Bijns (1493–1575) lashed out fiercely against Luther in her satirical poetry. And yet it was external factors, above all, that made the ideas of Luther so controversial in the Low Countries. The most prominent of these was the obstinate attitude of the central authorities, opting for intense persecution for

---

[8] Cited in Maria Elizabeth Kronenberg, 'Gemengde berichten uit de kringen van theologen en rederijkers te Antwerpen, Brussel en Gent (begin 16e eeuw)', in *Prosper Verheyden gehuldigd ter gelegenheid van zijn zeventigsten verjaardag 23 Oct. 1943* (Antwerp: Nederlandsche Boekhandel, 1943), p. 238: 'om elckerlijck te lesen, dyen 't believen sal'.

[9] Cited in Wim Vroom, *De Onze-Lieve-Vrouwekerk te Antwerpen. De financiering van de bouw tot de Beeldenstorm* (Antwerp and Amsterdam: Nederlandsche Boekhandel, 1983), p. 59: 'dat 't rumoer ende opine van Lutherus geregneert heeft'.

political reasons. The municipal authorities generally took a much more accommodating position: as long as the peace was not disturbed and social harmony not threatened, no-one had any bone to pick with the divergent religious opinions of the urban population.

Luther's ideas were received early on and avidly in Antwerp, which was rapidly developing into a commercial metropolis. As early as April 1518 books by Luther were offered for sale in the city, and in 1520–2 no fewer than twenty-two editions of his work came onto the Antwerp market, twelve in Latin and ten in Dutch. Luther's views and texts trickled in by way of German merchants coming and going in Antwerp. Moreover, Luther found a base of support in the recently established Augustinian monastery there. A number of its monks had studied with him in Wittenberg and evinced Lutheran views after their return to Antwerp. Concerned for the commercial interests of the town, Antwerp's municipal government reacted moderately. In 1522, however, the Augustinian monastery was closed after a powerful crackdown from the central authorities. With that measure taken, early Lutheranism lost its most important base of support in the Low Countries.

Nevertheless, small groups of the evangelically minded continued to come together, frequently under the leadership of a (former) priest. In doing so, it was typical that they did not derive all their views from Martin Luther alone. In this way a pluriform, eclectic Reformation movement arose, which was certainly not looking for any definitive break with the Catholic Church yet. The movement spoke to highly trained people in particular, such as clergy, schoolmasters and artists. When in 1527 the Council of Brabant prosecuted seventy-five people who had attended the sermons of the evangelical preacher Nicolaas van der Elst (d. 1528) in Brussels, more than half of the proceedings turned out to involve tapestry weavers, in addition to a considerable number of gold- and silversmiths, as well as painters (among them, the renowned Bernard van Orley (d. 1541)).

Anabaptism and Calvinism presented urban communities with entirely different challenges, from the early 1530s and from the 1540s to the 1550s respectively. In terms of doctrine and organisation, these movements were streamlined much better than the early evangelical movement. Both Anabaptists and Calvinists cultivated a clear group identity and formed underground congregations with their own preachers. The biblical fundamentalism of the Anabaptists – having arisen in the 1520s in south German and Swiss regions – translated into a rejection of the established social order, by refusing, for example, to take oaths or to carry arms. The Anabaptists believed passionately that the end of times was near and desired to follow literally in the footsteps of Christ. This radical message found most adherents in the lower social groups, often manual labourers in the textile industry. Anabaptism was popular, for example, in the textile town of Kortrijk. On account of their social profile and subversive notions, however, the Anabaptists faced stiff-necked persecution, which further strengthened their identification with the martyrdom of Christ. During the tumultuous 1530s, both the central and local authorities feared uprisings in the towns in the Low Countries – certainly after a large group of Anabaptists, coming primarily from the northern Low Countries, for a short time succeeded in installing a millenarian kingdom in the north German town of Münster during the years 1534–5, under the leadership of the baker Jan Matthijsz (d. 1534) and the tailor Jan van Leiden (d. 1536). After community property and polygamous marriage were introduced, the communal experiment met with bloody repression from a coalition of Catholic and Lutheran princes. An attempt in 1535 by a handful of Anabaptists who hoped to overthrow the town government of Amsterdam unarmed and even in the nude – reckoning on the help of God – proved to be in vain.

The Calvinists had a different social profile, which revolved around skilled to highly skilled artisans and small entrepreneurs. The representatives of the social middling groups probably perceived quite a few points of contact between their own corporate ideology and the biblical moralism of Calvin: a combination of collective and individual discipline, a strong work ethic and recognition of a patriarchally organised household as the social and economic keystone of society. Just as in the case of Lutheranism and Anabaptism, both the urban network in the Low Countries and the economic relations existing with urban centres in other regions played a major role in the spread of Calvinism. In the 1540s, Calvinist nuclei popped up in southern towns like Tournai, Lille and Valenciennes. The first genuine underground churches were established in Antwerp: a French-speaking congregation in 1554 and a Dutch-speaking one in 1555. In these early years there was clearly a 'French connection', with a direct line to Geneva. Yet the ties with the refugee churches of London, Emden and a number of towns in the German Rhineland became at least as important. After all, the refugee churches functioned as hiding places for persecuted co-religionists, training centres for preachers and financial bases of support for needy congregations. Moreover, forbidden books were smuggled into the Low Countries from a number of refugee centres, such as the east Frisian harbour town of Emden. A few pivotal figures from the Walloon Calvinist congregation of Antwerp arranged for the import of Francophone Calvinist literature. In doing so they made an appeal to commercial and familial relations in Frankfurt, Heidelberg, Geneva and Lyon. Examples of this type show how much Antwerp functioned as a hub for Calvinism in the Low Countries.

It is important to emphasise that, in the early decades, Calvinism was a phenomenon almost exclusive to the southern Low Countries. Typically, before the *annus mirabilis* of 1566, there were no Calvinist church consistories on the northern side of the great river delta. In that context, Zeeland, having church consistories in Middelburg and Veere, belonged to the sphere of influence coming from Flanders and Brabant, a pattern that has also been ascertained more than once already for the Middle Ages. Even in the southern Low Countries, though, there were considerable regional differences. Calvinism found its adherents in the towns in particular, but also in those rural regions that were intensely industrialised, such as the tapestry-weaving area around Oudenaarde and the linen industry area on the river Leie (Lys). Merchants and entrepreneurs from these parts regularly journeyed to Antwerp to sell their products, and there was a fairly large degree of mobility for labourers. The most striking example is that of the Westkwartier, the south-western corner of the county of Flanders, where the serge industry around Hondschoote was doing especially well in the sixteenth century (see Chapter 2). The industrial and commercial success of the region generated an improved standard of living among both labourers and peasants. This condition also translated into a substantial cultural infrastructure, with a dense network of rural schools and chambers of rhetoric, which in their turn facilitated the reception of Calvinism. In this region, economy, culture and religion clearly went hand in hand.

The Westkwartier was also the region where the most telling religious crisis in the Low Countries broke out, namely the *Beeldenstorm* ('Iconoclastic Fury', 1566). In the years and months before the *Beeldenstorm*, Calvinist open-air sermons had been delivered in the immediate vicinity of a number of large cities, which indicates that for many (and certainly for the authorities) there was a distinction between what was tolerated inside and outside the town walls. A furious sermon given by the preacher Sebastiaan Matte in Steenvoorde on 10 August 1566, however, was the starting gun for a chain of iconoclastic actions – some planned, some spontaneous – in which the interiors of churches and religious institutions were stripped of their 'papist idolatry'. After a few days, the iconoclasm spread from the Westkwartier to Antwerp, after which all the Low Countries were faced with the phenomenon. The greatest and most violent destruction of religious patrimony took place in Flanders, Hainaut, Brabant and Zeeland (with very heavy iconoclastic attacks in Antwerp, Ghent and Valenciennes), although some towns (such as Brussels and Bruges) were spared as a result of local circumstances.

Matters frequently proceeded in a much more controlled way in the north, because in towns like Leeuwarden, Groningen and Culemborg the authorities took it upon themselves to remove the images. In some cities, including Valenciennes, Tournai, Antwerp, 's-Hertogenbosch and Amsterdam, the Calvinists also tried to take over secular power, but those attempts rapidly fizzled out.

Most historians have reduced the events of 1566 to that one particular Wonder Year or *annus mirabilis*. Yet the impact of the *Beeldenstorm* reached much further. It revolved around an attack on urban religious culture as that had almost literally accumulated in the many churches and monasteries for centuries. As stated above, the religious views and social identity of townspeople – individuals, families and corporations – were inextricably woven together with one another; they were embodied in the many images of saints, relics, altarpieces, cult objects and so forth. The Calvinist iconoclasts forcefully condemned the Catholic community between the living and the dead, as well as every form of belief in the magical power of images. In their eyes salvation was a gift of God to the individual believer. For that reason, the iconoclasm is a telling illustration of the impact of religious ideas. At the same time it preeminently demonstrates how much piety was still an embodied piety in this period: the *Beeldenstorm* was an extremely physical reaction against the physical experience of Catholic devotion. Whether consciously or not, many iconoclasts also grabbed their artisans' tools in order to lay into the ecclesiastical interiors. In this way the religious violence recalled the artisans' raids against competitors from the late Middle Ages (see Chapter 2): religious and social repertoires thus remained strongly connected with one another.

The *Beeldenstorm* also heralded the beginning of the Dutch Revolt. Yet even though religion was an extremely important factor in the Revolt, the eventual outcome could not be predicted on its premises in the 1560s. The main focus of the Calvinist movement was, after all, in the southern Low Countries until the 1580s. During the years 1577–85, that concentration led to the most explicit experiment in the development of a 'civic religion', if we use the concept in its strict sense. In that period Calvinist regimes were installed by the burghers themselves in a number of cities in Flanders and Brabant, such as Brussels, Ghent, Antwerp, Mechelen and Bruges. The frequently used term 'Calvinist Republics' is in a sense misleading because these urban regimes formally continued to recognise the authority of the prince (first that of Philip II (1527–98), and later that of François of Anjou (1555–84)). In all other respects, however, the communal idea was burnished and furnished with strongly sacral implications.

The most genuine example of a 'Calvinist republic' is Ghent. There, in 1578, Calvinism became the only recognised religion. That led to further iconoclasm, a refurbishing of the churches – from white-washed Calvinist places of worship to munitions depots – and a partial expulsion of the clergy. Catholic processions were cancelled and replaced by Calvinist days of prayer. Poor relief and the school system were placed completely under the authority of the Calvinist municipal government and were thoroughly invested in as well, as demonstrated by the furnishing of a theological faculty in the former Dominican monastery. The belief in sacral identity was strong in the town. In the process a biblical kind of moralism became the norm: Sunday as a day of rest was to be strictly observed, while neighbourhood wardens watched over the observation of sexual morals. The range but also the limitations of this 'civic Calvinism', as it was called by Heinz Schilling, are clear from the stipulation that Catholic sacraments were forbidden in the town, even though burghers in Ghent were allowed to enter into marriage outside the municipal district, in order to avoid the sin of fornication.

The parallels with many German towns during the early (Lutheran) Reformation are clear. In other towns Calvinism never acquired the same status of 'civic religion'. Catholicism was indeed forbidden, but in Brussels and Antwerp rights were also granted to Lutherans. In Bruges the Calvinist experiment – which was looked upon, not entirely incorrectly, as a product imported from Ghent – led to more resistance. The Calvinists were more intensely on their guard therefore, too. Though the Procession of the Holy Blood was cancelled, the Holy Blood relic could not be violated, probably owing to the realisation that, for most of its burghers, the town of Bruges still derived its sacral identity from this valuable treasure. It is very difficult to estimate, however, how everything would have proceeded further had the cities mentioned not been retaken one by one by the governor-general Alexander Farnese (1545–92) in the name of King Philip II in 1584–5. A massive emigration of inhabitants to the northern towns, primarily in Holland and Zeeland, was the consequence. Economic motives did play a role in that process, yet it is good not to downplay religious considerations too much. It was no coincidence that many who left the southern Low Countries came to be in charge of the Reformed nuclei in the towns in the north.

In the southern Low Countries, a Catholic revival came about remarkably quickly. As Judith Pollmann has demonstrated, it was precisely the religious experiment of the 'Calvinist Republics' that brought about the radicalisation of Catholics, of whom a proportion – primarily clergy but also leading laity – had gone into exile. In their eyes, the Calvinists had undermined the religious foundations of urban society. When the

Catholic exiles returned after 1585, they contributed to the development of a renewed Catholic urban culture, with the support of religious orders like the Jesuits – who provided the stimulus, for example, for laypeople to become members of Marian sodalities. There was, however, also unexpected continuity with the Calvinist period, such as a strong emphasis on a religiously inspired education. From then on, bishops also had their sees in the most prominent towns of the southern Low Countries (see above, p. 134). In the meantime, old and new religious orders profited from the urban exodus by buying land, as a result of which a new phase of urban 'monasticisation' dawned around 1600. Certainly, this did not lead to a complete religious pacification. As of old, some craft guilds were opposed to the fiscal advantages that the monasteries enjoyed.

Epilogue

In spite of many qualifying remarks, the contours of a specific 'civic religion' in the Low Countries may nevertheless be discerned. The urban self-image was sustained by a religious discourse that was, however, constantly subjected to change. It has been pointed out that there is a connection with the development of the earliest forms of urban historiography and theatre. In a broader sense, too, literary texts can be found – not in abundance, certainly – which can be read as direct expressions of a 'civic religion'. The famous Gruuthuse and Van Hulthem manuscripts, for instance, both compiled around 1400, comprise a number of texts with an explicit urban ideology, such as *De zeven poorten van Brugge* ('The seven gates of Bruges') and *Hoemen ene stat regeren sal* ('How a city shall be ruled'). Another good example is the *Maghet van Ghend* ('Maiden of Ghent') by the Ghent poet Boudewijn van der Luere (*c.* 1382, transmitted in the Van Hulthem manuscript). In this narrative the city is presented allegorically as a maiden in an arbour (the marketplace), surrounded by the patron saints of the most important parishes, neighbourhoods, confraternities and guilds. The maiden's motto – 'Living purely and free/ Comes before gold, before precious stones'[10] – unswervingly evinces the desire for urban autonomy. The Gruuthuse and Van Hulthem manuscripts can be linked to the furious factional conflict in Bruges and Brussels in the years before and after 1400. It is no coincidence that this is also the period in which the need was felt more strongly than before to visualise urban unity in grandly staged civic processions.

---

[10] Cited in Joris Reynaert, 'Boudewijn van der Luere en zijn "Maghet van Ghend"', *Jaarboek de Fonteine*, 31.1 (1980–1), p. 124: 'Suver leven ende vri / Gaet voer gout, voer dierbaer stene'.

From the sixteenth century onwards, urban ideology also acquired a clearly recognisable visual translation. A nice example is the woodcut collection brought onto the market in 1524 by the Ghent printer Pieter de Keysere (d. *c.* 1547): in addition to a view of the townscape with the Maiden of Ghent in front of it, the three woodcuts comprise the coats of arms of the most prominent families among Ghent's *poorters* as well as of the craft guilds, which together represent the municipal authority. The painting by Pieter Claeissens the Elder (d. 1576) of the *Septem Admirationes Civitatis Brugensis* (*c.* 1550–1560) calls to mind the *Zeven poorten van Brugge*. It shows a contrived town with an idealised view of the seven most important religious and economic buildings in Bruges. De Keysere's woodcuts and Claeissens' painting not only refer to older material, but also point to a new humanist orientation towards the classics (see Chapter 8). The first humanist town description from the Low Countries is the *Libellus de Traiecto instaurato* (1485) by Matthaeus Herbenus (d. 1538), with a description of the monuments and structures of Maastricht. Humanist town anthems were strongest in Antwerp, though, where a number of paeans were published in the sixteenth century, from the hand of the town secretary Cornelius Grapheus (d. 1558), among others. Related to these is a series of Antwerp townscapes, such as the series of woodcuts from around 1515–18 in which this city on the river Scheldt is presented as a *Mercatorum Emporium*. There are also examples for other towns such as Amsterdam, but these genres experienced more substantial success from the seventeenth century onwards. Great humanist town histories, for example, were not yet written in the sixteenth century.

Few examples can be given of any urban historiography for the Low Countries region, for which the urban authorities directly served as patrons. There is the chronicle by Peter van Os (d. 1542), a town secretary from 's-Hertogenbosch, who during the years 1513–15 wrote and compiled that town's history from Adam and Eve to his own times. This chronicle, which was continued by other town secretaries, was conceived of as a practical working tool for the municipal government, with references to various cartularies. Somewhat comparable is the *Dagboek van Gent* ('Diary of Ghent'; late fifteenth century, with a continuation from the early sixteenth century), which describes the political events in Ghent and also contains copies of official documents. Held at the aldermen's house, it, like the German *Ratsbücher,* was probably kept up by town clerks. Most of the major historiographical projects, however, served a regional rather than a municipal purpose. Sometimes the municipal authorities were very clearly the engine driving such regional chronicles, as in the case of the Brussels *Voortzetting* ('Continuation',

1432/41) by the town pensionary Petrus a Thymo (d. 1474), a sequel in verse to the *Brabantsche Yeesten* ('The deeds [of the dukes] of Brabant') by Jan van Boendale (d. *c.* 1350). In other cases, such as in the *Flandria Generosa C* tradition, such direction is much less clear. In contrast, quite a lot of smaller chronicles by townspeople are preserved, as diverse as the *Annales Gandenses* by a Franciscan from Ghent (*c.* 1310), the *Récits d'un bourgeois de Valenciennes* (*c.* 1365) and the chronicle of the Groningen brewer Johan van Lemego (*c.* 1425). After the Dutch Revolt broke out, a large number of educated townspeople, from artisans' backgrounds as well, penned texts of this sort, frequently with the intention of making the political and religious upheavals more comprehensible.

From this perspective, what is true for 'civic religion' thus also holds true in a broader sense for urban ideology in the Low Countries. As opposed to other European regions, it is difficult to give too much weight to municipal governments. The often heterogeneously composed urban magistracies in the Low Countries did not succeed in making the same claim to legitimacy as their Italian or German counterparts, or in apportioning for themselves an undisputed sacral aura, either. From above, on the one hand, was the influence of the prince, which could not be disregarded. He had a strong sacral aura visible, for example, in the rhetoric derived from Antiquity and the Bible in the Joyous Entries. From below, on the other hand, there was a kind of creative input from broad strata of the population, who identified strongly with their town yet at the same time were in search of a familial or corporate identity tailored to them.

6 Urban Space: Infrastructure, Technology and Power

Claire Billen and Chloé Deligne

More Than Just Bricks and Mortar: A History of Infrastructure and Facilities

The cloth hall of Ypres, the town hall of Brussels, the Hospice Comtesse of Lille, the belfries of Tournai and Ghent, the *perron* (commemorative column) of Liège, the weigh house of Deventer, the town halls of Middelburg and Gouda: these are all buildings dating from the Middle Ages or the beginning of the early modern era, and even today they are considered to be among the most emblematic monuments of the towns mentioned. Many general surveys and much tourist literature provide information about those who designed or commissioned them, the various phases of their construction and their successive alterations or reconstructions throughout the centuries. Yet these buildings are more than simply testimonials to past architectural talent or to a historic lifestyle. This chapter looks 'beyond the buildings' and writes a social history of space in the city of the Low Countries.

The fundamental innovation regarding how urban space is thought about carries the imprint of postmodern anglophone geographers and historians, who themselves frequently drew their inspiration from French sociologists and philosophers such as Henri Lefebvre (1901–91) and Michel Foucault (1926–84). The so-called 'spatial turn' calls for one to look at the construction of a cloth hall, or of a town hall or of a town wall, no longer exclusively as a functional and architectural answer to specific urban needs, but additionally as a social production that is embedded into a space assembled from multiple layers of meaning. This relatively recent way of looking at space, and at urban space in particular, differentiates itself consciously from an older historiography in which 'urban facilities' are reduced to a list of services and infrastructure, as an expression of an urban society with increasingly better and more advanced facilities. Then, too, urban space is anything but 'neutral' space. It does not exist in and of itself, but is the result of sustained social production, defined by material constraints. It acquires mental shape in words and images as,

Urban Space: Infrastructure, Technology and Power

Figure 6.1 The course of the river Scheldt in Tournai, as depicted in 1622, in relation to an endless conflict between Tournai and a number of other towns that also used the same river for provisioning. The various alterations made to the river over the course of time can be seen: drainage systems, expansion of landing quays, a wooden bridge where mills have been constructed, the demarcation of canals with hedgerows and stone walls, the solidification of islands by means of planting, and so on. Free movement on waterways was obstructed in order to facilitate provisioning as well as collecting taxes. In Tournai, passage through the city was in the hands of the guild of the *piremans*: boatmen specialised in the transfer of cargo on small sloops.

for example, in cartographic representations. From that perspective, the erection of a cloth hall does not merely give expression to the desire on the part of the municipal authorities or the prince to promote or protect trade. It is a way of making propaganda for an existing political model via monumental symbols or, conversely, of moving consciously away from that model and opting for innovation. It is, in short, a chance to give civic ambitions material expression.

This chapter charts the material manifestation of the towns of the Low Countries in the Middle Ages and the early modern era. It seeks out the specificity and the shared characteristics of their spatial and material configurations, meanwhile putting emphasis on infrastructure and urban facilities. We will look at the ensemble of collective structures that support urban life and urban activities, and that at the same time outwardly represent urban space. In this minimalistic definition, the central concept is to be understood collectively with reference to the notion of urban community (see Chapter 4). It takes as its point of departure the basic proposition that urban societies in the Low Countries – precisely thanks to their infrastructure and collective services – have given shape to a particular urban landscape and urban space. The concept of 'infrastructure' means all types of facilities that aid the provisioning of the town, with regard to both transit and transport (roads, bridges, canalisation of waterways, water distribution systems) and organising markets (halls, market squares, weighing facilities, cranes). The concept of infrastructure is expanded to include both public buildings for political deliberations and the dispensing of justice (merchant halls, aldermen's houses (*schepenhuizen* or *Maisons de la Paix*), belfries) and also those which gave shape to mutual assistance, social care services and religious practices (almshouses, churches, chapels), as well as all manner of municipal defences (ramparts, fortifications, citadels).

Therefore, this overview cannot be limited to a merely material description, an inventory of the formal aspects of this infrastructure, or a list of specific regional architectural characteristics. It is indeed nonsensical to look at the formal aspects of an object or building without taking into account the society that produced it. When discussing urban facilities, inevitably the entire urban spatial context has to be considered. Only an exhaustive analysis in which the actual remnants are conceived of as end products of a social process allows for an understanding of the material specificity of the medieval and early modern town in the Low Countries. This specificity is followed across four processes that are inextricably connected with the development of a city: (1) the construction of a site; (2) the construction of a role for the centre; (3) the delineation of internal boundaries; and (4) the construction of a kind of social unity through the practice of *caritas*.

The Construction of an Urban Site

With four notable exceptions – Nijmegen, Maastricht, Tongeren and Tournai – it cannot be said that the sites that later became the towns of the Low Countries had urban characteristics as early as Antiquity or the Gallo-Roman period. The hesitant growth of the first urban settlements – which refers to the joint occurrence of a number of economic functions such as minting money, levying tolls and developing harbours or marketplaces, as well as any type of production oriented towards export – is indeed one of the most characteristic aspects of these provinces. The process took place first along three large rivers: the Maas and its tributaries from the sixth to the eighth centuries, including settlements like Dinant, Namur, Hoei, Maastricht and, in a subsequent phase, Liège; the Scheldt (seventh to ninth centuries), including the early years of Tournai and the development of Ghent and Antwerp; and the very vulnerable Rhine delta, including initially the *emporium* of Dorestad, which disappeared in the ninth century to the benefit of Tiel and particularly Utrecht. The connection between these river basins and urbanisation manifested itself not only in this first phase but also during the so-called feudal period that followed (843–c. 1100). The majority of the urban nuclei began to develop along the secondary river basins. These areas were connected to the three major rivers mentioned or had ready access to the sea (Arras, Saint-Omer, Douai, Brussels, Leuven, Mechelen, Aalst, Lille, Kortrijk, Bruges and Ypres). The growth of smaller urban nuclei can be associated with the re-flourishing of long-distance trade between the Carolingian period and the end of the eleventh century.

The emergence of these towns, however, cannot be ascribed just to the exceptional nature of the sites concerned. Being favourably situated along a river, on a protected, more elevated site, or at a highway junction never provides an adequate explanation for the development of an urban agglomeration with a unique commercial or artisanal role. In Namur, for example, jetties are some of the earliest infrastructural elements that urban archaeology has unveiled. Bridges – certainly across major rivers – are infrastructural elements, of course, that act as major attractions for population centres. Even so, one ought to guard against overestimating their role or seeing them as a guarantee of urban continuity. The first known bridge in the vicinity of Hoei dates from the first or second century. But it is found in the territory of Amay, several kilometres downstream from the urban site that would come to flourish during the Middle Ages. Information concerning the construction of bridges is almost non-existent before the ninth century and remains rare until the eleventh century. Very little is known, therefore, about those who commissioned them, in particular because it is often impossible to make a connection between archaeological finds and written testimonials. What is indeed clear, though, is that these large-scale building sites demanded considerable human and material investment.

From the tenth century onwards, the territorial princes were emphatically involved. Princes were generally able to claim their prerogatives over rivers and 'uncultivated areas'. By intervening on the landscape, the seigneurial princes killed two birds with one stone: they (re)organised their territory and they established their authority. Between the ninth and twelfth centuries, these sorts of operations were carried out by the counts of Flanders, Leuven, Hainaut and Namur, and by the prince-bishops of Liège. Seigneurial authority figures got involved in setting up important infrastructure elements, too, such as the Pont des Arches in Liège, for which Bishop Réginard provided the finance in the first half of the eleventh century. In developing such sites the princes were generally unable to act alone. The aid of local aristocrats, of major ecclesiastical institutions (which they themselves had frequently founded) and of an increasingly important merchant class proved to be indispensable in many cases. That assistance has been illustrated, for example, in the work of Paulo Charruadas on eleventh- and twelfth-century Brussels.

The development of trade routes along the river axes was coupled with the dissipation of the power of the central governments of the French king and the German emperor. Regional princes were able to strengthen their claims to legitimacy by investing in securing those trade routes, by making harbours more accessible and swampy areas more habitable, and by altering the course of waterways. As a result of this dynamic process, a kind of expertise developed in controlling water and manipulating hydrographic networks. Traces have been found of large-scale activity during the earliest periods (reckoning from the Carolingian period forward), with operations in the regions of Flanders and Holland as well as in the river Maas area. An example is the alteration of the arm of the river Maas at Liège at the time of Bishop Otbert (1091–1119).

The major canalisation works were carried out within the framework of ambitious harbour plans. The counts of Flanders from the house of Alsace (Thierry (Diederik) and Philip, 1128–91) and their immediate entourage (Chancellor Robert of Aire (Dover), d. 1174) or family (Matthew, count of Boulogne, d. 1173) orchestrated important works in Calais, Gravelines, Dunkirk, Nieuwpoort, Damme and Biervliet. They combined founding harbour towns along the coast both with draining swamps and salt marshes in the coastal area and with digging canals that connected with the hinterland, all of which sustained the early economic development of the county of Flanders. In the county of Holland, a similar development took place over the course of the thirteenth century. The count promoted the development of a navigable route from the Zuiderzee – literally broken open as a result of successive floods during the second half of the twelfth century – up to the river IJssel. Among other things, he provided a stimulus for digging a network of drainage canals – connected to river tributaries – as well as for constructing sluices. He also saw to the draining of swamps and peat bogs in the centre of the county. With its tollhouse, sluice and harbour, Gouda became the nexus of trade routes running west to east and north to south throughout Holland. This provided for competition with a similar network of waterways that the prince-bishop of Utrecht had laid out throughout his territories.

Generally, these major building sites have been associated with the concerns of transport and communication. Indeed, promoting and taxing the traffic in bulk goods and essential foodstuffs remained a persistent source of trepidation for princes in power. They wanted to gain a hold on trade circuits, for the benefit of their own towns and territories and to the detriment of those areas in the hands of a neighbouring prince. In specific terms, their strategies revolved around closing off a river network or protecting it against advancing armies. The towns themselves acted on their concerns as well. A nice example of this kind of municipal interest is found in the digging of the Lieve Canal, which connected Ghent with Damme from 1269 onwards. In this case, the town of Ghent took charge of the entire enterprise, acquired control over the canal and its banks, and did so for the entire route throughout the county of Flanders. The intention was to make the detour via Bruges superfluous and to bring Ghent directly into contact with overseas trade. Less ambitious but as precocious is the deepening and altering of the river Ieperlee from the middle of the thirteenth century onwards, whereby Ypres was connected to Nieuwpoort and the sea on the one hand, and to the river Leie (Lys) on the other. The stiff mutual competition among the towns could thoroughly thwart some of these undertakings. When in 1379 Bruges, with the support of Count Louis of Male (1330–84), took up the plan to connect its harbour directly with the river Leie by means of a canal, this idea was felt by the weavers and mariners of Ghent to be an immediate threat to the provisioning of their town, and just as much of an assault on their shipping privileges. The result was a violent reaction against opening the site, an incident that ushered in outright civil war in Flanders.

All this illustrates the capacity of urban society for moulding the geographical and ecological context to its own ends. It also shows, though, how political conflicts between towns could play both a stimulating and an inhibiting role. The history of Zeeland and Holland provides many examples. So, for instance, at the end of the fifteenth century (1492), the town of Gouda did not hesitate to undertake military action against the building site that Leiden, Haarlem and Amsterdam had set up in order to develop an alternative route through central Holland by means of a canal and sluices. That project would have circumvented the traditional route controlled by Gouda. In Zeeland, Middelburg fought for centuries to stop the further development of Arnemuiden and to acquire direct access to the sea for itself, whereby Veere and Vlissingen, in particular, were to be kept under. In 1536 Middelburg received permission to dig a canal and two sluices at its own expense, in addition to constructing a dry dock at the Walcheren roads. These considerable investments heralded the development of a seaport, accessible to larger ships, even though it was 5 kilometres inland. In Holland, Delft wanted to affirm its autonomy with respect to Rotterdam and Schiedam. In 1386, in order to secure access to the sea and the Nieuwe Maas, the town negotiated with Count Albert of Bavaria about digging a canal and developing an outer harbour, Delfshaven. This harbour remained under Delft's control until the end of the early modern era.

Nevertheless, this analysis of the hydrographic network cannot be limited to the study of waterways, rivers and canals. In any event, water was a fundamental given with many dimensions to it – as a source of energy, as a basic raw material for much artisanal activity and as an effective element of military defence. It was also necessary for getting rid of waste. In short, water is intimately interwoven with urban life. The importance of water as an agent for hydraulic energy (water mills) has long remained undervalued. Nevertheless, the installation of drive wheels on one and the same watercourse necessitated a series of difficult and delicate operations. Recent historical and above all archaeological research has exposed interventions of this sort by various cities. In this way, Dietrich Löhrmann has demonstrated, for instance, how altering a dead arm of the river Maas in Liège allowed various new mills to be put into operation around the year 1000. Vilvoorde was a much more modest town, but analogous considerations were at play there, too, when over the course of the twelfth century the small river Woluwe was redirected in order to provide water for several town mills. In the same period, the river Demer around Hasselt was also tackled.

What was vital was the infrastructural works that allowed water for domestic and industrial use to be supplied to the city. Water was essential for activities such as brewing, preparing animal skins, fulling and dyeing textiles, washing, and getting rid of waste. Operations were regularly needed to keep the requisite quantities available, both in the areas from which the town obtained its water supplies and also in the town itself, especially underground. This intervention implied installing and maintaining supply pipes, waste drainage, reservoirs, temporary storage sites and 'privies' (so-called *heymelicheden* or *secrets*). For all this infrastructure, municipal authorities were obliged to devise an arsenal of rules and regulations. To that end, both large and small towns developed an impressive set of applied knowledge. In the case of towns like Ypres, Namur, Binche, Nivelles and Brussels these practices are well known. From the thirteenth century onwards in Liège a sophisticated system was developed, the so-called *areines*, in which water released in the coal galleries located nearby was conduited to the town. A few of the best-known aldermen's families invested heavily in the development of this refined piping system.

Moreover, from the sixteenth century onwards, a series of experimental hydraulic machines were designed by engineers and specialised technicians, and financed by princes (as in Brussels) or major entrepreneurs (as in Antwerp). This practical application of scientific knowledge (see Chapter 8) also served for watering the private gardens of the elite. In this application, a basic need became a kind of social monopoly. From the end of the sixteenth century onwards, the pump engine in Brussels – set up with much effort to provide water for the park, the ducal palace and gradually the entire district in the neighbourhood of the court – heightened the prestige of living in the centre of town. In the years 1552–3 in Antwerp, the (in)famous businessman Gilbert van Schoonbeke acquired many adherents among the brewers – whom he wanted to bring together in a new town district – when he succeeded in assuring them of a supply of good-quality water, which was a scarcity in the metropolis at that time. An extensive and complex system of pumps, pipes and reservoirs allowed him to develop a monopoly on the water supply to the breweries, whereby he immediately acquired control over this important branch of industry.

All these technological novelties drove the value of the water sky-high and correspondingly increased the social and economic capital of those who provided it. Over the course of the fourteenth and fifteenth centuries, the inscriptions on the many monumental fountains erected by those in power in the towns were already emphasising the exceptional nature of the running water that flowed into the heart of the conurbations in abundance. In so doing, this iconography referred to religious symbols, moral values and local mythology. The analogy with the rivers in paradise and the sacrifice of Christ thus radiated out directly to the municipal government and the political programme.

The Development of Centres' Roles

The urbanisation process of the central Middle Ages consisted of the gradual growing together of different residential nuclei. In a prior stage they had frequently already had collective services of a much more rural nature: the presence of a commons (*dries*) and of common property, for example, the development of elements for defence (fortified moundworks and ramparts), and provision for religious services (chapels and churches) or for the marketplace. The intention behind having these elements grow together is the construction of a 'role for the centre' or, in other words, the creation of a new comprehensive space, filled with a certain rational structure and clearer to read – and all for a population as diverse as possible. If the history of urban infrastructure is interpreted in this way, then the outcome is a process that does not necessarily read like a major success story, inasmuch as that story was still unfinished in many towns at the end of the Middle Ages. Consider, in this regard, the many seigneurial enclaves that sometimes retained a distinct status in parts of cities until the end of the eighteenth century: the seigneuries of the canons' chapter and of the provost (*het kanunnikse en het proosse*) of Saint Donatian in Bruges, the seigneurie of the chapter of Saint Waudru in Mons, the seigneurie of the prince-bishop of Liège in Namur, the districts in Valenciennes that came under various lords. In this way, urban space was an arena in the conflict between unity, on the one hand, and respecting and affirming the unique character of these enclaves, on the other.

Municipal governments often struggled to incorporate parishes, neighbourhood districts and seigneuries; but, in some cases, faced with intense opposition, they chose to organise a kind of separation or even exclusion. The parish of 'Chapel Church' (Kapellekerk or Église de la Chapelle), characterised by artisanal activity, was founded outside the initial town ramparts of Brussels. It *was* included in the second set of ramparts from the fourteenth century, yet that did not prevent the continued existence of the first set of walls. As a result, the parish was at least visually separated from the centre of trade where the urban elite lived. In this way, the thirteenth-century Steenpoort ('Stone Gate') controlled traffic to and from the Kapellekerk district and the town centre. In the case of 's-Hertogenbosch, there is the Vughterdijk, a district which had a large concentration of artisans producing knives: this neighbourhood was surrounded by a second set of town walls, yet a gate still closed it off from the town centre inside the first set of ramparts.

Parish churches generally expressed the autonomy and individual character of these pre-urban nuclei. The early foundation of a collegiate church and its accompanying canons' chapter inside municipal territory by the prince or another seigneur generally had the effect of a new church assuming the role of primary church and parish. With this new ecclesiastical hierarchy a certain unification of religious space was also achieved (see Chapter 5). Moreover, the foundation of a canons' chapter frequently went hand in hand with the development or re-orientation of the castral district by the seigneur or prince, as can be demonstrated for towns like Bruges, Ghent, Leuven, Brussels and Lille. *Castrum* and canons' chapter, at times separated, though seldom very far removed from each other, furnished municipal territory with a new focal point, which then created the impetus for the emergence of new (artisanal) districts and new connecting routes, supplementing or replacing the existing infrastructure.

Settling in the vicinity of these ecclesiastical and princely focal points were families who had acquired local power as a result of their commercial fortunes or as a result of services to the princes. To that end, the families in the most important towns erected imposing fortified houses. Frequently these residences were imitations of – and sometimes outright challenges to – the symbols of princely or seigneurial power, as was the case with the castle of Geraard De Duivel in Ghent, the fortified stone palaces of patricians in Ghent and Brussels, and the houses with drawbridges in Liège. In contrast to the vast majority of common houses, these residences revolved around structures of (natural) stone and took up a considerable proportion of the built urban land. Frequently they were fortified, so as to be capable of offering resistance in the event of a clan war or escalating social unrest. They reflected the power of the urban patriciate, as owners of the original land, in that place where middling groups and artisans had not yet acquired any political rights (see Chapter 3). Even though they were conceived by private families, in many towns these fortified stone houses took on the role of providing a collective service in and of itself. Over the course of the twelfth to fourteenth centuries, the patrician stone residences were the setting for political consultations or for specific legal proceedings. It was there where the municipal accounts for the town of Mons were 'listened to' (*advisés*), that is to say, presented and approved.

Essential to the organisation of an urban space was the development of a street network. In many cases, control over that development initiated the conflicts between the dominant families who prevailed in specific districts, as in the case of the *vinâves* in Liège. Yet the claims to power made by princes, too, who were more than happy to pose as owners of uncultivated lands, provoked clashes with the urban communities that gradually cast themselves as protectors of public space, as in Brabant, for example. Respecting building lines, organising drainage, keeping the urban space clean and converting structures to stone (the architectural process of 'petrification' or *verstening*) increasingly became the exclusive competence of municipal governments from the fourteenth century onwards. In some towns, such as Leuven and Brussels, a distinct bursary was created within the municipal finance system. This separate office allowed the master-paviours (*cauchiedemeesters*) to maintain the streets, access routes, bridges, dykes and passageways. The primary concern of these municipal officials was, of course, to facilitate the flow of traffic to and from the marketplace, which can also be inferred from their authority in monitoring the municipal weigh house, as well as the hoisting cranes that were used for the loading and unloading of boats and carts. In Leuven these officials were charged, moreover, with the collection of specific import duties that needed to be paid at the town gates.

Yet there was more than just this material trepidation: an ideal city distinguished itself, after all, by the degree to which its street pattern was laid out in a regular manner and the level to which that network was kept clean. In the account of his travels from 1517, Antonio de Beatis writes of the visit of Cardinal Luigi d'Aragona (1475–1519) to Mechelen, describing the beauty, scale and careful layout of the streets and central squares: 'they are paved with small stones and their edges slope slightly downwards, so that no water or mud remains standing'.[1] For many municipal governments, monitoring the quality of the road network was nothing less than a matter of honour. Both in Leuven and in Brussels the special bursary for street-paving (*causiede*) received a striking number of testamentary gifts from private individuals, proving the extent to which well-off burghers were disposed towards supporting the layout of an urban road network.

The creation of a central market square, where commodities were exchanged in a controlled way, played a leading role. In spatial terms, the original marketplaces had frequently come into being as annexes to the site of seigneurial power. There are many examples of how the first marketplaces arose in the shadow of an ecclesiastical institution, a fortified site, a harbour and so forth: the market of Saint Waudru in Mons, the first harbour in Veurne, the fish market in Ghent at the foot of the Gravensteen castle, the market of Liège next to the Cathedral of Saint Lambert and the palace of the prince-bishop, to name just a few. In many towns this original marketplace was relocated over the course of the eleventh and twelfth centuries to a new site that soon grew into the 'grand (market-)place'. This process of relocation did not involve a simple expansion of the existing market square. Additionally, the place where the new market was proposed to be put was not arbitrary or connected with the availability of undeveloped space. Through a planned relocation, political powers – whether municipal or princely – created new sites having nothing to do with old power relations. In certain towns, such as Ypres and Ghent (its Vrijdagmarkt square), they went so far as to tear down existing developed premises so as to make a new marketplace possible. In other towns, such as Lille, Brussels and 's-Hertogenbosch, marshy, less inviting areas were drained, levelled and ultimately made suitable

---

[1] Madeleine Havard de la Montagne (ed.), *Le Voyage du cardinal d'Aragon en Allemagne, Hollande, Belgique, France et Italie (1517–1518) par Antonio de Beatis*, translated from the Italian in accordance with a manuscript from the sixteenth century, with introduction and annotation (Paris: Perrin et Cie, 1913), pp. 86–7.

for building, at the cost of major investments. In other towns, too, such as Mons, Namur and Diest, existing space was altered to accommodate the marketplace. In all these cases, then, more than merely functional answers were sought for a problematic lack of sites; delineation and differentiation of a totally new zone were the goal. In the fourteenth century, in towns like Deventer and Zutphen, expanded market and trade zones were elaborated on the edge of the old fortified centre, though separated from older centres of power. Every town developed its own emphasis in this process: sometimes different competitive marketplaces were retained, as in Ghent, but most of the towns privileged a large central marketplace (as in Gouda and 's-Hertogenbosch). But everywhere a similar sort of rationale can be found: distinct space was created, and embedded with new meaning.

To begin with, the organisation of markets involved wide-open spaces, in the middle of a street network, without much regularity, and traders' stalls were grouped according to the merchandise offered. The appearance of large merchant halls of the sort that still exist today was a long-term process. Such initiatives were a symbol of the town's identity, including emblematic monumental structures that reflected the honour and pride of the town and its prince. The municipal merchant halls occupied pride of place, but the weigh house, where traded goods were officially measured, was nearly as important (particularly in the county of Holland and in the prince-bishopric of Utrecht, as well as in Overijssel). At the start of the sixteenth century, the construction of a monumental weigh house on the Brink square in Deventer (1528) was an opportunity to refine the town with a remarkable building. The uppermost storeys served as presentation space: it was there that the visiting prince was paid tribute to and that the burghers swore their loyalty to King Philip II of Spain in 1555.

Like the marketplaces, the first merchant halls were generally an initiative that can be attributed to the prince or the town lord. These frequently involved wooden buildings, rather simple and purely functional. Essential commodities were offered for sale there: initially grain, then meat and fish, and finally textiles or other special products from local guilds, such as leather goods, footwear, furs and so forth. The halls were undoubtedly convenient for the traders and their clientele, yet they also allowed for the requisite monitoring and increased the effectiveness of taxation. The way in which the space in the halls was allotted internally shows how the guilds were organised among one another. This organisation reveals the process by which the occupation of a well-defined site was passed by inheritance within a family or a clan. From around 1300 onwards in Brabant, guild privileges mention how the prince refrained from personally favouring a close confidant with a specific site in the merchant hall. Butchers and cloth traders were the first to demand this right for themselves in Antwerp, Brussels and Mechelen, for example. In Ghent, the use of a meat market hall was a structural element in the organisation of the influential butchers' guild.

The significance of the founding of the first merchant halls can also be seen in the terminology used, such as *domus* and *hala*. The same nomenclature was used to indicate princely government buildings. In towns where any major power conflict raged, every lord had his own hall. In Mons, for instance, the canons' chapter of Saint Waudru and the count of Hainaut competed with each other. In Liège the Surlet clan succeeded in erecting its own cloth hall. The breakaway from conducting business in this way is found in the county of Flanders from the thirteenth century onwards, and in Brabant and Holland over the course of the fourteenth and fifteenth centuries. The process reflected the power of the municipal government and of certain groups from the textile industry, as in Ypres, Ghent, Brussels and Leuven. In smaller towns, groups that specialised in the meat industry were also included, as in Geldenaken, Zoutleeuw, Namur, Nivelles, Tongeren, Middelburg and Gouda.

The symbolic importance of the halls is also shown by their additional roles: as places where aldermen met, as sites where belfries were erected, as meeting places for guilds, as locations for celebrations or simply as storage places. Used efficiently in this way, such buildings were anchored in the urban 'mental geography', granting them a crucial role in the identity process. Beginning as soon as municipal authorities assumed the burden of financing and building the halls, specific architectural efforts were made to enhance their utilitarian function with an additional political and communicative layer. This was often non-existent when halls were erected by princes or lords. In this respect, the halls of Ypres are emblematic, all the more so because they date from a very early period (1260–1304). The halls in Bruges soon followed this example; the 'water hall' of that town (1283–97) was legendary for the fact that its lowest storey was accessible to barges and small boats.

The cloth halls of Leuven and Brussels were well known for their size – even though they fall far short of the exceptional length of the halls of Ypres (133 metres) and Bruges (95 metres) – but even more for their refined system of internal lighting. In both cases, the innovative elaboration of roofing occurred in such a way that it guaranteed optimal lighting. The way that light entered was essential for thoroughly checking the quality of the fabrics offered and particularly of the luxury textiles, for which both towns had stood in high regard internationally since the thirteenth century. For this reason, the city of Cologne sent a master carpenter to both towns in 1375 'ad videndum hallas ibidem' ('to see the halls there').[2] In Brussels, just as in Douai, the cloth hall was also the place where artisans put the finishing touches to the cloth at the customer's request. Halls of this sort needed to reflect the exceptional quality and reputation of the products offered there (see Chapter 8).

It must also be noted that the communal halls comprised new architectural elements that would become typical for many business sites in northern Europe. The integration of spatial scale, of functionality and of monumentality, the use of wooden pillars or of stone (or brick) columns, the technical virtuosity used to construct the roofs, the importance attached to how light entered, the large unified interior space: all these elements made up part of a totally new and fruitful building design. This conceptualisation can also be found in the churches of the mendicant orders and in the major municipal almshouses of the thirteenth and fourteenth centuries. Having light enter effortlessly into a public or commercial building reflects the ambition to make clear that what plays out inside the building is open and above board. It refers to the concern to fight fraud and to banish backroom politics as inimical to the general interest (see Chapter 4).

It is no coincidence that taking control of the merchant halls went hand in hand with initiatives by urban power elites to (re-)organise the marketplaces. At these central locations, a notable concentration of functional and symbolic buildings gradually arose, reflecting the ideals of municipal administrators in the late Middle Ages: town hall, belfry, town bell, fountains, *perron* (monumental column), a house of prayer for a leading urban confraternity, and so on. The most prominent inns can be found here, too, as well as the houses of the major traders and later also the halls of the most important guilds. Being pre-eminently presentation squares, they were equalised, subjected to rules, paved and kept clean as a priority by municipal services. Fountains or monumental cisterns made beneficial water available there. The commercial role was the prime one for these locations, but judicial activity also took place in this setting (see Chapter 4). Legislation was proclaimed from the steps of the town hall or of the *perron*, and political meetings were convoked there. As a tell-tale indicator of the fact that the central location in town reflected important political aims, princely power was materially represented there as well, as a counterweight to municipal power. In Brussels' case, this situation explains why the ducal Broodhuis (also known today as the

---

[2] Raymond Van Uytven, *Stadsfinanciën en stadsekonomie te Leuven van de XIIe tot het einde der XVIe eeuw* (Brussels: Koninklijke Vlaamse Akademie voor Wetenschappen, Letteren en Schone Kunsten van België, 1961), p. 387.

'King's House') – rebuilt as an administrative building and courtroom for cases reserved for the prince – was built on the Grand Place (Grote Markt). It also explains why, in 1423 in Lille, Duke Philip the Good had the Beauregard erected on the Grand Place there, in the vicinity of the *schepenhuis* ('aldermen's house') and the belfry.

In addition to this central infrastructure – in which the use of symbols, political signification, religious references, legal announcements and urban memory converged in a limited space – further components of urban facilities came to fulfil similar functions. In cities along an impressive river – the river Maas valley provides various examples – bridges did a similar job. It comes as no surprise, then, that they are depicted on some of the earliest municipal seals, being a reflection of technical ingenuity, municipal power and the unique commercial role of the town. In Dinant, the *pons publicus*, mentioned as early as 824, was provided with a tower where the aldermen met and the accounts and archives of the town were kept. Until 1374 it was prominently depicted on the town seal. In Namur, the bridge served as a belfry, too, as is shown in a comital tax book from 1289. Bridges were sites of exchange, of course, but also of legal demarcation, as in the customary law of Jambes (recorded at the end of the thirteenth century), where, 'sur le pont de Moeze dela le berfroit', those condemned to death were handed over to the higher jurisdiction of the town of Namur.[3]

The completion of the grand marketplace is a high point in the process of modelling urban space. Bringing such a major, central location into being went hand in hand with great investments in decorating the buildings involved. In this domain, an entire stylistic idiom came about in which both the ideals of burghers and the profane and religious values of the urban community were expressed. Aldermen's meetings, which took place outdoors or inside modest structures well into the twelfth and even thirteenth century, were with increasing frequency accommodated in specialised and generally prestigious buildings. The halls of Ypres and Bruges, which housed the municipal administration for a time, have already been mentioned above. In Namur the local aldermen's hall was the so-called Cabaret, the process of expansion of which, with its increasing complexity and ornamental renovation, can be followed throughout the thirteenth and fourteenth centuries. In Mons, the town hall gradually came into being during the fourteenth and fifteenth centuries, its basis being a major private residence that had been acquired

---

[3] Dieudonné Brouwers, *L'Administration et les finances du comté de Namur du XIIIe au XVe siècle. Sources, IV, Chartes et règlements, II, 1299–1337* (Namur: Wesmael-Charlier, 1914), p. 282.

by the town. It was patiently developed into a remarkable administrative centre (1458–77), a sign of municipal power and of its self-declared effective and beneficial relationship with comital power.

The developments in the construction and ornamentation of town halls went hand in hand, of course, with political and institutional innovations in municipal government (see Chapter 4). The entry of guilds into municipal power structures – over the course of the fourteenth century in the county of Flanders and in towns of the prince-bishopric of Liège; somewhat later in Brabant, Tournai and Holland – clashed with the structure of the old governmental buildings. The broader base for recruitment was reflected in the alteration of space in which new people in control met and discharged their duties. This development is very pronounced in Ghent from the beginning of the fourteenth century onwards and once again at the end of the fifteenth century, but also in Brussels over the course of the fourteenth century, when a second wing was built onto the town hall. The high tower added to the building (an architectural *tour de force* designed by the leading architect Jan van Ruysbroek) was imitated in many towns, such as Middelburg. It is interesting that construction of the tower is also mentioned in chronicles written in places located relatively far away (such as the Abbey of Floreffe). These construction projects coincide with the entry of guilds in Brussels into municipal government after the revolt of 1421. In this way, the new people in power made it obvious that they were able to uphold the elevated honour of the town better than any preceding government.

Naturally, by showing off their strength they wanted to legitimate their power as well. Sometimes grandstanding of this sort went against any economic rationale, as in Damme, where a monumental town hall was erected in the second half of the fifteenth century – at a moment when depopulation was evident. This building, which performed the functions of both aldermen's house and merchant hall, required an investment that went far beyond the capacities of the declining municipal revenues. In Ghent, both highpoints in expenditures for public works in the fifteenth century (for monumental new construction, to be more specific) coincided with periods of high political tension and of economic and social problems. In the generally much more peaceful town of Namur, where internal political conflicts scarcely occurred, the expenditure on public buildings remained comparatively modest. Namur succeeded in keeping costs under control, which directly benefitted the municipal debt. The northern town of Deventer experienced a period of economic prosperity in the fifteenth century. At that time, the municipal government invested in the construction of an impressive tower for the Collegiate Church of Saint Lebuinus. This tower served as a belfry and also housed a bell, called 'Jesus', on which its commissioners were mentioned by name, all of them members of the urban elite. During the same years, the town also took over the governance of the collegiate school. This appropriation by powerful burghers of monuments that in principle were part of the ecclesiastical and princely patrimony – the canons' chapter at Saint Lebuinus depended, after all, on the prince-bishop – was characteristic of towns along the river IJssel (see Chapter 5).

The trend of having effect take priority over effectiveness was common. Although the chronology may differ, there was no fundamental difference, unless seigneurial or princely influence was at work longer in smaller towns. The large towns set the tone, and interurban competition played a major role in improving these initiatives, a process which seems to have been influential in the entire urban network in a manner that was independent of the political boundaries. Mechelen derived its models from Bruges; Mons and Geraardsbergen imitated Brussels; Namur and Hoei did the same with regard to Liège; Leuven and Brussels were constantly attempting to outdo each other's accomplishments, as were Ghent and Tournai. In the sixteenth century, Antwerp's town hall inspired those of Vlissingen, The Hague and Emden. In the seventeenth century, Amsterdam would model its stock exchange on that of Antwerp. Plans, models and descriptions, but artisans and technicians, too, circulated among the towns, and in this way provided for a type of homogeneous monumental culture (see Chapter 8).

Additionally, there was interaction between Church and court, on the one hand, and the town on the other. The model of the covered hall inspired the construction of the large hall of government which Count Floris V of Holland erected in The Hague, and also the construction of those cloth halls that would come into being a few decades later in towns in Brabant. The very same model was used for the nearly infirmary of the Bijloke hospital in Ghent, which was built at the same time. When in 1452 Duke Philip the Good invited the town of Brussels to erect a large hall of government connected to his residence on Coudenberg hill, the construction site was staffed by the same artisans, masons and carpenters who were active at municipal sites. Mathieu de Layens, the architect of Leuven's town hall, also coordinated work on the Maison de la Paix in Mons, as well as on the Collegiate Church of Saint Waudru in the same town. After 1448 he relocated his business activity to Tienen, where, on the grand marketplace, the site for the chapel of the confraternity of Our Lady of the Lake awaited him.

What remains most evocative, though, is the career of the Keldermans or Van Mansdale family, which goes back to Jan Keldermans, the sculptor and stonecutter from Brussels who died in 1424/5. His descendants would remain active as sculptors and designers in the Low Countries well into the second half of the sixteenth century. They were involved in the construction of the Church of Saint Gummarus in Lier, as well as the town halls of Mechelen, Leuven, Gouda and Middelburg. Both the town and the lord of Bergen-op-Zoom called on the skills of Antonis Keldermans (d. 1512), who worked on the tower of the Church of Saint Bavo in Haarlem and who, with his son Antonis Jr, effected the enclosure of the square called the Baliënplein adjacent to the princely residence on Brussels' Coudenberg hill. This son would not only collaborate on the meat halls in Leuven and Middelburg but also design the new ducal Broodhuis ('King's House') in Brussels. This creation of a building that was centrally located on the Grand Place (Grote Markt) and represented the ducal power went hand in hand with his appointment as 'master workman of our lord the king' (*meester werkman ons heeren des conincx*). The appointment of other family members as 'town overseers' (*werkmeester van de stad*) in Mechelen, Leuven and Bergen-op-Zoom did not prevent them from remaining relatively mobile or from being active in princely commissions for Philip the Fair, Margaret of Austria and Charles V. Rombout Keldermans Jr (d. 1531) is undoubtedly the best known of the entire clan.

From the end of the fourteenth until the first third of the sixteenth century, Brabant architects also contributed to the spread of certain building materials. In combination with brick, these materials led to the dethronement of the centuries-old tradition of building with Tournai limestone in Flanders. The new building materials played an unmistakable role in unifying the urban landscape in the Low Countries. Sandstone from the region around Brussels and bluestone from Ecaussines, Arquennes and Feluy (on the boundary of Hainaut and Brabant) found their way into the county of Holland by water. The masons' marks of quarries and stonecutters can be found on buildings far into the north in Leiden, Haarlem, Egmond, Alkmaar and Gouda. Over the course of the sixteenth century, the preponderance of building material from Brabant decreased in the northern Low Countries in favour of stone from Bentheim or from the region around Namur. In tandem, new dynasties of architects appeared, yet what came to be called 'Brabantine Gothic' remained a specific variation of the flamboyant Gothic style, the nature of which is defined by the materials at hand in the region.

With regard to stylistic idiom and technique, the style remained a point of reference, even after the new canon of the Italian Renaissance had penetrated into the Low Countries. The gallery of the Antwerp stock exchange (1531) and the tower of the Collegiate Church of Our Lady in the same town became advertisements of the 'modern style', also called the Tertiary Gothic. Stock exchange and church tower, which also served as a belfry, wholly honoured the radiance of the new trading metropolis of north-west Europe. Oudenaarde's town hall, completed by Hendrik van Pede in 1530, is an almost perfect example of the feverish, innovative building activity in the period coinciding with the start of the reign of Charles V. As an example of Habsburg propaganda, the imperial crown that was lifted onto the tower demonstrated the new power relations. Those new conditions were less the result of deliberations than of centralising and authoritarian power relations between the state and the towns.

The development of a centre's role was not just a matter of spatial organisation or of architectural achievement; the effective use of space also has to be taken into account. An initial example is the operation of the town bells, a special and quite costly component of communication. How the urban community acquired the right to have bells has been documented for Tournai better than for any other town, as it involved a deliberate concession from the French king being added to the municipal charter of 1188. The bell was an essential component in horizontal communication among members of the urban population: it was able to call them together, warn of danger or draw attention to special legal actions in town. In Tournai the bell was eventually hung in a tower (known as a belfry by 1294 at the latest), although it had already been in use for various decades before it was transferred to this home. A fire necessitated the casting of new bells in 1392. As a result, Tournai's belfry gradually acquired the slender and richly ornamented features that still characterise the 70-metre-high tower.

The same height was planned for the belfry in Ghent, the fairly laborious construction of which seems to have been inspired by Tournai's tower. Bruges's belfry, connected to the cloth hall, was initially limited to a wooden structure that fell victim to a fire in 1280, along with the hall. The elegant stone tower with its familiar octagonal top stage – one of the main symbols of the town of Bruges – came about in various phases over the course of the fourteenth and fifteenth centuries. From the beginning of the thirteenth century onwards, Valenciennes had a belfry with bell tower: the building was erected on a busy traffic artery around 1222, but was relocated relatively soon to the Grand Place. In this case, the relocation revolved around a politically loaded act. Between 1222 and 1237 – the period in which Joan of Constantinople, the countess of Hainaut, consented to the re-design – the county was troubled by the episode of Baldwin the pretender. Claiming the countship, he had found significant numbers of adherents in Valenciennes in 1225, resulting in very tense frictions between the urban elite, who supported the countess, and the broader social groups. The history of the razing and rebuilding of the belfry can therefore be reinterpreted in the light of this episode, in the sense that it is a tell-tale indicator of how the town and the urban space were once again brought under control by the political elite, who triumphantly prevailed. It was also an important step in altering the grand marketplace, a process eventually completed over the course of the fifteenth century.

Accommodating the town bell in a belfry is not a phenomenon that characterised the Low Countries in their entirety; on the contrary, it remained limited to the region of Flanders, Hainaut and Tournai. The model doubtless originated in France, or certainly from the area of Picardy, and may have been inspired by Mediterranean campaniles. In the towns of Liège and Brabant (in the latter case, Lier constitutes an exception), the town bell was hung in a church tower. The choice of location did not fall to just any church, of course, but to the church most patronised by the elites, such as Saint Nicholas in the vicinity of Brussels' Grand Place, Saint Peter in Leuven, Our Lady in Antwerp, Saint-Pierre-au-Château in Namur, Saint Lebuinus in Deventer and Saint John in Gouda.

Using a town bell can be explained by the town's need to keep everyone across its entire territory informed in an accessible and simultaneous way, yet without being dependent on any sort of communication monopolised by seigneurial or ecclesiastical authorities. In most of the larger towns there is a definite transition from using a single bell to putting various bells into use, each with a unique sound and thus a particular use. There were distinct bells to announce the end of the (work-)day, or the opening and closing of market transactions. Sometimes they all rang together to warn of danger or to sound an alarm, or else to signal important legal events, such as executions. Other bells marked working hours, which indicates that the urban economy also impacted on the urban community's division of time. The patent for the work bell which the duke of Brabant awarded the burghers of Leuven in 1290 clearly illustrates the way in which workdays were altered to fit the interests of entrepreneurs and merchants. Urban time, which was so frequently emphasised, therefore did not necessarily exhibit cyclical or regular features. Even though time for working was already laicised, it was still an experience of time that was configured according to who had the say in town.

Only the clockwork and the clock hands, which were mounted on the town towers (as in Namur in 1393) or on the town hall (as in Mons around 1372 and in Brussels in 1441), showed a regular and 'objective' time to the population. Nevertheless, the practical impact of this innovation was limited: in spite of the clocks' central location and enclosure in representative buildings, the sound field was relatively modest. The cost and the peculiar nature of the clockwork contributed, of course, to the prestige and power of the belfry or the aldermen's house (*schepenhuis*). In Namur, the decision to install clockwork in the belfry was significantly borne in part by the count, 'which the inhabitants of Namur complained about, saying that it was not done with their consent'.[4] Ultimately, town and prince were able to reach an agreement whereby the costs of this new instrument were borne by both parties. In the first instance, though, it remained a testimonial to the comital ambition for demarcating the boundaries inside which the urban community was able to develop. Even the clash between the autonomy of the towns and the advancing power of the Habsburg state in the sixteenth century had a direct effect on the town bells. In towns that were increasingly subjected to princely authority – such as Tournai, Ghent, Bruges and Mechelen – mellifluous carillons were installed in the belfries, the sound of which was more connected to all manner of musical lines than had ever been the case with the more austere tolling bells, the so-called *banklokken*.

The extraordinary building activity that government administrators conducted throughout the thirteenth to sixteenth centuries ultimately resulted in a built space full of meanings that invite a multiplicity of readings. Conflicting interests could crystallise around public buildings or sites in town which expressed specific collective values. In this way, being in control of the belfry, town hall or most prominent market square became a central element in many collective strategies (see Chapter 4). In addition to these markers of urban space literally set in stone, there were also the more ephemeral processions, joyous entries and festivals of all kinds, which decorated the built space with temporary ornamentation and architecture. On occasions of this sort, the political messages were literally carried by *tableaux vivants*, painted sheets, inscriptions, torches and so forth (see Chapter 5). How these stagings were localised was also far from coincidental, but frequently the result of a carefully contrived political communication strategy, in which the most significant places in the town were promoted.

---

[4] Cited in Paul De Croonendael, *Cronicque contenant l'estat ancien et moderne du pays et conté de Namur. La vie et geste des seigneurs, contes et marquis d'icelluy, publié par le Comte de Limminghe* (Brussels: Fr.-J. Olivier, 1878–9), vol. II, p. 576: 'dont ceux de Namur se plaindarent disans que ce n'estoit pas de leur consentement'.

Demarcating Boundaries

The process of converting the town ramparts to stone (their 'petrification') had answered a similar need to pair utility with politics and ideology very early on. Even when the construction of town ramparts was done in the name of the prince, the input of the urban oligarchies was almost everywhere of great importance. Frequently the construction itself was a significant element in the way that the power of these elites evolved. In the same process, the town ramparts became an essential component in demarcating the legal identity of the town. They furnished the town with a defensive force, even in the presence of its own prince. Therefore both the incorporation and the exclusion of well-defined sites during the successive construction phases of town walls deserve a more thorough evaluation.

It is certainly not the case that the stone ramparts enclosing towns in the Low Countries at the end of the twelfth century and throughout the thirteenth, giving them a recognisable outward appearance, fulfilled only a military function. That role was already filled – frequently with great efficacy – by older structures, for example, palisades in tamped-down earth. In the case of large-scale fortification campaigns, there were other motivations at play, too: the concurrent ambitions of the prince and the local elites; the opportunity for developing a distinct tax system as well as an efficient municipal financial system; the control of social movements by providing temporary mass employment; the desire to incorporate or otherwise exclude certain outer districts; and the marking of certain economically important routes of access with imposing gates. Stone walls and monumental town gates richly appointed with towers and symbolic references were the first thing that a visitor to the town saw. They also very clearly defined the way in which the town was perceived by the outside world and how it made itself manifest with respect to its rural surroundings. It is from here, too, that the imagined landscapes originate in which the town – by means of its walls and towers and building density – distinguished itself as an island in the middle of a rolling and seemingly lifeless countryside. The outer districts – often densely populated and bustling with activity, half urban, half characterised by horticulture – are erased in the process. Whenever a siege occurred, these outer districts were often in effect destroyed or evacuated, but just as frequently they rose up again from their ruins. They were also of essential importance for the town: a cheap and occasional labour force could be accommodated in reserve there, and it was there that workshops were set up by influential entrepreneurs outside sometimes strict corporate controls. Moreover, these outskirts guaranteed nearby provision of food products from horticulture and modest animal husbandry, in addition to semi-finished industrial products.

Whether the result of social, political or military motivations, walls make unambiguously clear what is located inside and outside the town. For that matter, the audacious erection of a stone wall frequently disturbed a town's internal organisation. Routes of access became cut off or lost their significance; residences and houses were expropriated; the course of waterways was redirected; parishes and seigneuries were bisected. Frequently the end result was a new town alongside the entity surrounded by walls. If a second, more extensive set of ramparts demarcated the surrounded territory in a later stage, the 'new town' often retained its specific characteristics. The earliest maps from the second half of the sixteenth century show how many towns had retained their original set of ramparts. At that time the first set of ramparts had become internal walls and even the gates still made up part of the urban fabric. They frequently acquired a new role as weapons depots, prisons or residential complexes, though just as often they remained testimonials to earlier dividing lines. The case of Tournai illustrates this situation well: the course of the earliest, episcopal set of ramparts can still easily be seen on the map by Jacob van Deventer from the sixteenth century, while the belfry, grand marketplace and places where those in power in the commune stayed are all situated at the foot of this original set of town walls, yet clearly on the outer side of it. An analogous determination can be made for Brussels: the first set of ramparts from the thirteenth century excludes the densely populated artisans' district of 'Chapel Church' (Kapellekerk), even though this is found inside the route of the second set of ramparts from the fourteenth century. For thirteenth-century Bruges a similar sort of development can be reconstructed.

In addition to these complex functions, the ramparts of towns in the Low Countries had, of course, a primarily military role, which allowed them to stand up to sometimes lengthy sieges. From the thirteenth century onwards, these walls answered to all current technical demands and military necessities. Frequently they developed as bow-shaped structures fortified with earth: a relatively economical way of building with solid materials, which offered adequate resistance to undermining and to the earliest kinds of artillery. Traditions in this regard underwent fundamental alteration in the first half of the sixteenth century, though for political rather than technical reasons. Charles V and his councillors imposed the engagement of Italian architects and the use of new types of fortifications on the towns: centred, and equipped with bastions directed from a central citadel. These citadels exhibited an intense sort of spatial dominance, by which the prince threatened the town and kept an eye on it. Ghent's citadel, erected in 1540 on the site of the Abbey of Saint Bavo, largely reduced to rubble, offers one of the most telling examples of this kind of authoritarian exercise of power over a town. It is a spatial translation of the exemplary punishment that the emperor had imposed upon the rebellious town. As such an example, it had been preceded by similar interventions in many towns in the Low Countries, ever since the reign of Philip the Good. In a town like Lille, the royal fortress – which was closely connected to the model of the citadel – had been there since the end of the thirteenth century, as testimony to a lengthy siege of the town in the context of the war fought by King Philip IV 'the Fair' of France (1268–1314) and Count Guy of Dampierre (1226–1305) and the Flemish towns.

In Antwerp a new set of ramparts, which were laid out starting in 1543, and a citadel from the years 1567–72 threw up a serious obstacle to the spatial development of a town fully undergoing expansion. The gigantic costs, forced on the town by Charles V and the duke of Alva, imposed a heavy burden on the municipal finances and caused a delay in the expansion of new public services, which were necessary for the further administrative and commercial evolution of the town. The new town hall, which had been planned since the start of the sixteenth century, was built only in 1564, in a much more modest version altered to the circumstances. With its sober and sanitised design, the Renaissance style of the building satisfied the dominant fashion trends but also the considerably straitened budget.

From the thirteenth century to the sixteenth, a very large proportion of municipal funds was absorbed by fortification works, as they demanded constant alteration to match developments in firepower and in government policy. Given a princely patent as an incentive, they also served to enable an effective and efficient system of taxation, which was fundamentally inequitable, however, as it was based on indirect taxes that were levied on vitally important commodities. Once this system had been put into operation, a consolidated municipal debt also began to function, which in its turn laid the foundation for investments in monumental edifices and other structures. The connection between a generalised tax system and important architectural and urbanistic achievements obliged the urban elite – who ultimately commissioned most construction projects – to justify their expenditure as well as to invest their own funds in those projects. For that reason, sometimes the names of aldermen were mounted on town gates, as happened in Mons with the trader Jean de Bertaimont, whose name appeared next to that of the count of Hainaut on the Porte du Parc ('Park Gate') finished at the end of the thirteenth century. Another example is Claes Barbezaen, trader, financier and former town magistrate, who had his financial contribution immortalised in 1408 in the construction of the walls and towers of Bruges. In Liège, the tax collectors of the *fermeté* (a specific excise duty, the revenue from which was earmarked for financing defence works) demanded that their actions be recorded in an inscription on the new set of ramparts which were constructed after the destruction of the town by Charles the Bold's army in 1468. In completing a building project of this sort, there were of course also attempts to fill the entire population of a town with pride and joy. On the occasion of its inauguration, scenes of jubilation and distribution of wine, bread, baked goods and sweets were meant to encourage the taxpayers to identify with those in power and with these outward signs of municipal power.

Among those elements jointly making up municipal fortifications, town gates deserve particular attention. Frequently defence works started with the gates, whereas a stone wall literally remained in the works in progress, with the town's defence left to a set of earthen ramparts or a palisade, which could prove to be perfectly effective. In this way, giving pride of place to gates comes down to overvaluing the town's peculiar nature and to emphasising the power of municipal administrators to receive newcomers or deny them access. These gates – which of course were of great economic importance through the levying of tolls – were thus a component of a set of political instruments in which the keys were literally preserved or exchanged in moments of conflict or subjugation. In Brussels the gates came under the control of great patrician clans, who watched over and administered the buildings. In 1421, however, the guilds gained access to the municipal government, a fact which could occasion a re-allotment of the gates. In the cases of Bruges in 1436 and of Ghent in 1453, the punishment of the town by the prince (Philip the Good) saw to the dismantling of specific town gates. In Kampen on the river IJssel, in contrast, the gate for the grain market – through which the bishop of Utrecht traditionally entered the town – acquired distinct significance for the urban community after it was kept closed to David of Burgundy until he consented to set his seal on Kampen's municipal privileges.

The names of the gates generally referred to the direction or place they opened the way to, or to a patron saint. Their iconography and the literature about them demonstrate how they were able to express fundamental values of urban society. It is no coincidence that the influential Bruges society of the 'White Bear' (i.e. *Witte Beer*) referred to the seven gates of the town (one for each letter in its Middle Dutch name, *Brugghe*) in a poem composed on the occasion of their gathering on the eve of the feast of the Epiphany in 1414.

Caritas as the Key Component of Civic Unity

Among civic virtues, respect for unity, the practice of solidarity and love of one's neighbour played a crucial role as guarantees of social peace. This ideological mixture finds its ingredients in the political discourse of the elites, which can be traced back to the initial phases of the commune, in the values of the corporate organisations in which guilds set the tone, as well as in the apostolic ideal that the mendicant orders introduced into the town (see Chapters 3 and 4). From the point of view of urban infrastructure, this ensemble of values is best embodied by hospitals and shelters. From the twelfth century onwards, confraternities, individuals, ecclesiastical institutions and town magistracies established institutions that offered shelter to those who were poor, sick or travelling. Frequently this was just basic shelter, providing food, religious support and care for the dying. Few hospitals specialised in genuine medical help. And even fewer in number were those hospitals that opened their doors to a wide array of patients. The Saint John's hospitals in Brussels and Bruges, Our Lady or Saint Elisabeth's in Antwerp, the Bijloke hospital in Ghent, the Hospice of Saint Gilles in Namur and afterward its Grand Hospital are a few examples of this latter, more accessible category, the governance of which was rapidly assumed by municipal authorities.

More numerous are the institutions where shelter was targeted at specific categories of burghers. As the earliest institutions, the leprosaria deserve mention. In theory they were intended to shelter those members of the urban community who were kept out of the community, as a result both of the real danger of infection and of the taboo that was attached to their illness. The leprosaria were founded, then, literally at the edges of urban agglomerations. They were run by *donati*, oblates who came from the urban community. The hospital of Mont Cornillon in Liège is one of the earliest known institutions of this type, though most towns already had a leprosarium in the second half of the twelfth century or at the start of the thirteenth. At that time, with support from the bishops, those in power in the towns took over both economic control and the internal organisation of these institutions. Lepers were never very numerous in the Low Countries, and during the fourteenth and fifteenth centuries the leprosaria gradually became general hospitals, where isolation was no longer given priority. Old members as well as dependants of established burghers' families then found shelter there, as the well-documented example of the leprosarium of Terbank in Leuven shows.

One section of the hospitals that is difficult to quantify – probably the majority – was oriented towards members of specific guilds (fullers, weavers, tanners, blacksmiths and so forth), towards the representatives of specific clans, towards certain social categories (old clergy) or towards groups defined by gender (poor women, poor widows, former beguines, old men and so forth). Notwithstanding the dominant discourse and the importance placed on solidarity and fraternity, it turns out that the more the influence of guilds and other corporations increased, the more these values were put into practice only for the relatively limited groups of their own kind (see Chapter 3). Civic unity and mutual support, it appears, could only be achieved via the sum total of corporate initiatives.

Most hospitals were accommodated in individual buildings involving modest structures. They made but a humble stamp on the urban fabric, though from the perspective of the group related to their founders they took on essential roles as gathering places and hotspots for social support. In contrast, the major hospitals became points of reference for an entire neighbourhood, a role that they owed to the large infirmary plus chapel, refectory, dormitory for the religious community supporting them, imposing kitchens, repositories, dependent agricultural businesses, burial grounds and church. The Bijloke hospital in Ghent and Saint John's Hospital in Bruges are the most impressive testimonials to these major institutions. It is no coincidence, then, that these were also in the two largest towns in the medieval Low Countries. Their innovative architecture and well-developed facilities were a model for many important public buildings. These major hospitals represented an imposing kind of landownership and financial power, too, whereby their activity was not limited to supporting the homeless and the needy. They also functioned as credit institutions and as trustees for the property of third parties – primarily for the mendicant orders, with which they maintained close ties from the start. The major hospitals thus had multiple functions, which were inspired nonetheless by the ideals that their founders had in mind, as well as by what the Church and the mendicant orders commissioned.

From the first half of the thirteenth century onwards, these mendicant orders set themselves up on a massive scale in the most important towns of the Low Countries (see Chapter 5). In doing so, they were resolutely supported both by secular princes and by bishops. That support was indispensable, given the mistrust with which the traditional canons' chapters viewed the arrival of mendicant orders. From their very first settlement, Franciscans, Dominicans and Carmelites were also able to count on much support from the broader population. Their role was not limited to preaching and pastoral care, nor to recruiting new brothers from the milieu of merchants and artisans, nor to providing education. Their buildings – above all the large hall churches designed with preaching to the masses in mind – were also opened for guild meetings and to formal political assemblies. In 1291 the Dominicans from Ghent received a comital delegation, the town magistracy and representatives from the Ghent commonalty and from the other major Flemish towns with the objective of finding a way out of the very sensitive discussion that had arisen around the monitoring of the town's finances. In a subsequent phase, the accessibility of the mendicant orders' halls allowed certain mercantile wares – primarily tapestries and artworks – to be displayed and offered for sale to a broad public. Given that a considerable share of these objects would ultimately end up as a pious donation of some sort to the patrimony of ecclesiastical institutions, there was no talk of any discrepancy between this very specific function for the premises of Dominicans and Franciscans and the ideal of poverty that belonged to the core of their identity.

One of the most important interactions between the mendicant orders and the urban communities was incorporated in the directing and legitimating role that the Dominicans, in particular, played from the perspective of the many beguinages. These courtyards offered lodging to women (and very occasionally men) who chose to live communally in an apostolic sense, yet who still desired to remain laypeople (see Chapter 5). These communities of beguines and beghards occupied a distinct and mostly recognisable series of dwellings, inside which these pious souls were able to devote their lives to work, yet also to providing healthcare and even education. The textile sector particularly profited from the availability of this stable and regulated workforce, which proved to be less mobile than regular male and female labourers, who generally offered their labour on a weekly basis at the worksites provided for that purpose (see Chapter 2). The major court beguinages of Bruges and Ghent housed several hundred people in this manner. They made up part of the urban infrastructure and often became cities within the city, as it were, or at least in its immediate vicinity. In addition to these extensive communities, which were generally endowed by princes or important dignitaries, there were smaller communities that frequently went back to spontaneous communities founded by individuals, where a handful of beguines had lived communally. Founded mini-communities of this type seem to have been the rule in towns like Tournai and Liège but were also imitated in smaller towns like Hoei.

In summary, the complexity of the organisation of civic *caritas* can only be viewed with complete amazement. Those in power in the towns were far from the only players in this field, even though their representatives did everything possible to bring the most conspicuous and wealthiest institutions under their control. In most cases, though, distinct initiatives by individuals or collectives assumed the role of providing services. They were also the ones who awarded commissions for developing the imposing buildings that – like the grand trade halls and town halls – in their way each expressed the town's concern for the general interest. The fragmentation of interests and initiatives was precisely one of the most characteristic aspects of the urban infrastructure oriented towards *caritas*.

Conclusion

'The history of the late medieval city – the creation of urban identity, urban privileges, an urban "public" and an authority that acted in the name of the public – was to an important extent, a history of space.'[5] Urban infrastructure and facilities were both witnesses to the way in which this space came into being, as well as active agents in that process. In the towns of the Low Countries, the production of urban space was influenced to a large degree by the changing and uncertain power relations in politics and society. The competing claims to power of prince and town, the internal conflicts within the urban elites, the struggle between patrician families and artisans' guilds, the rivalries among individual ecclesiastical institutions: all these circumstances contributed to the maintenance of quasi-permanent building sites, ad to persistent alterations of existing buildings, of their functionality and, therefore, of the symbolically loaded messages they were considered to convey. Urban ideology has previously been described as the result of a kind of *bricolage*. This makeshift process also describes the way in which the infrastructure of the towns came into being and was developed. It does not mean, however, that the powerful political and moral sources of impetus at its foundation need to be minimalised, nor the means invested undervalued, much less the services that they provided negated. Instead, it involves reading the infrastructure of towns and their facilities – both in their realised as well as their projected form – as not being unambiguous. Indeed, this fundamentally hybrid nature may well be the most peculiar characteristic of urban space in the Low Countries.

That singular nature returns us to the theoretical points of departure introducing this series of observations about urban infrastructure. It has been demonstrated that the built space in the towns of the late medieval and early modern Low Countries was a bearer of ambiguous values. Yet this space remained a very distinct factor in local socio-political life. Once implanted, a specific infrastructure sent out its own messages, and

---

[5] Martha C. Howell, 'The spaces of late medieval urbanity' in Marc Boone and Peter Stabel (eds.), *Shaping Urban Identity in Late Medieval Europe* (Leuven and Apeldoorn: Garant, 2000), p. 19.

gave them a significance that in turn evoked collective behaviour – at times desired, and at other times not. Festivals as well as revolts and riots took place at certain well-defined sites, and they put into motion mechanisms of signification. Social groups or political factions had a sound knowledge of these mechanisms and could occasionally take advantage of them in order to claim legitimacy. Conversely, some population groups were excluded. Even the prince used space to reinforce his ambitions or to demonstrate his power. For those who lived in the towns, the urban infrastructure was an intensely experienced space. This aspect of experience was expressed via very diverse types of demonstrations, parades and processions that marked the public life of the towns (see Chapter 5). The urban landscape – a complex combination of built surfaces, routes, squares, waterways and monumental structures – therefore also constituted a public sphere in the philosophical sense. This space was intersected by enclaves with a status of their own. Yet, precisely as a result of the infrastructure and the many meanings it inherently bore, this space tended towards the essence of what a public space is supposed to be: a place where messages can be conveyed and where the answer to them can also be heard.

7 At Home in the City: The Dynamics of Material Culture

Inneke Baatsen, Bruno Blondé, Julie De Groot and Isis Sturtewagen

In recent decades, much attention has been paid in historical research to public space, and this volume is no different. Marketplaces, squares, town gates, streets and church buildings clearly functioned as nuclei of economic activities, everyday social contacts and religion. In addition, they constituted the setting for political exchange as well as urban rituals. It was these spaces that artisans, traders, municipal administrators, clergy and other townspeople voraciously employed to confirm, represent or negotiate identities, mutual relationships and the rights they had acquired or hoped to acquire (see Chapter 6). Major urban projects and architectural landmarks have always enjoyed preferential treatment in research on urban infrastructure and its layered space. Central to this chapter, however, is not the market square, the cloth hall, the bell tower, the guild house or the parish church, nor the everyday practices, festive processions, festivals and rituals in which individuals and groups appropriated public and semi-public spaces. Rather, we will leave the street behind and visit the inside of the urban dwelling. We will do this in order to picture its material culture and its residents. As we do so, not only will the material culture of the built 'house' move to the forefront, but the cultural and material construction of the 'home' will also be given prominence.

Among historians of consumption and material culture, it is usual to depict the seventeenth and eighteenth centuries as crucial eras in the transition towards the 'modern culture of consumption'. Jan de Vries, for example, identified the seventeenth-century northern Netherlands as an early cradle of the so-called 'modern consumer society'.[1] Essential to this transition were modifications in the manner and intensity of people's engagement in market-related activities. Perhaps most influential was De Vries's interpretation of this transition as a cultural phenomenon, emanating from the demand side, where the demand for 'old luxuries' slowly

---

[1] Jan de Vries, *The Industrious Revolution: Consumer Behavior and the Household Economy, 1650 to the Present* (Cambridge: Cambridge University Press, 2008).

Figure 7.1 Workshop of Robert Campin, *Annunciation Triptych*, c. 1427–1437 (central panel). In the interior constituting the setting for this Annunciation scene, we see a long *keerlys*, that is, a bench with a backrest that could be tilted. The majolica vase with white lilies in the middle of the table was a recognisable symbol for Mary. In the early fifteenth century, the representation of a religious scene in a burgher's residence was a novelty in the art of painting. That such a domestic setting was chosen illustrates the great significance of the home in the urban mindset.

shifted towards a cultural preference for 'new luxuries'. Whereas the 'old luxuries' were strongly oriented towards the 'conspicuous consumption' of a limited elite, it was these 'new luxuries' to which a socially more diverse group of consumers now gained access. From this perspective, the shifts in material culture betrayed changes in the definition of domesticity, comfort and pleasure. That model of consumption, according to

De Vries, was one in which large strata of the populace – and especially burghers and townspeople – could participate. This new way of consuming percolated down the lower echelons of society and united rather than divided, as new luxuries did not aim so much at uniqueness and distinction as at the multipliable. Inexpensive alternatives to many luxury goods appeared for a broader market, even though expensive, prestigious and conspicuous things were never completely eliminated from patterns of consumption. With that shift, the biggest hurdle in transitioning from an old model of consumption for nobles towards a new model of consumption for burghers was supposedly cleared.

De Vries was not the first though. In the nineteenth century, a comparable belief in the driving force of the urban environment inspired Jacob Burckhardt (1818–97) to identify late medieval Italy as a cradle of crucial material innovations.[2] Burckhardt – to some extent the 'inventor' of the Renaissance – called to mind an intimate connection between everyday life, material culture and the rise of Renaissance culture in Italy.[3] Richard Goldthwaite further embroidered upon this basic idea. He discovered in the Italian town a new mentality shaping the consumption of the urban nobility and patriciate. Over the course of the fifteenth and sixteenth centuries, the interiors and the decoration of Italian *palazzi* and *casae* gradually became more complex, more refined, richer and more luxurious. Not just the built *magnificenza* but also the *objets d'art*, the tableware and the furniture – that is to say, the *splendore* – increasingly contributed to the identity and sociability of the residents of Italian towns. In view of the fact that quite a few of the material innovations remained confined to the highest strata of society, the question remains whether an urban success story ought to be read into this narrative outright. In any case, Goldthwaite himself considered the income level in late medieval Italy to be too low and the distribution of wealth far too unequal for any broad consumption of this new material culture. Given their shared fascination for the 'urban background' of innovative models of consumption in two different contexts, however, both Jan de Vries and Richard Goldthwaite provide the ideal frame of reference for an overview of the material culture in the towns of the Low Countries.

The following pages set out the history of the urban house and of the ways in which material culture redefined domesticity, each time in a

---

[2] Jakob C. Burckhardt, *Die Kultur der Renaissance in Italien* (Basel: Verlag der Schweighauser'schen Verlagsbuchhandlung, 1860), translated as *The Civilization of the Renaissance in Italy*, ed. Peter Murray, trans. S.G.C. Middlemore (London: Penguin, 1990).
[3] Richard A. Goldthwaite, *Wealth and the Demand for Art in Italy, 1300–1600* (Baltimore: Johns Hopkins University Press, 1993).

different and unique way, specific to its context. On the production side of this narrative, the parallels with the industrial transformations and re-orientation of the Low Countries, as previously sketched, will stand out (see Chapter 2). This chapter provides an overview of the demand for goods that appeared and disappeared, as well as a survey of the economic sectors that moved to that rhythm. In addition, significant attention will be paid to the way in which the specific sociological composition of the town in the Low Countries (with its strong mercantile elites and substantial middling groups – see Chapter 3) influenced the region's material culture. It is argued that, during the Middle Ages and the sixteenth century, towns in the Low Countries played a crucial role in dynamics hitherto exclusively ascribed to Renaissance Italy or to the burgeoning consumer societies in Holland and England during the seventeenth and eighteenth centuries.

Residential Styles and Cultures

The story of the medieval urban residence is not easily written. Most houses from this period have disappeared from the contemporary streetscape, and over the centuries the few remaining ones with medieval traces have frequently been rebuilt so thoroughly that it is almost impossible to reconstruct their earliest residential cultures. Over the course of centuries, existing structures were replaced and adapted to the fashion of the period or to the changing needs of repeatedly new families and generations of residents. As a result, not only towns but also individual houses have been built out of different time-layers. Yet by making use of interdisciplinary research methods and by combining different types of sources, some crucial features of medieval residential culture can still be brought to light. The architectural history of the physical and typological characteristics of houses can be supplemented with research on post-mortem inventories. These inventories tell us even more about the internal organisation of the residential space, about the orientation and spatial positioning of the rooms, and about the presence of furniture and household effects which gave those rooms their cultural significance.

There is especially little known about the first houses in the centres of the earliest urban settlements. In all probability, most of them were rectangular wooden structures with limited functional partitioning. An open hearth at the centre was the structure's main heating and cooking source, and smoke from its fire was vented through the roof. From the eleventh century onwards, things started to change. Within the city walls of the *portus* of Ghent, land-owning merchants and traders had already settled in large stone houses with thick sturdy walls and several storeys, erected in Tournai limestone (see Chapter 3). Large parts of Brabant, too, saw an early implementation of building with stone, as natural stone was relatively inexpensive to obtain locally. Conforming to the Romanesque architectural style, these kinds of houses had few or only very small window openings, with limited light entering the rooms. Alongside these rare stone residences, most houses were built in wood, sometimes in combination with clay. Gradually, however, municipal authorities realised that stone structures offered much better resistance to fire hazards.

The process of so-called 'petrification', or building in stone, experienced a similarly gradual evolution and was, moreover, one that chronologically seems to have varied in terms of town and region. In Utrecht, petrification took off as early as the thirteenth century through both new construction and renovation of older structures. The same goes for the towns of the river IJssel region in the northern Netherlands, where brick was used for the construction of residences from the thirteenth century. After the great fire in the city of Zwolle in 1324, the *stadboek* (i.e. city codex, or records) stipulated that thenceforth roofs were to be 'cover[ed] with tile or with slate' (*decken zal met pannen oft mit leyen*) and no longer with flammable thatch or straw. In Bruges, too, from the thirteenth century onwards, straw roofs were replaced by hard roofs for reasons of fire prevention. However, in Leiden, even though bricks were used relatively early here, compared to other parts of the county of Holland, it was not until 1450 that it was stipulated that all façades and partition walls were thenceforth to be built in stone. Near the end of the fourteenth century, the process of building in stone was in some places encouraged by municipal governments which subsidised petrification. The magistracy in Antwerp, for example, decided in 1546 to issue a ban on constructing wooden house fronts and subsidies were provided for those who replaced their wooden house fronts with stone ones. But until well into the nineteenth century this prohibition did not prevent the existence and construction of such wooden structures.

Urban growth and the gradual development in housing from freestanding (detached) residences to connected (terraced) buildings on the street also required elaborate intervention from the authorities regarding ('common') stone walls shared by two residences, openings for light in the side walls, roof gutters, and overhanging storeys on the street side. The countless conflicts that were fought out before the aldermen's bench in Bruges as a result of disagreements between neighbours give an idea of the need for clear regulations – both for preventing possible fire hazards and for confronting architectural chaos and conflicts. Living together in towns continually dictated and redefined the boundaries of public, semi-public and private space.

While the initial layout of urban residences still looked simple, throughout the late medieval period it increasingly diversified, and that was the case – as will be discussed – for interior design as well. Buildings grew ever higher, with spacious attic storeys, upstairs rooms, lofts and mezzanines or so-called 'hanging' rooms (*hangende camere*). Moreover, brick house-front structures allowed for larger window openings, whereby the rooms on the street side were able to benefit from more natural light. In the meantime, the hearth was shifted to the side wall and, with the introduction of a mantelpiece and chimney, became able to heat multiple rooms at the same time, as fireplaces on different storeys could be connected via the central flue. As a result, the accommodation of all core household activities (cooking, eating, sleeping, working) was no longer assigned to the same space. In more spacious residences – and gradually in more modest dwellings as well – secondary fireplaces were created, whereby the largest hearth increasingly functioned as a cooking facility. Chafing dishes, stoves, bed warmers and charcoal burners further contributed to the spread of heat in the house.

To a great extent, lighting and heating amenities determined the functions a room could fulfil. The reception of guests, for instance, preferably took place in well-heated and adequately lit rooms, where the natural daylight that entered via the windows was backed up by a vast arsenal of candles, oil lamps, candelabra, chandeliers and in some cases mirrors as well. Attic and cellar spaces were primarily used for storing supplies (frequently thought of in terms like 'apple loft' (*appelzolder*) or 'grain loft' (*corenzolder*)) and could be rented out separately to merchants and artisans. The idea of a functional specialisation of space has frequently been put forward in scholarly literature. In more spacious houses, different residential functions such as cooking, sleeping or dining were increasingly concentrated within areas specifically intended for performing that role. But in late medieval and early modern practice this phenomenon seems to have been only partially adopted. For example, the *chambre ou l'on dine* (dining room) in a fifteenth-century Bruges residence accommodated comfortable armchairs, cupboards and a bed with decorative bedding, in addition to a table and chairs. That arrangement suggests that even such a quite specialised space, in spite of its name, was not used just for taking meals but fulfilled important status functions as well (see pp. 212–13). Frequently referred to in post-mortem inventories, the *cuekene* (kitchen), too, could be the site of multiple household functions, despite the clear semantic reference to the activity of preparing or 'cooking' food. The presence, for example, of paintings, parlour games and prestigious seating betrays the fact that quite a few kitchens were much more than mere places in which to work and cook. Such furnishings would later also be translated, for that matter, into the phenomenon of 'conspicuous kitchens', so-called 'grand kitchens' in wealthier households of sixteenth-century Antwerp. In these more affluent households, such conspicuous kitchens were only sporadically slept in, unlike those of many (nuclear) families with fewer spatial possibilities, and contrary to the prestigious *neerkamers* (the main public reception rooms) in these buildings.

Such was the case in 1592, in the kitchen of *De Blauwe Schaar* ('The Blue Shears') – the residence in The Hague of the broadcloth cropper Andries Pieterszoon van Dalem – where people were cooking, eating and also sleeping. The front of his house – approximately 3.5 metres wide – was entirely occupied by the artisan's shop, with its cropper's equipment (including the shears, combs and cards), sales counter and workbench, as well as, among other things, scaffolding and a 'piece of wood with some of his wares hanging from it' (*houtgen daer wat cramerij aen hangt*). With pewter tableware, copper pots and kettles, a handful of silver, and even a few pieces of golden jewellery, Andries was firmly positioned in urban society's middling groups where, based on his occupational profile, one would expect him to be. Dinner in his kitchen took place at a folding table, and sleeping in a bedstead, which, thanks to curtains, still offered some privacy. Washing and cooking were done in the back kitchen, where, again, less prestigious tools for cooking, washing and preserving food were stored. Shop and kitchen together scarcely measured more than about 21 square metres.

Multiple occupation was a necessity for many people in the medieval town. Quite a few people occupied only one room, which in some cases had to be shared with others. For many individuals, the one room that they rented (and sometimes even shared) was the place where their entire indoor lives played out. At the other end of the spectrum were the genuine or would-be nobility, who occupied roomy, fortified stone residences in town, the so-called 'tower houses' (see Chapter 3). The taxes that were levied in some places on the rental value of residences give a clear picture of the unequal social distribution of 'residential quality'. In the city of 's-Hertogenbosch, the wealthiest 20 per cent of the residents paid 50 per cent of the total estimated rental value, whereas the poorest 20 per cent of the people brought in scarcely 3 per cent during the early sixteenth century. Moreover, only a minority of the urban populace owned their own residence, a fact which had major consequences. For the few lucky enough to own a dwelling, immovable property constituted a nice source of income. Property could also be mortgaged with rents, thus serving as leverage for economic activities: property owners acquired easy (and cheap) access to the capital market.

The flexibility of residential styles and living patterns was translated into the spatial layout of the medieval dwelling, which in many cases was still quite adaptable to changing occasions, events and conditions. Parts of the interior walls of the rooms consisted of wooden panels which could relatively easily be taken down or added to. In that way, the number of rooms per floor and the size of those rooms could be adjusted. For a long time the same flexibility actually affected the dwelling itself. All things considered, it is no coincidence that, in quite a few customary law stipulations, a distinction was drawn between the land and the wooden (and, as such, easily taken down and movable) structures on it. Moreover, people moved relatively frequently, which certainly had an influence on the furnishings and the design of residences.

At Home in the City

Some historians have described the canal houses in seventeenth-century Holland as the cradle of 'domesticity', regardless of the fact that domesticity was rather unconsciously created and experienced. Even so, in spite of the major social differences in residential cultures called to mind above, quite a few sources suggest that the burgher's house in a medieval town had long been much more than a mere 'roof over his head'. Yet we can ascertain that domestic culture throughout the Middle Ages developed very rapidly, and that this evolution happened both in terms of design and furnishings and in terms of (residential) comfort. Consequently, this process not only applied to interior home decoration and furnishing but encompassed all other domains of the material culture. The following pages engage with this extension of material wealth, and we will argue that many historians have probably emphasised too heavily a discernible fault line between medieval and (early) modern material culture and consumption patterns. An attempt will be made to connect the urban societies of the Low Countries before 1600, their diversified goods and service economies, and the specific models of behaviour and consumption which developed there. As a result, this chapter's scope reaches beyond charting the changing idiom of materiality in the medieval town of the Low Countries.

In its book of ordinances (the so-called *keurboek*) of 1384, Antwerp, as yet a small city, witnessed the agreement upon so-called *stadsvoordeel*, or 'forward shares as deemed by the municipality', among an entire array of stipulations made in customary law. 'Forward shares between husband and wife' (*Tvordeel tusschen man ende wijf*) is nothing less than a list of household objects to which the surviving spouse was legally entitled after the death of the partner. The list therefore provides a kind of standard inventory of household goods which were defined by the *communis opinio* as proper and necessary for a decent standard of living. The list from 1384 does not look impressive, yet it is already telling. It contained some thirty objects, among them a table with a tablecloth, a chair with a seat cushion, a box or chest, a pot, kettle, pan, frying pan, hot iron, gridiron and more of these kinds of objects for everyday use. From all of these objects, and a few others not mentioned here, surviving spouses had the right to lay aside the 'best' items for themselves in the event of the death of their partners. The same logic applied to the generally quite expensive and symbolically important bed and its appurtenances, as well as to the best clothes 'that one wears to church on Easter, Pentecost, and Christmas' (*alsi Paeschdagh, Sinxendaghs, ende Kerstdaghs ter kerken mede gheet*). These kinds of stipulations speak volumes about the central position that the *culture des apparences* occupied in medieval society.

If this *stadsvoordeel* is now put next to the list that was drawn up in the Antwerp *Compilatae* at the end of the sixteenth century, a world of material difference is encountered. The *Compilatae* lists more than 200 items, of which many seem to have been rather marked in terms of luxury. Those who found themselves widowed at the end of the sixteenth century even had the right to a *verkeerbert* (a board game, not unlike backgammon), waffle iron, chestnut pan and so forth. That the 'best painting along with its frame' also made up part of the *stadsvoordeel* sufficiently expresses the place that decorative semi-luxury items such as paintings had already come to occupy in the urban mindset at that time. In principle, this latter *stadsvoordeel* remains silent about what people actually possessed; after all, these types of documents were drawn up by those who were not poor themselves, and as such were constructed according to somewhat elitist ideas of necessity. Recent research makes clear, however, that, early in the sixteenth century, paintings already constituted a vital part of the standard interior design of burghers' living quarters. Not just paintings, but in general all goods listed in this growing list of goods in the *stadsvoordeel*, translate into an increasingly varied and generally also wealthier material culture.

Innovations in Products and Processes

The diversification of material culture was possible only as a result of an entire series of innovations in products and processes which cannot be detached from the larger economic history of the Low Countries in this period (see Chapter 2). Herman Van der Wee described the diversification of the late medieval economy as a creative response to an industrial challenge. In the late Middle Ages, in his view, the decline of the traditional textile industry was absorbed by a dynamic diversification in the supply of goods and services with high added value. As both producers and consumers, prosperous urban middling groups were a crucial component of this process of reconversion. Wim Blockmans and Walter Prevenier also discerned a model of consumption for burghers as a response to a large-scale economic challenge and re-orientation. In contrast to what the major, actual social polarisation within the late medieval and sixteenth-century town might suggest, the new material culture supposedly derived its power from a larger sales market in broader social strata. Not only were the extensive urban middling groups relatively wealthy, but they also profited from the numerous innovations in products and processes. These innovations brought things of a diverse nature within arm's reach of increasingly large and socially more varied groups of people. It is difficult to attach a precise chronology to the expansion and diversification of the material culture. What is certain, though, is that this development proceeded haltingly. New products seldom completely drove out old objects immediately. Such processes rarely travelled along linear routes, nor could they be fitted into a few simple trends. Yet, by taking a step backwards, a number of important patterns do become discernible.

Undoubtedly, the most striking characteristic was the gradual diversification of material culture. Not only did more and more objects conquer the market, but their style and workmanship ('fashion') also diversified. Such variety also applied to the many functions and meanings that objects were able to fulfil. A nice illustration of that process of diversification can be found in furniture designed for storage, of which the chest or trunk was the basic type that dominated between 1100 and 1300. Trunks or chests were not only easily movable – which made them eminently suited to the practice of residing and relocating described above – but they were also multi-functional and could be decorated with exquisite woodcarving, frequently inspired by architectural styles. For centuries thereafter, both the trunk and the chest would continue to occupy an important place in domestic interiors. Yet, over the course of the fourteenth century, cupboards and *dressoirs* joined their company, both of which had actually grown out of the chest as a piece of furniture. As was the case for its Francophone analogue just mentioned, a *tresoor* is nothing more than a chest on high legs, with or without doors (creating so-called *sloten*, akin to the erstwhile sense of 'closets') and furnished underneath with a shelf on which ewers or platters were displayed. Semantically related to 'treasury', this piece of furniture probably derived its name from the custom of keeping in it valuable possessions, such as financial assets and deeds to property, money, jewels, devotional objects, precious tableware or the best cloth. Their special significance for status is illustrated by the fact that these *dressoirs* were frequently located in the space for receiving guests or in the vicinity of the most important bed and the dining table. In this regard, *dressoirs* were also frequently decorated with woodcarving, such as floral ornamentation, Gothic arches, linenfold panels and/or artfully carved lattice-work ventilation.

The new kinds of storage furniture that came to enlarge the array of options in the second half of the sixteenth century – in addition to the *teljoorberd* (literally 'plate-board'), *glazenberd* (glasses cupboard), *tinschaprade* (pewter-ware cupboard) and *kleerschaprade* (clothing cupboard) – included various types of writing bureaux, like the *cantoir*, *comptoir* or *cabinet*. This last item became *the* pre-eminent showpiece of storage furniture for prosperous townspeople. It combined the functions of a *dressoir* and a desk, but was valued above all for its superior decorative workmanship and its use of new, expensive and frequently exotic materials, such as ebony, silver, copper and curiosities like coral, tortoiseshell and ivory.

As regards seating, similar developments arose, in which the common bench, armchairs, three-legged stools and *schabbellen* (this plural being related to the Italian furniture term *sgabelli*), as well as settees, set the tone for a long time. One piece of seating furniture that was quite common in urban interiors during the fourteenth and fifteenth centuries was the *zittekist* ('bench-chest') or *lys*. Laying colourful cushions on it or draping a bench covering over it could enhance the comfort of this banquette, which also served as storage furniture. Just like the armchair, *lys*-banquettes could be found pretty much everywhere in residential spaces, as seen in the famous Merode triptych (*c*. 1430) or the Saint Barbara wing of the *Werl Altarpiece* (1438), where a specific type of *lys* is depicted. This often exquisitely worked bench was called a *keerlys* or *wendlys* (literally, a 'turn-*lys*'), referring to the backrest that could be rotated, allowing its users the option of sitting with their backs or their faces towards the fire – an innovation, moreover, that was refined throughout the fourteenth and fifteenth centuries and that rendered this furniture very popular among prosperous townspeople. Individual chairs, too, found their way in: one luxury chair that could sometimes be found in the finest rooms from the late sixteenth century onwards was the so-called 'Spanish chair'. Although quite popular in Antwerp, its spread in the Low Countries at that time did not really take off. In confiscation inventories in Mechelen, for instance, these types of chairs are occasionally found, but to a far lesser extent than was the case in Antwerp.

Large commercial towns did frequently take a leading role in the material diversification process, as they possessed the necessary infrastructure, knowledge, access to resources, and capital. That role can be determined from the fact that, for example, decorative and refined tableware made of red earthenware developed more rapidly in Bruges than in Oudenaarde, where the older and merely utilitarian grey variety held on longer. In the end, even the broad strokes of the history of earthenware betray a steadily increasing process of diversification. Until the beginning of the thirteenth century, earthenware stood out by virtue of its austerity, simplicity and multi-functionality. For instance, as found many times in archaeological excavations, the *kogelpot* –a spherical or globe-shaped pot with a small opening – was used not only for cooking but also as a storage pot or a chamber pot. The smallest specimens were supposedly even used as goblets. On account of its inability to be glazed, grey earthenware was also considerably limited in its possibilities for use, which further resulted in a rather limited choice of sorts and shapes. Turning up from the thirteenth century onwards, 'red earthenware' derived its name from clay containing iron that oxidised during firing, giving the resulting pottery a reddish blaze. Local red earthenware could be glazed and was much more readily decorated, lending itself to the production of more complex and varied shapes with a wider variety of uses. As a reaction, the gamut of objects enlarged: plates, bowls and platters but also roof tiles and interior tiling were brought onto the market in diverse shapes, sorts and sizes. With the entry of 'highly ornamented earthenware' finished with colourful glazing, the decorative possibilities and the array of choices became even larger. Bowls of all manner of sizes, pans for preparing specific dishes and disposable goblets – the so-called *drinckuyt* (roughly, 'drink-up'), a small single-serving vessel – came onto the scene.

No sector of the material culture remained untouched by the process of diversification. What applied to furniture and tableware could also be said of the clothes that people wore. The diversification in the supply of woollen fabric had already spread centuries prior to the sixteenth, with worsted fabrics from the 'draperies légères' ('light draperies') and with the import of less expensive English kerseys. By the end of the sixteenth century the array of choices in fabric had become remarkably varied. In the spring of 1575, for example, dozens of kinds of fabric were offered for sale in Antwerp's global market, ranging from precious silver or gold brocade, through fine silk material like velvet, satin and damask, to broadcloth and inexpensive woollen fabric. The big change, however, came with the steadily increasing popularity and broader application of mixed materials, including fustian, which was woven from a combination of linen and cotton, and semi-silk materials like grosgrain, bombazine, camlet and so-called *trijp* (velvet with a base fabric of linen). In addition, sixteenth-century price lists show that silk, just like wool, was available in all manner of types and grades of quality, and so did not necessarily have to be exceptionally expensive. The large supply of affordable textiles also opened up options for new textile processing. Gradually there arose a preference for surface embellishment, such as silk and pearl embroidery, appliqué with lace, galloon and metallic thread, and cutting out or slashing the fabric in order to create decorative patterns.

Over the course of the late Middle Ages and the early modern era, in addition to the increasing diversity in fabrics, greater attention was paid to the cut of clothing. Jan van Boendale, the clerk to Antwerp's aldermen, wrote about this new awareness in his *Bouc van der Wraken* ('Book of Vengeance', *c.* 1346): 'The women wear long clothes that gird them so tightly that the shape of their private parts becomes visible, by which they lead men to impurities.' Concerning men, the same Boendale remarked: 'The men wear clothing so short that it just reaches their private parts.'[4] This short clothing for men, which supposedly arose under the influence of changes in military equipment, was not without effect. The Flemish textile industry had already experienced a period of decline in the late thirteenth century, but was hit even harder as a result of this fashion. In order to fit the clothing nicely to the shape of the body, new advanced tailoring techniques were needed. In the end, clothing patterns became increasingly complicated. Formerly only a square front and back panel were needed, supplemented with two sleeves and *geren* (gores), that is, wedges or triangles to give the tunic more volume. The new cut, on the other hand, required multiple numbers of these three geometric parts in the pattern. Shifts in fashion did not escape religious circles either. As can be read in 'The seven enclosures' ('De zeven sloten', 1346), Jan van Ruusbroec's treatise on guidelines for monastic life, the pattern of the clothing closely followed the shape of the body, 'as if it were sewn to their skin'.[5] Clothing became tighter, and simultaneously there appeared yet another major innovation: button, hook and lace-up closures. These

---

[4] Original text: 'Vrouwen draghen cledre lanc, daer si in sijn ghepranct, datment daer dore merct ghereyt die vorme herre schamelheyt, daer si die manne mede leyden te gheloesder loesheyden' and 'Die manne draghen cledere mede cort tote hare scamelhede', cited in Ferdinand Augustijn Snellaert (ed.), *Nederlandsche gedichten uit de veertiende eeuw* (Brussels: M. Hayez, Drukker der Koninklijke Akademie, 1869), p. 372.

[5] Original text: 'oft ane hare vel ghenaeyt ware', cited in Léonce Reypens and Marcellus Schurmans (eds.), *Werken van Jan van Ruusbroec, Deel III* (Amsterdam and Mechlin: De Spieghel and Het Kompas, 1934), p. 118, translated as Jan van Ruusbroec, *Opera omnia*, vol. II: *Vanden seven sloten. De septem custodiis*, ed. G. de Baere (Turnhout: Brepols, 1989).

small, frequently decorated closures pointed the way towards a fashion that was 'receptive to accessories', a tendency that over the following centuries would only increase in importance.

The growing number of options that consumers could choose from the markets for durable consumer goods was the result of an entire series of product and process innovations. As we have illustrated for the pottery industry, both product type and workmanship, decoration and price tag were going through immense transitions, adapting to new expectations. The transition from the manuscript to the printed book is another well-known example, just as the printed engraving had previously opened up unprecedented possibilities for broader dispersal and other uses of the 'image' in society. The market for paintings, too, was able to develop into a kind of mass market only as a result of the fact that painters were able to step up their productivity by, among other things, starting to produce in series and by entering into collaborative connections that benefitted labour productivity. In the sixteenth century, large numbers of frequently inexpensive paintings were ready-made.

The same process was avidly applied to the market for clothing. By the fifteenth century, head coverings like caps and bonnets were made-to-stock and exported. A good example of this dedicated ready-made production can be found in the case of the Antwerp hat-maker Cornelis van Buyten (1568), who counted in his stock, among other things, 'twelve satin hats', 'three hundred and twenty children's hats' and 'three-and-twenty men's hats of fine felt'.[6] Even producers of other accessories, such as makers of stockings, purses, gloves, belts and maunches, were already venturing into serial production in the Middle Ages. As the sixteenth century progressed, ready-made clothing was increasingly offered on the market, and included even coats and cloaks. As a result of not having to be tailored to size and also because savings could be achieved in the elimination of contacts between client and clothier, ready-made clothing was of course much less expensive. Various levels of price and quality made their appearance, and more people gained access to items of clothing that had previously been expensive and exclusive.

Design

A conspicuous, common thread, not entirely distinct from the innovations in products and processes outlined above, is the increasing economic and cultural importance of design and decoration as a factor of

[6] State Archives Brussels, Kwitanties van de Rekenkamer te Brussel, T576 – 3614, fol. 1v (22 March 1568).

innovation. While even the earliest pieces of furniture – like, for example, the chests and trunks discussed above – were artfully decorated in one way or another, gradually the construction of furniture became finer, lighter and more varied; the woodcarving on *dressoirs* and cupboards became deeper and the compositions more light-hearted. In addition, new materials and techniques made their appearance, whereby domestic furniture contributed in an ever more expressly decorative manner to the layout of the rooms. In the second half of the sixteenth century, the rise of inlay techniques – the so-called *intarsia* – crossed over from Italy, and different pieces of diverse wood types were incorporated into mosaics – *marqueterie* – in furniture. Italian architectural treatises like those of Leon Battista Alberti (1404–72), Sebastiano Serlio (1475–1554) and Andrea Palladio (1508–80) not only inspired builders but also influenced the artistic production of furniture. New decorative styles and an extensive idiom of ornamentation were put into print by, among others, Cornelis Floris de Vriendt (1514–75) and Hans Vredeman de Vries (1526–1609). The latter – himself a cabinet-maker by training – published a book of models in 1573, with different pieces of furniture and decorative elements, especially for cabinet-makers, entitled: 'Various cabinetry such as portals, armoires, buffets, bed frames, tables, chests, chairs, benches, *sgabelli*, towel rails, "glasses-cupboards" and many other kinds of products, all being very nicely ordered and drawn' (*Verschyden schrijnwerck als portalen, kleerkasten, buffetten, ledikanten, tafels, kisten, stoelen, bancken, schabellen, hantdoex-rollen, glasberden en veel andre soorten van wercken, alles zeer aerdich geordonneert en geteyckent*).

The continuing changes in style and production could, coincidentally, provide for a good number of boundary disputes between the artisans' guilds. Returning to Bruges, there is an interesting example from the middle of the sixteenth century. In 1554, a dispute was fought out before the municipal aldermen's bench between the cabinet-maker Gillis vanden Coornhuuse and Pieter vander Heyde, dean of the turners' guild. The latter had dragged Gillis before the court because Gillis had made *and* sold a bed that was finished with turned posts. But turned products, so he argued, belonged traditionally to the domain of the turners' guild and not to that of the cabinet-makers. Gillis defended himself, though, by claiming that these posts were only a component or *accessoire* for the piece of furniture. The production of larger beds simply fell to the cabinet-makers' guild. Moreover, as Gillis contended,

those people from the turners' guild did not understand the craft of architecture to create these posts, here targeted by calumny, or any others properly and proportionally (making his defence this way), since there were diverse and distinct forms, the one Tuscan, the other Doric, the other Ionic, some Corinthian and some Composite.[7]

By his own account, he should thus be allowed to make turned woodwork, certainly for the sake of the aesthetics of the piece of furniture and by virtue of his underlying knowledge. The ultimate outcome was that the complaint by Vander Heyde as dean of the Bruges turners was rejected.

Yet, although these kinds of boundary disputes suggest the contrary, within a late medieval urban market structure, vertical and horizontal collaboration among the guilds and a certain commercial flexibility were still often necessary and practised. Moreover, in many cases the municipal government also tolerated such cooperation. This allowed more flexible reactions to the increased demand for new 'symbiotic products', such as painted mirrors, which were jointly fabricated by different guilds.

Perhaps no sector better illustrates the importance of this decorative tendency than the art sector itself, in which paintings had ultimately become an important element of interior design. It would be wrong, however, not to keep in mind the impact of other, more modest forms of decorative art. From the sixteenth century onwards, majolica pieces turn up more frequently in the probate inventories. In Antwerp, majolica makers, not coincidentally, came under the Guild of Saint Luke, associated with artists. Aesthetics and the cultural taste of both the producer and the consumer led the way in this sector, after all. Majolica from the southern Netherlands, also called *gleiswerk*, would become a preliminary high point of this new aesthetic and would find its way from here to north-west and northern Europe. In one of its earliest phases, this colourfully painted earthenware, covered with a tin glaze, was still imported from Spain and Italy. In the fourteenth century, primarily the noble and very affluent consumers would be able to take pleasure in this Mediterranean-imported product with its polychrome decoration. When a local majolica industry was set up in Antwerp under the influence of the Italian merchant Guido di Savino around 1508, this luxury product slowly but surely came within the reach of the urban middling groups.

---

[7] In the original: 'dat die van den ambochte van de draijers hemlieden niet en verstonden an de conste van architecture, omme behoorlicke ende proportionalicke (ghelijck hij verweerere dede) te werckene de ghecalengierde ofte andere pilaren, bij dat die waren van diversche ende distincte figuren, de eene Tuscania, de andere Dorica, de andere Ionica, de zommeghe Corinthia ende de zommeghe Composita', cited in Arthur Van De Velde, *De ambachten van de timmerlieden en de schrijnwerkers te Brugge, hun wetten, hun geschillen en hun gewrochten van de XIVe tot de XIXe eeuw* (Ghent: Koninklijke Vlaamse Academie voor Taal- en Letterkunde, 1909), pp. 144–5.

Archaeological finds suggest that majolica producers frequently began creating items of lower quality, with simple, geometric decorations. By bringing the pieces known as *biscuits*, which were fired only once and left unglazed, onto the market, they even offered majolica specifically for the less financially strong middling groups. Yet, inside the house, majolica frequently landed in places where it could be admired. Spots like the mantelpiece, where once goods of silver and pewter had been put out for show, were now also used to display the household's most exquisite majolica and porcelain.

Majolica platters demanded a certain *diligencia* from their users. Archaeologists have determined that the painted top surfaces of these plates often did not show any scratches, suggesting that they were used neither for cutting food nor as individual dinner plates at the table. Rather they were used for serving food or for showing status, when displayed on the *dressoir*. At the beginning of the seventeenth century, majolica's success story was cut short by the growing popularity of porcelain, which was initially imported into these lands bit by bit, but started to be shipped on a large scale from the Twelve Years' Truce (1609–21) onwards. Porcelain, 'Delftware' and faience would assume a central role in the so-called 'consumer revolutions' of the seventeenth and eighteenth centuries. Yet the economic and mental grid for this success had already been drawn up centuries before.

Extremely valuable and desirable silver objects were reserved for the better-off households only, yet from the middle of the fourteenth century onwards pewter objects, such as jugs and platters, became a desired alternative. Pewter products had the advantage of being resistant to the acids in certain foods, and meals served in pewter vessels also kept hot longer. Even so, a high price tag was still attached to the possession of pewter table- and serving-ware. Pewter was no precious metal, of course, but it had sufficient intrinsic value to fulfil monetary roles, just as silver did. 'Old products' (*oud werck*) could be melted down into new tableware at the smithy and, in this way, be made more valuable in accordance with the prevailing aesthetic parameters.

It was in the fifteenth century, in particular, that the social playing field of this formerly still quite exclusive tableware started to widen considerably as a result of a marked increase in purchasing power. As the 'silver of the middling groups', pewter reached more people, and it did so in larger quantities. Thus, for instance, the less well-off Catherine, widow of Jan de Rike from Bruges, possessed 'twelve pewter platters' in 1444.[8] In

---

[8] State Archives Brussels, Chambre de Comptes, n° 13774, 1444, fol. 40r-v: 'douze plateaulx d'estain'.

addition to three graduated pewter jugs, the well-to-do spouse of Jehan le Carlier, Tanne, possessed another 'six pewter plates'.[9] Even the less well-off townspeople started to afford pewter tableware for themselves from the fifteenth century onwards. In the case of the lower social classes of the urban populace, this table service would frequently be kept for special occasions or for display purposes, whereas a number of sixteenth-century inventories of wealthier Antwerp residents suggest that it was increasingly classed as standard equipment. Significantly, pewter objects were sometimes categorised under 'everyday goods' (*dagelijksen*). For the sixteenth century, it was primarily bowls, platters, saucières, spoons and smaller plates that translated the popularity of pewter onto the table. In particular, the very common pewter plates (*teljooren*) point to a more refined and individual food culture.

Social Boundaries

The relative prosperity of the urban populace and the increase in the array of choice for products in all price categories eventually provided for mobility and the transgression of social boundaries. Precisely because quite a few 'social boundaries' appeared to be on a loose footing, and because it is frequently unclear what different scholars mean by terms such as 'burgher', 'middling group', 'elite' and so forth, it is no sinecure to indicate exactly who consumed what. Clothing, for example, is particularly considered to be a reflection of someone's gender, marital status, moral identity and social standing. Yet the social reality is often shown to be much stronger than the moral norm. In everyday life, the use of clothing was so irregular and varied that a genuine consensus concerning who was allowed to wear what was never entirely reached. It was also common in that regard for the townspeople in the Low Countries to have considerable purchasing power. In the middle of the fifteenth century, Jan van Dixmude 'quoted' the French queen as allegedly saying in the year 1301 that 'the women of Flanders are clothed like queens and princesses'.[10] The quotation was recycled by the nineteenth-century Romantic author Hendrik Conscience, after which it began to lead a life of its own. Yet, while it has more to do with fiction than with history, the

---

[9] State Archives Brussels, Chambre de Comptes, n° 13773, 1441, fol. 95r–v: 'six plats d'estains'.
[10] In the original: 'de wyfs van Vlaenderen zin ghecleet ghelyc coninghinnen ende princessen', cited in Jean-Jacques Lambin (ed.), *Dits de Cronike ende Genealogie van den Prinsen ende Graven van den Foreeste van Buc dat heet Vlaenderlant, van 863 tot 1436, gevolgd naer het oorspronkelyk handschrift van Jan van Dixmude* (Ypres: Lambin en zoon, 1839), pp. 157–8.

clothing of well-to-do burghers from the major Flemish cities of Ghent, Bruges and Ypres – not coincidentally prominent centres of production for luxury textiles – must indeed have been lavish in this period. In areas like the Holy Roman Empire, Italy, France and Great Britain, numerous sumptuary laws were enacted, laws that laid down who was allowed to wear what and, above all, who was not allowed to wear some types of clothing. Such attempts to restrain social transgressions by means of legislative texts were virtually absent for the most part in the Low Countries, and the few examples that exist reflect protectionist concerns rather than social considerations.

Although the exact reason for this relative absence is not entirely clear, it cannot be ruled out that the strong position of towns in Flanders and Brabant with respect to their territorial lords was responsible to a certain degree. A case in point arose in 1497. In that year, Philip the Fair (1478–1506) drew up a sumptuary law that regulated the wearing of velvet and silk. Although the proposed aim of these laws was the protection of the local textile industry, in practice it was also the prince's intent to regulate the line dividing the clothing of the nobility and that of wealthier burghers. Strikingly enough, in their translation of this sumptuary law from 1497, the authorities in Bruges assumed that citizens (*poorters*), too, and even well-to-do artisans were allowed and able to permit themselves this kind of clothing. This was also the everyday reality. Non-ennobled families of *poorters*, traders and successful entrepreneurial artisans excelled in appropriating a material culture that reflected the ambition of *vivre noblement* ('living nobly'). The social acceptance of this lifestyle says much about the purchasing power of the wealthiest townspeople, though it is also true that outward appearances did not fundamentally contribute to the recognition of noble status.

The so-called social transgressions, to which sumptuary laws applied the brakes, were not only the result of increased purchasing power but also the effect of the lively markets for second-hand products. Clothing was expensive but also durable, such that it retained a large portion of its value. In auctions or in the shops of second-hand clothing sellers, garments could start a second, third or umpteenth life – eventually even outside their original social milieu. A few sumptuary laws, like those of Charles V (1500–58) in 1550, safeguarded the boundaries within the elites. Yet these laws completely missed the rise of less expensive woollen fabrics and linen, which by this time were, at the bottom of the market, fundamentally redefining the character of the concept of 'luxury' itself.

While the town exerted a great attraction for the nobility (see Chapter 3), 'urban nobility' also appealed to the lifestyle of the wider urban populace. Noblemen with town residences were a strong role model in social terms. In The Hague of the early fifteenth century, a man such as Frank van Borselen (*c.* 1395–*c.* 1470), count of Oostervant, lord of Voorne, Zuilen and Sint-Maartensdijk, led a conspicuous lifestyle in which, among other things, the display of precious silver and pewter played a major role, in addition to the requisite show of heraldry. Van Borselen had the grounds of his house in The Hague surrounded by a wall with crenellations and a gate, so making the contrast with the single-storey, wooden buildings in what was then still more a village immediately clear. Certainly from the middle of the fifteenth century onwards, the Burgundian process of state-building, as well as the ducal policy of maintaining a physical presence, provided a major stimulus for the luxury industries in the Low Countries themselves. Conspicuous careers in the service of the prince could result in ennoblement, as happened with Peter Bladelin (*c.* 1410–1472). He even achieved the foundation of the town of Middelburg (in Flanders), near his newly built castle. While the effects of such courtly manifestations were often less spectacular, they were no less important. Later on, court cities such as Mechelen and Brussels would be strongly stimulated by the presence of a residential court, as well as important central institutions (see Chapter 8).

It is clear, however, that the wealth of the material culture and product differentiation were, to an important extent, directed by the need to supply new social markets beyond the boundaries of the urban elites as well. Take again, for example, the market for paintings. Without denying the role of the nobility in developing new profane genres like the portrait, the landscape or the fauna painting, it is clear that urban middling layers played a key role in the increasing popularity of diverse new genres such as the landscape, the still life of the market or kitchen, the peasant satire and the genre painting. The typical town/burgher ethos was never far away in the sermonising morality piece, as it was marketed by Hieronymus Bosch (*c.* 1450–1516), for instance – imitated in Antwerp on a quasi-industrial scale. It was no coincidence, then, that research into probate inventories from the sixteenth century shows that the urban middling groups themselves constituted an extremely important sales market for the artistic production from these regions.

As previously discussed, majolica was brought onto the market in all kinds of variations and price bands. Something similar happened in the silk industry: in the course of the sixteenth century, the Low Countries developed their own alternative to Italian silk imports. Focussing on the domestic production of inexpensive silk resulted in more people being able to afford luxuries of this kind. This situation is also clearly shown in an analysis of the confiscated goods of Protestants fleeing the city in the years after the Iconoclasm (1566). In spite of the fact that quite a few of those people sentenced in absentia will have either taken things along with them in their flight or parted with them quickly, silk fabrics were anything but an exception in the households of Ghent and Antwerp. In both cities, even quite a few 'ordinary' shopkeepers and master artisans possessed silk. They owned small accessories as well as garments decorated with ribbons and trimmings, in addition to entire pieces of clothing, all of which were completely fabricated from both more and less precious silk fabrics.

Savoir Vivre

Yet consuming alone was not enough to gain social recognition, just as *vivre noblement* did not in any way suffice to gain access to the Second Estate. Much more was needed than merely a full purse for one to be able to belong to the core of urban society. When Albrecht Dürer (1471–1528) was the guest of local painters in Antwerp in 1520, he described with great amazement the silver service from which the food was dished out.[11] Yet, this kind of 'conspicuous display' of silver tableware was by no means a guarantee of social approval. Rather, according to an Antwerp etiquette book from 1484, it was above all the 'good manners one employs at table, whether man or woman, which are much better than silver or gold'.[12] As indicated earlier, social inequality and mechanisms for inclusion and exclusion were nurtured by codes of conduct and by culture, which people were able to acquire. Putting on a show, then, happened not so much with silver pitchers and platters as with bodily, 'mannered' actions. From the late fifteenth century onwards, as a result of the up-and-coming printing press, among other things, increasing numbers of treatises on civility appeared in the vernacular. The popularity of translated and repeatedly reprinted versions of the *De Civilitate Morum Puerilium Libellus* (1530) of Desiderius Erasmus (c. 1466–1536), and the *Galateo* (1558) by Giovanni Della Casa (1503–56) points to the growing interest from a broader audience in the subtle know-how of a well-mannered dining culture. In 1546, Erasmus' precepts even appeared in

---

[11] Albrecht Dürer, *Le Journal de voyage d'Albert Dürer dans les Anciens Pays-Bas (1520–1521)*, ed. Jan-Albert Goris and Georges Marlier (Brussels: La Connaissance, 1970), p. 58. See also Roger Fry (ed.), *Durer's Record of Journeys to Venice and the Low Countries* (Boston: Merrymount Press, 1913), p. 38.

[12] Cited in Christianne Muussers, 'Vette handen en vieze tafellakens' in Andrea van Leerdam, Orlanda Lie, Martine Meuwese and Maria Patijn (eds.), *Kennis in beeld. Denken en doen in de Middeleeuwen* (Hilversum: Verloren, 2014), p. 72: 'goede manieren, die welc men ter tafelen sal hantieren, het sy man oft wijff, ionck oft out, die veel beter sijn dan silver of gout'.

the vernacular in the form of a text with questions and answers, entitled *Goede manierlijcke seden* (roughly 'well-mannered customs'), a popular translation of his handbook in Latin from sixteen years before.

Certain topics were simply deemed necessary in the case of practising good table manners. So, for example, the development of the table knife and the tablespoon during the fifteenth century demanded some manual dexterity and, thus, the training of the table companion. In any case, the use of certain utensils almost automatically resulted in a slower food culture as well, which in turn was linked to refinement and distinction. Appropriate table manners *and* the accompanying tableware became important ingredients for an urban *habitus* in which status did not revolve so much around wealth or possession as around taste and cultural training. The importance can hardly be exaggerated: both in the private sphere and in public associations, for many years conviviality had already played a key role in forging social relationships and constructing identities.

The 'table' itself was seen as the symbol of sociability, of togetherness and – perhaps less explicitly – of Christian charity. It is not without reason that it also lies at the origins of urban institutions like 'table-master', 'poor table' and 'table of the Holy Ghost', which attempted to a certain extent to compensate for the lack of social security for widows, orphans and paupers. The great importance of conviviality is evident in the many (semi-)public banquets, feasts and drinking parties which maintained and strengthened the social fabric of the town. Occasionally that could also get out of hand: in the by-laws for the guilds of Saint-Omer (1072–83) and Arras, for example, quite a few rules are recorded for reining in physical and verbal violence induced by such joint drinking parties. Tellingly, the banquet for many corporate associations and confraternities was also an obligatory social investment. Many rhetoricians' chambers, guilds and confraternities seized on the festive banquet as a strategic instrument for their own objectives. So it was in 1498, for example, during a contest among town confraternities that De Fonteine ('The Fountain'), the rhetoricians' chamber in Ghent, organised a banquet for the other participating chambers. The Violieren ('Gillyflowers') from Antwerp, too, and the Peoene ('Peonies') from Mechelen 'nurtured' their social contacts annually by organising a festive banquet held outdoors. Yet not only on the public stage but also indoors, conviviality associated with dining played a central role.

The meaningful way in which people handled domestic objects can be revelatory for their cultural ideologies and social aspirations. In addition to an important symbolic and cultural value, many of these objects had a practical and functional value-in-use. An intriguing piece of furniture that serves as an illustration of this multi-layered nature of household objects is the bed. Beds can easily be seen as necessary basic furniture, yet they derived their value at least as much from their highly symbolic and emotional character. The high economic value of a bed had to do not only with the quality of the wood used for producing it but also with the bed linens. A number of sheets, a colourful bedspread, smaller head-cushions, a *peluwe* or larger cushion (akin to a 'pillow') to support those using it and also, in certain cases, a number of bed curtains all made up part of the standard bedclothes. Although beds could be quite expensive, most townspeople still had a respectable number of them in their houses, and until well into the sixteenth century it remained common to furnish more prestigious spaces with at least one bed. Since the social standing of the sleeper determined the shape, the material, the decoration and the location of the bed, the variation in the type of wood, in size and in workmanship was extensive. In this regard, the marriage bed was generally larger, furnished more richly with fabrics and placed closer to the fireplace than, for example, the beds of children, maidservants, pages, apprentices or occasional visitors.

In a number of towns, such as Oudenaarde, it was customary for a daughter to receive a bed and its appurtenances as a gift from her parent(s) or guardian on the occasion of her majority. This gift must be seen not only in an economic but also in a symbolic context. It is no coincidence either that furniture for sleeping, along with its concomitant linens, turns up with relative frequency in wills, where it is given to cherished family members and even to personal servants. It is striking in that regard how gender-sensitive such gifts could be. In most cases, beds and their appurtenances – sheets, bedspreads, cushions and pillowcases – were given to young female relatives, whereas young men were more readily remembered with clothing, money or tools. In the municipal customary law of Oudenaarde, among other towns, marriage itself was invariably expressed in terms of *bedde* ('bed'), as in 'father and mother being of undivided [i.e. same] bed' (*vader ende moeder 't bedde gheheel sijnde*) so as to indicate that the parents were joined in marriage. In other words, the bed was simply the symbol of the marriage, the house and the creation of a home. It is no wonder that, until well into the sixteenth century, bed frames fulfilled a prominent role in the more prestigious spaces of the house for receiving guests. They seem to have determined the reception ritual as well. In treatises on civility, the distance of a visitor with respect to the bed was taken as a measure of his or her degree of acceptance into the confidence of the household.

That material culture plays a key role in developing ideologies, role models, identities and power relationships is nowhere better illustrated than in dress. By the use of a specific colour and appliquéd insignia or emblems, clothing was frequently a visual confirmation of membership of guilds or confraternities and of administrative or military positions. Its signal value becomes very clear in the case of certain marginalised groups such as Jews, lepers and prostitutes, who by order of the municipality – and later also by order of the state – were obliged to wear certain recognisable insignia. In Mons (Bergen) in the fifteenth century, for example, 'girls of loose morals' had to wear an oblique yellow band on their right shoulder, while in Ghent in 1491, procurers and procuresses were sentenced to wearing a red band on the back of their sleeves.

The close link between dress and the performance of (a certain) identity is evident in the *Livre des trois vertus* (*Book of the Three Virtues*), in which Christine de Pizan (c. 1364–1430) reminds her readers that 'each woman [should] wear such clothing as indicates her husband's and her rank'.[13] When the Leiden University professor Paulus Merula wrote a letter to his bride-to-be in 1589, he worded it as follows: 'The task of the wife also consists of maintaining moderation in her clothing in accordance with her standing and the worthiness of her husband.'[14] The meaning that was assigned to clothing differed for men and women, although on a more subtle level. So, for example, the head covering of a woman (ideally) signalled her marital status. Well-off married women wore their best head scarves and prettiest headdresses on high holy days, and when they 'went a-dancing'. As a day-to-day head covering, the *hovetcleet* (literally 'head-cloth') remained the norm for the entire late Middle Ages. Even widows wore this modest head covering, as long as a *wimpel* (neck-cloth) was added that covered the throat. Dark, austere clothing and the *falie* – a mostly black cloth mantle worn over the head and shoulders – were found with strikingly higher frequency in the probate inventories of widows.

Over the course of the sixteenth century, the head covering of women became noticeably freer and lighter – a development that had already made its appearance in the fifteenth century, albeit in a minor way. The veils that covered the throat and neck were omitted with increasing frequency, and instead of an entire *hovetcleet* smaller cowls and caps came into use. Young, unmarried girls mostly wore their hair uncovered, either

---

[13] Christine de Pisan, *The Treasure of the City of Ladies: Or the Book of the Three Virtues*, ed. and trans. Sarah Lawson, rev. edn (London: Penguin, 2003), p. 149. The original French text appears in Christine de Pisan, *Le Livre des trois vertus*, ed. Charity Cannon Willard (Paris: Champion, 1989), p. 178.

[14] Cited in *Kronijk van het Historisch Gezelschap te Utrecht, Vierde Jaargang* (Utrecht: Kemink en zoon, 1848), p. 80: 'De taak van de vrouw bestaat ook hieruit dat ze matigheid houdt in haar kleding al naargelang haar status en de waardigheid van haar man.'

loose or in braids. Overall, for women, clothing seems to have played a key role in expressing sexual chastity. Any outfit that was too sumptuous inevitably evoked an image of impurity. 'Great dishonour and shame befalls women who find pleasure in being dressed posh and made up.' Those are the words of Christine de Pizan in her *Livre de la Cité des Dames* (*Book of the City of Ladies*), which became quite popular in its Middle Dutch translation as well. 'For,' she continues, 'one says that they do that to draw the attention of men and have them fall in love with them.'[15]

Material Culture and the City

Although more research is needed, we have been able to unveil the interplay between urban societies of the Low Countries before 1600, their diversified goods and service economies, and the specific models of both conduct and consumption that developed there. In contrast to what current historiography would have us believe, no sharp break is discernible between urban patterns of consumption in the Low Countries of the Middle Ages through the 'long' sixteenth century and those of the 'consumer revolutions' of the seventeenth and eighteenth centuries. In the medieval town, the house gradually became the setting for a fashionable and more diversified material culture. Apart from social polarisation, the late medieval and sixteenth-century town also welcomed growing possibilities for social mobility. In the long run, this meant that the new material culture derived its strength not just from the conspicuous consumption pattern of the wealthier urban elites – with or without their aspirations to nobility. Rather, the middling groups, too, claimed their place as consumers, both of luxury goods and of less expensive alternatives that were coming onto the market.

The experience of the historian who, from a distance, takes the measure of processes that flow across centuries differs fundamentally

---

[15] Cited in Noor Versélewel de Witt Hamer and Miriam Oort (eds.), *De stede der vrauwen. Een diplomatische transcriptie van de Middelnederlandse vertaling (1475) van Christine de Pizans 'Livre de la cité des dames' (1405)*, unpublished text, digitally available at: www.dbnl.org/tekst/pisa001nver01_01/ and as a PDF file at: www.dbnl.org/tekst/pisa001nver01_01/pisa001nver01_01.pdf, fol. 246r: 'groote onneere ende schaemte zo gheeft men toe alzulke vrauwen die hem zeluen verwanen ende vermaken zo vutnemende zo propre te wezene van hueren habijten ende van hueren pareerselen. want men zegt dat doen omme de aentreckelheden vanden mannen. ende omme die te bringhene tot hueren minnen' (last accessed 13 May 2016). An English edition of this text can be found in Christine de Pisan, *The Book of the City of Ladies*, ed. and trans. Earl Jeffrey Richards, rev. edn (New York: Persea, 1998).

from that of the contemporary. Throughout the entire period, all manner of goods – even gifts – fulfilled crucial monetary roles, much more so than is customary today. They could be used for giving, bartering, pawning, selling, stealing and then fencing. The importance of that monetary convertibility is nicely shown in wills and testaments, in which children, family members, servants or friends were frequently remembered with a cherished object. In Ghent on 20 January 1410, the widow of Gheeraard van Ghistele remembered her maidservant with the following: a garment with coloured or grey-coloured lining, or 30 shillings Flemish.[16] In addition to the inevitable symbolic and emotional values that these kinds of testamentary dispositions represented, it is striking that the gifts were often expressed quite dispassionately in monetary equivalents as well. The beneficiaries of these bequests were able to draw the equivalent value in money without much difficulty. Similarly, it happened that an eminent guest who had received a silver platter as a gift from the municipal government in Antwerp promptly converted that same platter to its sales value without evidently insulting his hosts by doing so.

Yet, as the array of material products became more varied and complex, and as decoration and design began to play a bigger role to the detriment of the intrinsic quality of the raw materials used in furniture and clothing, the product market lost much of its medieval 'transparency'. More generally speaking, changes in fashion and social transgressions continually evoked resistance and even moral indignation – a fact nicely illustrating how cultural 'legibility' was not always as great for everyone in terms of the changing material culture. On the contrary, consuming had to be learned. As times advanced, the accent shifted perhaps even more from mere 'possessing' towards proper 'using' – the tasteful way in which goods were taken care of – and towards manners that could be shown by correctly using and discussing those things. While goods might perhaps have been more affordable, taste could frequently throw up a subtle yet at least as effective social barrier. What is more, as material culture began to presuppose increasingly refined behavioural repertoires or knowledge of aesthetic norms, it often became an additional social barrier. Between town and country, for instance, major differences arose. These were articulated in the same way (and to a certain degree

---

[16] 'Item ghevic joncfrouw die tot doot van mi met my wonen sal I keerel met bonte of grauwe ofte 30 schellingen groot der over.' Cited in Julie De Groot, 'Zorgen voor later? De betekenis van de dienstperiode voor jonge vrouwen in het laatmiddeleeuws Gent herbekeken', *Stadsgeschiedenis*, 6.1 (2011), p. 14.

materially as well) in cultural codes, such as marginalising the peasant as coarse and uncivilised (see Chapter 3).

In that regard, it is also immediately clear that the history of material culture cannot be reduced to a narrative of changing technologies, industrial reconversions, relative prices and monetary equivalents. Major cultural and social movements leave traces behind in a changing idiom of materiality. It is no coincidence that the fifteenth century, with its religious internalising, simultaneously prompted a strong externalising of religious behaviour (see Chapter 5), and was equally characterised by the mass production of devotional collectables. At the dining table, the idiom of style in the changing food culture gave direction to sociability, and vice versa. The medieval house not only underwent an important 'change towards stone' – a literal 'petrification' – but in terms of material design it was also a home in which a variegated palette of values was utilised and aspired to. This shift entailed much more than what was merely socially representative, which, for the sake of simplicity, historians have frequently reduced it to.

At the heart of this narrative stands the burgher, who is admittedly vaguely defined in the current state of research. In particular, few documents have been transmitted from poorer families who often sublet a room in impoverished circumstances, simply because they left nothing behind that was worth recording, bequeathing, stealing, reselling or recycling. Comparable inequalities can also be registered within the urban hierarchy and geography of the Low Countries. Quite a few economic historians acknowledge a gradual process of economic polarisation, as, for example, in the case previously described, whereby 'Spanish' chairs still emerged at first, and above all, in sixteenth-century Antwerp. In particular, the genuine luxury industries became increasingly monopolised by the larger towns, enjoying considerable 'economies of agglomeration' in the urban hierarchy. Something similar – *mutatis mutandis* – seems to have played on the demand side as well. Inhabitants of Middelburg in Zeeland, for example, bought their most exclusive luxury objects in the larger cities of the river Scheldt delta basin, such as Antwerp or Ghent, where they also found a kind of cultural model.

It would be wrong to coin local differences in material culture exclusively in terms of being ahead or lagging behind. Yet it is well known that emigrants from Flanders and Brabant who found a new place to live in Holland after 1585 distinguished themselves from the local population through their material culture and codes of conduct. The silk clothing, paintings and other exquisite things they sometimes brought with them were perceived by some as refined, by others as rather conceited and arrogant. In no time, however, the 'Brabantine model' became the trendsetter in the northern Netherlands. All of these phenomena demonstrate that the material culture of the Low Countries in the Middle Ages and the 'long' sixteenth century went at different speeds temporally, socially and spatially. The larger towns of the southern Netherlands, with their luxury and rural industries, had been at the geographic core for a long time. It is there that the foundation was laid for the 'new luxury' consumption model that would become so important in seventeenth-century Holland.

8 Education and Knowledge: Theory and Practice in an Urban Context

Bert De Munck and Hilde de Ridder-Symoens

In 1892, in his history of the origins of the University of Douai, founded in 1559, the French historian Georges Cardon wrote about the Renaissance and the state of schools in the Low Countries in the first half of the sixteenth century:

> The French Renaissance is the history of a school or of a few writers. In the Low Countries the Renaissance is the history of an entire people. No great names – if we except Erasmus – no great literary works; poets few in number and without talent; yet, by contrast, many scientists, scholars, writers, as well as useful institutions, printing presses, schools, rhetoricians' chambers. The culture of the mind scarcely seems to fit this people of artisans, merchants or municipal administrators. What do they look for in a book? Information rather than any intellectual pleasure. It has value only as a practical instrument or a political weapon.[1]

This quotation does a good job of summing up the components that have to be taken into account in a chapter about training and education in the Low Countries and the role of towns and townspeople in it. It suggests that there was a relatively broad base of literate, skilled and educated people in the towns of the Low Countries, but that they thought principally in terms of practicality and functionality. Indeed, more recent research has shown that urban culture in the Low Countries was especially receptive both to neo-Latin influences from humanists and to the development of literature and scholarship in the vernacular. In that culture it was not just a matter of 'trickle-down processes' but also of

---

[1] 'La Renaissance Française est l'histoire d'une école ou de quelques écrivains. Dans les Pays-Bas, la Renaissance est l'histoire de tout un peuple. Pas de grands noms, si nous exceptons Érasme, pas de grandes œuvres littéraires; des poètes peu nombreux et sans talent; au contraire, beaucoup de savants, d'érudits, d'écrivains, et d'institutions utiles, imprimeries, écoles, chambres de rhétorique. La culture de l'esprit ne semble guère convenir à ce peuple d'artisans, de marchands ou d'administrateurs de cités. Que cherchent-ils dans un livre? Des renseignements plutôt qu'un agrément pour l'esprit. Il n'a de valeur que comme instrument de travail ou arme de parti.' Georges Cardon, *La Fondation de l'Université de Douai* (Paris: Alcan, 1892), pp. 1–2.

Figure 8.1 Woodcut from the Antwerp guild of Saint Luke, first half of the sixteenth century. Allegorical representation of the Antwerp guild of Saint Luke and the chamber of rhetoric De Violieren (which was incorporated in the painters' guild). In the middle, Saint Luke is painting the Blessed Virgin with Christ. Above this scene is De Violieren's motto 'Gathered out of benevolence' ('Wt ionsten versaemt'). This image is framed by female representations of the virtues of Memory and Eloquence and of two of the liberal arts, Music and Rhetoric. Below, the coats of arms of Antwerp are shown together with a winged ox, which also refers to Saint Luke. This representation expresses the intellectual ambitions in the milieu of visual artists and rhetoricians.

developments in which the gap was closed from the bottom up between the development of the mind and the more practical aspects of administration and production.

From a political perspective it is striking that the urban nuclei playing a central role in this book were characterised by hybrid forms of administration, in which representatives from the noble elites, patricians, jurists and artisans rubbed shoulders (see Chapter 4). From an economic point of view, these individuals are well known for developing luxury and service industries, such as the medical sector (see Chapter 2). This situation, too, led to cross-fertilisation between the world of the mind and the world of practical action. As will be seen below, the development of new technologies and products went hand in hand with a rapprochement between the liberal and the mechanical arts. Whereas a number of artists and wealthier or better-trained artisans acquired aspirations to belong to the learned and literate world of the liberal arts, the physical and manual knowledge of the mechanical arts gradually came to be seen as a legitimate form of access to the knowledge of divine creation.

In addition, it is important to bear in mind that these developments played out over the long term. This chapter will make clear that what are known as the Renaissance and humanism must not be understood as a fault line but, on the contrary, need to be situated within a broader tradition of the development of knowledge in the towns of the Low Countries. Moreover, it will argue that a juxtaposition between intellectual developments and transformations in the application of that knowledge must not be taken as a point of departure. On the one hand, intellectual currents like humanism and the Reformation strongly influenced (artistic) production as well as political and legal administration. On the other hand, merchants and municipal authorities frequently provided the stimulus for innovation in knowledge by way of investment in the training of engineers and skilled labourers. They founded municipal schools, colleges and libraries, as well as becoming patrons of knowledge that could be applied in shipbuilding, navigation, cartography, mathematics and optics, instrument manufacture, hydraulic engineering, surveying, architecture, mining and so on.

The university towns of Leuven and above all Leiden, after 1575, played a very important role in all this, as did the printers' town of Antwerp. Moreover, genuine mediators between the 'learned intellectual workers' and the 'manual workers' are to be found among the artists. During the fifteenth and sixteenth centuries, a great many of them gradually distanced themselves from 'manual labourers' and, under the influence of humanism, began to align themselves with the world of letters. Together with other skilled artisans they associated in rhetoricians' chambers – among other organisations – and formed the guilds for *amateurs* of drama and poetry. Other groups of mediators were the printers and publishers, always searching for new printing techniques and frequently forming the axis of an intellectual network; and schoolmasters, who might be organised into a craft guild (as in Antwerp and Middelburg), but who at the same time were supervised by an ecclesiastical representative who had to keep watch over 'proper doctrine'.

Perhaps the most important form of learning, certainly in quantitative respects, was the practical, manual learning on the shop floor, which was omnipresent long before the existence of the so-called 'Latin' (i.e. humanities-oriented) schools, universities and rhetoricians' chambers. From an economic perspective, 'learning while doing' was a necessity for many, because children who went to school cost a lot of money, not only directly but also by way of income foregone. On the shop floor, learning happened via 'trial and error', which is certainly not to say that it was of less value because of that. Recent research has even indicated that the scientific revolution during the seventeenth century has to be understood precisely as a bottom-up process, in which the practical knowledge of artisans and artists was of great importance. After all, the scientific revolution can be summarised as a shift from deductive thinking and dialectic reasoning towards generating knowledge by means of experimentation and observation, two practices which artisans and artists had been good at as early as the Middle Ages. Moreover, 'learning while doing' does not rule out the fact that there were handwritten sets of instructions in the vernacular circulating in the day-to-day practice of, for example, medicine.

In short, it is important to look at the development of knowledge in towns in an integrated manner as well as over the longer term, paying attention both to teaching and training practices and also to institutional developments. Hereafter this examination will be carried out, successively, for primary education; learning on the shop floor; reading culture and the practical use of books; secondary education (in the humanities); and higher (university) education. In each section we will examine the role of urban actors and institutions as well as the tensions between intellectual knowledge and practical training. The last section will look at intellectual activity in secular and ecclesiastical courts and the interaction between court, university and town.

Reading, Writing and Arithmetic

Given the decentralised political structures and the relatively high degree of political participation from middling groups in the Low Countries, literacy was a necessary skill for many. In addition, certain economic activities compelled merchants and artisans to acquire skills in reading, writing and arithmetic. Around the year 1200 a merchant from Huy sent his son Abundus to the Abbey of Villers in Brabant 'in order to become competent there in conducting commercial transactions as well as recording notes on his father's debts'.[2] The son fell under the spell of monastic life and belles-lettres (or *bonae litterae*) to such an extent that, to the great displeasure of his father, he declined to become a merchant, choosing instead to be a monk. For the merchant father from Hoei, the problem was that at that time he had no option other than a monastery school or a canons' chapter: they had a monopoly on education until parish schools were set up in the newer towns. The only alternative for the merchant was to hire a cleric as a private teacher. To prevent their sons from taking up a religious vocation, then, and chiefly to enable them to receive instruction that was genuinely useful for any future merchant-entrepreneur or master artisan, a number of townspeople lobbied for a new type of school.

The solution was to take the organisation of education into their own hands. That task was not simple, however, because it affected the monopoly position of the Church. As early as the last quarter of the twelfth century, a struggle broke out between the comital collegiate chapter of Saint Pharaildis, attached to the court of the count of Flanders, and the patriciate in Ghent concerning the right to hold classes. What this group needed was for its sons to learn reading, writing, arithmetic, bookkeeping and correspondence in the vernacular, as well as for them to acquire enough Latin for administration and international trade; religious instruction was not a priority for urban burghers during this period. In Ghent, as in most towns, a compromise was reached. In addition to the official schools of the parish, the chapter and the monastery or convent, which were all hugely expanding their curriculum offerings, anyone who considered himself or herself competent to do so was free to open a school. To that end, a prospective 'free' schoolmaster (or schoolmistress) made a contract with the municipal magistracy. The agreement set out the rights and duties of both sides in writing. The so-called *scholaster* or 'scholastic' – a canon from a chapter who was responsible for the

---

[2] Cited in Henri Pirenne, 'L'instruction des marchands au Moyen Age', *Annales d'histoire économique et sociale*, 1 (1929), p. 20.

instruction – or the pastor retained the right to visitation, and the schoolmaster or schoolmistress had to hand over a percentage of his or her earnings to the chapter or presbytery.

In this way, during the Middle Ages, facilities for education were established in almost all towns for boys and girls, rich or poor. Elementary education was provided in the so-called *cleyne* (i.e. 'small') school or, *Dietsche* (= Dutch-language) lower or primary school, also called the 'writing school' (*schrijfschool*). There, both boys and girls learned reading, writing and, in the event, arithmetic in the vernacular. Religion was of course also part of the programme, and in the better schools some Latin was taught. In addition, certain schoolmasters began to cater specifically for traders, entrepreneurs and artisans. In the Dutch-language area, these kinds of schools were called *French* or *Walloon* schools (*Fransche* or *Walsche scholen*) because French was also part of the programme. Thanks to the existence of a schoolmasters' guild owning a wealth of documents, there is a lot of information about the sixteenth-century curriculum offerings in the commercial metropolis of Antwerp, including an indication of the textbooks used. In addition to modern languages (French, German, Italian, Spanish, English), bookkeeping, commercial accounting, geography, correspondence and courses of that sort were offered. In the seventeenth century these vocational schools flourished hugely in the north, though they died back in the south.

In Flanders, Brabant and Hainaut, private initiative played a major role in the development of primary education, as records for towns such as Douai, Lille, Valenciennes, Oudenaarde, Bruges and Ghent show. That does not mean that the municipal authorities did not supervise curriculum offerings and their quality. Certainly, from the fifteenth century onwards, such aspects were watched over so that as many children as possible might enjoy education. Guardians of orphans or semi-orphans, for example, had to promise to 'make the children go to school to learn virtue and honour'.[3] In cases where parents were not able to underwrite this elementary education, the towns provided free instruction. A town either paid a salary to a municipal educator (male or female), or it paid the cost of tuition to independent or 'free' schoolmasters. It was the municipal authorities in the northern provinces, though, which had the largest revenues, where more public municipal schools were established or more parochial schools were taken over. For example, shortly after 1400, Gouda's magistracy guaranteed to a schoolmaster named Kerstkyn an income equivalent to the tuition of 300 pupils.

---

[3] Cited in Marianne Danneel, *Weduwen en wezen in het laat-middeleeuwse Gent* (Leuven and Apeldoorn: Garant, 1995), p. 30: 'ter scolen doen gaen, duecht ende eere leeren'.

New humanist views concerning the duty of authorities to train their populations to be virtuous, dutiful and industrious subjects were introduced, mainly in the first half of the sixteenth century. Humanist pedagogues, however, pretty much exclusively concerned themselves with the humanities and university education. Their interest in elementary education centred in particular around poor relief and codes of conduct, which were supposed to instil etiquette and a sense of citizenship into pupils. They hardly ever expressed themselves concerning vocational education. Under the influence of humanists like Juan Luis Vives (1492/3–1540), the author of *De subventione pauperum* (1526), they saw to it, above all, that those in need were employed. To that end, begging was forbidden and support was provided only to those paupers who were incapable of working (see Chapter 3). By extension, occupational training, including apprenticeship contracts, was encouraged, and many towns established vocational schools for orphans and those without (financial) means. To what extent even the poorest were encouraged to learn reading and writing remains to be seen. Some orphanages saw to it that their children acquired these basic skills, yet contracts for apprenticeships and outsourcing show that such acquisition was frequently limited to a few hours' worth of lessons on Sundays in connection with religious instruction. In other words, rather than emancipation by way of education, the Sunday schools seem to have revolved around a kind of disciplinary activity instead. In any case, on the shop floor the task of the poor and of orphans was frequently the carrying out of simple and low-paid preparatory work, in the textiles sector, among other industries.

In many other jobs, the ability to read and write was often not needed, in view of the infrequent use of handbooks and sets of instructions – at least by those pupils who would not have the chance of ever becoming master artisans themselves. But for others, reading, writing and arithmetic were necessary basic skills. While independent entrepreneurs needed to keep up a system of bookkeeping – however rudimentary it might be – there were practice-oriented works in circulation for people from specific artisans' circles: guidebooks for surgeons and midwives, medical instructions concerning pestilence and pharmaceutical prescriptions, merchants' and artisans' textbooks, dictionaries and language books, surveying books and so forth. Altogether, then, large groups of artisans seem to have been capable of reading and writing and seem to have had a basic knowledge of arithmetic. It was among the unskilled labourers that genuine illiteracy was mainly found.

This is not to say, however, that craft guilds themselves encouraged reading and writing. In the fifteenth century in the painters' guild in Ghent, masters were obliged to teach their apprentices to read and write, albeit for extra payment. Yet that kind of remuneration was an exception. The teaching of those skills took place primarily in the smaller schools mentioned earlier, by private schoolmasters. That was also true for orphans, foundlings or poor children, who were placed with a master artisan by parochial charities. In the *Bogardenschool* (a municipal school for the poor) in Bruges, for example, regular education ended at the age of thirteen. In accordance with his aptitude, a young man was then contracted to a master to learn a vocation.

Teaching and Discipline

Despite the growing laicisation of education during the Middle Ages, religious authorities never lost their influence on educational activity, while the Reformation also provoked a lot of tensions. Heresy trials show that many of those from the middling groups – and chiefly from the artisans' milieu – were tried for the crime of reading and possessing heretical books (see Chapter 5). According to his trial dossier, Hector van Dommele, a hat-maker (*bonnetier*) who was actively involved in the first evangelical group in Bruges around 1525, read Latin and could cite numerous biblical texts with references from memory. He possessed an extensive library containing primarily Lutheran writings. No wonder that the Catholic and later also the Protestant authorities emphasised the importance of education. In their schools, young minds were prepared and trained for the priesthood or the ministry, and brothers for monastic orders were recruited from various social groups. Even the secular authorities were aware of the possibilities that education offered for cultivating a sense of citizenship, a work ethic and codes of conduct. In other words, training, education, edification and discipline are difficult to distinguish from one another.

The Brethren of the Common Life (see Chapter 5), who fought for the education of those with few opportunities, perhaps best personified this complexity in educational philosophy. Unique to their system was the fact that, instead of genuine schools, they founded boarding houses, also called *bursae* or *convicts*, the latter term deriving from the Latin for 'living together' or 'society' (*convictus*). Thus, the Brethren set up homes for poor students (*domus pauperum*) in Delft, Deventer, Gouda, Utrecht, Doesburg, Nijmegen, Groningen, 's-Hertogenbosch, Liège and Brussels, among other places. In some towns, in addition to the home for poor children, they ran a home for paying schoolchildren (*domus divitum*), as in 's-Hertogenbosch. The pupils in these boarding schools led a monastic life; discipline was strict and daily life was inspired by religion. Erasmus, who had himself gone to schools run by the Brethren in Deventer and 's-Hertogenbosch, had bad memories of them. The boarders in the *convicten* of the Brethren of Common Life went to local schools. Whereas well-off children paid the regular tuition fees, the brothers themselves provided the school fees for poor children.

Special measures existed even before this time for poor children, but that did not stop education for them remaining firmly tied to the business cycle. If things went well economically, many children took lessons. In periods of crisis, though, there was not only not enough money to pay tuition fees, but children also had to earn money themselves from a very young age. Schooling came second in that case. In order to deal with this problem, from the thirteenth century onwards schools for the poor were established in most towns across the Low Countries. These were often called *écoles des Bons Enfants* or, transposing the French into the vernacular, *Bonnefanten-* or *Bonifantenschool*. The teachers were on the payrolls of the towns. These schools mostly combined instruction in reading and writing with vocational education. Under the influence of new notions concerning poor relief and regulations about begging, their numbers increased hugely in the sixteenth century (see Chapter 3). The duty to set up a school for the poor in each parish – or, if such did not exist, to provide free education to poor children – was even included in the decrees of the Council of Trent (1545–63). Parents who did not send their children to school were excluded from receiving alms.

The major entanglement between teaching and religious edification resulted in gratis education in day schools as well as in Sunday schools. Antwerp got its first Sunday school in 1526, and Emperor Charles V would expand this form of education across all the Low Countries by ordinance in 1531. Poor children who could not go to school during the week had to receive free elementary education and religious instruction on Sundays and holidays. The provincial Council of Mechelen (1570) stipulated that each parish was obliged to set up a Sunday school, which would include instruction in reading and writing. In 1565 Tournai began to make up for the continuing lack of day schools. There, boys and girls between the ages of seven and fourteen received lessons in reading, writing and the catechism on Sundays. Even adults who had not had any schooling at all were able to receive religious and moral education in addition to lessons in reading and writing.

All of this had little to do with the development of (applied) scientific and technological knowledge. Humanists like Vives were also concerned about primary vocational training. In the fifteenth and sixteenth centuries, the need was increasingly felt for adequate vocational education, yet even that was primarily instigated for social and moral motives. For that reason, homes for orphans and foundlings established occupational schools of their own. Boys and girls were educated in religion, reading and writing, but they learned a trade there as well. By teaching a craft, these schools wanted in fact to be self-sustaining. Under the direction of overseers, boys learned baking, brewing, tailoring or making shoes, for example. The intention was that these boys would later find work as artisans or in industrial centres. In separate schools, girls received education in sewing, knitting, washing, ironing and other domestic skills, equipping them for work in the textiles sector or as domestic help. In practice, though, these occupational schools were not a great success, and they were anything but flourishing. It proved to be more profitable to place children into apprenticeships with private craftsmen and women. This system was especially expanded during the early modern era, which led to the exploitation of cheap child labour.

Vocational Education: Learning on the Shop Floor and the Role of Craft Guilds

The most widespread form of learning was no doubt learning on the shop floor, and by trial and error. This frequently took place in one's own father's business and thus formed part of the broader training for becoming a respectable burgher. If one was not taught in the family business, then not only did training take place under another master, but the apprentice frequently lodged with him as well. In that case the master acted to a certain extent as a substitute father – *in loco parentis* – such that there was once again a kind of far-reaching connection between training and upbringing. That tie made sense from an economic point of view because artisans guaranteed the quality of their products not only by their skills but also by their honesty. What counted for their clients was principally the intrinsic value of those products: that is to say, the quality and the content of the raw materials they used. Frequently that quality was difficult to judge with the naked eye – consider alloy in the case of silver, the proportion of tin to lead in pewter, the type of wood used and so on – such that the client depended on the trustworthiness of the manufacturer.

For the majority of artisans, learning was based on fairly matter-of-fact written or verbal agreements that differed in accordance with the context and the power relations at the time. The length of the apprenticeship, the size of the apprenticeship fees, the terms of payment, the responsibilities in case of the illness of the apprentice or the death of the master, and clauses in connection with breach of contract were all negotiated between two private parties, namely, the master and the parents or guardians of the apprentice. Moreover, the length of the apprenticeship was linked not only to the instructional content and the trade's degree of difficulty but also to the finances of the apprentice's parents or guardians. Poorer apprentices were sometimes apprenticed for longer periods and paid their masters in the form of free labour after they had learned the craft. Another continually recurring source of concern was breach of contract, which could be counteracted by requiring payment to be made beforehand or by clauses that stipulated that the apprenticeship fees still needed to be paid if the apprentice ran off. For his part, the master guaranteed that the apprentice would indeed be taught and that he would not be exploited by being required to carry out merely repetitive or domestic tasks.

In the course of the fifteenth and sixteenth centuries, this system was standardised and institutionalised to an increasing degree by the craft guilds. Gradually an obligatory minimum term for apprenticeships (which was the same for everyone in the same guild in the same town) was required, as well as a standard master's test. Given these uniform practices, according to some economic historians craft guilds supposedly guaranteed that apprentices would not run off prematurely. Among other things, the obligatory term of apprenticeship and the frequently recurring prohibition in the statutes against recruiting runaway apprentices (or against snatching them away by offering better contractual provisions) would have seen to it that masters were certain of a return on their investment. For their part, apprentices would have been better protected against exploitation thanks to the required masterpiece, whereby the instructional content was objectified.

It is far from certain, however, that the introduction of a formal apprenticeship system by craft guilds can be entirely ascribed to the economic need to overcome the mistrust between the apprentice's connections and the master – even more so, given the fact that more often than not there are no quantitative data concerning breach of contract and the average length of apprenticeship. Qualitative research even suggests that requiring a uniform term of apprenticeship and a standardised master's trial also had something to do with overseeing entry into the group as well as into the town. In the earliest ordinances of craft guilds (from the fourteenth and fifteenth centuries) there is as yet no discussion of any required term of apprenticeship or of any uniform master's trial. In Antwerp, the administrators of the craft guild were originally only obliged to let the municipal government know whom they were allowing to enter. An equal minimum term of apprenticeship for each new master does not appear in the ordinances until sometime during the fifteenth century.

There is frequently no talk of any masterpiece, either. In general, a uniform and standardised 'master's test' was not introduced until the (long) sixteenth century, and most probably has to be linked to the disappearance or failure of a number of informal mechanisms for entering a profession, rather than to an inadequate system for learning on the shop floor. Artisans often had to deal with attempts by alien or 'false' entrepreneurs and traders to meddle with the production themselves. Instead of merely buying products from masters, they tried to recruit apprentices, journeymen and frequently also other masters. For this last problem, a required term of apprenticeship and a uniform masterpiece seem to have offered a solution. Such requirements served to prevent traders or other 'false' entrepreneurs from being able to become masters themselves after the obligatory term of apprenticeship by means of fictitious contracts with a master. Even the fact that apprentices lodged with their masters as required by the craft guilds needs at least in part to be interpreted in this framework.

These developments formed part of a broader trend towards textualisation, formalisation and bureaucratisation in urban society (see Chapter 4). Craft guilds cultivated values like equality, mutual assistance and 'friendship', and in that spirit they organised collective activities such as masses and festivals for their patron saints. In the fifteenth and sixteenth centuries, these values were already coming under considerable pressure, however. Contributions in kind for the patron saints' festivals, such as wine and wax, were replaced by monetary contributions to the funds of the craft guild or to the poor box, while collective activities like banquets were done away with. In the meantime, maximum limits on the size of businesses were lifted; thus differences between large and small masters were permitted. In the northern provinces, where, owing to later urbanisation, the artisans' trades were in any case less anchored in urban society and municipal political structures, the religious and cultural dimensions of craft guilds entirely disappeared into the background after the Reformation. There the emphasis came to lie much more on poor relief.

Concerning the nature of knowledge in a narrower sense, learning on the shop floor was mostly limited to what Joel Mokyr calls 'prescriptive knowledge', that is, knowing how something has to be done in order to achieve a certain result, without understanding via the physical sciences why a certain effect results (so-called 'propositional knowledge').[4]

---

[4] Joel Mokyr, *The Gifts of Athena: Historical Origins of the Knowledge Economy* (Princeton: Princeton University Press, 2002).

Traditionally, it has been assumed that there was a strong distinction made in the Middle Ages between the liberal and the mechanical arts, whereby the mechanical arts occupied an inferior position. That did not stop the relationship between the two being subject to change. Whereas the accumulation of knowledge for most townspeople was a physical (tactile and visual) process in which dealing and becoming familiar with raw materials played a central role, from the thirteenth century onwards there were certainly intellectuals whose interests went further. Like the Franciscan brother Roger Bacon (*c.* 1214–1294), they were interested in the mechanical arts on account of the importance of experimentation – not just for the sake of societal well-being but also because it offered access to divine grace. From the late fifteenth century, in particular, the distinction between university-trained intellectuals and artisans came under pressure.

In the medical sector, among others, a kind of rapprochement took place between practical and intellectual knowledge. A number of surgeons distanced themselves not only from quack doctors but also from barbers and surgeons who limited themselves to blood-letting, removing kidney and bladder stones and other manual operations, without knowledge of the classical Galenic theories or of Latin. The former group sometimes took lessons at university or, more informally, with academically trained physicians or *doctores*. Between 1538 and 1542 in Antwerp, there was even a surgeons' school established within the surgeons' guild. Central to this training were the anatomy lessons that student surgeons had to have with the *prelector* (a sworn town physician) for two years. Even university-trained physicians looking for practical experience took these anatomy lessons. This training took place under the aegis of, among others, Andreas Vesalius (1514–64), a physician from Brabant who called Galenic teachings into question by way of experimentation and observation. A subsequent step in this professionalisation and quality control was the establishment of *collegia medica* during the seventeenth century. Physicians in Antwerp started the initiative with the establishment of the first municipal medical college in 1620, of which recognised medical care providers (physicians, surgeons and apothecaries) were members. The Antwerp initiative was imitated in most large towns and a few smaller ones, in both the south and the north.

In artists' circles, too, attitudes changed with regard to manual versus mental labour. While groups like majolica manufacturers as well as gold- and silversmiths adopted techniques, templates and product designs from the Italian Renaissance, some artists distanced themselves from what they started calling 'mere handicraft' (see Chapter 7). That is what Antwerp sculptors did around 1600. Following a long process that had begun at the end of the fifteenth century, they broke away from the guild of the *Vier Gekroonden* (the 'Four Crowned Martyrs'), which governed a number of occupations in the building sector, in order to find accommodation in the artists' guild. In doing so, the sculptors consciously made a distinction between the *officio mechanico* of the bricklayers and their own *conste* (roughly, their 'artistic know-how'), which they saw as being related to painting and architecture. These occupations gradually came together under the heading *arti del disegno* because, on the one hand, drawing and composition were required and, on the other, classical and Italian models played a role. Even this process was already underway long before the sixteenth century. Associating painters and architects with *vrije* (liberal) arts like geometry had been up for discussion in Italy from at least the early fifteenth century onwards.

The greater importance of theory and the greater distinction between execution and design do not mean, however, that the mechanical arts simply lost importance and prestige. There are also indications that the expansion of luxury industries and the development of urban material culture provided precisely for greater appreciation of those who made attractive artefacts (see Chapter 7). Whereas some artists applied a distinction between *fecit* and *invenit*, the values and approaches of artisans – experimentation, practical experience, observation – became important in scientific circles.

However it may have been, learning remained a process that in the main played out on the shop floor. That was also the case for the technical and vocational training of engineers, surveyors, cartographers and navigators, which was still structurally not very organised in the fifteenth and sixteenth centuries. It was not until the end of the sixteenth century – chiefly in the Dutch Republic, though with input from specialists who had fled from the south (see p. 251) – that these types of training were seen as forms of higher education.

Handbooks and '*Artes*-Literature'

Reading and writing skills became steadily more important in the late Middle Ages. That was certainly true for municipal administration, yet the question to what extent this also applied to the shop floor and to conducting business is more difficult to answer. Jan Luiten van Zanden has floated the proposition that the cradle of the modern knowledge economy was the urban centres of the Low Countries. In addition to the effective system of learning, as organised by the craft guilds, the reason for this origin would have to be sought in the spread of the printing press and a relatively low interest rate, both of which supposedly gave rise to a lower price for knowledge (printed matter) and better access to learning on the shop floor (via apprenticeship contracts).

In comparison with the rest of Europe, the Low Countries certainly possessed a dense network involving printer-publisher-booksellers, as these occupations were normally combined in the fifteenth and sixteenth centuries. Thanks to the extensive humanist school network and the presence of a university in Leuven in the duchy of Brabant, quite a lot of entrepreneurs ventured to start up printing houses. Between 1470 and 1480 the first printers in the Low Countries started doing business. In 1473 the first book to be printed in the Low Countries appeared in Aalst. Willem Heijting has statistically calculated that between 1477 and 1492 one tenth of the total European book production was carried out in the Low Countries.

Because bringing out new works presupposed considerable knowledge, printer-publishers worked together with specialists who could supply the right texts and subsequently prepare them for publication and who, in the event, corrected them during printing. In the sixteenth century, the importance of these functions increased, in particular in larger firms. At Dirk Martens and in the printing house of Plantin, scholars like Peter Gillis (1486–1533), Cornelis Kiliaen (1529–1607) and Justus Lipsius (1547–1606) even occupied key positions. Printer-publishers also maintained good relations with other cultural institutions, such as schools, universities and ecclesiastical institutions to which their authors were for the most part connected. In Deventer, Alexander Hegius, the rector of the Latin school, even lodged with the printer Richard Pafraet (1455–1512). Like the makers of books in the Middle Ages, the practitioners of the book trade – the 'scribes', the 'printmakers' and others like them – usually joined an existing guild, mostly the Guild of Saint Luke, which traditionally linked artists together.

The printing press was also capable of bringing a larger audience into contact with handbooks and sets of instructions – in short, with written 'knowledge'. Certainly in administrative and business circles there was a great need for that information. In the major towns during the late Middle Ages, specialised schools arose for the training of merchants and bookkeepers, yet these institutions probably expected their pupils to be acquainted with some general knowledge already. Like artisans, merchants in particular predominantly learned their trade on the shop floor. After an apprentice had been sufficiently taught at home how to conduct business, and if he possessed the required aptitude, he was sent to domestic and foreign business branches to prepare him for

Education and Knowledge

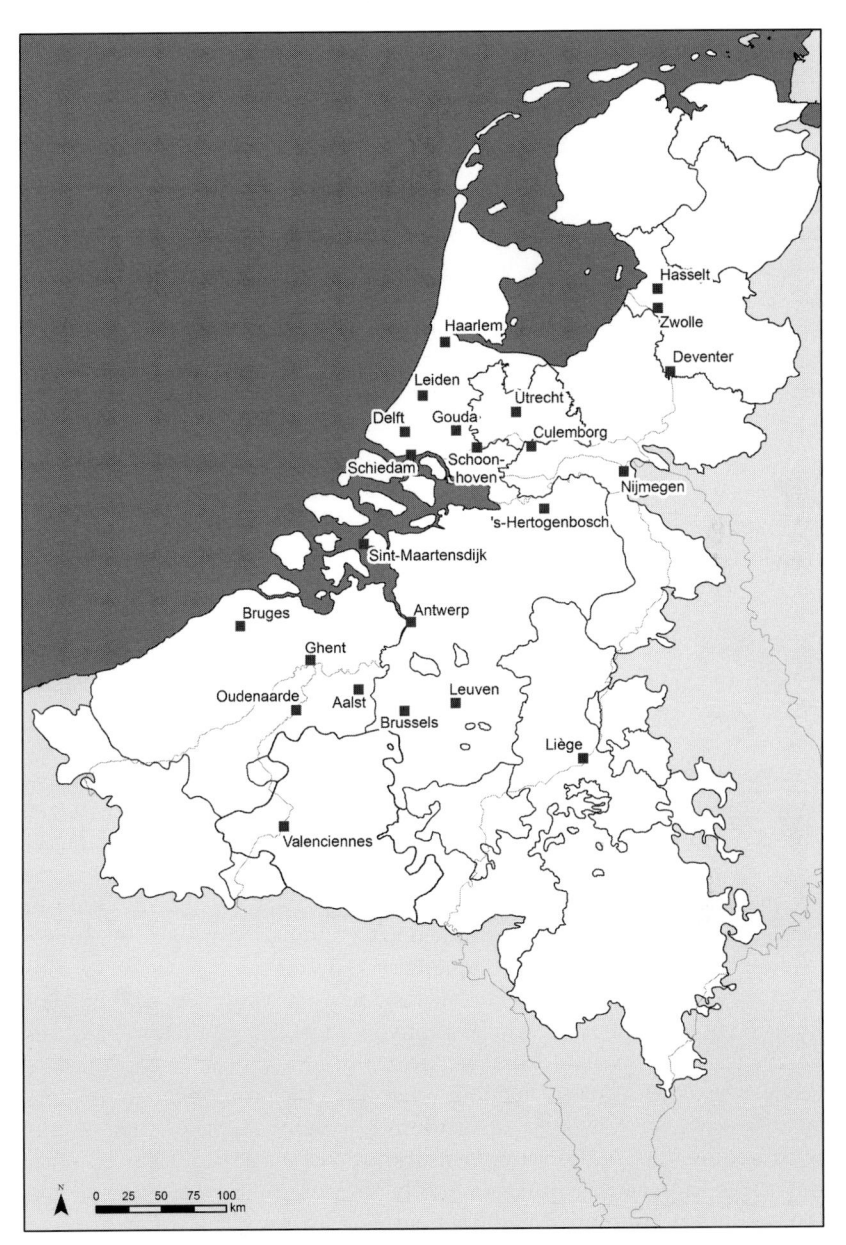

Figure 8.2 Printing centres in the fifteenth century.

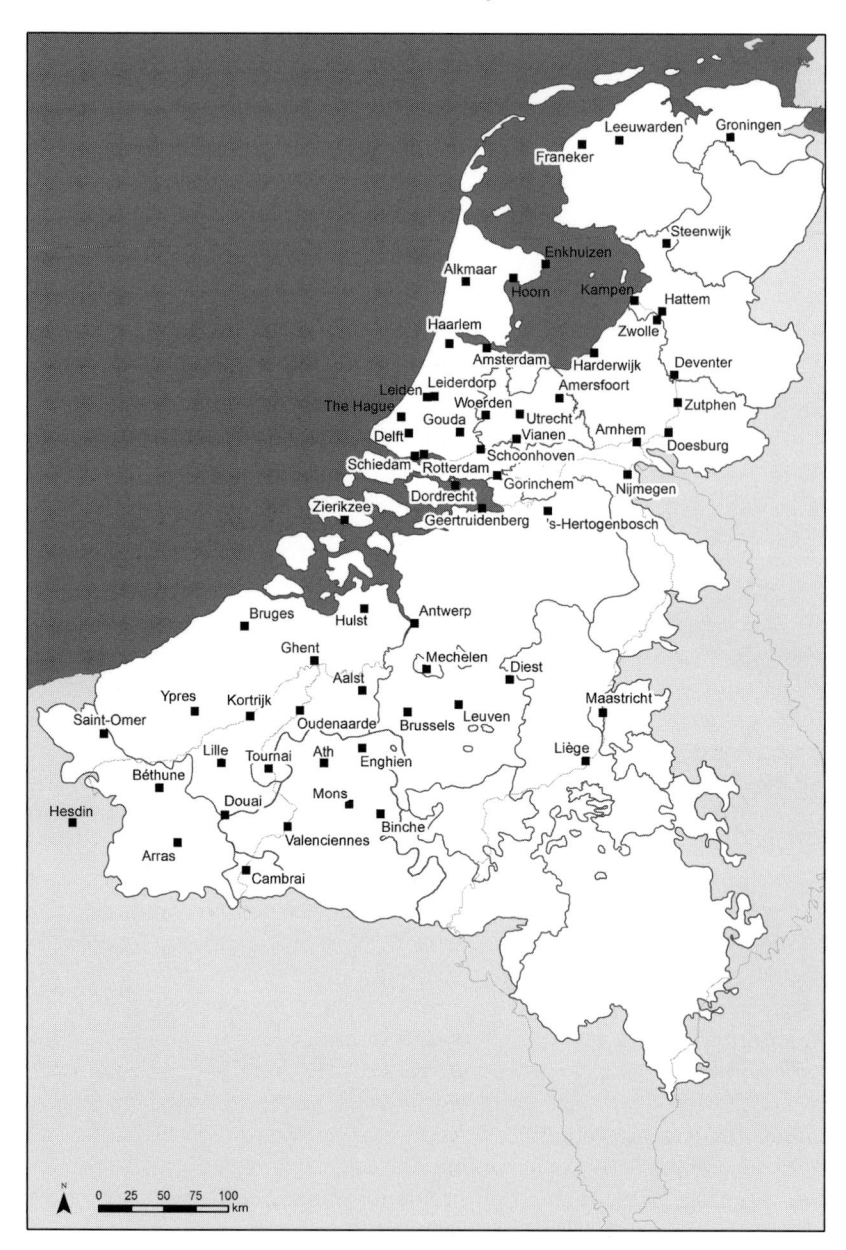

Figure 8.3 Printing centres in the sixteenth century.

international trade, among other things by learning other languages. Yet after one's apprenticeship one could equally well become competent in various European languages, mathematics, bookkeeping and business correspondence by way of handbooks. As early as the fourteenth century, textbooks were being produced for merchants in many versions in Italy (*Pratica della Mercatura*). From Italy, they were imported to the Low Countries, where they were translated and adapted. In Bruges, the *Livre des mestiers* or *Bouc vanden Ambachten* (*Book of Trades*, c. 1340), experienced great success as a conversation book for learning French. In his travel narrative from the 1590s, the Englishman Fynes Moryson (1566–1630) pointed to the important economic significance of a knowledge of languages for the inhabitants of the Low Countries:

And it standes with reason, that they who are very industrous in traffique, and having litle of theire owne to export, (except lynnen) doe trade most with the Commodityes of other nations, should themselves learne many languages, whereas other Nations have not the same reason to learne the Flemish tounge. And by reason of the Flemings generall skill in strange languages, strangers may passe and trade among them though they cannot speake a worde of the vulgar toung.[5]

In other sectors, too, as early as the fourteenth and fifteenth centuries, handwritten handbooks in Latin and in the vernacular were circulating, namely the so-called '*artes*-literature', which can also be described as trade and scientific literature. This comprised, among other things, works about surgery, gynaecology, biology, alchemy, magic, astronomy and astrology, as well as chronology, architecture, agriculture and marine navigation. The printing press provided for both an unprecedented upscaling in production and a considerable drop in the price of knowledge. In sixteenth-century Antwerp, a flourishing market for educational books of this sort was growing. For many printer-publishers, schoolbooks constituted an important part of their income.

Another question is whether reading and writing became more important in the professional lives of manual labourers as well. Initially, publishers produced predominantly older titles, namely, classical texts. In the fifteenth century, Latin works were printed chiefly for use in schools, as were devotional works in the vernacular (see Chapter 5). Much also depended on the context. Three-quarters of Gouda's production in the 'era of incunabula' was religious in nature, whereas Antwerp's printers in the same period specialised more in science and languages,

---

[5] Charles Hughes (ed.), *Shakespeare's Europe: A Survey of the Condition of Europe at the End of the 16th Century Being Unpublished Chapters of Fynes Moryson's Itinerary (1617)*, 2nd edn (New York: Blom, 1967), p. 378 (first published London: Sherratt and Hughes, 1903).

and especially in schoolbooks. During the sixteenth century, the supply expanded considerably, and there was a flood of handbooks, textbooks, etiquette books and do-it-yourself books in Dutch and French. Books were printed in all price categories. The cheapest Latin schoolbooks cost between one and three *stuivers*; for better books, the outlay was three to six *stuivers*. For comparison, a proofreader who did not lodge at the Plantin printing house earned between eight and twelve *stuivers* per day, while an in-house corrector earned more.

Taken altogether, then, books seem to have been relatively inexpensive, yet that is certainly not to say that they were commonplace for artisans. There are few indications that artisans used books on the shop floor. Handbooks seem to have played a significant role, however, for larger entrepreneurs and businessmen, given that they frequently concerned languages, bookkeeping, mathematics, geography and navigation. Recipes seem to have been limited to specific niche sectors, such as working silver, dyeing textiles and gold leather production – and even there it remains to be seen whether the author of any set of instructions truly had artisans in mind as a target audience rather than an audience of hobbyists and pseudo-scientists who were also involved in alchemy and natural philosophy. Books circulated mainly among artists and among entrepreneurs in the field of luxury production (like gold- and silversmiths), as well as within the medical sector (surgeons and apothecaries). Whereas the former group used models (Italian, among others), surgeons and apothecaries came more and more frequently into contact with academic knowledge from the *medicinae doctores* via handbooks and pharmacopoeias (in Latin and the vernacular). It was in these circles that a group gradually emerged which emancipated itself both from the 'mechanical arts' associated with the shop floor and from the scholastic and classical knowledge of the monastic schools and universities. In this 'midfield' there arose a need for reading matter for relaxation, but also for personal development.

It was in this way, then, that the production of texts in the vernacular was stimulated. The milieu of the artistic trades was permeated through and through with humanist principles, and many rhetoricians, too – of whom a majority came from an artisanal milieu – were oriented towards humanism (see Chapter 5). Indeed, the Low Countries played an important role in the development of vernacular humanism, a concept that has received much attention only in the most recent decades, though it continues to evoke controversy. What is certain is that, thanks to improved and expanded education in Latin and the circulation of translations of both classical authors and neo-Latin humanists, the body of thought and scientific knowledge from the classical era was received and even appropriated by broader strata of the population. Thus, for example, interest in and openness to language and culture are confirmed by the testimonials of travellers, among whom the best known is undoubtedly the Italian Lodovico Guicciardini (1521–89). Guicciardini was amazed that nearly everyone in the Low Countries – even the simple peasant – could read and write, and that so many spoke foreign languages (French, German, English, Italian and others), even though they had never been abroad. In much the same wording in his chronicle about the 'rebellion de Flandres', *maestro* Pedro Cornejo (*c.* 1536–1590) expressed his amazement about the inclination towards studying and the knowledge of languages he found. In 1531, Jacob de Meyere (1491–1552), a historian from Belle (now Bailleul in France), was similarly amazed about the passion for letters and the love for study which were dominant all over Flanders, such that there was barely a town or village where a famous schoolmaster was not active.

For that reason, the art of printing should be associated with intellectual and humanist developments rather than economic growth – and with the social mobility of a number of artisans' and artists' sons who outgrew the mechanical arts and became architects, for example. For some groups, the late fifteenth and sixteenth centuries were a period of great social mobility, certainly until the Dutch Revolt. To an increasing degree, a proper course of classical training was felt to be necessary for an artist with ambitions. There were careers also set aside for artists with a Latin education, especially in the administration and the judiciary. In this way, the study of classical languages led to prestige, social differentiation and better social positions in church, town and state. At the same time, intellectual developments could also give rise to innovations in the economy. This is certainly the case in the arts sector, where the influence of the Italian Renaissance provided for product innovations that presupposed a more classical form of schooling (see Chapter 7). For architects, mathematics became indispensable; painters needed to have a sense of optics (perspective), anatomy, chemistry and physics (raw and finished materials); for sculptors, mathematics and a knowledge of materials proved to be necessary. It is clear, moreover, that all artists from the Renaissance onwards had to become acquainted with classical history and mythology. Thanks to familiarisation with the world of Antiquity and with the roots of the Christian faith, broader strata of the population came into contact with the world of Christian humanism. Latin schools, printing houses, municipal governments, cultural and religious organisations, artists' ateliers: there were so many places where burghers could be found searching for knowledge about Antiquity, a deeper religious life and moral and ethical standards adapted to ever-changing urban life.

By this time, within the rhetoricians' movement there was the notion that the uneducated – namely those who had no part in the internationally oriented, (neo-)Latin scholarly world – could develop into 'poets' and 'rhetoricians' within the chambers of rhetoric: that is, they could evolve as learned persons who could even hold their own with 'learned doctors, master artisans and major writers'.[6] In-depth religious knowledge, too, was essential for rhetoricians in their edification as socially engaged burghers (see Chapter 5). At Latin schools and universities, the seven liberal arts – which included the 'trivium' – were propaedeutic subjects that provided access to knowledge of the higher sciences. That is how they were also seen in rhetoricians' circles. The foundation of the education programme for a rhetoricians' chamber consisted, therefore, of elements from grammar, logic and rhetoric, making up the trivium. These topics began with the improvement of new members' elementary reading and writing techniques. According to the statutes of the rhetoricians' chamber of Aalst (1539), for example, it was thus expected that the 'instruction' in the chamber would help members 'in becoming more skilled and more competent in reading, writing and pronouncing than they had been'.[7] That such betterment was expected not only in Aalst is shown in many later testimonials from the village of De Lier in the county of Holland, as sworn before investigators of the High Court (i.e. *Hof*) of Holland in 1604. A twenty-year-old member declared that he had joined the chamber to 'learn to write and read' better – by copying dramatic works, for example.[8] Apart from exercises of this sort in writing technique, they also learned 'to compose and produce' works themselves inside the chamber, as was formulated in the statutes for the chamber of the village of Oudenbosch in the duchy of Brabant in 1548.[9] Another fundamental component of the didactic programme was exercises in speaking (with an emphasis on 'pronunciation') and listening. After the middle of the sixteenth century, the emphasis was increasingly laid upon learning to speak fluently in flawless, unadulterated Dutch.

In the process, the activities of these rhetoricians and other corporately organised groups were interwoven with their urban context. While artisans mostly worked at the front of the house and in that way were visible to clients and the public, the activities of rhetoricians can also be seen as

---

[6] Arjan van Dixhoorn, *Lustige geesten. Rederijkers in de Noordelijke Nederlanden in de vijftiende, zestiende en zeventiende eeuw* (Amsterdam: Amsterdam University Press, 2009), p. 137: 'doctuers, meesters ende grote clercken'.

[7] Ibid., p. 134: 'int lesen, scriven ende prononchieren nutter en bequamer te wordene dan zij gheweest en zijn'.

[8] Ibid.

[9] Ibid.

distributing knowledge and know-how to their public. Rhetoricians were closely involved in the organisation of town festivals, such as pageants (*ommegangen*) and 'Joyous Entries' (see Chapter 5). They wrote the scripts and texts, declaimed those texts before honoured guests and put on theatrical performances. Their knowledge of biblical texts and mythological material was a great help to them in doing so. The case of the rhetoricians also confirms that it is difficult to maintain a strict distinction between economic and intellectual or cultural developments. What is generally referred to under the heading of the Renaissance was carried out by middling groups that evolved intellectually yet at the same time were economically active as artists and manufacturers in the luxury sectors. In that sense some intellectual developments can be seen as economic innovations, although the degree to which these developments were linked to economic expansion remains subject to debate. What is clear, however, is that in this case urban actors and institutions played an especially dynamic role.

The 'Latin' School: A Link Between Elementary and Higher Education

Beginning with 'secondary' education, the role of urban actors becomes clearer, though for that reason no less ambiguous. A kind of tension remained between schooling for general education and practical vocational training. Choosing between the two was strongly correlated with the parents' vocations, as well as with whether they carried out intellectual or manual labour. It was not a purely financial question but also an intellectual one. Among the master artisans there were more wealthy people than, for example, among municipal functionaries or schoolmasters of a Latin school. Nevertheless, the latter groups sent more sons to university than the master artisans. The preparatory step for that level was the Latin school. As early as the Middle Ages, the chapter schools' monopoly as providers of advanced general education had been broken. The demand by burghers for secondary education for laymen was very great. Instruction was increasingly seen as essential and as a matter that fell within urban competences. For that reason, multiple parish schools – where Latin and the subjects of the trivium (grammar, rhetoric and logic) or the seven liberal arts (that is, mathematics, geometry, astronomy and music, in addition to trivium topics) were taught – developed into municipal Latin schools or grammar schools (*Grote School*) in the larger and more dynamic towns. Sometimes the town took over existing schools at monasteries or chapters, so as to acquire oversight of the quality of the education. Such appropriation happened during the sixteenth century, and included most of the schools that had been in the hands of the Brethren of the Common

Life, among others, if they were not taken over by regular orders. In other towns, the chapters transferred their *scholastrie* or school supervision to the town; the chapter school was refashioned into a municipal Latin school. In Mechelen this change happened as early as 1450 because the scholastics (*scholasters*) were no longer able to carry out their duties properly. This was partly a consequence of the accumulation of ecclesiastical prebends, which led to them being frequently absent from their posts.

The laicised Latin schools initially followed the methods of the chapter schools. Under the influence of Johan Cele, the rector or head of the Latin school in Zwolle, however, fundamental changes came about in secondary education. Cele set out the ground rules for classical secondary education. Around 1400 this school in Zwolle had between 800 and 1,000 pupils. In keeping with tradition, the schoolchildren there received joint or individual, targeted instruction, but because that kind of instruction was not very efficient, the pupils were divided into eight classes, according to their level of knowledge and not their age. A class did not have to correspond to an academic year. If the child had finished learning the material for a specific class, he could then go on to a subsequent one or, conversely, take longer than one year to graduate from a class.

Girls were usually not admitted to Latin schools, or to universities, although there were exceptions. In 1320 Duke John III of Brabant promulgated an ordinance in which he expanded and regulated the number of municipal schools in Brussels: nine primary schools (five for boys and four for girls) and two Latin schools (one for boys and one for girls). Girls also attended Latin schools in Emmerich, Gouda, Hattem and Culemborg in the fifteenth century, as well as in Sittard in the sixteenth century. More generally speaking, parents who aspired to a classical kind of training for their daughters could avail themselves of the lessons offered in the better convent schools or by a private tutor, if the father did not believe himself to be called to train his daughters. Humanist pedagogues such as Erasmus and Vives were interested in the education of women. They held that women should be literate in order to become better Christians and burghers, to be able to bring up their children properly for the first seven years and to be pleasant conversationalists for their husbands and visitors. Women with intellectual needs and aspirations were also allowed to be initiated into the *bonae litterae*, though not at public schools. Erasmus and Vives thus took a more restrictive view of what was actually happening in urban practice.

All kinds of indirect sources, such as diaries, travel accounts and surveys, show that the number of schools increased considerably during the sixteenth century. In addition to the public schools provided by the municipality or by chapters or religious orders – which had all been modernised in accordance with the guidelines of humanist pedagogues – numerous private schools with humanist-trained schoolmasters arose. Towns of some size soon had more than one Latin or grammar school, which of course had financial consequences for the public schools. As compensation, the heads of schools or rectors as well as their deputy headmasters had to donate 1 per cent per pupil to the rector of the municipal Latin school. Home schooling was another option. Of course this instruction was reserved only for those who were financially most secure, but even they often opted for a good Latin school, with an eye to the *aemulatio* or competition that the humanists considered of paramount importance, at least for boys.

Thus, for example, the number of schools in Ghent increased enormously in the first half of the sixteenth century. According to the diary of Cornelis (1516–67) and Philips van Campene (d. after 1571), at the beginning of the sixteenth century the town had only two to three Latin schools, albeit each with 200–300 pupils. One of these schools was that of the Brethren of the Common Life, the other the private school of the poet-humanist Eligius Hoeckaert (*c.* 1488–1544), himself a pupil of the printer-humanist Robert de Keysere (d. 1532). Around 1565, according to Van Campene, there were at least twelve Latin schools, though each now had only twenty to thirty pupils. In Antwerp, too, the five chapter schools (the so-called *papenscholen*) supported by the town did not keep private individuals from offering private Latin instruction. Of the Latin schoolmasters registered in the schoolmasters' guild in the sixteenth century, twenty-four were employed in private schools and twenty in public schools. In the university town of Leuven, leading humanists like Vives and Adrianus Barlandus gave private instruction independently of the faculty of arts. The demand for education based on classical texts and the study of neo-Latin authors was considerable, and humanists gladly satisfied that need. It also helped them to acquire a higher income.

Even smaller towns were willing to invest in Latin education. It brought prestige to a town and gave young people the opportunity to obtain a good education close to home. Nonetheless, it was frequently a very heavy financial burden for towns with a population of less than 5,000 to maintain a Latin school. Tuition fees were not able to cover the cost of the rector and the deputy headmaster(s), and the town had to jump in. The municipal government in Geraardsbergen, for instance, had taken over the Latin school of the Brethren of the Common Life in 1539. In 1594–5, when the town wanted to bring back Joos Schollaert (1565–1608) from Halle as *regent*, it promised to pay 180 pounds as his annual salary. The money was recouped from various municipal institutions (the municipal treasury, the 'Holy Spirit' rhetoricians' chamber, the leprosarium and the treasury of religious services). The financial pressure on the municipal treasury proved to be too great, however, and in 1629 the Latin school was taken over by the Benedictine Abbey of Saint Adrian. Other municipal governments or impassioned inhabitants did not succeed in setting up Latin education in their own towns. Deinze, among other places, failed in this respect. Nevertheless, the numerous small humanities schools made it possible for even less well-to-do parents to pay for schooling that prepared children for university. Moreover, there were numerous local scholarships available, which the town magistrates and burghers had set up for children in secondary schools. Indeed, there is a direct correlation between the presence of a Latin school and the number of university students from any given town. Geraardsbergen and Arnhem, in a positive sense, and Deinze and Eeklo, in a negative sense, are good examples of that interrelationship.

Sadly, even upon closer inspection it is not possible to say what percentage of the male population enjoyed a humanities education. In addition, there are no sources available to enable any quantitative study to be made. The increase in schools sketched above does suggest, however, that the humanist (and reformational) body of thought was able to permeate into large areas of the population, certainly well into artisans' circles. Via an indirect route, above all thanks to biographical information and data that relate to cultural life, one dare say that – certainly in the tertiary sector, but also at the level of masters from the wealthier craft guilds, in particular the luxury industries – knowledge of the *bonae litterae* was reasonably widespread in the sixteenth century. That is not to say in any sense, however, that this dissemination has to be seen as a merely intellectual development. What is striking about classical education in urban circles is its practical orientation, the consequence of the specific response that the Low Countries provided to humanist education. In Italy and France both humanist pedagogy and the expansion of education were strongly targeted at the aristocracy, with the intention of constituting an intellectual elite. Humanists in the Low Countries opted for a body of humanist thought disseminated more broadly and inspired by Christianity, which penetrated deep into the middling groups of artisans as well.

Higher Education

What role did the urban centres in the Low Countries ultimately play in higher education? A distinction has to be drawn here between higher vocational education and university education, although overlaps can also be detected. As a result of the development of the humanist model of education, the boundary between secondary and higher education became sharper. Until around 1500, boys left the Latin school on average at the age of thirteen or fourteen, and went on to become more competent in the liberal arts at the arts faculty of the university located closest to them. Before the establishment of a university in Brabant – at Leuven in 1425 – Paris (from around 1200 onwards) and Cologne (from 1388 onwards) were the centres most often chosen. Because of the increasing quality of education in the Latin schools – a consequence of the better intellectual level of the teachers – schoolchildren gradually began to study for longer at the Latin school in their own town or region. Around the age of seventeen or eighteen they then left for university with a thorough knowledge of the *trivium*. Thus the university faculty of arts was able to extend its own level of teaching in terms of content and, for example, start to specialise more in the *quadrivium*. In these developments, though, urban actors seem to have played a relatively small role, aside from the fact that universities were of course founded in towns in the Low Countries, too.

In spite of early urbanisation, however, provinces in the Low Countries were rather late in investing in universities of their own. The initiative did not come from the urban milieu either, although there was indeed a need for academically trained personnel there. Until the larger influx of university students during the first half of the sixteenth century, it was sometimes necessary to appoint jurists 'from outside' because there were none at hand in the towns themselves. From the thirteenth century onwards, in order to rectify this shortcoming, young people were already being assisted with scholarships in the larger towns. The town accounts of Bruges and Ghent testify to this subsidising process. So, for example, the municipal accounts in Ghent from 1352 to 1358 mention 'Item paid to master Jan vanden Rake, to help him with his studies in Paris, 40 pounds'.[10] Private individuals also supported scholarship recipients. In his last will and testament dated 24 January 1276, Arnold van Maldeghem, a canon of Tournai, left 150 pounds per year for poor students who were qualified but did not have the (financial) means to study at the University of Paris or elsewhere. The Abbey of Saint Peter in Ghent had to pay these scholarships out of earnings from lands that Arnold had left to it. There is evidence of payments well into 1406.[11]

---

[10] Cited in Frans De Potter, *Gent, van den oudsten tijd tot heden. Geschiedkundige beschrijving der stad*, rev. edn (Brussels: Uitgeverij Kultuur, 1975), vol. IV, p. 163: 'Item betaalt aan meester Jan vanden Rake, thulpen siere studen te Parijs, 40 ponden' (first published Ghent: Annoot-Braeckman, 1886).

[11] Ferdinand François Joseph Lecouvet, 'L'instruction publique au Moyen Age. I: l'abbaye de Saint-Pierre à Gand et l'université de Paris', *Messager des sciences et des arts de la Belgique* (1855), pp. 171–9.

From the last decades of the fourteenth century, princes aspired to a university of their own for the training of provincial and local officials, clergy and physicians. As early as 1422, the duke of Burgundy, Philip the Good, founded a university at Dole in Franche-Comté. His nephew, Duke John IV of Brabant, followed his example and founded the first university in the Low Countries in 1425 in Leuven, the former capital of Brabant. This was done in collaboration with the town and the collegiate chapter of Saint Peter, following the model set by the universities of Paris and Cologne. In 1432 the theological faculty was added to the faculties of arts, law and medicine. Under the influence of Erasmus, among others, and the numerous enthusiastic and gifted humanists who lived in the Low Countries, the *studium generale* (the customary name for a university during this period) in Leuven became a centre of humanism that attracted up to 10 per cent of its students from other countries.

University education was reserved for only a small minority of townspeople in the main. Depending on the region, around 1500, the number of young males in Europe who obtained a university education stood between 1 and 2.5 per cent. For various reasons, the Low Countries scored relatively highly in that regard. Higher education flourishes best in an urban region where there are sufficient financial means at hand to pay for these kinds of studies, where a local intellectual habitus exists, where – linked with those structures, practices and sensibilities – family traditions of education have grown, and where pre-university and university education can be undertaken without too much effort. The Low Countries satisfied all those conditions.

And yet the need for academically trained people in the Low Countries was relatively small. What need did a large- to medium-sized town in 1500 have for those trained at university? From the fourteenth century onwards, the requirements were: one or two pensionaries, university-trained officials who gave legal advice to the city council; anywhere between one and several secretaries and/or registrars, very often jurists; at least one town attorney, always a jurist; at least one town physician, a *doctor medicinae*; and at least one *magister artium* for the Latin school. For the most part, prosecutors and legal notaries did not have university degrees until the sixteenth century. From then on, the number of those trained at university increased owing to the large supply of graduates. Furthermore, there was always a use for some young people who had gone to university for a few years, had received their *baccalaureat* and were therefore useful for all manner of administrative tasks. Of course the administrative capitals – such as Brussels, Mechelen, Lille, Ghent, The Hague, Utrecht and Groningen, as well as the episcopal cities – had a greater need for jurists. It must also be remembered, though, that officials and judges in these administrative centres were not recruited solely from their own towns. In addition, there were numerous clergy with academic titles, who could end up in cathedral and collegiate chapters, in ecclesiastical courts and administration, and also in pastoral care. Research into the intellectual background of pastors in the late Middle Ages and the sixteenth century has demonstrated that their intellectual training was generally good. Until around 1500 many municipal officials (secretaries and pensionaries) still had a religious status. They were mostly university-trained canons, who saw this function as an initial step in a career in the service of the provincial or central government.

In short, given an average career lasting ten to fifteen years for each position, a typical town with about 5,000 inhabitants did not have to find even one jurist a year in order to satisfy its needs. Big towns with more than 50,000 inhabitants of course needed more university-trained people. Ghent, for instance, with about 50,000 inhabitants in the sixteenth century, was able to fulfil its administration requirements with five or so new jurists per year. Antwerp was probably able to employ a few more in the sixteenth century. Detailed research shows that, during the long sixteenth century, on average approximately twenty people from Antwerp left for university each year – the largest number for any town in the Low Countries. From the middle of the sixteenth century onwards, a town like Antwerp (with about 100,000 inhabitants) evidently had so many university-trained people that this figure possibly helps to explain the large number of academics (39 per cent) who held seats on the aldermen's bench. Indeed, from the late fifteenth through to the Dutch Revolt, there are many examples which illustrate the upward social mobility among graduates there, in particular among jurists, and certainly among those who had studied abroad.

All this suggests that this higher education had a practical and applicable purpose as well. The professional officials became the architects of institutional reorganisations following the Roman/humanist model. They improved the legal procedures and the municipal system of justice to such a degree that they became less vulnerable to appeal – from the provincial courts, among others. Given this authority, the larger towns could take more responsibility in the case of the so-called *hoofdvaart*, a system in which smaller towns without university-trained legal personnel sought advice from larger towns. These trained officials were also in a better position to defend themselves politically and judicially against the authority of the central government. They spoke the same language as the princely councillors; they had often attended the same classes at university and had acquired the same political and legal ideologies.

For its part, higher vocational education did not really develop in the Low Countries until the seventeenth and eighteenth centuries, first in the north and much later in the south. A school for marine navigation existed in Amsterdam in 1586. Its major supporter was Petrus Plancius, also known as Platevoet (1552–1622), who came from Dranouter in the county of Flanders. He was one of numerous cartographers who had migrated to the north. In Leiden in 1600, at the request of Stadtholder Maurice of Nassau, the *Duytsche Mathematicque* (roughly, the 'Dutch Mathematics Programme') was set up, a special school for the training of military engineers, surveyors and fortifications architects, ancillary to the university. At the birth of this school, too, there was a Fleming present: Simon Stevin (1548/9–1620), a mathematician from Bruges. The lessons were taught in Dutch, which at that time was still relatively uncommon.

Interactions between Court, University and Town

In addition to the educational institutions (schools and universities) and the printing houses, the secular and ecclesiastical courts constituted a third milieu in which science was carried out and knowledge transmitted during the Middle Ages. Because the physical sciences had hardly any place in the schools, scientific treatises in translation were studied by individual researchers, who were frequently connected to princely and episcopal courts. Medieval princes surrounded themselves with military personnel, engineers, architects, diplomats, legal scholars, pastors, secretaries, artists, physicians, surgeons, servants and so-called 'wise people'. Together they constituted the court household. Discoverers, translators and authors of new texts also travelled around and were recruited as teachers, as makers of horoscopes and prophecies, to practise medicine and to make new mathematical calculations. In the process, observations could also be made that were necessary for their own research. Being employed at court irrefutably had many advantages. Courts enjoyed their own jurisdiction – just as the Church and universities did – and they even offered a kind of legal immunity, a sort of diplomatic status. Until the late Middle Ages, the courts were itinerant, and they were only temporarily important for the towns where they were residing, although this changed greatly during the period studied in this volume.

Although courts and court culture are not traditionally associated with urban culture, research into late medieval literature and art in the

Low Countries has resulted in an entirely different picture. There was more interaction between court and town, courtiers and burghers than had previously been assumed. The courts in the Low Countries were powerful magnets for culture in town. In the city of Brussels – and in Mechelen, to a somewhat lesser degree – there are good examples of this interplay. Until the accession of Philip the Good in 1419, the Burgundian dukes resided more often than not in Burgundy or Paris and only sporadically in towns of the Low Countries. As a result of the enormous territorial expansion of the Burgundian realm in the Low Countries under Philip, the focal point was relocated to Flanders and Brabant, and a permanent residence became a necessity for housing the central legal, financial and political institutions, among other things. From 1430 onwards, the palace on Brussels' Coudenberg Hill became the permanent residence, and Brussels the de facto capital of the Burgundian Netherlands. The city shared that status with Mechelen, a residential town favoured by princely widows and regents. Both Mechelen and Brussels experienced the beneficial influence of the court, for example, in the local growth of luxury industries, and the court's establishment there was an important factor in the shift of the economic focal point from Flanders to Brabant (see Chapter 2).

That influence reached even further, however. An important aspect for the town was the 'civilising' role of the court. Although the introduction of new templates for conduct and etiquette is increasingly ascribed to urban middling groups, townspeople frequently mirrored court culture with aristocratic aspirations (see Chapter 3). Courtiers set the tone and defined etiquette and fashion. Artists, poets and scholars found employment there thanks to an intricate patronage system, and became important mediators of 'courtesy' in the urban milieu. Court artists received commissions not only from the court but also from wealthy urban nobles and burghers, who for their part could be a source of inspiration for the court artists. All these elements are found at the court of Philip the Good, the Burgundian duke from 1419 to 1467. This duke not only organised glittering banquets at the palace on Coudenberg Hill but was also present at town festivals such as the famous pageant on the Sunday before Pentecost. In order to please both the ducal entourage and the broader urban audience in a more permanent manner, the city of Brussels decided to appoint a town painter around 1435. Its choice went to Roger de la Pasture from Tournai, known in Brussels as Rogier van der Weyden.

Historians cannot agree whether Duke Philip himself harboured intellectual interests or whether he was only in it for the prestige. However, if he did not himself possess any genuine scientific ambitions, he still created a climate in which science could flourish. Any prince who could afford it surrounded himself with physicians and astrologers, of whom many had a predilection for scientific experimentation and gratefully made use of the court library, which was well supplied with medical treatises. Consider, for instance, the Van Wesele clan, medical doctors in the service of the Burgundian-Habsburg dynasty, of whom Vesalius is the best known, though not the only one to publish. Joannes de Wesalia (d. 1472) – who came from Wesel and was Vesalius' great-grandfather – was professor of medicine from 1429 to 1447 at the university of Leuven, as well as court astrologer to Philip the Good. He ended his career as Brussels' town physician.

At the same time as the court lost its itinerant nature and bureaucratisation of the administration continued to become steadily stronger, the university town of Leuven developed a dynamic of its own. In the first half of the sixteenth century the university there became a centre of scientific humanism. The *collegium trilingue* (Trilingual College), set up under the influence of Erasmus and in the will of his friend the councillor Jeronimus Busleyden (1470–1517), offered much more than Latin, Greek and Hebrew, the three languages of the Bible. It was one of the most important international centres for the study of everything that involved the *bonae litterae*. Leuven's mathematics school, too, had an international reputation. Specialists in astronomy, chronology, cosmography, mathematics, geography, cartography and so forth from across the whole of the Low Countries and beyond worked together there fruitfully with mathematical and nautical instrument makers and with trained surveyors. Without a doubt, the most prominent among the instrument makers was the goldsmith Gaspar van der Heyden (à Myrica) (*c.* 1496–1549) who, together with Leuven cartographers, designed globes and mathematical instruments. What is striking is the multifaceted nature of the sixteenth-century scientists. Among the most eminent was Gemma Frisius (1508–55) – physician, mathematician, geographer, astronomer and instrument maker. In addition to atlases and globes, he devised astronomical instruments, and he wrote scientific treatises. In them he developed, among other things, the principle of the *camera obscura*. His pupil, Gerard Mercator (1512–94) – even in his own era called the Flemish Ptolemy – was a scientific cosmographer, cartographer, instrument maker and engraver.

In the meantime, Mechelen and Antwerp were developing as commercial centres for cartography. Painters, engravers, printers and publishers saw to it that the knowledge developed in Leuven was broadcast and commercialised. One of the most renowned among them is the mapmaker Jacob van Deventer (1500/5–1575), who settled in Mechelen after studying medicine, mathematics and surveying at Leuven. Between 1536 and 1545 he criss-crossed the Low Countries to make maps of five provinces (Brabant, Holland, Guelders, Friesland and Zeeland), which are now considered to be the first reliable survey maps. Around 1560, thanks to this experience, Philip II commissioned him to map all the towns in the Low Countries. These maps had to be very reliable, in case it was necessary to lay siege to rebellious towns. The indication of gates and fortifications, of tall buildings and the structures built up around the towns was essential, so that the Habsburg soldiers could orient themselves correctly. Of approximately 300 town maps produced by Deventer (all on a scale of around 1 : 8,000), 222 have been preserved.

In order to properly understand the dynamics concerning education and the development and spread of practical and theoretical knowledge, they also need to be viewed on a regional level. For the Low Countries it is clear that much changed as a result of the religious wars, which brought into play a brain drain from the south to the north. From 1575 onwards, the northern provinces had their own Calvinist academy (the humanist term for a university) at Leiden, which could provide the rebellious provinces with preachers, jurists, physicians and masters in the liberal arts. This university was strongly directed by Leiden's pragmatically minded magistracy, and thus succeeded in acquiring and maintaining a tolerant character. The result was that it became one of the highest-ranking institutions, internationally and scientifically, in the seventeenth century. Technically skilled artisans, too, migrated to Zeeland and Holland to start applying their knowledge productively. Migrants from the southern Low Countries founded craft guilds and chambers of rhetoric there and had a major influence on the artistic and literary culture of their host towns. That does not necessarily mean that the development and circulation of knowledge came to a standstill in the southern provinces. Courts, towns, Latin schools, craft guilds, small schools and orphanages remained important centres for the education of the young and the generation and development of knowledge. In the seventeenth century, not only would (art) academies come about there, but the Catholic (Counter-)Reformation in general and the Jesuits in particular would also provide for a new sort of élan extending far beyond the boundaries of the southern Low Countries.

Conclusion

Employing economic jargon, it can be stated that there was a strong sort of 'human capital' present in the towns of the Low Countries. The towns generally had a large supply of low-threshold forms of education for acquiring skills in reading, writing and arithmetic, yet also for education in languages, bookkeeping and additional subjects of this sort. Literacy and numeracy were, therefore, relatively high. From an economic perspective, learning on the shop floor was more important, because technical and manual skills, including knowledge of new products, were what made the difference. That kind of knowledge, too, was well represented in the towns dealt with in this chapter. Yet the question still very much remains to what extent the municipal authorities and institutions themselves were responsible for that knowledge. Craft guilds frequently prescribed terms of apprenticeship and defined the masterpieces to be made, but in practice learning was still a matter of agreements between masters and (the party of the) apprentices. The craft guilds did possibly have a number of favourable effects on economic problems – they provided for a higher kind of trust between the contracting parties and guaranteed product quality – but, at the same time, the existence of craft guilds had disadvantages. Entry into them was frequently expensive, while their regulations were generally oriented towards demarcating market segments and guarding privileges. Moreover, attracting technical knowledge was probably much more important than producing it locally. That priority is suggested by the connection between economic growth and immigration and by the systematic attempts on the part of municipal authorities to lure highly trained people during periods when things were in decline – by awarding patents and monopolies, gratis infrastructure, exemptions from taxes and the like. In any case, the most dynamic industries in the southern Low Countries in the sixteenth century were strongly influenced both by technologies and by kinds of products developed elsewhere – if they were not actually introduced by immigrants, as was the case with glass and majolica in sixteenth-century Antwerp. The great importance of migration further demonstrates that knowledge was directly conveyed via people more than on paper, except where it concerned models and templates, which could make the difference in the art and luxury sectors.

In addition to economic and administrative consequences, a broad and high level of literacy influenced intellectual, religious and scientific life more generally. Certainly from the sixteenth century onwards, in many schools of higher education there was room for experimental research and for instruction targeted at practice, as was the case for physicians and for jurists – the latter through the study of indigenous princely and customary laws. These developments played out against the background of changing relationships between practical and theoretical knowledge, or between mechanical arts and liberal arts. In intellectual and scientific circles, observation and experimentation became more important, at the expense of the Aristotelian ideals of deduction and *disputatio*, which were cultivated at universities. Yet, at the same time, in the circles of the most prestigious and influential artisans and artists, processes were underway in which physical and experiential knowledge of a matter was suppressed by more abstract and more schematic thinking. In that sense, scientific thinking and the shop floor seem to have grown towards each other in the long term, a fact which is confirmed by recent studies concerning the seventeenth-century scientific revolution.

For the large majority of artisans this convergence did not mean that they acquired a higher status; sometimes the opposite was the case. Thanks to economic prosperity and the political and religious emancipation of urban middling groups in the Low Countries, intellectual, cultural, artistic and spiritual aspirations were created that allowed upward mobility for the highly skilled portion of artisanal groups. Yet the gap with common manual labourers probably became greater at the end of the period studied here. Via the channels described above, the urban middling groups got the opportunity to participate actively in humanist – or, more generally speaking, intellectual – activities. What was traditionally seen as high and even learned culture became more broadly accessible, not least as a result of language instruction and the increased accessibility of writings in translation from other languages. The increase in schools and informal networks implies that the body of thought from the Reformation, too – which, along with humanism, shared a concern for (Christian) sources – was able to permeate large strata of the population, certainly well into the better-trained artisans' circles. The role of the chambers of rhetoric in this process also cannot be denied (see Chapter 5).

In other words, this is not a linear narrative of progress about an increasingly well-educated urban population. Poor and socially weak groups of the population encountered disciplinary action, while they were looking at an increasingly high threshold of refined codes of conduct. Although religious values and norms were taught together with reading and writing in Sunday schools, the pressure increased to learn an economically useful trade and a well-honed work ethic either from a master artisan or in vocational schools connected with orphanages. Even within the urban middling groups themselves, new distinctions were applied. From the fifteenth century onwards, painters, sculptors and architects marked a distinction between 'art' and 'craft', in which art was associated more with the liberal arts and the world of scholars, on account of the need for knowledge of perspective and geometry, as well as familiarity with the classical visual idiom. In view of the greater importance of drafting and design in material culture in a broader sense, a distinction gradually emerged between artisans who were capable of designing their own products and those who only carried out the plans of others.

To what extent knowledge and the acquisition of knowledge may or may not be called 'urban' in this regard is another question. The knowledge of particularly middling groups must be seen expressly in an urban context. Craft guilds cultivated in every sense an ideal in which being a master was intimately connected to the political status of being a *poorter* (roughly, 'citizen' – see Chapter 4). Artisans also explicitly connected their technical knowledge and skills to the urban (public and political) context in their visual culture and rituals, by referring, for example, to the tools of their trade on craft guild banners. As far as the 'learned' and scientific milieus are concerned, an evolution towards a more urban mentality seems to have gradually taken place, whereby the increasing importance of the printed text and the scientific experiment went hand in hand with a specific type of honesty, respectability and *civilité*. On the one hand, those who were more highly trained were firmly attached to the town, and they participated actively in its economic, political and cultural life. On the other hand, they were also well at home in the broad international world of culture, art and science, the so-called republic of letters.

Over the long term, cultural consumption became a widespread phenomenon of the Low Countries, albeit channelled and censured in the south as a consequence of the Counter-Reformation. For ecclesiastical and secular authorities, schools and education were extremely important weapons in the moral and religious disciplining of the population – at the expense of intellectual freedom. Certainly for the lower strata, both the ecclesiastical authorities and to a certain degree their secular counterparts saw those disciplinary actions as more important than the acquisition of knowledge. Thus, during the seventeenth century, the literacy of the south regressed, unlike that in the north, which had risen considerably. In the north, burghers' ideals were spread so widely that the strict Calvinist morality was tempered, and economy, education, culture and science acquired more latitude.

9 Epilogue: The Legacy of the Medieval City in the Low Countries

Bruno Blondé, Marc Boone and Anne-Laure Van Bruaene

In the seventeenth century, the Dutch Republic outstripped rival European economies in almost every possible way. In 1995 a team of prominent historians reflected upon the causes and consequences of this so-called 'Dutch Miracle'. According to the editors of *A Miracle Mirrored: The Dutch Republic in European Perspective*, the specificity of the Dutch Golden Age can briefly be summarised as a deviant model in European state formation.[1] While elsewhere centralised nation-states gained momentum in the seventeenth century, the Dutch Republic followed a different path, one of decentralised power and a decentralised urban system that constituted its crucial building material. Internally as well, the Dutch cities were marked by complex but equilibrated 'checks and balances'. Even though many studies have seen the light since and Dutch historians have continued to reflect upon the role of towns in society, this analysis is still very relevant today.[2] In fact, it builds upon a central claim by Johan Huizinga, who in his classic *Dutch Civilisation in the Seventeenth Century* typified the Netherlands as a 'bourgeois society'.[3]

The present book has unveiled the path-dependency of the Dutch Golden Age on the society that developed in the urban core of the Low Countries (Flanders, Brabant and Holland-Zeeland) in the centuries prior to the Dutch Revolt. However diverse the economies, built spaces, social structures and cultures of individual cities in the different eras and areas of the Low Countries, internally, the utmost defining characteristic of the Low Countries' city was a complex social balance marked, on

---

[1] Karel Davids and Jan Lucassen (eds.), *A Miracle Mirrored: The Dutch Republic in European Perspective* (Cambridge: Cambridge University Press, 1995).
[2] Maarten Prak, *The Dutch Republic in the Seventeenth Century: The Golden Age* (Cambridge: Cambridge University Press, 2005).
[3] Johan Huizinga, *Dutch Civilisation in the Seventeenth Century, and Other Essays*, ed. Pieter Geyl and F.W.N. Hugenholtz (London: Collins, 1968).

Figure 9.1 Dirck Jacobsz, *Group Portrait of the Guild of the 'Kloveniers'*, 1529/1559. The middle panel of this group portrait was painted in 1529 and shows the seventeen members of the Amsterdam guild of the *kloveniers*, who exercised with arquebuses. The side panels were added in 1559. This painting was destined for the rooms of the *kloveniers* and expresses their sense of male pride and collective honour.

the one hand, by relatively decentralised power and distributed income, and, on the other, by its strong and resilient middling sort of people.

These defining characteristics of Low Countries' urban society cannot be disconnected from the geographical conditions that shaped it. Pointing to geographical and ecological conditions in order to interpret long-term developments is, of course, always a hazardous exercise. The case of Holland can serve as an example here. Holland was an early and heavily urbanised region. It was endowed with a massive stock of cheap energy, especially the abundant supply of peat and the availability of wind power. Yet, its economic fate was also heavily influenced by major ecological challenges that accompanied the struggle against the sea and especially the soil settling of the peat regions, which eventually fostered a process of soil exhaustion and endangered crop growing. This ecological challenge forced the agricultural economy to adjust. Paradoxically, the challenge strengthened a process of agricultural and industrial specialisation, away from grain growing, eventually stimulating economic productivity and interregional exchange.

In short, it was both ecological opportunities and threats that shaped the economy and society of the Low Countries. These caveats notwithstanding, the present book demonstrates that the imprint of the basic geological and geographical opportunities and threats to the economy and society of the Low Countries, and especially to its urban network, was significant. Indeed, access to the sea, combined with a delta of major European rivers and a dense network of connecting rivers and canals, is the crucial feature for understanding the specificity of the urbanisation in this region, as Wim Blockmans had earlier argued.[4] In pre-industrial economies, the cost of transport was often a real bottleneck for the development of dense urban agglomerations. Cities not only produce luxuries for long-distance trade but also need to be built, fuelled and fed, a process that requires the transportation of large volumes, in this period inevitably with an unfavourable weight : value ratio. Hence, access to the sea and inland waterways delivered the essential foundation for the urbanisation of the Low Countries. Cheap maritime transport and inland river navigation allowed cities and their hinterlands – each with its specific social agro-system – to maximise productivity gains through processes of agricultural, industrial and service specialisation. This system was brought to near-perfection in the seventeenth-century Dutch Republic, when a sophisticated and dense system of barges on newly dug *trekvaarten* (waterways), suitable for the mass transport of inhabitants of different social classes, was established in the Netherlands.

We argue that cheap access to transport not only fostered economic growth and urbanisation. It also fundamentally impacted upon the social structure of the cities in the Low Countries by enabling large numbers of people, goods and ideas to flow from one place to another. In the Low Countries, abundant and relatively cheap transport was also a crucial requirement for the large middling groups to prosper and engage in culture and public life. Throughout this book, we have witnessed the resilient nature of these urban middle groups, however diversified and difficult they are to grasp from a sociological viewpoint. Present-day Belgium and the Netherlands, in spite of the substantial differences that exist between the two countries, are still largely path-dependent upon these medieval roots. Compared to neighbouring European nations, both countries have been sheltered in recent years from pronounced social polarisation, as they have continued to share relatively low income inequalities. Yet, at the same time, the urban middle groups themselves reproduced social inequalities, and they continue to do so today. In political, social and cultural discourse, urban citizens increasingly marginalised people who fell below the material and cultural thresholds of decent bourgeois life. Moreover, the permanence of an ideology of the 'common good' notwithstanding, vested interest groups did not necessarily promote general welfare all the time. In this way, affluence and 'civilisation' came – and still come – at a considerable social cost. Present-day Belgium, for instance, fails dramatically to absorb poorer people and migrants into its economy.

---

[4] Wim Blockmans, *Metropolen aan de Noordzee. De geschiedenis van Nederland, 1100–1560* (Amsterdam: Uitgeverij Bert Bakker, 2010), p. 17.

In spite of an educational system that is financially accessible to lower income groups, the social drop-out remains considerable.

For better or worse, the Low Countries were essentially an urbanised society with large and diversified middling groups. Another crucial feature of the urban hierarchy that developed along the mentioned transport grid was its essentially multi-nuclear nature. In the course of the late Middle Ages and the sixteenth century bigger urban nuclei witnessed the strongest urbanisation gains, as was the case elsewhere in the rest of urban Europe. They were able to expand their political influence and economic power, and achieved significant accumulation of wealth. International trade and economies of agglomeration account for the metropolitan development of the major gateway cities, Bruges, Antwerp and Amsterdam. Yet, at no point in time did the Low Countries witness the development of an urban hierarchy coming close to a primacy model, dominated by one giant metropolis, as happened, for instance, in Castile, England and France. No single town was able to combine court, university, important administrative institutions and major cultural industries with a privileged position in sea trading, servicing and industrial production. While Leuven and Leiden flourished as university towns, Mechelen, Brussels and eventually The Hague were marked by the presence of a court. Meanwhile Bruges, Antwerp and Amsterdam fulfilled vital commercial gateway functions, and a string of industrial cities like Ghent, Ypres, Douai and Haarlem developed as well. As a result, the urban network was marked by both economic competition and cooperation.

Unsurprisingly, then, the specific nature of the urban network in the Low Countries also heavily influenced its political profile. In the course of the long twelfth century – the crucial period when Western societies developed their own pathways – an urban communal movement manifested itself in several episcopal cities in present-day northern France. This communal movement aimed at political emancipation from the traditional ecclesiastical and feudal lords and had a direct impact on the most northern part of the kingdom of France: the county of Flanders. The crisis of succession in 1127–8 (we are familiar with it thanks to the well-known account by Galbert of Bruges) turned out to be a Flemish version of this communal revolution. Yet, whereas in France the king succeeded in channelling the energy unleashed by these communes to his own advantage, in the end broadening his power base, the communal movements in the Low Countries followed a quite different path. The regional powerbrokers (counts in Flanders, Namur, Holland and Zeeland and dukes' succession in Brabant) never succeeded in controlling the political ambitions of the cities within their territories, as became clear in the course of the fourteenth century from the many revolts and successions crises in the different principalities.

During the Middle Ages the composition of the urban elites also underwent fundamental change: an originally closed, almost hereditary, group of patricians made room for a heterogeneous urban elite including representatives of guilds and corporations, and regional noblemen succumbing to the charms of urban life. All of these groups finally identified to a greater or lesser extent with fundamental urban interests. Figuring among these interests were monetary stability, commercial privileges, the right to judge one's fellow citizens and the care for judicial protection of both city dwellers and their properties.

City and prince were, however, not the only conflicting powers. One of the characteristics of the political and social history of the Low Countries was the recurrence of internal conflicts between groups within cities, a 'little' tradition of revolt that simultaneously fuelled the 'great' tradition of opposing the prince.[5] The two types of revolt were interconnected, ideologically as well as organisationally, and, although not unique to the Low Countries, they proved to be stronger than anywhere else in Europe. The degree of urbanisation and of connectivity in a relatively limited territory can explain this. The geographical constraints of the Low Countries prevented the development of city-states as in other equally urbanised regions in northern and central Italy. The efficient network of navigable waterways and the relatively short distances between the towns resulted in a different trajectory. Eventually in the Low Countries, urban cooperation proved to be more efficient, although this insight was only progressively gained after numerous internal conflicts among cities. As a result, the political ambitions of the Valois dukes of Burgundy (ruling the Low Countries from the last quarter of the fourteenth century onwards) were thwarted by the urban political culture of participation in decision-making. The ongoing process of political unification, reinforced by dynastic opportunities, may have led to an almost complete personal union of the principalities of the Low Countries (some ecclesiastical enclaves excepted), yet it also provoked a number of open and armed confrontations between prince and city. These conflicts only occasionally resulted in a straightforward victory for one of the parties. Even when the prince won a decisive military victory, he still had to bargain with the cities' representatives, given the fiscal powers they possessed.

---

[5] Marc Boone, Maarten Prak, Rulers, patricians and burghers: the great and little tradition of urban revolt in the Low Countries in Karel Davids, Jan Lucassen, *A Miracle Mirrored. The Dutch Republic in European Perspective* (Cambridge, 1995), pp. 99–134.

One should not, however, underestimate the impact of political serendipities, as they also help to explain fundamental economic and geographical changes in the urban network. The demise of Bruges as a commercial hub in favour of Antwerp at the end of the fifteenth century was reinforced by the confrontation that set mainly the Flemish cities in opposition to Habsburg power, but was also influenced by the secular shift of political power from Flanders to Brabant. More importantly, three-quarters of a century later, the combination of military power (and political contingency), religious zealotry and uncustomary financial demands by the Habsburg sovereign resulted in the relocation of the economic heart of the Low Countries, this time away from Antwerp to Amsterdam.

The dialectics of social and political conflicts in the cities and the repeated confrontations between city and prince resulted in a deepening of the praxis of consultation and communication. Furthermore, one must also underline that the remarkably strong literacy of urban populations of the Low Countries facilitated the elaboration of an urban ideology and offered tools to express political and social claims. If one characteristic of the Dutch Republic of the seventeenth century stands out, it may well be the incessant internal divisions within cities and between cities. Paradoxically, it reinforced a distinct preference for negotiations and deliberations as a means to an (albeit often temporary) end to conflict. It also explains the impact of so-called 'representative institutions' in the Low Countries. The 'scabini Flandriae', who as 'national' delegates represented the great Flemish cities in the course of the thirteenth century; the 'Members of Flanders' in the fourteenth and fifteenth centuries; the Estates in each principality; and the Estates General from their birth in the 1460s – all incorporated the ambition of urban power elites to put their mark on the way that their society was organised.

This ambition was not, of course, unique to the Low Countries. However, contrary to what was the rule in France, England or the German Empire (where the prince took the initiative to call for a meeting and decided on its agenda), in the Low Countries, the subjects acquired the right to convene on the topics they deemed worthy of discussion. The pinnacle of this development was undoubtedly the so-called Act of Abjuration (1581), in which the rebels deposed King Philip II as ruler. In this document, the Estates General declared that they could no longer put their trust in the king, and therefore refused to recognise him any longer as their righteous lord. This took place long before the English Glorious Revolution (1688) or the American and French revolutions. The Act of Abjuration may echo the speech given on behalf of the burghers of Ghent by Iwein van Aalst against the ambition of the French candidate for succession in the county of Flanders (the Norman nobleman William Clito) in 1128, though it would be false to suggest any linear and teleological evolution between the two events. What is clear, however, is that an ongoing and complex process of political conflict – within cities and between city and prince – led to the gradual refinement of arguments, reinforcing the position of both urban elites and middling groups alike.

Unsurprisingly in such a political field, cities invested heavily in maintaining and constructing their collective memories, which proved very helpful. In the course of the Revolt of the Netherlands in the late sixteenth century, old medieval privileges – for example, the set of privileges granted by Mary of Burgundy in 1477 to the Estates General, to the estates of several principalities (Flanders, Brabant, Hainaut and Holland-Zeeland) and to some individual cities (Ghent and Bruges) – were searched for in the archives and multiplied, thanks to the new medium of the printing press. These fifteenth-century privileges served as a direct source of inspiration for the Act of Abjuration. The hallmark of the old cities of the ancient Low Countries as urban democracies that we owe to Henri Pirenne is no longer accepted as such and has been deconstructed by recent research. What remains is the insight that the urban network of the Low Countries harboured a number of political experiments, concerning both the relationship between cities and prince, and the often conflicting relations between social and economic groups within the cities.

To a large extent, the tensions between cooperation and conflict determined the economic and political organisation of the Low Countries. The town halls and belfries that testify to the circulation of architectural knowledge and models and a clearly developed sense of civic pride are still visible today. At the same time, these tensions created a specific urban culture that drew its meaning from the constant exchange of values, practices and ideas inside and outside the urban network. This was epitomised in the ritual exchanges between towns, among other things through participation in joint civic processions. In the fifteenth century, official delegations from the towns of Flanders, Artois, Hainaut and Brabant participated in the Procession of Our Lady in the episcopal city of Tournai. In this sense, the urban religious culture differed considerably from the Italian model, where city-states like Venice or Florence aggressively imposed the civic symbols and rituals of the leading city on the towns and villages of their *contadi*. In the Low Countries, besides large cities, many smaller towns organised renowned processions or maintained famous pilgrimage sites, which were visited annually by secular and religious dignitaries, as well as ordinary devotees from other towns and from the surrounding region or even beyond.

Even more particular to the Low Countries was its competitive culture of public display. This derived certainly from the omnipresence of the corporative model, which, through the agency of craft and merchant guilds and religious confraternities, stood at the root not only of the organisation of industry and trade but also of lay devotion and cultural display. Sports and literary performance were increasingly dominated by urban corporations, respectively elite jousting companies and the shooting guilds, and the chambers of rhetoric, which were mainly composed of middle-class citizens. From the thirteenth century onwards, numerous urban jousts, competitions of crossbow guilds and theatre or poetry contests were held, often between guilds from different towns. Corporations defending the honour of their hometown tilted at the ring, shot at the popinjay or performed farces and morality plays at central marketplaces in the presence of cheering urban crowds. These sportive and literary exchanges reflected the constant economic interactions within the urban network and can be seen as part of 'an economy of symbolic exchange'. The invitations to these events that were sent to neighbouring towns underlined values such as friendship, brotherhood and harmony and avoided every allusion to actual economic competition or political friction. In this sense, these contests contributed in an important way to the social and cultural integration of the Low Countries.

The Burgundian-Habsburg princes were quick to recognise the political value of a cultural model that highlighted reciprocity and cooperation, and they willingly patronised public competitions. Some princes, from Duke Philip the Bold to Emperor Charles V, participated in person as honorary members of crossbow guilds. Therefore, these urban meetings in which local elites and the middling sort of people played a central role were appropriated from the late fourteenth century onwards as part of the Burgundian-Habsburg 'theatre state', which also included elaborate joyous entries and celebrations of dynastic births, marriages and peace treaties in sumptuous ceremonies that temporarily transformed urban space.

The reverse of the model was, ironically, that the considerable investment in urban and corporative honour also caused numerous frictions among guilds and among the cities they represented. At the end of the thirteenth century, the count of Flanders even had to intervene in a violent conflict between the cities of Douai and Lille, after a joust in the first city had got out of hand, while in the sixteenth century the small towns of Herentals and Turnhout in Brabant fought out a bitter legal battle about the precedence of their respective places in the competitions of the shooting guilds and the chambers of rhetoric. Significantly, conflicts about precedence or about who deserved the first prize were always between neighbouring cities or between towns that matched each other in political status and competed in trade or production. Therefore, sports, theatrical performance and even religious ritual could bring communities closer together but also inflame rivalries in the political and economic domains.

The urban culture of the Low Countries derived its characteristics from the interactions and conflicts not only between established corporations but also between less formally organised social groups. Accordingly, the dazzling achievements in the luxury industries – the visual arts in particular – were the result of a constant process of emulation and distinction between courtiers and citizens with different social status. This was most clear in cities where the prince (Bruges, Brussels, Ghent, Lille, Mechelen and The Hague) or a bishop (Utrecht, Liège, Cambrai and Tournai) resided, temporarily or more permanently, where they cultivated a splendid court life and promoted art production. Courtiers followed the model of their prince or high prelate by building impressive stone residences and commissioning similar furniture, textiles, books and paintings. Affluent patricians and guildsmen in their turn imitated these courtiers, but also acted as innovators. This dialectic process stimulated constant strife in these fashionable cities for a renewal in materials, style and subject matter. This is also demonstrated by the strong urban influence in the shaping of the art markets in the fifteenth and sixteenth centuries. Foreign merchants, like Giovanni Arnolfini and Tommaso Portinari in Bruges, contracted both secular and religious paintings. In the field of the visual arts, the role of collective investment cannot be denied either. Corporations pooled their funds to commission impressive altarpieces, giving middle-class citizens access to the top layer of the art market. Rogier van der Weyden executed the *Descent from the Cross* (*c.* 1435, now in the Prado Museum) for Leuven's crossbow guild, while Dirk Bouts painted the *Last Supper* (1464–8) for the Corpus Christi confraternity in the same city. In a similar vein, membership of civic corporations could bring significant volumes of work, as was the case for Hieronymus Bosch, who was a member of the prestigious Our Lady Confraternity in Den Bosch, or Jan van Scorel, who portrayed himself as one of the brothers of the Jeruzalem confraternity of Haarlem (*c.* 1528).

The importance of collective investment in the pictorial and architectural arts is most clear in a pictorial tradition that would become emblematic for the Dutch Golden Age, but that had developed from the fifteenth century onwards: the group portrait. Typical in this genre are the portraits of civic militia that express male honour and urban resilience. Around 1500 an anonymous master portrayed the members of the crossbow guild of Mechelen assembled in devotion around their patron Saint George, who, in deference to the ruling dynasty, has the facial features of Duke Philip the Fair. In 1529 Dirck Jacobsz painted a secular group portrait for the meeting hall of the guild of the *kloveniers* (who exercised with arquebuses) in Amsterdam (Figure 9.1). Although the group portrait gained popularity in the seventeenth century, it is not difficult to see that its roots lay in the civic culture of the late medieval Low Countries, which tried to overcome the many challenges of a highly competitive urban economy, a fragmented political landscape and intense social inequality by upholding an ideology that highlighted the moral authority of the group and the common good of the wider urban community. Through collective patronage, the middling groups could thus rival the urban elites, courtiers and foreign merchants as investors in specific forms of art, while at the same time strengthening the exclusion of lower-class groups. Of course, many more or less subtle status distinctions in clothing, housing, diet and *savoir vivre* remained. Yet, a strong corporative identity allowed the middling groups to participate fully in and even dominate urban culture.

As is crystal clear, even today the Netherlands and Belgium owe much to this medieval legacy of conflict, competition and cooperation in and between cities. While it would be wrong to frame history in deterministic terms, it is also true that the middling groups continue to struggle to defend their position in society, often reinforcing structural patterns of path-dependency.[6] Yet, balances of power can abruptly change. Hence, implicit and explicit concerns about threats to the social position of the middling sort of people are a recurrent topos in the histories of the Low Countries, one that has powerfully echoes today. Indeed, technological evolutions and global changes challenge the social architecture of our urbanised societies. Yet, so far, structural societal features inherited from the medieval legacy of the Low Countries and the long-lasting 'strategies' of the middling sort have proved remarkably resilient.

---

[6] Godfried Engbersen, Erik Snel and Monique Kremer (eds.), *De val van de middenklasse? Het stabiele en kwetsbare midden* (The Hague: Wetenschappelijke Raad voor het Regeringsbeleid, 2017).

Select Bibliography

Chapter 1

Billen, Claire and Marc Boone, 'L'histoire urbaine en Belgique: construire l'après-Pirenne entre tradition et rénovation', *Città & Storia*, 5.1 (2010), pp. 3–22.

Blockmans, Wim, *Metropolen aan de Noordzee. De geschiedenis van Nederland, 1100–1650* (Amsterdam: Bert Bakker, 2010) (see also the special forum discussing this topic in *BMGN-Low Countries Historical Review*, 127.2 (2012), pp. 75–96).

Blok, Dirk Peter, Walter Prevenier, Daniel Jeen Roorda et al. (eds.), *Algemene geschiedenis der Nederlanden*, 15 vols. (Haarlem: Fibula-Van Dishoeck, 1977–83).

Boone, Marc, 'Cities in late medieval Europe: the promise and curse of modernity', *Urban History*, 39 (2012), pp. 329–49.

Clark, Peter, *European Cities and Towns, 400–2000* (Oxford: Oxford University Press, 2009).

Clark, Peter (ed.), *The Oxford Handbook of Cities in World History* (Oxford: Oxford University Press, 2013).

Davids, Karel and Jan Lucassen (eds.), *A Miracle Mirrored: The Dutch Republic in European Perspective* (Cambridge: Cambridge University Press, 1995).

Lucassen Leo and Wim Willems (eds.), *Living in the City: Urban Institutions in the Low Countries, 1200–2010* (New York and London: Routledge, 2012).

Pirenne, Henri, *Les Villes et les institutions urbaines*, 2 vols. (Paris: Alcan, 1939).

Prak, Maarten and Jan Luiten van Zanden, *Nederland en het poldermodel. De economische en sociale geschiedenis van Nederland, 1000–2000* (Amsterdam: Bert Bakker, 2013) (see also the special forum discussing 'The Netherlands and the polder model' in *BMGN – Low Countries Historical Review*, 129.1 (2014), pp. 90–133).

Taverne, Ed, Len de Klerk, Bart Ramakers and Sebastian Demski (eds.), *Nederland stedenland. Continuïteit en vernieuwing* (Rotterdam: nai010 uitgevers, 2012).

Weber, Max, *The City* (New York: Free Press, 1958) (part of *Wirtschaft und Gesellschaft*; critical edn: *Wirtschaft und Gesellschaft: Grundriss der verstehenden Soziologie* (Tübingen: Mohr-Siebeck, 1956)).

Websites

www.eauh.eu (European Association for Urban History).
www.historiaurbium.org (International Commission for the History of Towns).

Chapter 2

Blockmans, Wim, 'The creative environment: incentives to and functions of Bruges' art production' in Maryan W. Ainsworth (ed.), *Petrus Christus in Renaissance Bruges: An Interdisciplinary Approach* (New York and Turnhout: Metropolitan Museum of Art and Brepols, 1995), pp. 11–20.

Metropolen aan de Noordzee. Geschiedenis van Nederland, 1100–1555. (Amsterdam: Bert Bakker, 2010).

'Regionale Vielfalt im Zunftwesen in den Niederlanden vom 13. bis zum 16. Jahrhundert' in Knut Schulz (ed.), *Handwerk in Europa vom Spätmittelalter bis zur Frühen Neuzeit* (Munich: Oldenbourg, 1999), pp. 51–63.

Boone, Marc and Walter Prevenier, *La draperie ancienne des Pays-Bas: débouchés et stratégies de survie (14e–16e siècles)* (Leuven and Apeldoorn: Garant, 1993).

Dambruyne, Johan, *Corporatieve middengroepen. Aspiraties, relaties en transformaties in de 16de-eeuwse Gentse ambachtswereld* (Ghent: Academia Press, 2002).

De Munck, Bert, 'Gilding golden ages: perspectives from early modern Antwerp on the guild debate, c. 1450–c. 1650', *European Review of Economic History*, 15 (2011), pp. 221–53.

'One counter and your own account: redefining illicit labour in early modern Antwerp', *Urban History*, 37 (2010), pp. 26–44.

Technologies of Learning: Apprenticeship in Antwerp from the 15th Century to the End of the Ancien Régime (Turnhout: Brepols, 2007).

De Munck, Bert, Steven Laurence Kaplan and Hugo Soly (eds.), *Learning on the Shop Floor: Historical Perspectives on Apprenticeship* (London and New York: Berghahn Books, 2007).

Deceulaer, Harald, *Pluriforme patronen en een verschillende snit. Sociaal-economische, institutionele en culturele transformaties in de kledingsector in Antwerpen, Brussel en Gent, 1585–1800* (Amsterdam: IISG, 2001).

DuPlessis, Robert S. and Martha C. Howell, 'Reconsidering the early modern urban economy: the cases of Leiden and Lille', *Past and Present*, 94 (1982), pp. 49–84.

Epstein, Stephan R., 'Craft guilds, apprenticeship and technological change in pre-industrial Europe', *Journal of Economic History*, 58 (1998), pp. 684–713.

Epstein, Stephan R. and Maarten Prak (eds.), *Guilds, Innovation, and the European Economy, 1400–1800* (Cambridge: Cambridge University Press, 2008).

Howell, Martha C., *Commerce before Capitalism in Europe, 1300–1600* (Cambridge and New York: Cambridge University Press, 2010).

Lecuppre-Desjardin, Elodie, *Le royaume inachevé des ducs de Bourgogne (XIVe–XVe siècles)* (Paris: Belin, 2016).

Lesger, Clé, *Handel in Amsterdam ten tijde van de Opstand. Kooplieden, commerciële expansie en verandering in de ruimtelijke economie van de Nederlanden ca. 1550–ca. 1630* (Hilversum: Verloren, 2001).

Lis, Catharina and Hugo Soly, 'Different paths of development: capitalism in the Northern and Southern Netherlands during the late Middle Ages and the early modern period', *Review*, 20.2 (1997), pp. 211–42.

Worthy Efforts: Attitudes to Work and Workers in Pre-Industrial Europe (Leiden: Brill, 2012).

Lis, Catharina, Jan Lucassen, Maarten Prak and Hugo Soly (eds.), *Guilds in the Early Modern Low Countries: Work, Power and Representation* (Aldershot: Ashgate, 2006).
Lucassen, Jan and Maarten Prak, 'Guilds and society in the Dutch Republic 16th–18th centuries' in Stephan R. Epstein, H.G. Haupt, C. Poni and H. Soly (eds.), *Guilds, Economy and Society: Proceedings of the Twelfth International Economic History Congress, Session B* (Madrid: Fundación Fomento de la Historia Ecónomica, 1998), pp. 63–77.
Munro, John H., 'Industrial transformations in the north-west European textile trades, c. 1290–c. 1340: economic progress or economic crisis?' in Bruce M.S. Campbell (ed.), *Before the Black Death: Studies in the 'Crisis' of the Early Fourteenth Century* (Manchester: Manchester University Press, 1991), pp. 110–48.
Medieval woollens: textiles, textile technology, and industrial organisation, c. 800–1500' in David Jenkins (ed.), *The Cambridge History of Western Textiles* (Cambridge: Cambridge University Press, 2003), pp. 181–227.
'Medieval woollens: the Western European woollen industries and their struggles for international markets, c.1000–1500' in David Jenkins (ed.), *The Cambridge History of Western Textiles* (Cambridge: Cambridge University Press, 2003), pp. 228–324.
Textiles, Towns and Trade: Essays in the Economic History of Late-Medieval England and the Low Countries (Aldershot and Brookfield, VT: Variorum, 1994).
Murray, James M., *Bruges, Cradle of Capitalism, 1280–1390* (Cambridge: Cambridge University Press, 2005).
Nicholas, David, *The Metamorphosis of a Medieval City: Ghent in the Age of the Arteveldes, 1302–1390* (Lincoln, NE: University of Nebraska Press, 1987).
Sicking, Louis, *Neptune and the Netherlands: State, Economy, and War at Sea in the Renaissance* (Leiden and Boston: Brill, 2004).
Soly, Hugo, 'The political economy of guild-based textile industries: power relations and economic strategies of merchants and master artisans in medieval and early modern Europe', *International Review of Social History*, 53 (2008), supplement, pp. 45–71.
Sosson, Jean-Pierre, 'Les métiers: norme et réalité. L'exemple des anciens Pays-Bas méridionaux aux XIVe et XVe siècles' in Jacqueline Hamesse and Colette Muraille-Samaran (eds.), *Le Travail au Moyen Age. Une approche interdisciplinaire* (Louvain-la-Neuve: Publications de l'Institut d'Études Médiévales, 1990), pp. 339–48.
Stabel Peter, 'Compositions et recompositions des réseaux urbains des Pays-Bas au bas Moyen Age' in Elisabeth Crouzet-Pavan and Elodie Lecuppre-Desjardin (eds.), *Villes de Flandre et d'Italie. Relectures d'une comparaison traditionnelle*. (Turnhout: Brepols, 2007), pp. 29–64.
Dwarfs among Giants: The Flemish Urban Network in the Late Middle Ages. (Leuven and Apeldoorn: Garant, 1997).
'Guilds in the late medieval Low Countries: myth and reality of guild life in an export-oriented environment', *Journal of Medieval History*, 30 (2004), pp. 187–212.
'Urban markets, rural industries and the organization of labour in late medieval Flanders: the constraints of guild regulations and the requirements of

export oriented production' in Bruno Blondé, Eric Vanhaute and Michèle Galand (eds.), *Labour and Labour Markets between Town and Countryside (Middle Ages–19th Century)* (Turnhout: Brepols, 2001), pp. 140–57.

Stein, Robert, *Magnanimous Dukes and Rising States: The Unification of the Burgundian Netherlands, 1380–1480* (Oxford: Oxford University Press, 2017).

Taverne, Ed, Len de Klerk, Bart Ramakers and Sebastian Demski (eds.), *Nederland stedenland. Continuïteit en vernieuwing* (Rotterdam: nai010 uitgevers, 2012).

Thijs Alfons K.L., 'Antwerp's luxury industries: the pursuit of profit and artistic sensitivity' in Jan Van Der Stock (ed.), *Antwerp: Story of a Metropolis, 16th–17th Century* (Antwerp: Snoeck-Ducaju and Zoon, 1993), pp. 105–13.

'Structural changes in the Antwerp industry from the fifteenth to the eighteenth century' in Herman Van der Wee (ed.), *The Rise and Decline of Urban Industries in Italy and the Low Countries (Late Middle Ages–Early Modern Times)* (Leuven: Leuven University Press, 1988), pp. 207–12.

Van 'werkwinkel' tot 'fabriek'. De textielnijverheid te Antwerpen (einde 15de–begin 19de eeuw) (Brussels: Gemeentekrediet van België, 1987).

Van Bavel, Bas, *Manors and Markets: Economy and Society in the Low Countries, 500–1600* (Oxford: Oxford University Press, 2010).

Van Bavel, Bas and Jan Luiten Van Zanden, 'The jump start of the Holland economy during the late medieval crisis, c. 1350–1500', *Economic History Review*, 57 (2004), pp. 503–32.

Van der Wee, Herman, *The Growth of the Antwerp Market and the European Economy (fourteenth–sixteenth centuries)* (The Hague: Martinus Nijhoff, 1963).

'Industrial dynamics and the process of urbanization and de-urbanization in the Low Countries from the late Middle Ages to the eighteenth century' in Herman Van der Wee (ed.), *The Rise and Decline of Urban Industries in Italy and the Low Countries (Late Middle Ages–Early Modern Times)* (Leuven: Leuven University Press, 1988), pp. 307–81.

'Structural changes and specialization in the industry of the southern Netherlands, 1100–1600', *Economic History Review*, 28 (1975), pp. 203–21.

Van Uytven, Raymond, 'Splendour and wealth? Art and economy in the Burgundian Netherlands', *Transactions of the Cambridge Bibliographical Society*, 10 (1992), pp. 101–24.

Chapter 3

Aerts, Erik, 'Economie, monnaie et société dans les Pays-Bas méridionaux de Charles Quint' in Wim Blockmans and Nicolette Mout (eds.), *The World of Emperor Charles V* (Amsterdam: Koninklijke Nederlandse Akademie van Wetenschappen, 2004), pp. 201–26.

Blockmans, Wim P., 'The social and economic effects of plague in the Low Countries', *Belgisch Tijdschrift voor Filologie en Geschiedenis*, 58 (1980), pp. 833–63.

Blockmans, Wim P. and Walter Prevenier, 'Poverty in Flanders and Brabant from the fourteenth to the mid-sixteenth century: sources and problems', *Acta Historiae Neerlandicae*, 10 (1978), pp. 20–57.

Blockmans, Wim P., Ingrid De Meyer and Jacques Mertens, *Studiën betreffende de sociale strukturen te Brugge, Kortrijk en Gent in de 14e en 15e eeuw*, 3 vols. (Kortrijk and Heule: UGA, 1971).

Blondé, Bruno, *De sociale structuren en economische dynamiek van 's-Hertogenbosch, 1500–1550* (Tilburg: Stichting Zuidelijk Historisch Contact, 1987).

Blondé, Bruno and Jord Hanus, 'Beyond building craftsmen: economic growth and living standards in the sixteenth-century Low Countries: the case of 's-Hertogenbosch (1500–1560)', *European Review of Economic History*, 14.2 (2010), pp. 179–207.

Boone, Marc, *Gent en de Bourgondische hertogen ca. 1384–ca. 1453: een sociaal-politieke studie van een staatsvormingsproces* (Brussels: Koninklijke Vlaamse Academie van België voor Wetenschappen en Kunsten, 1990).

—— 'State power and illicit sexuality: the persecution of sodomy in late medieval Bruges', *Journal of Medieval History*, 22 (1996), pp. 135–53.

Brand, Hanno, *Over macht en overwicht. Stedelijke elites in Leiden (1420–1510)* (Leuven and Apeldoorn: Garant, 1996).

Buylaert, Frederik and Sam Geens, 'Social mobility in the medieval Low Countries, 1100–1600' in Sandro Carocci and Isabella Lazzarini (eds.), *Social Mobility in Medieval Italy (1100–1500)* (Rome: Viella, 2018), pp. 77–99.

Carlier, Myriam, *Kinderen van de minne? Bastaarden in het vijftiende-eeuwse Vlaanderen* (Brussels: Paleis der Academiën, 2001).

Carlier, Myriam and Peter Stabel, 'Questions de moralité dans les villes de la Flandre au bas Moyen Age: sexualité et activité urbaine (bans échevinaux et statuts de métiers)' in Jean-Marie Cauchies and Eric Bousmar (eds.), *'Faire Banz, edictz et statuts': légiférer dans la ville médiévale* (Brussels: Publications des Facultés universitaires Saint-Louis, 2002), pp. 241–62.

Dambruyne, Johan, *Corporatieve middengroepen. Aspiraties, relaties en transformaties in de 16de-eeuwse Gentse ambachtswereld* (Ghent: Academia Press, 2002).

Danneel, Marianne, *Weduwen en wezen in het laat-middeleeuwse Gent* (Leuven and Apeldoorn: Garant, 1995).

De Moor, Tine and Jan Luiten van Zanden, 'Girl power: the European marriage pattern and labour markets in the North Sea region in the late medieval and early modern period', *Economic History Review*, 63 (2010), pp. 1–33.

Gunn, Steven, David Grummitt and Hans Cools, *War, State and Society in England and the Netherlands, 1477–1559* (Oxford: Oxford University Press, 2007).

Hanus, Jord, *Affluence and Inequality in the Low Countries: The City of 's-Hertogenbosch in the Long Sixteenth Century, 1500–1650* (Leuven: Peeters Publishers, 2014).

Hoppenbrouwers, Peter, 'Maagschap en vriendschap: een beschouwing over de structuur en de functies van verwantschapsbetrekkingen in het laat-middeleeuwse Holland', *Holland*, 17 (1985), pp. 69–108.

Howell, Martha, *The Marriage Exchange: Property, Social Place, and Gender in Cities of the Low Countries, 1300–1550* (Chicago and London: University of Chicago Press, 1998).

Hutton, Shennan, *Women and Economic Activities in Late Medieval Ghent* (Basingstoke: Palgrave, 2011).

Kittell, Ellen E. and Mary A. Suydam (eds.), *The Texture of Society: Medieval Women in the Southern Low Countries* (New York: Palgrave MacMillan, 2004).

Lestocquoy, Jean, *Aux origines de la bourgeoisie. Les villes de Flandre et d'Italie sous le gouvernement des patriciens, XIe–XVe siècles* (Paris: Presses Universitaires de France, 1952).

Lis, Catharina and Hugo Soly, *Poverty and Capitalism in Pre-Industrial Europe* (Hassocks: The Harvester Press, 1979).

Lis, Catharina, Jan Lucassen, Maarten Prak and Hugo Soly (eds.), *Guilds in the Early Modern Low Countries: Work, Power and Representation* (Aldershot: Ashgate, 2006).

Munro, John, *Textiles, Towns and Trade: Essays in the Economic History of Late Medieval England and the Low Countries* (Aldershot: Ashgate, 1994).

Nicholas, David, *The Domestic Life of a Medieval City: Women, Children and the Family in Fourteenth-Century Ghent* (Lincoln, NE: University of Nebraska Press, 1985).

Noordegraaf, Leo, *Hollands welvaren? Levensstandaard in Holland, 1450–1650* (Bergen: Octavo, 1985).

Noordegraaf, Leo and Jan Luiten Van Zanden, 'Early modern economic growth and the standard of living: did labour benefit from Holland's Golden Age?' in Karel Davids and Jan Lucassen (eds.), *A Miracle Mirrored: The Dutch Republic in European Perspective* (Cambridge: Cambridge University Press, 1995), pp. 410–37.

Pirenne, Henri, *Les Villes et les institutions urbaines* (Paris: Alcan, 1939).

Prevenier, Walter (ed.), *Le prince et le peuple. Images de la société du temps des ducs de Bourgogne, 1384–1530* (Antwerp: Mercatorfonds, 1998).

Proeve 't al, 't is prysselyck. Verbruik in Europese steden (13de–18de eeuw). Liber amicorum Raymond Van Uytven (Antwerp: UFSIA, 1998).

Rousseaux, Xavier, 'Crimes, pouvoirs et societies (1400–1800): anciens Pays-Bas et principauté de Liége' in Marie-Sylvie Dupont-Bouchat and Xavier Rousseaux (eds.), *Crimes, pouvoirs et societies (1400–1800). Anciens Pays-Bas et principauté de Liège* (Kortrijk: Heule, 2001), pp. 15–82.

Ryckbosch, Wouter, 'Economic inequality and growth before the industrial revolution: the case of the Low Countries (fourteenth to nineteenth centuries)', *European Review of Economic History*, 20 (2015), pp. 1–22.

Soltow, Lee and Jan Luiten Van Zanden, *Income and Wealth Inequality in the Netherlands, 16th–20th Century* (Amsterdam: Het Spinhuis, 1998).

Sosson, Jean-Pierre, 'Les XIVe et XVe siècles: un âge d'or de la main d'oeuvre? Quelques réflexions à propos des anciens Pays-Bas méridionaux' in Jean-Marie Cauchies (ed.), *Aspects de la vie économique des pays bourguignons (1384–1559). Dépression ou prospérité* (Basel: Centre européen d'études bourguignonnes (XIVe–XVIe s.), 1987), pp. 17–39.

Stabel, Peter, *Dwarfs Among Giants: The Flemish Urban Network in the Middle Ages* (Leuven: Garant, 1997).

Tits-Dieuaide, Marie-Jeanne, 'Les tables des pauvres dans les anciennes principautés belges au Moyen Age', *Tijdschrift voor Geschiedenis*, 88 (1975), pp. 562–83.

Van Caenegem, Raoul C., Albert Demyttenaere and Luc Devliegher (eds.), *De moord op Karel de Goede* (Leuven: Davidsfonds, 1999).
Van der Wee, Herman, 'The economy as a factor in the revolt of the southern Netherlands' in Herman Van der Wee (ed.), *The Low Countries in the Early Modern World* (Aldershot: Variorum, 1993), pp. 264–78.
The Growth of the Antwerp Market and the European Economy (Fourteenth–Sixteenth Centuries) (The Hague: Martinus Nijhoff, 1963).
Van Steensel, Arie, 'Recent historiography on the nobility in the medieval low countries', *History Compass*, 12 (2014), pp. 263–99.
Van Werveke, Hans, 'La famine de l'an 1316 en Flandre et dans les régions voisines', *Revue du Nord*, 41 (1959), pp. 5–14
Vercauteren, Fernand, *Luttes sociales à Liège, XIIIe et XIVe siècles* (Brussels: Renaissance du livre, 1943).
Verhulst, Adriaan, *The Rise of Cities in North-Western Europe* (Cambridge: Cambridge University Press, 1999).

Chapter 4

Arnade, Peter, *Beggars, Iconoclasts, and Civic Patriots: The Political Culture of the Dutch Revolt* (Ithaca and London: Cornell University Press, 2008).
Realms of Ritual: Burgundian Ceremony and Civic Life in Medieval Ghent (Ithaca and London: Cornell University Press, 1996).
Benders, Jeroen, *Bestuursstructuur en schriftcultuur. Een analyse van de bestuurlijke verschriftelijking in Deventer tot het einde van de 15de eeuw* (Kampen: IJsselacademie, 2004).
Bertrand, Paul, *Les écritures ordinaires. Sociologie d'un temps de révolution documentaire (entre royaume de France et Empire, 1250–1350)* (Paris: Publications de la Sorbonne, 2015).
Blockmans, Wim, *Metropolen aan de Noordzee. De geschiedenis van Nederland, 1100–1560* (Amsterdam: Bakker, 2010).
Blockmans, Wim and Walter Prevenier, *The Promised Lands: The Low Countries under Burgundian Rule, 1369–1530* (Philadelphia: University of Pennsylvania Press, 1999).
Boone, Marc, *A la recherche d'une modernité civique. La société urbaine des anciens Pays-Bas au bas Moyen Age* (Brussels: Éditions de l'Université de Bruxelles, 2010).
'The Dutch Revolt and the medieval tradition of urban dissent', *Journal of Early Modern History*, 11 (2007), pp. 351–75.
'Les gens de métiers à l'époque corporative à Gand et les litiges professionnels (14ième–15ième siècles)' in Marc Boone and Maarten Prak (eds.), *Individual, Corporate and Judicial Status in European Cities (Late Middle Ages and Early Modern Period)* (Leuven: Garant, 1996), pp. 23–47.
Braekevelt, Jonas, Frederik Buylaert, Jan Dumolyn and Jelle Haemers, 'Factional conflict in late medieval Flanders', *Historical Research*, 85 (2012), pp. 13–31.
Carlier, Myriam and Peter Stabel, 'Questions de moralité dans les villes de la Flandre au bas Moyen Age: sexualité et activité législative urbaine (bans échevinaux et statuts de métiers)' in Jean-Marie Cauchies and Eric Bousmar

(eds.), *'Faire bans, edictz et statuz': légiférer dans la ville médiévale. Sources, objets et acteurs de l'activité législative communale en Occident, ca. 1200–1500* (Brussels: Publications des Facultés universitaires Saint-Louis, 2001), pp. 241–62.

Cohn, Samuel, *Lust for Liberty: The Politics of Social Revolt in Medieval Europe, 1200–1425. Italy, France, and Flanders* (Cambridge, MA: Harvard University Press, 2006).

Cox, Joost, *'Hebbende privilege van stede'. De verlening van stadsrechtsprivileges in Holland en Zeeland (13de–15de eeuw)* (The Hague: Sdu Uitgevers, 2011).

Crombie, Laura, *Archery and Crossbow Guilds in Late Medieval Flanders* (Woodbridge: Boydell and Brewer, 2016).

Dubois, Sébastien, Bruno Demoulin and Jean-Louis Kupper, *Les Institutions publiques de la principauté de Liège (980–1794)* (Brussels: Algemeen Rijksarchief, 2012).

Duerr, Hans Peter, *Nudité et pudeur. Le mythe du processus de civilisation* (Paris: Maison des sciences de l'homme, 1988).

Dumolyn, Jan, 'The legal repression of revolts in late medieval Flanders', *Tijdschrift voor Rechtsgeschiedenis*, 68 (2000), pp. 479–521.

Dumolyn, Jan and Jelle Haemers, '"A bad chicken was brooding": subversive speech in late medieval Flanders', *Past and Present*, 214 (2012), pp. 45–86.

'"Let each man carry on with his trade and remain silent": middle-class ideology in the urban literature of the late medieval Low Countries', *Cultural and Social History*, 10 (2013), pp. 169–89.

'Patterns of urban rebellion in medieval Flanders', *Journal of Medieval History*, 31 (2005), pp. 369–93.

Elias, Norbert, *Über den Prozeß der Zivilisation. Soziogenetische und psychogenetische Untersuchungen*, 2 vols. (Basel: Haus zum Falken, 1939), translated as *The Civilizing Process: State Formation and Civilisation* (Oxford: Blackwell, 1982).

Godding, Philippe, *La Législation ducale en Brabant sous le règne de Philippe le Bon (1430–1467)* (Brussels: Académie royale de Belgique, 2006).

Haemers, Jelle, *De strijd om het regentschap over Filips de Schone. Opstand, facties en geweld in Brugge, Gent en Ieper (1482–1488)* (Ghent: Academia Press, 2014).

For the Common Good: State Power and Urban Revolts in the Reign of Mary of Burgundy (Turnhout: Brepols, 2009).

'Révolte et requête: les gens de métiers et les conflits sociaux dans les villes de Flandre (XIIIe–XVe siècle)', *Revue Historique*, 677 (2016), pp. 27–55.

'Social memory and rebellion in fifteenth-century Ghent', *Social History*, 36 (2011), pp. 443–63.

Hemptinne, Thérèse de and Walter Prevenier, 'Les actes urbains, témoins d'une conscience identitaire', *Histoire Urbaine*, 35 (2012), pp. 7–33.

Howell, Martha, *Commerce Before Capitalism in Europe, 1300–1600* (Cambridge: Cambridge University Press, 2010).

Lantschner, Patrick, *The Logic of Political Conflict in Medieval Cities: Italy and the Southern Low Countries, 1370–1440* (Oxford: Oxford University Press, 2015).

Lecuppre-Desjardin, Elodie, *La Ville des cérémonies. Essai sur la communication politique dans les anciens Pays-Bas bourguignons* (Turnhout: Brepols, 2004).

Leupen, Piet, *Philip of Leyden: A Fourteenth-Century Jurist* (The Hague and Zwolle: Leiden University Press and W.E.J. Tjeenk Willink, 1981).

Select Bibliography

Mareel, Samuel, *Voor vorst en stad. Rederijkersliteratuur en vorstenfeest in Vlaanderen en Brabant, 1432–1561* (Amsterdam: Amsterdam University Press, 2010).
Muchembled, Robert, *Une histoire de la violence. De la fin du Moyen Age à nos jours* (Paris: Seuil, 2008).
Le Temps des supplices. De l'obéissance sous les rois absolus (XVe–XVIIIe siècle) (Paris: Colin, 1992).
Pleij, Herman, *Het gevleugelde woord. Geschiedenis van de Nederlandse literatuur 1400–1560* (Amsterdam: Bert Bakker, 2007).
Prak, Maarten, 'Citizens, soldiers and civic militias in late medieval and early modern Europe', *Past and Present*, 228 (2015), pp. 93–123.
Prevenier, Walter, 'Utilitas communis in the Low Countries (13th–15th centuries): from social mobilisation to legitimation of power' in Elodie Lecuppre-Desjardin and Anne-Laure Van Bruaene (eds.), *De Bono Communi: The Discourse and Practice of the Common Good in the European City, 13th–16th centuries* (Turnhout: Brepols, 2010), pp. 205–16.
Prevenier, Walter and Thérèse de Hemptinne (eds.), *La Diplomatique urbaine en Europe au Moyen Age* (Leuven: Garant, 2000).
Schulz, Knut, *Denn sie lieben die Freiheit so sehr ... Kommunale Aufstände und Entstehung des europäischen Bürgertums im Hochmittelalter* (Darmstadt: Wissenschaftliche Buchgesellschaft, 1992).
Stein, Robert, *Magnanimous Dukes and Rising States: The Unification of the Burgundian Netherlands, 1380–1480* (Oxford: Oxford University Press, 2017).
Stein, Robert and Judith Pollmann (eds.), *Networks, Regions and Nation: Shaping Identities in the Low Countries, 1300–1650* (Leiden: Brill, 2010).
Van Dijck, Maarten F., 'De stad als onafhankelijke variabele en centrum van moderniteit. Langetermijntrends in stedelijke en rurale criminaliteitspatronen (1300–1800)', *Stadsgeschiedenis*, 1 (2006), pp. 7–26.
Van Herwaarden, Jan, 'Opgelegde bedevaarten. Een populaire praktijk in de laatmiddeleeuwse Nederlanden', *Madoc*, 24 (2010), pp. 241–9.
Van Leeuwen, Jacoba, *De Vlaamse wetsvernieuwing. Een onderzoek naar de jaarlijkse keuze en aanstelling van het stadsbestuur in Gent, Brugge en Ieper in de Middeleeuwen* (Brussels: KVAB, 2004).
Van Oostrom, Frits Pieter, *Wereld in woorden. Geschiedenis van de Nederlandse literatuur, 1300–1400* (Amsterdam: Prometheus, 2013).
Van Uytven, Raymond, *Het dagelijks leven in een middeleeuwse stad. Leuven anno 1448* (Leuven: Davidsfonds, 1998).
Watts, John, *The Making of Polities: Europe, 1300–1500* (Cambridge: Cambridge University Press, 2009).
Weis, Monique (ed.), *Des villes en révolte. Les 'républiques urbaines' aux Pays-Bas et en France pendant la deuxième moitié du XVIe siècle* (Turnhout: Brepols, 2010).

Chapter 5

Arnade, Peter, *Beggars, Iconoclasts and Civic Patriots: The Political Culture of the Dutch Revolt* (Ithaca: Cornell University Press, 2008).
Bange, Petty, *Een handvol wijsheden. Eenvoudig geloof in de vijftiende eeuw: De Spieghel ofte reghel der kersten ghelove* (Nijmegen: Valkhof Pers, 2000).

Select Bibliography

Bijsterveld, Arnoud-Jan, *Laverend tussen Kerk en wereld. De pastoors in Noord-Brabant 1400–1570* (Amsterdam: Vrije Universiteit Uitgeverij, 1993).

Bogaers, Llewellyn, *Aards, betrokken en zelfbewust: de verwevenheid van cultuur en religie in katholiek Utrecht, 1300–1600* (Utrecht: Levend Verleden, 2008).

Brinkman, Herman, *Dichten uit liefde: literatuur in Leiden aan het einde van de Middeleeuwen* (Hilversum: Verloren, 1997).

Brown, Andrew, *Civic Ceremony and Religion in Medieval Bruges, c. 1300–1520* (Cambridge: Cambridge University Press, 2011).

Callewier, Hendrik, 'De papen van Brugge. De seculiere clerus in een middeleeuwse wereldstad (1411–1477)', unpublished PhD thesis, Katholieke Universiteit Leuven (2011).

Christman, Victoria, *Pragmatic Toleration: The Politics of Religious Heterodoxy in Early Reformation Antwerp, 1515–1555* (Rochester, NY: Rochester University Press, 2015).

Crouzet-Pavan, Elisabeth and Elodie Lecuppre-Desjardin, *Villes de Flandre et d'Italie (XIIIe-XVIe siècle). Les enseignements d'une comparaison* (Turnhout: Brepols, 2008).

De Rock, Jelle, 'Beeld van de stad: picturale voorstellingen van stedelijkheid in de laatmiddeleeuwse Nederlanden', unpublished PhD thesis, Universiteit Antwerpen (2011).

Decavele, Johan, *De dageraad van de Reformatie in Vlaanderen (1520–1565)*, 2 vols. (Brussels: Koninklijke Academie, 1975).

Duke, Alastair, *Dissident Identities in the Early Modern Low Countries*, ed. Judith Pollmann and Andrew Spicer (Aldershot: Ashgate, 2009).

Dumolyn, Jan, 'Une idéologie urbaine "bricolée" en Flandre médiévale: les *Sept portes de Bruges* dans le manuscrit Gruuthuse (début du XVe siècle)', *Belgisch Tijdschrift voor Filologie en Geschiedenis*, 88.4 (2010), pp. 1039–84.

Folkerts, Suzan, 'Te "duncker" voor liken? Middelnederlandse Bijbelvertalingen vanuit het perspectief van de gebruikers', *Jaarboek voor Nederlandse Boekgeschiedenis*, 18 (2011), pp. 155–70.

Goudriaan, Koen, 'De derde orde van Sint-Franciscus in het bisdom Utrecht: een voorstudie', *Jaarboek voor Middeleeuwse Geschiedenis*, 1 (1998), pp. 205–60.

'Het einde van de Middeleeuwen ontdekt?', *Madoc*, 8 (1994), pp. 66–75.

Jonckheere, Koenraad, *Antwerp Art after Iconoclasm: Experiments in Decorum, 1566–1585* (Brussels: Mercatorfonds, 2012).

Kuys, Jan, *Kerkelijke organisatie in het middeleeuwse bisdom Utrecht* (Nijmegen: Valkhof Pers, 2004).

Lavéant, Katell, *Un théâtre des frontières. La culture dramatique dans les provinces du Nord aux XVe et XVIe siècles* (Orléans: Paradigme, 2011).

Lawrence, Clifford Hugh, *Kloosterleven in de Middeleeuwen in West-Europa en de Lage Landen* (Amsterdam: Pearson Education Benelux, 2004).

Lecuppre-Desjardin, Elodie, *La Ville des cérémonies. Essai sur la communication politique dans les anciens Pays-Bas bourguignons* (Turnhout: Brepols, 2004).

Marnef, Guido, *Antwerp in the Age of Reformation: Underground Protestantism in a Commercial Metropolis, 1550–1577* (Baltimore and London: Johns Hopkins University Press, 1996).

'Civic religions' in Ulinka Rublack (ed.), *The Oxford Handbook of the Protestant Reformations* (Oxford: Oxford University Press, 2017), pp. 546–64.

Meijns, Birgitte, 'Veelheid en verscheidenheid: de kanonikale instellingen in het graafschap Vlaanderen tot circa 1155', *Trajecta*, 9 (2000), pp. 233–51.

Nissen, Peter (ed.), *Geloven in de Lage Landen. Scharniermomenten in de geschiedenis van het christendom* (Leuven: Davidsfonds, 2004).

Oosterman, Johan, *De gratie van het gebed. Overlevering en functie van Middelnederlandse berijmde gebeden*, 2 vols. (Amsterdam: Prometheus, 1995).

Pleij, Herman, *Het gevleugelde woord. Geschiedenis van de Nederlandse literatuur 1400–1560* (Amsterdam: Bert Bakker, 2007).

Pollmann, Judith, *Catholic Identity and the Revolt of the Netherlands 1520–1635* (Oxford: Oxford University Press, 2011).

Ramakers, Bart, *Spelen en figuren. Toneelkunst en processiecultuur in Oudenaarde tussen Middeleeuwen en Moderne Tijd* (Amsterdam: Amsterdam University Press, 1996).

Schepers, Kees (ed.), *1517–1545: The Northern Experience. Mysticism, Reform and Devotion between the Late Medieval and Early Modern Periods*, special issue of *Ons Geestelijk Erf*, 87.1–2 (2016).

Schilling, Heinz, *Civic Calvinism in Northwestern Germany and the Netherlands: Sixteenth to Nineteenth Centuries* (Kirksville, MO: Sixteenth Century Essay and Studies, 1991).

Simons, Walter, *Cities of Ladies: Beguine Communities in the Medieval Low Countries, 1200–1565* (Philadelphia: University of Pennsylvania Press, 2001).

Stad en Apostolaat. De vestiging van de bedelorden in het graafschap Vlaanderen (circa 1225–circa 1330) (Brussels: Koninklijke Academie voor Wetenschappen, Letteren en Schone Kunsten van België, 1987).

Speakman Sutch, Susie and Anne-Laure Van Bruaene, 'The Seven Sorrows of the Virgin Mary: devotional communication and politics in the Burgundian-Habsburg Low Countries (*c*. 1490–1520)', *Journal of Ecclesiastical History*, 61.2 (2010), pp. 252–78.

Speetjens, Annemarie, 'A quantitative approach to late medieval transformations of piety in the Low Countries: historiography and new ideas' in Robert Lutton and Elisabeth Salter (eds.), *Pieties in Transition: Religious Practices and Experiences, c. 1400–1640* (Aldershot and Burlington, VT: Ashgate, 2007), pp. 109–26.

Stein, Robert, *Politiek en historiografie. Het ontstaansmilieu van Brabantse kronieken in de eerste helft van de vijftiende eeuw* (Leuven: Peeters, 1994).

Trio, Paul, *Volksreligie als spiegel van een stedelijke samenleving. De broederschappen te Gent in de late middeleeuwen* (Leuven: Universitaire Pers, 1993).

Trio, Paul and Marjan De Smet (eds.), *The Use and Abuse of Sacred Places in Late Medieval Towns* (Leuven: Leuven University Press, 2006).

Van Bruaene, Anne-Laure, *Om beters wille. Rederijkerskamers en de stedelijke cultuur in de Zuidelijke Nederlanden (1400–1650)* (Amsterdam: Amsterdam University Press, 2008).

Van Bruaene, Anne-Laure, Koenraad Jonckheere and Ruben Suykerbuyk (eds.), *Beeldenstorm: Iconoclasm in the Low Countries*, special issue of *BMGN-Low Countries Historical Review*, 131.1 (2016).

van Dixhoorn, Arjan, *Lustige geesten. Rederijkers in de Noordelijke Nederlanden (1480–1650)* (Amsterdam: Amsterdam University Press, 2009).
Van Engen, John, *Sisters and Brothers of the Common Life: The Devotio Moderna and the World of the Later Middle Ages* (Philadelphia: University of Pennsylvania Press, 2008).
Van Herwaarden, Jan, *Between Saint James and Erasmus: Studies in Late-Medieval Religious Life: Devotion and Pilgrimage in the Netherlands* (Leiden: Brill, 2003).
Van Luijk, Madelon, *Bruiden van Christus. De tweede religieuze vrouwenbeweging in Leiden en Zwolle, 1380–1580* (Zutphen: Walburg Pers, 2004).
Verhoeven, Gerrit, *Devotie en negotie. Delft als bedevaartplaats in de late middeleeuwen* (Amsterdam: Vrije Universiteit Uitgeverij, 1992).
Vroom, Wim, *Financing Cathedral Building in the Middle Ages: The Generosity of the Faithful* (Amsterdam: Amsterdam University Press, 2010).
Waite, Gary, *Reformers on Stage: Popular Drama and Religious Propaganda in the Low Countries of Charles V, 1515–1556* (Toronto: Toronto University Press, 2000).
Weis, Monique (ed.), *Des villes en révolte. Les 'Républiques urbaines' aux Pays-Bas et en France pendant la deuxième moitié du XVIe siècle* (Turnhout: Brepols, 2010).

Chapter 6

Arnade, Peter, Martha Howell and Walter Simons, 'Fertile spaces: the productivity of urban space in northern Europe', *Journal of Interdisciplinary History*, 32.4 (2002), pp. 518–48.
Baudoux-Rousseau, Laurence, Youri Carbonnier and Philippe Bragard (eds.), *La Place publique urbaine du Moyen Age à nos jours* (Arras: Artois Presses Université, 2007).
Bertrand, Paul, *'Commerce avec Dame Pauvreté'. Structure et fonctions des couvents mendiants à Liège XIIIe–XIVe siècle* (Geneva: Droz, 2004).
Billen, Claire, 'Dire le bien commun dans l'espace public: matérialité épigraphique et monumentalité du bien commun dans les villes des Pays-Bas à la fin du Moyen Age' in Elodie Lecuppre-Desjardin and Anne-Laure Van Bruaene (eds.), *De Bono Communi: The Discourse and Practice of the Common Good in the European City (13th–16th c.)* (Turnhout: Brepols, 2010), pp. 71–88.
Blockmans, Wim, 'Urban space in the Low Countries, 13th–16th centuries' in Alberto Grohmann (ed.), *Spazio urbano e organizzazione economica nell'Europa medieval. Atti della session C 23, 11th International Economic History Congress, Milano, 12–16 settembre 1994* (Naples: ESI Edizioni Scientifiche Italiane, 1994), pp. 163–76.
Boone, Marc, 'Urban space and political conflict in late medieval Flanders', *Journal of Interdisciplinary History*, 32.4 (2002), pp. 623–8.
Boone, Marc and Elodie Lecuppre-Desjardin, 'Espace vécu, espace idéalisé dans les villes des anciens Pays-Bas bourguignons' in Alain Dierkens, Christophe Loir, Denis Morsa and Guy Vanthemsche (eds.), *Villes et villages. Organisation et représentation de l'espace. Mélanges offerts à Jean-Marie Duvosquel* (Brussels: Le livre Timperman, 2011), pp. 111–28 (= *Revue Belge de Philologie et d'Histoire*, 89).

Select Bibliography

Boone, Marc and Peter Stabel (eds.), *Shaping Urban Identity in Late Medieval Europe* (Leuven and Apeldoorn: Garant, 2000).

Boucheron, Patrick and Jean-Philippe Genet (eds.), *Marquer la ville. Signes, traces, empreintes du pouvoir (XIIIe–XVIe siècle)* (Paris: Publications de la Sorbonne, 2013).

Cauchies, Jean-Marie, 'Le "cri" et l'espace urbain: bretèches et publication dans les villes des anciens Pays-Bas' in Alain Dierkens, Christophe Loir, Denis Morsa and Guy Vanthemsche (eds.), *Villes et villages. Organisation et représentation de l'espace. Mélanges offerts à Jean-Marie Duvosquel* (Brussels: Le livre Timperman), 2011, pp. 167–89 (= *Revue Belge de Philologie et d'Histoire*, 89).

Charruadas, Paulo, *Croissance rurale et essor urbain à Bruxelles. Les dynamiques d'une société entre ville et campagnes (1000–1300)* (Brussels: Académie royale de Belgique, 2011).

Classen, Albrecht (ed.), *Urban Space in the Middle Ages and Early Modern Age* (Berlin: De Gruyter, 2009).

Coomans, Thomas, 'Belfries, cloth halls, hospitals and mendicant churches: a new urban architecture in the Low Countries around 1300' in Alexandra Gajewsli and Zoë Opacic (eds.), *The Year 1300 and the Creation of a New European Architecture* (Turnhout: Brepols, 2007), pp. 185–202.

Crang, Mike, 'Spaces in theory, spaces in history and spatial historiographies' in Beat Kümin (ed.), *Political Space in Pre-Industrial Europe* (Farnham and Burlington, VT: Ashgate, 2009), pp. 249–66.

De Jonge, Krista, '"Scientie" et "experientie" dans le gothique moderne des anciens Pays-Bas' in Monique Chatenet, Krista De Jong, Ethan Matt Kavaler and Norbert Nussbaum (eds.), *Le Gothique de la Renaissance. Actes des quatrièmes Rencontres d'architecture européenne, Paris 12–16 juin 2007* (Paris: Picard, 2011), pp. 199–216.

De Spiegelere, Pierre, *Les Hôpitaux et l'assistance à Liège (Xe–XVe siècles). Aspects institutionnels et sociaux* (Geneva: Droz, 1987).

De Waha, Michel, 'De la collaboration à la confrontation: enceintes urbaines et châteaux princiers dans les villes des anciens Pays-Bas' in Philippe Contamine, Nicolas Faucherre, Gilles Blieck and Jean Mesqui (eds.), *Le Château et la ville* (Paris: CTHS, 2002), pp. 161–77.

Deligne, Chloé, *Bruxelles et sa rivière. Genèse d'un territoire urbain (1200–1800)* (Turnhout: Brepols, 2005).

'Edilité et politique: les fontaines urbaines dans les Pays-Bas méridionaux au Moyen Age', *Histoire Urbaine*, 22 (2008), pp. 77–96.

'Powers over space, spaces of powers: the constitution of town squares in the cities of the Low Countries (12th–14th century)' in Marc Boone and Martha Howell (eds.), *The Power of Space in Late Medieval and Early Modern Europe: The Cities of Italy, Northern France and the Low Countries* (Turnhout: Brepols, 2013), pp. 21–8.

Deligne, Chloé, Claire Billen and David Kusman, 'Les bouchers bruxellois au bas Moyen Age: profils d'entrepreneurs' in Serge Jaumain and Kenneth Bertrams (eds.), *Patrons, gens d'affaires et banquiers. Hommages à Ginette Kurgan-van Hentenrijk* (Brussels: Le livre Timperman, 2004), pp. 69–92.

Dietrich-Strobbe, Irène, '"Chacun doit gaignier et prouffiter du prince": Lille ou le laboratoire d'une politique monumentale bourguignonne' in Elisabeth Crouzet-Pavan and Jean-Claude Maire Vigueur (eds.), *L'Art au service du prince. Paradigme italien, expériences européennes (vers 1250–vers 1500)* (Rome: Viella, 2015), pp. 143–61.

Foucault, Michel, *Surveiller et punir. Naissance de la prison* (Paris: Gallimard, 1975), translated as: *Discipline and Punish: The Birth of the Prison* (New York: Random House, 1975).

Haemers, Jelle and Elodie Lecuppre-Desjardin, 'Conquérir et reconquérir l'espace urbain: le triomphe de la collectivité sur l'individu dans le cadre de la révolte brugeoise de 1488' in Chloé Deligne and Claire Billen (eds.), *Voisinages, coexistences, appropriations. Groupes sociaux et territoires urbains (Moyen Age–16e siècle)* (Turnhout: Brepols, 2007), pp. 119–42.

L'Initiative publique des communes en Belgique. Fondements Historiques (Ancien Régime). 11e colloque International de Spa, 1–4 septembre 1982 (Brussels: Crédit Communal de Belgique, 1984).

Jacobs, Thibaut, 'Des hôpitaux de Métiers à Bruxelles? Nouvelles perspectives sur la charité et la bienfaisance en milieu urbain à la fin du Moyen Age', *Revue Belge de Philologie et d'Histoire*, 91 (2013), pp. 215–56.

Köhl, Sascha, 'Platz, Stube, Haus: die Anfänge der Bauaufgabe Rathaus in Brabant', *Rathäuser und andere Kommunale Bauten. Jahrbuch für Hausforschung*, 60 (2010), pp. 117–28.

Laleman, Marie-Christine, 'Espaces publics dans les villes flamandes au Moyen Age: l'apport de l'archéologie urbaine' in Marc Boone and Peter Stabel (eds.), *Shaping Urban Identity in Late Medieval Europe* (Leuven and Apeldoorn: Garant, 2000), pp. 25–41.

Lecuppre-Desjardin, Elodie, *La Ville des cérémonies. Essai sur la communication politique dans les anciens Pays-Bas bourguignons* (Turnhout: Brepols, 2004).

Lefèbvre Henri, *La Production de l'espace* (Paris: Anthropos, 1974), translated as *The Production of Space* (Oxford: Blackwell, 1991)

Leroux, Laure, *Cloches et société médiévale. Les sonneries de Tournai au Moyen Age* (Louvain-la-Neuve: Ciaco-i6doc.com, 2011).

Paquay, Isabelle, *Gouverner la ville au bas Moyen Age. Les élites dirigeantes de la ville de Namur au XVe siècle* (Turnhout: Brepols, 2008).

Sicking, Louis, 'Sleutels tot de zee: havensteden en hun infrastructuur in de Nederlanden in de late middeleeuwen. Een verkenning', *Tijdschrift voor Zeegeschiedenis*, 25.1(2006), pp. 3–9.

Simon-Muscheid, Katharina, 'Städtischer Zierde-gemeiner Nutzen-Ort der begegnungen: öffentliche Brunnen in Mittelalterlichen Städten' in Helmut Bräuer and Elke Schlenkrich (eds.), *Die Stadt als Kommunikationsraum. Beiträge zur Stadtgeschichte vom Mittelalter bis ins 20. Jahrhundert. Festchrift für Karl Czok zum 75. Geburtstag* (Leipzig: Leipziger Universitätsverlag GMBH, 2006), pp. 699–720.

Simons, Walter, *Stad en apostolaat. De vestiging van de bedelorden in het graafschap Vlaanderen (ca. 1225–ca. 1350)* (Brussels: Koninklijke Academie voor Wetenschappen, Letteren en Schone Kunsten van België, 1987).

Soly, Hugo, *Urbanisme en kapitalisme te Antwerpen in de 16de eeuw. De stedebouwkundige en industriële ondernemingen van Gilbert van Schoonbeke* (Brussels: Crédit Communal de Belgique, 1977).

Sosson, Jean-Pierre, 'Le bâtiment: sources et historiographie, acquis et perspectives de recherches (Moyen Age, début des temps modernes)' in Simonetta Cavacocchi (ed.), *L'edilizia prima della rivoluzione industriale secc. XIII–XVIII. Atti della Trentaseiesima Settimana di Studi, 26–30 aprile 2004, Istituto Internazionale di Storia Economica F. Datini Prato* (Florence: Le Monnier, 2005), pp. 49–108.

'Politique économique et "innovation": l'exemple des infrastructures (Brabant, Flandre. Fin XIIe–XVe siècles)' in Hans-Joachim Schmidt (ed.), *Tradition, Innovation, Invention. Fortschrittsverweigerung und Fortschrittsbewusstsein im Mittelalter. Freiburger Kolloquium 15–17 März 2001* (Berlin: de Gruyter, 2005), pp. 143–59.

Stabel, Peter, 'The market place and civic identity in late medieval Flanders' in Marc Boone and Peter Stabel (eds.), *Shaping Urban Identity in Late Medieval Europe* (Leuven and Apeldoorn: Garant, 2000), pp. 43–64.

Van der Heijden, Manon, Elise van Nederveen Meerkerk, Griet Vermeersch and Martijn van der Burg (eds.), *Serving the Urban Community: The Rise of Public Facilities in the Low Countries* (Amsterdam: Aksant, 2009).

Van Uytven, Raymond, 'Flämische Belfriede und Südniederländische städtische Bauwerke im Mittelalter: Symbol und Mythos' in Alfred Haverkamp (ed.), *Information und Kommunikation und Selbstdarstellung in Mittelalterlischen Gemeinden* (Munich: Oldenbourg, 1998), pp. 125–59.

Verhulst, Adriaan, *The Rise of Cities in North-West Europe* (Cambridge: Cambridge University Press, 1999).

Volti, Panaiota, *Les Couvents des ordres mendiants et leur environnement à la fin du Moyen Age: le nord de la France et les anciens Pays-Bas méridionaux* (Paris: CNRS, 2003).

Wurtzel, Ellen, 'Defense, authority, and city limit: the fortifications of Lille in the late Middle Ages', *Jaarboek voor Middeleeuwse Geschiedenis*, 14 (2011), pp. 150–82.

Xhayet, Geneviève, *Réseaux de pouvoir et solidarité de parti à Liège au Moyen Age (1250–1468)* (Geneva: Droz, 1997).

Yante, Jean-Marie, 'Créations et aménagements de voies d'eau dans les Pays-Bas (XIIIe–XVIe siècles). Quelques jalons', *Revue Belge de Philologie et d'Histoire*, 94 (2016), pp. 973–82.

Chapter 7

Alexandre-Bidon, Danièle, Françoise Piponnier and Jean-Michel Poisson, *Cadre de vie et manières d'habiter (12e–16e siècle). 8e Congrès international de la Société d'archéologie médiévale (Paris, 11–13 octobre 2001)* (Caen: Crahm, 2006).

Baatsen, Inneke, 'A bittersweet symphony: the social recipe of dining culture in late medieval and early modern Bruges (1438–1600)', unpublished PhD thesis, University of Antwerp (2016).

Baatsen, Inneke and Bruno Blondé, 'Antwerp and the "material Renaissance": exploring the social and economic significance of crystal glass and majolica in the sixteenth century' in Catherine Richardson, Tara Hamling and David Gaimster (eds.), *The Routledge Handbook of Material Culture in Early Modern Europe* (London: Routledge, 2017), pp. 436–51.

Bessemans, Lutgarde (eds.), *Leven te Leuven in de late Middeleeuwen* (Leuven: Stedelijk Museum Vander Kelen-Mertens, 1998).

Blockmans, Wim and Esther Donckers, 'Self-representation of court and city in Flanders and Brabant in the fifteenth and early sixteenth centuries' in Wim Blockmans and Antheun Janse (eds.), *Showing Status: Representation of Social Positions in the Late Middle Ages* (Turnhout: Brepols, 1999), pp. 81–111.

Blondé, Bruno and Wouter Ryckbosch, '"In splendid isolation": a comparative perspective on the historiographies of the material Renaissance and the consumer revolution', *History of Retailing and Consumption*, 1.2 (2015), pp. 105–24.

Bloom, James J., 'Why painting?' in Neil De Marchi and Hans J. Van Miegroet (eds.), *Mapping Markets for Paintings in Europe, 1450–1750* (Turnhout: Brepols, 2006), pp. 17–34.

Buskirk, Jessica, '"Salve Maria Gods Moeder Ghepresen": the Salve Regina and the vernacular in the art of Hans Memling, Anthonis De Roovere, and Jacob Obrecht' in Joost Keizer and Todd M. Richardson (eds.), *The Transformation of Vernacular Expression in Early Modern Arts* (Leiden and Boston: Brill, 2012), pp. 59–97.

Buylaert, Frederik, Wim De Clercq and Jan Dumolyn, 'Sumptuary legislation, material culture and the semiotics of "vivre noblemen" in the county of Flanders (14th–16th centuries)', *Social History*, 36 (2011), pp. 393–417.

Buylaert Frederik, Jelle De Rock and Anne-Laure Van Bruaene, 'City portrait, civic body, and commercial printing in sixteenth-century Ghent', *Renaissance Quarterly*, 68.3 (2015), pp. 803–39.

Crane, Susan, *The Performance of Self: Ritual, Clothing and Identity During the Hundred Years War* (Philadelphia: University of Pennsylvania Press, 2002).

Crawford, Joanna, 'Clothing distributions and social relations' in Catherine Richardson (ed.), *Clothing Culture, 1350–1650* (Aldershot: Ashgate, 2004), pp. 153–78.

De Clercq, Wim, Jan Dumolyn and Jelle Haemers, '"Vivre noblement": material culture and elite identity in late medieval Flanders', *Journal of Interdisciplinary History*, 38 (2007), pp. 1–31.

De Coo, Jozef, 'A medieval look at the Merode Annunciation', *Zeitschrift für Kunstgeschichte*, 44 (1981), pp. 114–32.

Deceulaer, Harald, *Pluriforme patronen en een verschillende snit. Sociaal-economische, institutionele en culturele transformaties in de kledingsector in Antwerpen, Brussel en Gent, 1585–1800* (Amsterdam: Stichting beheer IISG, 2001).

De Groot, Julie, 'At home in Renaissance Bruges: material and domestic cultures in a city in decline, 1438–1600', unpublished PhD thesis, University of Antwerp (2017).

De Staelen, Carolien, 'Spulletjes en hun betekenis in een commerciële metropool. Antwerpenaren en hun materiële cultuur in de zestiende eeuw', unpublished PhD thesis, University of Antwerp (2007).

De Witte, Hubert (ed.), *Brugge onder-zocht. Tien jaar stadsarcheologisch onderzoek, 1977–1987* (Bruges: VZW Archeo-Brugge, 1988).

Dijkstra, Jeltje, 'The Brussels and the Merode Annunciation reconsidered' in Susan Foister and Susie Nash (eds.), *Robert Campin: New Directions in Scholarship* (Turnhout: Brepols, 1996), pp. 95–104.

Dumortier, Claire, *Céramique de la Renaissance à Anvers: de Venise à Delft* (Brussels and Paris: Éditions Racine and Les Éditions de l'Amateur, 2002).

Eames, Penelope, *Furniture in England, France and the Netherlands from the 12th to the 15th Centuries* (London: Furniture History Society, 1977).

Friedman, John Block, *Brueghel's Heavy Dancers: Transgressive Clothing, Class, and Culture in the Late Middle Ages* (New York: Syracuse University Press, 2010).

Goldstein, Claudia, *Pieter Bruegel and the Culture of the Early Modern Dinner Party* (Aldershot: Ashgate, 2013).

Hand, John Oliver, Catherine A. Metzger and Ron Spronk, *Prayers and Portraits: Unfolding the Netherlandish Diptych* (New Haven and London: Yale University Press, 2006).

Howell, Martha, *Commerce Before Capitalism in Europe, 1300–1600* (Cambridge: Cambridge University Press, 2010).

Martens, Maximiliaan P.J., 'Some aspects of the origins of the art market in fifteenth-century Bruges' in Michael North and David Ormrod (eds.), *Art Markets in Europe, 1400–1800* (Aldershot: Ashgate, 1998), pp. 19–27.

Martens, Maximiliaan P.J. and Natasja Peeters, 'Paintings in Antwerp houses (1532–1567)' in Neil de Marchi and Hans J. Van Miegroet (eds.), *Mapping Markets for Paintings in Europe, 1450–1750* (Turnhout: Brepols, 2006), pp. 35–53.

Munro, John, 'The anti-red shift – to the dark side: colour changes in Flemish luxury woollens, 1300–1550' in Robin Netherton and Gale R. Owen-Crocker (eds.), *Medieval Clothing and Textiles 3* (Woodbridge: The Boydell Press, 2007), pp. 55–96.

Nuechterlein, Jeanne, 'The domesticity of sacred space in the fifteenth-century Netherlands' in Andrew Spicer and Sarah Hamilton (eds.), *Defining the Holy: Sacred Space in Medieval and Early Modern Europe* (Aldershot: Ashgate, 2008), pp. 49–79.

Reynolds, Catherine, 'Reality and image: interpreting three paintings of the Virgin and Child in an interior associated with Campin' in Susan Foister and Susie Nash (eds.), *Robert Campin: New Directions in Scholarship* (Turnhout: Brepols, 1996), pp. 183–95.

Sarti, Raffaela, *Europe at Home: Family and Material Culture, 1500–1800* (New Haven: Yale University Press, 2002).

Stabel, Peter, 'Selling paintings in late medieval Bruges: marketing customs and guild regulations compared' in Neil De Marchi and Hans J. Van Miegroet (eds.), *Mapping Markets for Paintings in Europe, 1450–1750* (Turnhout: Brepols, 2006), pp. 89–103.

Sturtewagen, Isis, 'All together respectably dressed: fashion and clothing in Bruges during the fifteenth and sixteenth centuries', unpublished PhD thesis, University of Antwerp (2016).

Van der Wee, Herman, 'Industrial dynamics and the process of urbanization and de-urbanization in the Low Countries from the late Middle Ages to the eighteenth century. A synthesis' in Herman Van der Wee (ed.), *The Rise and Decline of Urban Industries in Italy and in the Low Countries (Late Middle Ages–Early Modern Times)* (Leuven: Leuven University Press, 1988), pp. 307–82.

Van Uytven, Raymond, *Het dagelijks leven in een middeleeuwse stad. Leuven anno 1448* (Leuven: Davidsfonds, 1998).

'Splendour or wealth: art and economy in the Burgundian Netherlands', *Transactions of the Cambridge Bibliographical Society*, 10 (1992), pp. 101–24.

Van Winter, Johanna M. (ed.), *Spices and Comfits: Collected Papers on Medieval Food* (Turnhout: Prospect Books, 2007), pp. 318–29.

Veeckman, Johan and Sarah Jennings (eds.), *Majolica and Glass from Italy to Antwerp and Beyond: The Transfer of Technology in the 16th–Early 17th Century* (Antwerp: Stad Antwerpen, 2002).

Vermeylen, Filip, *Painting for the Market: Commercialization of Art in Antwerp's Golden Age* (Turnhout: Brepols, 2003).

Wolversperges, Thibaut, *Meubelkunst in België, 1500–1800* (Brussels: Racine, 2000).

Chapter 8

Blockmans, Wim, 'The Burgundian court and the urban milieu as patrons in 15th century Bruges' in Michael North (ed.), *Economic History and the Arts* (Cologne, Weimar and Vienna: Böhlau, 1996), pp. 15–26.

Bot, Petrus Nicolaas Maria, *Humanisme en onderwijs in Nederland* (Utrecht and Antwerp: Spectrum, 1955).

Bousmar, Eric, 'La cour de Bourgogne et l'humanisme avant Érasme: influences et rencontres manquées?' in *Renaissance bourguignonne et Renaissance italienne: modèles, concurrences* (Neuchâtel: Publications du Centre Européen d'Etudes Bourguignonnes, 2015), pp. 41–64.

Cormack, Lesley B., Steven A. Walton and John A. Schuster (eds.), *Mathematical Practitioners and the Transformation of Natural Knowledge in Early Modern Europe* (Cham: Springer, 2017).

Cuijpers, Peter M.H., *Teksten als koopwaar. Vroege drukkers verkennen de markt. Een kwantitatieve analyse van de productie van Nederlandstalige boeken. Tot circa 1550 en de lezershulp in de seculiere prozateksten* (Nieuwkoop: De Graaf, 1998).

Davids, Karel, 'Apprenticeship and guild control in the Netherlands, c. 1450–1800' in Bert De Munck, Steven L. Kaplan and Hugo Soly (eds.), *Learning on the Shop Floor: Historical Perspectives on Apprenticeship* (London and New York: Berghahn Books, 2007), pp. 65–84.

'The bookkeeper's tale: learning merchant skills in the northern Netherlands in the sixteenth century' in Koen Goudriaan, Jaap van Moolenbroek and Ad Tervoort (eds.), *Education and Learning in the Netherlands 1400–1600. Essays in Honour of Hilde de Ridder-Symoens* (Leiden: Brill, 2004), pp. 235–76.

De Bie, Annelies and Bert De Munck, 'Learning on the shop floor in the Spanish Netherlands' in Sven Dupré, Bert De Munck, Werner Thomas and Geert Vanpaemel (eds.), *Embattled Territory: The Circulation of Knowledge in the Spanish Netherlands* (Ghent: Academia Press, 2015), pp. 51–72.

Select Bibliography   283

De Kerf, Raoul and Bert De Munck, 'Cities as centres of innovation in the Spanish Netherlands' in Sven Dupré, Bert De Munck, Werner Thomas and Geert Vanpaemel (eds.), *Embattled Territory: The Circulation of Knowledge in the Spanish Netherlands* (Ghent: Academia Press, 2015), pp. 25–50.

De Munck, Bert, 'Corpses, live models, and nature: assessing skills and knowledge before the industrial revolution. Case: Antwerp', *Technology and Culture*, 51.2 (2010), pp. 332–56.

'From brotherhood community to civil society? Apprentices between guild, household and the freedom of contract in early modern Antwerp', *Social History*, 35.1 (2010), pp. 1–20.

Technologies of Learning: Apprenticeship in Antwerp from the 15th Century to the End of the Ancien Régime (Turnhout: Brepols, 2007).

De Munck, Bert and Hugo Soly, 'Introduction: learning on the shop floor in historical perspective' in Bert De Munck, Steven L. Kaplan and Hugo Soly (eds.), *Learning on the Shop Floor: Historical Perspectives on Apprenticeship* (London and New York: Berghahn Books, 2007), pp. 3–32.

de Ridder-Symoens, Hilde, 'The changing face of centres of learning 1400–1700' in Alasdair A. MacDonald and Michael W. Twomey (eds.), *Schooling and Society: The Ordering and Reordering of Knowledge in the Western Middle Ages* (Leuven: Peeters, 2004), pp. 115–38.

'Maranos and universities in the Renaissance Netherlands', *History of Universities*, 27.1 (2013), pp. 20–49.

'Het onderwijs te Antwerpen in de zeventiende eeuw' in Walter Couvreur (ed.), *Antwerpen in de XVIIde eeuw* (Antwerp: Genootschap voor Antwerpse Geschiedenis, 1989), pp. 221–50.

'La sécularisation de l'enseignement aux anciens Pays-Bas au Moyen Age et à la Renaissance' in Jean-Marie Duvosquel and Erik Thoen (eds.), *Peasants and Townsmen in Medieval Europe: Studia in honorem Adriaan Verhulst* (Gent: Snoeck-Ducaju and Zoon, 1995), pp. 721–38.

de Ridder-Symoens, Hilde and Jan Roegiers, 'Lecture tools at the Leuven faculty of arts from its origin (1425) until the end of the seventeenth century', *Annali di Storia delle Università Italiane*, 19.1 (2015), pp. 25–43.

De Universiteit te Leuven 1425–1985 (Leuven: University Press, 1986).

Dupré, Sven and Christine Göttler (eds.), *Knowledge and Discernment in the Early Modern Arts* (New York: Routledge, 2017).

Elkhadem, Hossam, 'Aperçu de l'état du savoir scientifique à l'époque bourguignonne' in Jean-Marie Duvosquel, Jacques Nazet and André Vanrie, *Mélanges André Uyttebrouck* (Brussels: Archives et Bibliothèques de Belgique, 1996), pp. 259–66.

Farr, James R., *Artisans in Europe, 1300–1914* (Cambridge: Cambridge University Press, 2000).

Gruys, Jan Albert and Clemens de Wolf (eds.), *Thesaurus 1473–1800. Nederlandse boekdrukkers en boekverkopers. Met plaatsen en jaren van werkzaamheid* (Nieuwkoop: De Graaf, 1989).

Lamont, Koen, *Het wereldbeeld van een zestiende-eeuwse Gentenaar Marcus van Vaernewijck* (Ghent: Maatschappij voor Geschiedenis en Oudheidkunde, 2005).

Long, Pamela O., *Artisan/Practitioners and the Rise of the New Sciences, 1400–1600* (Corvallis, OR: Oregon State University Press, 2011).
Mokyr, Joel, *The Gifts of Athena: Historical Origins of the Knowledge Economy* (Princeton: Princeton University Press, 2002).
Pettegree, Andrew and Malcolm Walsby (eds.), *Netherlandish Books: Books Printed in the Low Countries and Dutch Books Printed Abroad before 1601* (Leiden and Boston, Brill, 2011).
Post, Regnerus Richardus, *Scholen en onderwijs in Nederland gedurende de Middeleeuwen* (Utrecht and Antwerp: Spectrum, 1954).
Ramakers, Bart (ed.), *Understanding Art in Antwerp: Classicising the Popular, Popularising the Classic 1540–1580* (Leuven: Peeters, 2011).
Roberts, Lissa, Simon Schaffer and Peter Dear (eds.), *The Mindful Hand: Inquiry and Invention from the Late Renaissance to Early Industrialisation* (Amsterdam: KNAW, 2007).
Santing, Catrien, '"Liberation from the trivial yoke": Dutch Renaissance educators and their cultural and socio-political objectives' in Jan Willem Drijvers and Alasdair A. MacDonald (eds.), *Centres of Learning: Learning and Location in Pre-Modern Europe and the Near East* (Leiden: Brill, 1995), pp. 315–27.
Smith, Pamela H., *The Body of the Artisan: Art and Experience in the Scientific Revolution* (Chicago and London: University of Chicago Press, 2004).
Stabel, Peter, 'Social mobility and apprenticeship in late medieval Flanders' in Bert De Munck, Steven L. Kaplan and Hugo Soly (eds.), *Learning on the Shop Floor: Historical Perspectives on Apprenticeship* (London and New York: Berghahn Books, 2007), pp. 158–78.
Valleriani, Matteo (ed.), *The Structures of Practical Knowledge* (Cham: Springer, 2017).
Van Bruaene, Anne-Laure, *Om beters wille. Rederijkerskamers en de stedelijke cultuur in de Zuidelijke Nederlanden (1400–1650)* (Amsterdam: Amsterdam University Press, 2008).
van Dixhoorn, Arjan, 'Literary cultures and public opinion in the early modern Netherlands' in Jan Bloemendal, Arjan van Dixhoorn and Elsa Strietman (eds.), *Literary Cultures and Public Opinion* (Leiden: Brill, 2011), pp. 1–35.
  Lustige geesten. Rederijkers in de Noordelijke Nederlanden in de vijftiende, zestiende en zeventiende eeuw (Amsterdam: Amsterdam University Press, 2009).
  'Writing poetry as intellectual training: chambers of rhetoric and the development of vernacular intellectual life in the Low Countries between 1480 and 1600' in Koen Goudriaan, Jaap van Moolenbroek and Ad Tervoort (eds.), *Education and Learning in the Netherlands 1400–1600. Essays in Honour of Hilde de Ridder-Symoens* (Leiden: Brill, 2004), pp. 201–22.
Van Zanden, Jan Luiten, *The Long Road to the Industrial Revolution: The European Economy in a Global Perspective* (Leiden: Brill, 2009).
Vandommele, Jeroen, *Als in een spiegel. Vrede, kennis en gemeenschap op het Antwerpse Landjuweel van 1561* (Hilversum: Verloren, 2011).
Wesseling, Ari, 'Latin and the vernaculars: the case of Erasmus' in Jan Bloemendal (ed.), *Bilingual Europe: Latin and Vernacular Cultures – Examples of Bilingualism and Multilingualism c. 1300–1800* (Leiden: Brill, 2015), pp. 30–49.
Willemsen, Annemarieke, *Back to the Schoolyard: The Daily Practice of Medieval and Renaissance Education* (Turnhout: Brepols, 2008).

Index

Aachen, 117
Aalst, 29, 35, 109, 234, 240
   gateway, 165
Aardenburg, 117
Abbenbroek, 150
Abundus, 224
administration, municipal, 99–101, 107, 118–20, 175, 220, 247
   chirograph, 99–100
agriculture, 4, 7, 13, 26, 29, 33, 34, 37, 38, 43, 47, 62, 78, 218, 256
Aire-sur-la-Lys, 63
Alberghi, family, 76
Albert I of Bavaria, 168
Alberti, Leon Battista, 206
aldermen's house, 164, 176, 177, 182
Alkmaar, 88, 179
alliance between towns, *see* league of towns
almshouse, 18, 89, 164, 175
Alva, duke of, 185
Amay, 165
Ameide, Wouter, 41, 54
Amsterdam, 6, 28, 44, 51, 258, 260
   gateway, 14, 29, 38, 44, 56, 57, 258
   market, 35, 37, 41, 42, 43, 44
   religion, 155, 157
   schools, 248
   town accounts, 160
   urban network, 11, 26, 28, 30, 39, 79, 167
   urban space, 178
Anabaptism, 154
anti-clericalism, 140–1, 151
Antwerp (province), 26
Antwerp (town), 37, 40, 50, 55, 89, 237, 247, 258, 260
   art, 49, 50, 59, 123, 125, 142, 152, 200, 202, 207, 211, 212, 213, 218, 232, 252
   consumption, 199, 204, 209, 212
   craft guilds, 53, 55, 86, 114, 174, 223

Eiermarkt, 59, 61
elite, 71, 73, 76, 110, 169, 198
gateway, 14, 29, 38, 43, 44, 55, 56, 57, 165, 258
market, 5, 19, 30, 40, 41, 42, 44, 47, 55, 59, 81, 85, 87, 156, 205, 218, 250
middling groups, 85, 88, 89, 150, 152
municipal government, 92, 106, 114, 154, 196, 217, 247
Our Lady, Chapter of, 179
Our Lady, Church of, 142
Our Lady, hospital of, 187
population, 27, 59, 80
princely interaction, 11, 56, 107, 112, 113, 114, 119
religion, 132, 145, 153, 154, 155, 156, 157, 158
Saint Elisabeth, hospital of, 187
Saint George, Church of, 153
Saint James, Church of, 153
Saint James, parish of, 135
schools, 222, 225, 228, 232, 237, 243
Stock exchange, 178, 179
textile industry, 42, 203
town accounts, 96, 160
town hall, 178, 185
urban network, 10, 11, 21, 26, 28, 30, 33, 39, 40, 41, 45, 79, 260
urban society, 59, 60, 79, 135, 142, 187, 212
urban space, 120, 178, 179, 181, 185
Antwerpen, *see* Antwerp
Anvers, *see* Antwerp
archaeology, urban, 165, 168, 203, 208
architecture, urban, 6, 18, 41, 162, 174, 178–80, 192, 196, *see also* house, urban
   Brabantine Gothic, 179
   petrification, 171, 183, 196, 218
   regulations, 196
   Tertiary Gothic, 180
urban planning, 6

285

Aristotle, 253
Armentières, 29, 40, 41, 49
Arnemuiden, 167
Arnhem, 9, 244
Arquennes, 179
Arras
  art, 50, 147
  craft guilds, 69, 213
  elite, 64
  gateway, 165
  municipal government, 109
  population, 27
  princely interaction, 105
  town accounts, 99
  urban network, 10, 29, 79
art, 49, 50, 154, 189, 194, 207, 232, 249, 252, 263
  church music, 132, 143
  embroidery, 50
  glass, 252
  gold- and silversmiths, 154, 232
  jewellery, 201
  majolica, 207, 211, 232, 252, *see also* material culture:tableware
  painting, 49, 154, 200, 205, 207, 211, 218, 263
  porcelain, 208, *see also* material culture:tableware
  sculpture, 49, 178, 232
  stonecutting, 178, 179
  tapestry, 50, 54, 82, 154, 189
  woodcut, 50, 160
Artesia, *see* Artois
artisans, 46, 48, 59, 68, 87, 112, 157, 178, 198, 210, 220, 226, 232, 233, 238, 244, 251, 253, *see also* guilds, craft
  apprenticeship, *see* education: apprenticeship
  master artisans, 33, 50, 55, 70, 125, 148, 212, 226, 241
Artois, 24, 37
  economic development, 29, 35
  market, 56, 57
  municipal government, 64
  population, 27, 80
  religion, 261
  textile industry, 42, 57, 69
  urban network, 10, 30, 38, 49, 79
  urban society, 78
arts, 222
  artes-literature, 237
  liberal, 222, 232, 233, 241, 253
  mechanical, 222, 232, 233, 253
Ath, 102
Atlantic Rim, 26

autonomy, municipal, 16, 62, 96, 107, 114, 159, 258, 264
  enclave, 62, 137, 169–70, 183, 189
  legal autonomy, 101

Bacon, Roger, 232
Baldwin the pretender, 180
Baldwin, count of Flanders (VIII) and Hainaut (V), 102
Baltic Sea, 26, 35
Baltics, 34, 37, 41, 44
Barbezaen, Claes, 185
Barlandus, Adrianus, 243
Bartolus of Sassoferrato, 101
beguinage, 137, 189
behavioural codes, *see* manners, urban
belfry, 18, 100, 121, 162, 174, 175, 176, 177, 180–1, 182, 184, 261
Belgium, 3, 4, 5, 6, 7, 28, 30, 51
bell, town, 175, 178, 180–1, 192
Bentheim, 179
Bergen-op-Zoom, 40, 149, 179
  urban space, 179
Bergen-op-Zoom, lords of, 179
Bergues, 29, 132
  Saint Martin, Chapter of, 132
Berlin, 28
Biervliet, 29, 166
Bijns, Anna, 125, 153
Billen, Claire, 7
Binche, 168
Black Death, 48, 75, 77
Bladelin, Peter, 211
Blankenberge, 37
Blockmans, Wim, 201
Bode, family, 76
Boendale, *see* van Boendale, Jan
Bois-le-duc, *see* 's-Hertogenbosch
Bolsward, 136
Borgloon, 103, 117
Borluut, Elisabeth, 141
Borluut, family, 65, 66
Bosch, Hieronymus, 211
bourgeoisie, 4, 15, 194, 255, 257
Brabant, 3, 9, 10, 12, 16, 19, 21, 24, 26, 34, 39, 42, 43, 69, 80, 86, 107, 123, 132, 178, 249
  art, 148, 149, 150, 240, 251
  consumption, 218, 219
  craft guilds, 52, 56, 69, 173, 177
  economic development, 34, 56, 82, 86, 179
  elite, 73, 224
  market, 30, 40, 47, 56, 57
  municipal government, 65, 100, 109
  population, 27, 35, 80

Index

princely interaction, 11, 12, 96, 107, 113, 123, 171, 181, 210, 249, 258, 261
religion, 135, 138, 154, 156, 157, 261
schools, 225, 232, 234, 242, 245, 246
textile industry, 36, 43, 49, 57, 69
town accounts, 161
urban network, 10, 26, 27, 30, 38, 39, 45, 49, 79, 181, 260
urban society, 78, 92, 255
urban space, 174, 196
Breda
textile industry, 43
British Isles, 34, 47
Brouwershaven, 72
Brown, Andrew, 147
Bruegel the Elder, Pieter, 59
Bruges, 3, 9, 17, 41, 50, 91, 102, 112, 126, 147, 174, 180, 237, 258
art, 49, 50, 125, 141, 149, 203
belfry, 180
Beursplein, 41
Bogardenschool, 227
cloth hall, 78, 176, 180
consumption, 197, 208
craft guilds, 53, 55, 103, 114, 206, 207
elite, 64, 66, 72, 186
gateway, 14, 38, 39, 42, 44, 55, 56, 165, 167, 258
market, 19, 30, 37, 39, 40, 41, 42, 46, 47, 54, 82, 174
middling groups, 68, 71, 84, 85, 145, 147, 188, 210
municipal government, 63, 91, 106, 109, 111, 123, 159, 176, 196, 210
population, 27, 46, 80
princely interaction, 107, 112, 114, 119, 170, 182, 186, 248, 263
religion, 104, 132, 136, 137, 146, 156, 157, 158, 189, 227
Saint Donatian, Chapter of, 132
Saint John, Hospital of, 187
schools, 225, 227
textile industry, 41, 42, 78
town accounts, 86, 87, 90, 99, 159, 245, 261
urban network, 10, 28, 29, 33, 39, 40, 41, 79, 113, 260
urban society, 124, 136, 186, 187
urban space, 160, 170, 178, 180, 184, 196
water hall, 174
Wisselbrug, 41
Brugge, *see* Bruges
Brussel, *see* Brussels
Brussels, 5, 40, 132, 168, 169, 186, 249, 250
art, 49, 50, 123, 126, 149, 153, 249
Baliënplein, 179
Broodhuis, 175, 179
Chapel Church, 170, 184
Coudenberg, 178, 179, 249
craft guilds, 114, 174
elite, 73, 171, 211
gateway, 165
Grand Place, 176, 179, 181
market, 172, 174, 175
middling groups, 150, 154
municipal government, 111, 121, 159, 171, 174, 246
population, 27
princely interaction, 11, 30, 107, 114, 121, 166, 169, 170, 175, 249, 263
religion, 137, 145, 156, 157, 158
Saint John, Hospital of, 187
Saint Nicholas, Church of, 121
schools, 227, 242
Steenpoort, 170
textile industry, 30, 45, 82
town accounts, 96, 160
town hall, 162
urban network, 10, 11, 26, 30, 45, 79
urban society, 118, 187
urban space, 120, 162, 170, 172, 177, 178, 179, 181, 182, 184, 249
Bruxelles, *see* Brussels
buitenpoorter, see citizenship: outburgher
Burckhardt, Jacob, 194
burgher, *see* citizenship
Burgundian-Habsburg dynasty, 7, 11, 17, 150, 260, 262
Busleyden, Jeronimus, 250
Buylaert, Frederik, 105

Cailleu, Colijn, 149
Calais, 55, 166
Calvin, John, 155
Calvinism, 120, 154–6, 157, 251, 254
Calvinist Republics, 157
Cambrai, 63, 263
gateway, 131
princely interaction, 131
religion, 137, 146
Campine, 26, 42, 43
canal, 167
canalisation, 167, 168
capital (territory), 10, 11, 28, 246, 249
Cardon, Georges, 220
caritas, 187–90
Carlier, Myriam, 103
Castile, 258
Catholicism, 17, 128
Cele, Johan, 242

chambers of rhetoric, 15, 17, 93–5, 122, 124–6, 146, 150, 151–2, 213, 220, 223, 240, 251, 253, 262
Champagne, 39, 47, 56
Charles the Bold, 102, 119, 120, 186
Charles the Good, 63, 107
Charles V, emperor, 11, 91, 100, 112, 114, 120, 179, 180, 184, 185, 210, 228
Charruadas, Paulo, 166
church (building), 121, 132, 142–4, 156, 164, 170, 181, 188, 192
Church (institution), 136, 140, 150, 166, 172, 190, 204, 227, *see also* parish
  authority, 103, 131
  bishop(ric), 11, 62, 186
  chapter, 132, 170, 188
  heresy, 138, 227
    persecution, 153, 155
  liturgy, 132, 140, 142
citadel, 120, 164
citizenship, 54, 68, 71, 81, 128, 160, 176, 194, 199–201, 210, 218, 226, 227, 229, 242, 260, *see also* bourgeoisie
  'outburgher', 35
city, episcopal, 17, 70, 258
city republic, 114, 127
city-state, 16, 21, 28, 128, 259, 261
civic religion, 128, 132, 159, 161
civilising process, *see* manners, urban
Claeissens, Pieter the Elder, 160
Clark, Peter, 5
clergy, 11, 61, 62, 68, 130, 132–5, 154, 158, 188, 227
  privileges, 140
cloth hall, 162, 163, 174, 180
codes of conduct, *see* manners, urban
cohesion, social, 63, 69, 104, 255, *see also* society, urban
Cologne, 9, 27, 174, 245, 246
  university, 245, 246
Comines, 90
commodities, 32, 40, 42, 46, 48, 56–7, 83, 172, 173, *see also* economy, urban
communal identity, *see* identity, urban
commune, 14, 61–3, 68–9, 96–8, 107, 109, 128, 136, 145, *see also* ideology, urban
  communal movement, 62–3, 107, 131, 258
  conjuratio, 96, 109
community, urban, *see* commune
conflict, political, 167, 177, 181, 260, 261
conflict, social, 14, 21, 63, 69–71, 92, 94, 98, 171, 260

confraternities, 69, 74, 130, 136, 137, 140, 143, 144, 152, 175, 178, 213, 215, *see also* religion, urban
  charity, 69, 144
  devotion, 69
  hospital, 144
Conscience, Hendrik, 209
consumption, 19, 46, 72, 86, 192–4, 199, 201, 205, 208, 216–18, 219, 254, *see also* law: sumptuary law; material culture
conviviality, *see* sociability
Cornejo, Pedro, 239
corporate system, 17, 69, 74, 81, 111, 130, 144, 147, 151, 161, 183, 187, 259, 262
  inclusiveness–exclusiveness, 74, 91
corporations, *see* corporate system
court, 150, 248, 258, 264, *see also* prince
  court-urban culture, 248, 263
  etiquette, 249
Courtrai, *see* Kortrijk
Couthereel, Pieter, 112
craftsmen, master, *see* artisans: master artisans
crime, 91, 93, 104, 105, 120, 121
  confiscation, 97, 211
  corporal punishment, 105
  exile, 97, 105, 106, 123
  libel, 106, 121
  monetary fine, 106, 121
  pacification, 104–6
  punitive pilgrimage, 105, 106
Cruppelant, family, 73
Culemborg, 157, 242

Damme, 36, 98, 110, 122, 166, 167, 177
Danube (river), 10
David of Burgundy, 186
de Beatis, Antonio, 172
de Bertaimont, Jean, 185
de Brimeu, Guy, lord of Humbercourt, 119
de Castelein, Matthijs, 146
de Cordes, family, 55
de Deken, Willem, 119
De Doppere, Rombout, 125
de Jonghe, Jan, 120
de Keysere, Pieter, 160
de Keysere, Robert, 243
de la Pasture, Roger, *see* van der Weyden, Rogier
de Layens, Mathieu, 178
De Lier, 240
de Marke, Collard, 41
de Meyere, Jacob, 239
de Montigny, Nicolas, 72

Index

De Moor, Tine, 75
de Mortaigne, Eulard, 72
de Pizan, Christine, 215
de Rike, Catherine, widow of Jan, 208
De Rock, Jelle, 66
de Roovere, Anthonis, 124, 149
de Scutelaere, family, 112
de Vries, Hans Vredeman, 206
de Vries, Jan, 27, 192, 194
de Weert, Jan, 123
de Wesalia, Joannes, 250
Deinze, 36, 148, 244
Delfshaven, 168
Delft
  art, 142, 208
  market, 44, 47
  middling groups, 152
  religion, 138, 150, 151
  schools, 227
  textile industry, 51
  town accounts, 100
  urban network, 11, 26, 30, 168
Della Casa, Giovanni, 212
Demer (river), 168
demography, 21, 62
  demographic stagnation, 9
  mortality, 79–81
  population decline, 48, 75, 78, 80, 85, 177
  population density, 22–6, 40, 43, 257
  population growth, 75, 80
  population number, 24, 26–8, 40, 45, 60, 81
  resilience, demographic, 79
  surplus mortality, 32, 81
  urban population, 139
Den Bosch, *see* 's-Hertogenbosch
Dender (river), 32
Dendermonde, 52, 117, 121
  religion, 146
Des Marez, Guillaume, 5
Deventer, 9, 146, 234
  Brink, 173
  gateway, 39, 44
  market, 173
  religion, 136, 138, 139
  Saint Lebuinus, Church of, 177, 178, 181
  schools, 227
  town accounts, 96
  urban network, 27
  urban space, 162, 173, 177, 181
  weigh house, 162
Dhondt, Jan, 4
di Savino, Guido, 207
Diest, 79, 97, 149, 173

Diksmuide, 29, 49, 89, 145, 148
Dinant, 4, 27, 90, 110, 120, 165, 176
discipline, 95, 104, 115, 122, 254, *see also* manners, urban
discourse, 14, *see also* ideology, urban
  political, 12, 98, 126, 182, 187
  religious, 159
  social, 61, 257
Doesburg, 227
Dole, 246
  university, 246
domain, feudal, 32, *see also* lord, feudal
Dordrecht, 9
  craft guilds, 56, 70
  gateway, 38, 44
  market, 30, 36, 41
  municipal government, 123
  religion, 135, 138, 139
  town accounts, 100
  urban charter, 24
  urban network, 10, 27, 30, 79
Dorestad, 165
Douai, 51, 220
  cloth hall, 175
  craft guilds, 48, 54, 68, 110
  elite, 64
  gateway, 165
  market, 175, 258
  municipal government, 109
  population, 27
  religion, 132
  Saint Amatus, Chapter of, 132
  schools, 225
  textile industry, 45
  town accounts, 99
  university, 220
  urban network, 10, 29, 79
  urban society, 77, 78, 104
d'Outremeuse, Jean, 131
Dranouter, 248
Drenthe, 28
Duffel, 43, 49
Dunkerque, *see* Dunkirk
Dunkirk, 29, 37, 79, 166
Dürer, Albrecht, 212
Dutch Revolt, 9, 16, 80, 100, 128, 157, 255, 261

Ecaussines, 179
economy, urban, 13, 31, 45, 57, 264, *see also* agriculture; commodities; consumption; finances, municipal; luxury products; standard of living; textile industry; trade
  capitalism, 84–5
  commercialisation, 33

economy, urban (cont.)
  competition, 51, 57, 167, 262
  construction, 179
  decline, 30, 204
  demand, 195
  diversification, 82, 92, 201
  division of labour, 62, 71
  employment, 183
  export, 20, 39, 40, 46–7, 50, 51, 54, 57, 64, 78, 82, 90, 164
  finances
    banking, 41, 46
    brokery, 41, 54, 74, 83
    capital market, 43
    credit institution, 188
    financial history, 5
    fiscality, see prince
    speculation, 65
    stock exchange, 178, 179
    tax, see finances, municipal
    transactions, financial, 41
  free market, 51
  growth, 15, 42, 55, 57, 58, 59, 75, 83, 86, 92, 255, 256, 257
  import, 80, 207, 211
  income pooling, 34, 65, 86
  industry, 44, 45, 64, 79
    brewing, 57, 168, 169
    brick production, 46, 65
    gold- and silversmiths, 50, 74
    salt-processing, 29, 46
    shipbuilding, 57
    weapons, 50
  innovation, 50, 53, 55, 56–8, 205
  institutions, economic, 51
  knowledge economy, 20, 233
  labour
    manual, 111, 125, 155
    skilled, 13, 14, 32, 40, 48, 86, 109, 155
    supply, 85, 86
    unskilled, 47
    wage, 54, 59, 85, 87
  manufacturing, 17, 45, 78
  market economy, 9, 13
  market infrastructure, 39, 51
  market interdependence, 35, 38
  marketplace, 33, 82, 164, 171, 192
  'product life cycle', 47
  protectionism, 52, 210
  regulation, economic, 37, 51, 56, 69, 78, 95
  services, 32, 46, 72, 222
  skill premium, 14, 20
  specialisation, 44, 50, 57, 82, 256, 257
  unemployment, 83, 90
  wages, 20, 26, 48, 80, 85–7, 111

Edam, 88
education, 20, 33, 152, 220, 258
  apprenticeship, 20, 51, 52, 229, 237, see also artisans
  exclusion, 230
  masterpiece, 20, 230, 231
  discipline, 21, 226
  home schooling, 242, 243
  intellectuals, 253
  learning on the shop floor, see education: vocational training
  philosophy, educational, 227
  primary education, 225, 242
  secondary education, 241
  vocational training, 223, 226, 228–9, 241, 244, 248, 253
Eeklo, 46, 87, 89, 244
Egmond, 179
Eijsden, 97
Elburg, 28
Elias, Norbert, 93
elite, urban, 15, 63–8, 70, 74, 83, 111, 115, 123, 169, 183, 190, 193, 200, 211, 244, 259, 261, 264
  identity, 64
  regent class, 56
Emden, 155, 178
Emmerich, 242
England, 9, 11, 43, 47, 50, 56, 79, 81, 85, 195, 258, 260
Enkhuizen, 44, 46
entrepreneurs, 14, 50, 54, 59, 84, 87, 155, 169, 181, 226, 231, 238, see also trade: merchants
epidemics, 79
  plague, 77, 85, see also Black Death
Epstein, Stephan R., 53
Erasmus, Desiderius, 151, 212, 220, 227, 242, 246, 250
Espinas, Georges, 144
Etienne of Tournai, 131
Everaert, Cornelis, 125, 149

family, 66, 67, 69, 74, 143, 161, see also demography; women
  celibacy, 75
  children, 75
  European marriage pattern, 75, 77
  extended family, 75, 89, 104
  ideology, 15
  inheritance, 76, 78
  kin, 74, 76
  lineage, 66, 76
  marriage, 75, 76, 78, 104, 214
  nuclear family, 75, 77
famine, see food: crisis

Index

Far East, 44
Farnese, Alexander, 56, 158
Favresse, Félicien, 5
Feluy, 179
feudalism, 66
Fexhe, 113
finances, municipal, 5, 67, 68, 98, 111, 171, 185, 243
  accountability, 185
  accountancy, 101
  control mechanism, 111
  debt, 185
  expenditure, 177
  revenues, 67, 101, 185
  tax, 67, 72, 81, 87, 89, 98, 110, 116, 123, 140, 167, 173, 183, 185
Flanders, 1, 3, 7, 9, 10, 12, 19, 20, 24, 27, 28, 31, 34, 36, 37, 43, 46, 99, 109, 126, 167, 249, 260
  art, 148, 149, 150, 239
  consumption, 209, 218
  craft guilds, 48, 52, 53, 56, 69, 177
  economic development, 29, 30, 33, 35, 36, 40, 56, 82, 86, 166, 167, 179
  elite, 72, 73
  market, 41, 47, 56, 57, 80, 81
  middling groups, 72
  municipal government, 63, 65, 91, 99, 109
  population, 27, 35, 46, 80
  princely interaction, 11, 63, 102, 113, 147, 165, 166, 210, 224, 249, 258, 261
  religion, 132, 135, 138, 145, 156, 157, 261
  schools, 225, 248
  textile industry, 34, 36, 41, 42, 43, 47, 49, 57, 69, 89, 156
  urban network, 10, 26, 30, 39, 45, 49, 79, 89, 181, 260
  urban society, 77, 78, 84, 92, 255
  urban space, 174
Floreffe, 177
Florence, 28, 261
Floris (de Vriendt), Cornelis, 206
Floris V, count of Holland 178
food, 31, 34, 80, 183, *see also* consumption; economy, urban
  beer, 34, 35, 46, 47, 86, 110
  bread, 35, 86
  crisis, 65, 79, 80
    Great Hunger, 48, 80, 81
  dairy products, 34
  fish, 173
  grain, 34–5, 37, 44, 65, 80, 110, 118, 123, 173, 256
  herring, 34
  meat, 34, 84, 173, 174
  price, 59, 86, 118
  wine, 34, 123
Foucault, Michel, 162
fountain, 169, 175
France, 3, 7, 11, 29, 30, 34, 37, 39, 73, 79, 80, 81, 114, 181, 185, 210, 239, 244, 258, 260
Franche-Comté, 246
Francis of Anjou, 157
Frankfurt-am-Main, 40, 155
freedom, personal, 62, 66, 72, 78
  serfs, 24
freedoms, municipal, *see* privileges, municipal
French Flanders, 43
frictions, social, *see* conflict, social
Friesland, 28, 33, 148, 152, 155, 251
Fris, Victor, 115
Frisius, Gemma, 250
fuel, 47, 65, 256
Fynes, Moryson, 237

Galbert of Bruges, 63, 107
Ganshof, François-Louis, 5
Gembloux, 107
Genappe, 96
Geneva, 155
Genoa, 76
Gent, *see* Ghent
geography, 10, 256, 259
  geographic shift, 9, 13, 31, 40, 44, 57, 58, 260
Geraardsbergen, 35, 109, 178, 243, 244
  Saint Adrian, Abbey of, 244
German Empire, 9, 39, 40, 123, 130, 154, 155, 158, 161, 210, 260
Germany, 3
Ghent, 3, 5, 6, 18, 37, 114, 144, 148, 149, 177, 210, 226
  art, 50, 160
  belfry, 18, 162, 180, 182
  Bijloke hospital, 178, 187, 188
  Citadel, 120, 185
  consumption, 212, 217
  craft guilds, 37, 52, 84, 99, 103, 110, 114, 116, 117, 167, 174
  elite, 64, 65, 66, 67, 105, 109, 171, 224
  fish market, 172
  gateway, 29, 39, 165, 167
  Geeraard de Duivelsteen, 171
  Gravensteen, 172
  Great Beguinage, 138
  market, 37, 172, 173, 218, 258
  middling groups, 65, 68, 88, 98, 144, 149, 152, 188, 213

Ghent (*cont.*)
  municipal government, 37, 91, 109, 111, 112, 123, 167, 174, 189, 215, 246, 247
  population, 27, 90
  princely interaction, 102, 107, 112, 113, 114, 119, 120, 170, 182, 185, 186, 260, 263
  religion, 132, 135, 136, 137, 138, 140, 145, 156, 157, 158, 188, 189
  Saint Bavo, Abbey of, 185
  Saint Nicholas, Church of, 18
  Saint Peter, Abbey of, 245
  Saint Pharaildis, Chapter of, 224
  schools, 224, 225, 243
  textile industry, 41, 45
  town accounts, 90, 99, 100, 102, 115, 159, 160, 161, 245, 261
  urban network, 10, 28, 29, 79, 113
  urban society, 35, 36, 78, 104, 187
  urban space, 120, 162, 177, 178, 180, 195
  Vrijdagmarkt, 172
Gillis, Peter, 234
Godding, Philippe, 95
Golden Age, 6
Goldthwaite, Richard, 194
Gouda
  art, 142
  gateway, 47, 166, 167
  market, 44, 47, 173, 174
  middling groups, 143
  municipal government, 143
  religion, 237
  Saint John, Church of, 143
  schools, 225, 227, 242
  textile industry, 51
  town hall, 162
  urban network, 11, 167
  urban space, 162, 179, 181
Goudriaan, Koen, 139
government, municipal, 31, 55, 63, 67, 69, 73, 95, 109, 128, 136, 147, 154, 157, 158, 160, 171, 174, 176–7, 187, 196, 207, 225, 252, 256, *see also* institutions; municipal; law, municipal
  'annuality rule', 109
  bench of aldermen, 67, 70, 101, 103, 106, 176, 196, 206, 247
  Brede Raad, 114
  coalition, 112
  corruption, 67, 95, 114, 116, 119, 122, 123, 126
  election, 111, 112
  legitimation, 106, 177, 191

  maladministration, 115, 124
  oligarchy, 115
  public office, 73
    alderman, 73, 99, 106, 107, 111, 119, 168, 174, 176, 185
    burgomaster, 119
    town sheriff, 73
    town council, 64, 67, 69, 70, 73, 102
Grapheus, Cornelius, 160
Gravelines, 166
Great Privilege, 100
Groningen, 6, 28, 136, 138, 246
  princely interaction, 11
  religion, 157
  schools, 227
  town accounts, 161
Grote, Geert, 138, 139
Guelders, 1, 28, 47, 56, 139, 148, 251
Guicciardini, Lodovico, 79, 88, 239
guilds, craft, 14, 48, 50–6, 67, 69, 70, 74, 83, 88, 90, 91, 95, 97, 100, 111–12, 114, 116, 118, 119, 123, 130, 136, 140, 144, 146, 159, 160, 173, 174, 175, 177, 186, 187, 188, 190, 206, 213, 215, 226, 230, 231, 244, 251, 252, 254, 259
  almshouse, 54
  altar, 54
  autonomy, 69, 98, 110, 111
  butchers, 174
  chapel, 54
  guild house, 54, 117, 192
  guildhall, 64
  hallmark, 51, 52
  identity, 143, 161, 264
  jurisdiction, 103–4
  painters, 226
  political power, 112
  privileges, 111, 120, 173
  religion, 143
  river shippers, 37
  social security, 91
  subcontracting, 54, 55
  training, 51, *see also* education
  values, 231
guilds, merchants', 41, 63, 78, 130, 136, 262
guilds, military, 15, 74
guilds, shooting, 143, 262
Guy of Dampierre, 185

Haamstede, 150
Haarlem, 179
  market, 43, 44, 47, 258
  middling groups, 88
  religion, 136, 138
  Saint Bavo, Church of, 179

Index 293

textile industry, 44, 46, 51
urban charter, 24
urban network, 11, 26, 30, 79, 167
habitus, urban, *see* manners, urban
Habsburg, *see* Burgundian-Habsburg dynasty
Hagebaert, Thomas, 106
Hageland, 42
Hainaut, 10, 26, 28, 100, 102, 179, 180
   art, 147, 148
   craft guilds, 56
   economic development, 35, 56
   elite, 72, 73
   municipal government, 63, 91, 99, 102, 185
   population, 27, 80
   princely interaction, 165, 261
   religion, 135, 156, 261
   schools, 225
   textile industry, 36, 42, 57
   urban network, 38, 49, 181
   urban space, 174
Halle, 243
Hamburg, 57
Harderwijk, 28
Hasselt, 97, 111, 168
Hattem, 242
Hegius, Alexander, 234
Heidelberg, 155
Heijting, Willem, 234
Herbenus, Matthaeus, 160
Herentals, 43, 82
Herk-de-Stad, 118
Heuvelland, 41, 42
hierarchy, urban, 38, 45, 218, 258, *see also* urbanisation
   large town, 26, 79, 90, 148, 218
   medium-sized town, 26, 28, 79, 89
   metropolis, 21, 258
   small town, 28, 29, 54, 79, 89, 148, 165, 243, 261
   subordinate network, 39, 41, 44
high-quality products, *see* luxury products
hinterland, *see* town–countryside relationship
Hoeckaert, Eligius, 243
Hoeken, faction, 76, 112
Holland, 1, 7, 9, 12, 19, 24, 26, 28, 37, 46, 47, 67, 69, 73, 100, 240, 251
   art, 142, 148, 150, 151, 251
   consumption, 195, 199, 218, 219
   craft guilds, 48, 56, 70, 177
   economic development, 30, 33, 34, 35, 43, 44, 46, 56, 57, 65, 70, 82, 166, 173, 179
   elite, 70, 73, 76
   gateway, 166
   market, 44, 47, 57
   middling groups, 240
   municipal government, 100
   population, 45
   princely interaction, 12, 102, 112, 166, 258, 261
   religion, 132, 135, 138, 139, 150, 158
   textile industry, 46, 57
   urban charter, 24
   urban network, 10, 11, 26, 27, 30, 38, 39, 49, 79, 167, 168
   urban society, 76, 88, 255
   urban space, 174, 178, 196
Hondschoote, 40, 43, 49, 54, 55, 156
Honin, faction, 112
Hoorn, 44, 46
hospital, 178
house, urban, 68, 192, 195, 196, 197, *see also* architecture, urban
   architecture, 195, 196
   brick house, 179, 196
   domesticity, 192, 194, 199
   functional specialisation of space, 199
   kitchen, 197, 198
   price, 71, 86
   property, 198
   renting, 59, 197, 198
   residential culture, 46, 199
   shop, 198
   stone house, 171, 195, 263
Howell, Martha, 104
Hugh of Chalon, 112
Hugonet, Guillaume, 119
Hulst, 29
human capital, 13, 51, 52, 251
humanism, 20, 160, 220, 222, 226, 238, 243, 244, 246, 250, 253
   Christian humanism, 239
Huy, 24, 27, 46, 96, 100, 111, 112, 165, 178, 189, 224
   town accounts, 96

Iberian peninsula, 39, 42
iconoclasm, 140, 158
   Iconoclastic Fury, 120, 156
identity, dress, 215
identity, parochial, 132
identity, urban, 1, 3, 13, 16, 61, 62, 66, 98, 99–101, 120, 125, 126, 131, 136, 157, 173, 174, 190, 192, 194, 214
   urban, memory, 100, 261
ideology, urban, 15, 69, 76, 92, 125, 126, 136, 159, 161, 175, 176, 182, 183, 186, 190, 218, 260, 261
   bien commun, *see* common good
   civility, 212, 214, 264

ideology, urban (*cont.*)
  common good, 97–8, 99, 110, 114, 123, 175, 190, 257, 264
  corporatism, 69
  correct government, 123
  openness, 10
  political culture, 126, 258, 259
  political philosophy, 98, 123
    political body, 54
  res publicae, 114
  sacralisation, 145
  subversion, 120, 121
Ieperlee (river), 167
IJssel (region) 9, 138
IJssel (river), 9, 27, 29, 30, 31, 39, 56, 138, 166, 178, 186, 196
Ile-de-France, 29
Imperial Flanders, 37
industrial revolution, 4, 30
industrialisation, 29, 195, *see also* economy, urban
inequality, social, 15, 63, 70, 75, 88, 92, 169, 198, 212, 257, 264, *see also* polarisation, social
infrastructure, urban, 62, 163, 164, 165, 168, 176, 191
  bridge, 18, 164, 171, 176
  castrum, 170
  citadel, 184
  crane, 171
  fortification, 18, 120, 164, 172, 173, 185, 251
  harbour, 122, 166
  jetty, 165
  marketplace, 172, 175, 176, 181, 184, 192
  road, 164, 167, 183
  streets, 171, 192
  tollhouse, 166
  town, gate, 3, 66, 170, 172, 183, 185, 186, 192, 251
  town, walls, 1, 71, 120, 156, 162, 164, 170, 195
institutions, central
  supreme court, 11
institutions, municipal, 4, 5, 41, 94, 99, 247, 260, *see also* government, municipal
Italy, 1, 4, 16, 22, 28, 50, 56, 79, 81, 120, 130, 131, 144, 149, 194, 195, 206, 207, 210, 233, 237, 244, 259

Jambes, 176
Janssens, Lenaert, 121
Jerusalem, 149
Jodoigne, 107, 174
John III of Brabant, 242
John IV of Brabant, 246

John of Bavaria, 100
John the Fearless, 100, 102, 112

Kabeljauwen, faction, 76, 112
Kampen, 9, 27, 139, 143, 186
Keldermans, Antonis, 179
Keldermans, family, 178
Keldermans, Jan, 178
Keldermans, Rombout, 179
Kempen, *see* Campine
Kerstkyn, schoolmaster, 225
Kiliaen, Cornelis, 234
knowledge, 13, 20, 168–9, 220–54
  arithmetic, 224, 226
  bonae litterae, 244, 250
  bookkeeping, 224, 225, 234
  cartography, 250
  experimentation, 232, 250, 253
  foreign languages, 237, 239
  geography, 225
  humanities, 226, 244
  innovation, 14, 182, 200
  literacy, 16, 220, 224, 226, 228, 233, 240, 252, 260
  numeracy, 252
  prescriptive vs propositional knowledge, 231
  rhetoric, 240
  science, 250
  technology, 169, 176, 250, 252
  writing, 224, 226, 228, 233, 240
Kortenberg, 113
Kortrijk, 40
  craft guilds, 53
  gateway, 165
  middling groups, 72
  princely interaction, 113, 119
  religion, 145, 155
  textile industry, 33, 43, 46
  town accounts, 87
  urban society, 35, 36

laicisation, 130, 227
Lanchals, Pieter, 123, 124
land-owning class, 14
Latin, 220, 224, 237–9, 243
  education, 20
  handbooks, 237
law, municipal, 15, 95–6, 98, 101, 110, 168, 175, 210, 259
  administration of justice, 66, 109, 110, 176, 247
  canon law, 95
  court, 35
  customary law, 24, 96, 103, 107, 114, 199, 214

Index

law development, 93, 97, 99
legal, identity, 183
legal, services, 41, 171
oral tradition, 96–7
peace and order, 97, 102
property rights, 5, 68, 259
Roman law, 95, 110
sumptuary law, 19, 210
textualisation, 96, 99, 231
town charter, 95, 100, 180
urban charter, *see* privileges, municipal
voluntary judicial jurisdiction, 99–101
le Carlier, Tanne, spouse of Jehan, 209
league of towns, 113
   Council of Kortenberg, 113
Leeuwarden, 136, 157
Lefebvre, Henri, 162
Leiden, 44, 51
   art, 142
   consumption, 215
   craft guilds, 48, 54, 70
   elite, 65, 67, 72, 73, 105
   market, 43, 44
   princely interaction, 102, 248
   religion, 251
   schools, 222, 251, 258
   textile industry, 44, 46, 51
   urban charter, 24
   urban network, 11, 26, 30, 79, 167
   urban space, 179, 196
Leie, 31, 32, 37, 79, 156, 167
Leuven, 5, 9, 45, 125
   art, 50, 148, 250
   craft guilds, 53, 97, 110, 118
   elite, 109, 112
   gateway, 165
   market, 30, 42, 47, 174
   meat hall, 179
   municipal government, 104, 111, 171, 174
   population, 27
   princely interaction, 107, 114, 165, 170
   religion, 132, 137, 145
   Saint Peter, Chapter of, 246
   schools, 222, 234, 243, 245, 246, 250, 251, 258
   Terbank, leprosarium, 187
   textile industry, 30, 43
   town accounts, 86, 96, 104, 106
   town hall, 179
   university, 222, 243, 250
   urban charter, 24
   urban network, 10, 26, 79
   urban society, 104, 187
   urban space, 172, 178, 179, 181
Levant, 44

Liège (prince-bishopric), 3, 7, 10, 12, 24, 100, 102, 111, 113
   art, 148
   craft guilds, 56, 177
   princely interaction, 12, 113, 165
   urban space, 170
Liège (town), 3, 5, 100, 120, 162, 166, 168, 171, 263
   art, 50
   Beguinage, 137
   craft guilds, 69
   elite, 109, 171, 186
   gateway, 131, 165
   market, 46, 172
   Mont Cornillon, Hospital of, 187
   municipal government, 106, 111
   perron, 96, 162
   Pont des Arches, 166
   Prince-Bishop's Palace, 172
   princely interaction, 119, 120, 131, 166
   religion, 137, 138
   Saint Lambert, Cathedral of, 172
   schools, 227
   town accounts, 90, 96, 100, 109, 131
   urban network, 27
   urban society, 135, 187
   urban space, 174, 178, 181, 189
Lier, 50, 79, 82, 90, 107, 114, 149, 179, 181
   Saint Gummarus, Church of, 179
Lieve (canal), 167
Lille, 176, 185
   art, 50, 146
   Beauregard, 176
   gateway, 39, 165
   Grand Place, 176
   Hospice Comtesse, 162
   market, 55, 82, 172
   municipal government, 63, 109, 246
   population, 27
   princely interaction, 170, 263
   religion, 135, 145, 155
   royal fortress, 185
   schools, 225
   textile industry, 41, 43
   town accounts, 100
   urban network, 10, 29, 79
   urban space, 162
Limburg, 28, 97, 112
Lipsius, Justus, 234
literacy, *see* knowledge
literature, 16, 94, 105, 122–6, 141, 148, 151, 159, 205
   poetry, 16, 122, 152, 153, 220, 223, 262
   religious texts, 141, 152, 155
   urban history, 131, 159, 160
Lo, 145, 148

Löhrmann, Dietrich, 168
Lokeren, 37
London, 6, 11, 28, 47, 64, 155
Loon, 28
lord, feudal, 24, 62, 96, 102, 114, 172, 173, 258, 260, *see also* seigneurie
seigneurial obligations, 35
Louis of Male, 167
Louis of Nevers, 119, 120
Louvain, *see* Leuven
Lower Lorraine, 107
Lucassen, Leo, 6
Luigi d'Aragona, 172
Luther, Martin, 152, 153, 154, 155, 158, 227
Lutheranism, 158
Luxembourg (country), 1, 7
Luxembourg (principality), 11, 113
Luxembourg (town), 114, 119
luxury products, 19, 20, 22, 46, 50, 51, 72, 82, 174, 200, 210, 211, 218, 222, 238, 249, 252, 257, 263
Lyon, 135
Lys, *see* Leie

Maaseik, 43
Maastricht, 46, 116, 164, 165
　Saint Servatius, Chapter of, 131
　town accounts, 131, 160
　urban network, 27
Madrid, 28
Maerlant, *see* van Maerlant, Jacob
Malthus, Thomas, 75, 86
manners, urban, 19, 93, 122, 212, 217, 226, 227, 253, 264, *see also* discipline
　civilising process, 93–5, 257
　dining culture, 212
　etiquette book, 212
Margaret of Austria, 179
marginalisation, 91, 215, 218, 257
　Jews, 215
　lepers, 215
　prostitution, 103, 215
Martens, Dirk, 234
Mary of Burgundy, 70, 100, 114
material culture, 13, 19–20, 72, 192, 194, 201, 216, *see also* consumption; luxury products; economy, urban
　clothing, 19, 84, 87, 139, 200, 203, 204, 205, 209–10, 215, 218
　decoration, 19, 200, 202, 203, 204, 205, 217
　design, 19, 205, 217, 254
　diversification, 203, 209, 211, 217
　fashion, 46, 49, 204, 217

furniture, 19, 50, 194, 195, 199, 201, 202, 205–7, 214, 218, 263
gifts, 217
household objects, 195, 199
paintings, *see* art
pewter objects, 208–9, 211
probate inventories, 195, 200, 202, 207, 209, 211
secondary markets, 210
silver objects, 208, 211, 212, 217
tableware, 19, 194, 201, 203, 205, *see also* art: majolica; art: porcelain
testament, 217
textiles, 203, 263
Matilda of Flanders, 102
Matte, Sebastiaan, 156
Matthew of Boulogne, 166
Matthijsz, Jan, 155
Maurice of Nassau, 248
Maximilian of Austria, 40, 81, 114, 121, 125
Mechelen, 213, 250
　art, 50, 149, 202
　craft guilds, 69, 110, 114, 117, 174
　elite, 110, 211
　gateway, 165
　Great Beguinage, 138
　market, 42, 81, 250
　middling groups, 152
　municipal government, 111, 121, 246
　population, 27
　princely interaction, 11, 102, 114, 182, 249, 263
　religion, 132, 138, 157
　schools, 228, 242
　textile industry, 30, 43, 45
　town accounts, 90, 97
　urban network, 26
　urban society, 76, 118
　urban space, 172, 178, 179
Medemblik, 44
medicine, 232, 238
Menen, 40, 49, 53, 55
Mercator, Gerard, 250
merchants, *see* trade
Merula, Paulus, 215
Mesen, 120
Meuse (river), 4, 7, 10, 22, 26, 28, 29, 30, 31, 32, 34, 39, 46, 57, 164, 166, 168, 176
Middelburg (Flanders), 211
Middelburg (Zeeland), 177
　craft guilds, 223
　elite, 73
　market, 72, 174, 218
　meat hall, 179

Index

municipal administration, 100
population, 45
religion, 135, 138, 156
town hall, 162, 177, 179
urban network, 167
urban space, 162, 179
middle class, *see* middling groups
middling groups, 14, 15, 18, 21, 32, 46, 57, 63, 65, 67, 68, 71, 74, 75, 83, 88, 92, 95, 101, 111, 122, 124, 125, 126, 144, 145, 147, 148, 152, 155, 195, 198, 201, 207, 208, 211, 224, 227, 241, 244, 249, 253, 256, 257, 261, 262, 264
  identity, 71
  work ethic, 227
migration, 9, 57, 81, 89, 199, 257
  emigration, 9, 158
  immigration, 13, 31, 32, 43, 59, 68, 69, 81, 93, 186, 218, 252
  'life-cycle migration', 32
Milan, 120
mobility, social, 15, 21, 65, 216, 239, 247, 253
Mokyr, Joel, 231
monasticism, 135–40, 151, 154, 159, 227
  cloister, 137
  'via media', 137, 138
Mongolian steppe, 80
Monnet, Pierre, 130
Mons, 28, 50, 170, 173, 215
  elite, 73
  Maison de la Paix, 164
  market, 172
  municipal government, 91, 176
  Porte du Parc, 185
  Saint Waudru, Chapter of, 170, 174
  Saint Waudru, Church of, 178
  Saint Waudru, market of, 172
  town accounts, 90, 96, 171
  urban space, 174, 178, 181, 185
Mont, Hannin, 106
morality, 103, 104, 106, 122, 148, 158, 217, 254
  sexuality, 122, 216
Muchembled, Robert, 93, 94, 105
Münster, 155

Naarden, 81
Najemy, John, 96
Namur (county), 7, 56, 165
  princely interaction, 258
Namur (town), 24, 168, 176
  Cabaret, 176
  craft guilds, 53
  gateway, 165
  Grand Hospital, 187
  market, 46, 173, 174
  municipal government, 116, 176, 177
  princely interaction, 114
  religion, 132, 137
  Saint Gilles, Hospice of, 187
  Saint-Pierre-au-Château, Church of, 181
  town accounts, 96
  urban network, 27
  urban society, 187
  urban space, 165, 170, 176, 178, 179, 181, 182
Naples, 28
neighbourhood, 59, 74, 76
Netherlands, 3, 5, 6, 7, 28, 30, 44, 62, 70, 71, 73, 74, 84
  art, 141, 207
  consumption, 192, 219
  princely interaction, 249
  religion, 128, 132
  textile industry, 43
  urban network, 79, 131
  urban space, 196
network, social, 67, 104
  clan, 75, 76, 77, 171
  faction, 76, 109, 112, 125, 159
  social security, 104, 188
new institutional economics, 41
New World, 20, 38, 42, 44, 85
Nieuwkerke, 49, 53, 54, 55
Nieuwpoort, 29, 37, 110, 145, 148, 149, 166, 167
Nijmegen, 9, 44, 164, 227
  urban network, 27
Nivelles, 96, 107, 114, 168, 174
nobility, 14, 15, 61, 68, 71–4, 166, 194, 210, 212, 216, 259
  gentry, 68
  knights, 73
Normandy, 147
North Sea, 9, 26, 27, 37

Oostende, *see* Ostend
Oosterbant, 211
Oosterman, Johan, 141
Orléans, 98
Ostend, 37, 79
Otbert of Liège, 166
Othée, 100
Oudenaarde, 40, 50, 214
  art, 50, 203
  craft guilds, 116
  middling groups, 146
  municipal government, 214
  princely interaction, 112

Oudenaarde (*cont.*)
  religion, 145
  schools, 225
  textile industry, 33, 43, 46, 156
  town hall, 180
  urban network, 29
  urban society, 35, 147
  urban space, 180
Oudenbosch, 240
Oudenburg, 145, 148
Overijssel, 1, 28, 47, 148
Oversticht, 139

Pacification of Ghent, 114
Pafraet, Richard, 234
Palladio, Andrea, 206
Paris, 11, 27, 28, 29, 120, 245, 246, 249
  university, 245, 246
parish, 18, 62, 89, 91, 96, 132, 137, 142, 170, 192, 228
  identity, 132
  pastoral care, 132, 142
  table of the Holy Spirit, *see* poverty: poor table
patriciate, 66, 171, 186, 194, 224, 259, *see also* elite, urban
periphery, 28, 34
perron, 96, 162, 175
Petrarch, 131
Petrus a Thymo, 161
Philip II Augustus, king of France, 109
Philip II, king of Spain, 114, 120, 157, 158, 173, 251
Philip IV the Fair, king of France, 111, 185
Philip of Alsace, 166
Philip of Cleves, 121
Philip the Bold, 102
Philip the Fair, 179, 210
Philip the Good, 102, 112, 118, 176, 178, 185, 186, 246, 249, 250
Picardy, 35, 37, 57, 99, 107, 147, 181
piety, lay, 140–5, 157, 262
Pirenne, Henri, 3, 4, 5, 49, 51, 66, 111, 115
Plancius (aka Platevoet), Petrus, 248
Plantin, Christophe, 234, 238
Pleij, Herman, 93, 94, 95
Po Valley 28
polarisation, social, 15, 21, 61, 68, 70, 87, 101, 128, 201, 216, 218, 257, 259
polder model, 6
Pollmann, Judith, 158
poorter, *see* citizenship
Poperinge, 29, 49, 52
Portugal, 40
poverty, 21, 71, *see also* caritas; parish
  beggary, 59, 91, 228
  charity, 63, 89–90, 213
  discipline, 89, 92
  discourse, 14, 89, 91
    deserving poor, 91
    undeserving poor, 61, 91
  orphans and foundlings, 228
  poor (social category), 14, 21, 59, 63, 80, 187, 257
  poor relief, 89, 91, 132, 143, 158, 228, 231
  poor table, 90
  poorhouse, 90
  vagrancy, 59, 92
Prevenier, Walter, 201
prince, 12, 15, 81, 112, 119, 161, 165, 175, 260, 261
  central authorities, 68, 94, 105, 107, 112, 114, 118, 153, 165, 248, 258
  Concessio Carolina, 113
  fiscality, 110, 259
  princely residence, *see* court
  state-building, 105, 180, 182, 185, 211, 255
principality, 3, 7
principality, ecclesiastical, 131, 258
printing, 223, 239, 254
  book production, 49, 152, 205, 220, 234, 263
  educational books, 234
  engraving, 205
  pamphlets and flyers, 121
  printing press, 20, 142, 212, 220, 233, 237
  publishing, 223, 234
privileges, municipal, 11, 22, 36, 72, 113–14, 126, 167, 180, 259, 261, *see also* law, municipal; law, municipal:town charter
proletarisation, 48, 51, 68
property (land), 33, 36, 64, 68
  'betrayal of the bourgeoisie', 65
  rents, 64
Protestantism, 17, 120, 128, 211
provisioning, urban, 32
Prussia, 35, 37, 57
Ptolemy, 250

Ramakers, Bart, 146
ramparts, town, 169, 170, 183, 185, *see* infrastructure, urban: town, walls
raw materials, 26, 31, 32
  charcoal, 46
  coal, 46
  lime, 65
  linen, *see* textile industry

Index

metals, 34, 46, 57
natural stone, 34, 46, 171
  bluestone, 179
  limestone, 179, 196
  sandstone, 179
peat, 34, 46–7, 57, 65, 110, 166, 256
wood, 34
wool, 34, 42, 49
rebellion, urban, *see* revolt, urban
Reformation, 17, 114, 128–30, 151, 154, 222, 227, 231, 244, 253
Réginard of Liège, 166
religion, urban, 16, 64, 140, 148, 157, *see also* clergy; Church (institution); parish
  beguine movement, 17, 76, 137–8
    beghards, 138
  Catholic revival, 158, 159
  Devotio Moderna, 17, 138, 141
  economy of salvation, 141, 152, 157
  Marian devotion, 153
  mendicant orders, 17, 90, 99, 110, 118, 135, 175, 187, 188
    ideal of poverty, 135
    pastoral care, 135
    women, 137
  Our Lady of the Seven Sorrows, 150
  pluriformity of religious ideas, 153, 154
  religious, culture, 17
  religious experience, 141, 144
  religious orders, 130, 159, 251
  spiritual vs material, 130, 140, 141, 142, 144, 157, 218
  Third Order, 138
Renaissance, 20, 179, 194, 220, 222, 232, 239, 241
Republic, 6, 16, 44, 45, 115, 233, 255, 260
republicanism, 16
retail, 78, 87, 88
revolt, urban, 11, 16, 69, 70, 97, 98, 107, 109–13, 115–21, 123–5, 127, 259
rhetoricians, *see* chambers of rhetoric
Rhine (river), 9, 10, 22, 27, 29, 31, 34, 35, 39, 41, 70, 113, 155, 165
Rhône (river), 10
rights, municipal, *see* privileges, municipal
riot, urban, *see* revolt, urban
rituals, urban, 13, 192, 261
  'joyous entries, 113, 182, 241, 262
  ommegangen, *see* rituals, urban: pageants
  pageants, 54, 145, 146, 149, 241, 249
  tableaux vivants, 146, 182
  processions, 17, 54, 130, 145, 150, 158, 159, 182, 191, 261
    network, 149
  town festival, 241

river, 9–11, 31, 165, 166, 168, 178, 256, *see also* transport
  delta, 9, 256
  network, 9, 167, 256, 259
Robert of Aire, 166
Rocamadour, 106
Roeselare, 49
Rome, 66
Ronse, 42, 49
Rotterdam, 44, 46
  urban network, 168
Rupel (river), 118

's-Hertogenbosch
  craft guilds, 118
  gateway, 39
  market, 42, 85, 172, 173
  municipal government, 111
  population, 27
  princely interaction, 112, 113
  religion, 119, 139, 157
  schools, 227, 228
  textile industry, 43
  town accounts, 86, 87, 88, 100, 160
  urban charter, 24
  urban network, 10, 79, 87
  urban society, 198
  urban space, 170
  Vughterdijk, 170
Saint-Omer
  craft guilds, 213
  elite, 64, 109
  gateway, 165
  municipal government, 63
  population, 27
  princely interaction, 105
  textile industry, 45
  town accounts, 63, 99
  urban network, 10, 29, 79
  urban society, 71
Scheldt (river), 10, 22, 27, 31, 32, 37, 40, 79, 160, 165, 218
Schiedam, 138, 168
Schilling, Heinz, 158
Schollaert, Joos, 243
schools
  Bonnefantenschool, 228
  Brethren of the Common Life, 227, 242
  chapter school, 241–2
  convent school, 242
  grammar school, *see* Latin school
  humanist school, 234
  Latin school, 238, 240, 241–4, 245
  monastery school, 224
  municipal school, 20, 222, 242, 243
  parish school, 224, 241

schools (*cont.*)
  private school, 20, 243
  religious school, 158, 159, 178, 188, 226
  scholastic, 224, 242
  schoolbooks, 226, 234–8
  schoolmasters, 148, 154, 223, 224
  Sunday school, 228, 253
  trade school, 20
scientific revolution, 20, 223, 253
Scotland, 47
sea, 256, *see also* transport
  fishing, 29, 43, 57
  harbour, *see* port
  port, 37, 43, 72, 79, 166, 167
  shipping, 37, 167
seigneurie, 7, 11, 73
self-governance, *see* autonomy, municipal
Serlio, Sebastiano, 206
Sersanders, Daneel, 112
Sforza, dynasty, 120
Simons, Walter, 136, 137
Sint-Maartensdijk, 211
Sint-Niklaas, 37
Sint-Truiden, 9, 103, 117, 118
Sittard, 242
Sluis, 29
Smeken, Jan, 149, 150
sociability, 213
  dining culture, 213, 218
society, urban, 60–1, 154, 216, 256, 257
  culture des apparences, 200
  diversity, 62, 83, 128, 169
  harmony, *see* cohesion, social
  social boundaries, 209, 210, 217
  social resilience, 15, 61, 79, 256, 257, 264
  social transgressions, *see* society, urban: social boundaries
  solidarity, 71, 74, 89
  three estates, 61
Soignies, 97
Soly, Hugo, 86
space, urban, 13, 18, 68, 71, 139, 162, 164, 176, 190, 196, 262
  cartography, 163
  marketplace, 96, 132, 262
  meanings of space, 162–3, 173, 182, 190, 191
  mental geography, 174
  morphology, 46
  public sphere, 139, 148, 191
  relocation, 172, 180
  social topography, 71
  spatial turn, 18, 162, 190
  toponymy, 71
Spain, 34, 114, 173, 207
square, 117, 124, 164, 172, 179, 192

Stabel, Peter, 103
stability, social, *see* cohesion, social
standard of living, 85–6, 156, 200, 209, *see also* economy, urban
  cost of living, 80
  golden age of labour, 46
  purchasing power, 48, 84, 85–7, 208, 209, 210
  wages, *see* economy, urban
staple rights, 36–7
Stavoren, 28, 96
Steenvoorde, 156
Stevin, Simon, 248
Surlet, family, 174
Switzerland, 154

Taverne, Ed, 6
tension, social, *see* conflict, social
territory, boundary, 10, 44
territory, princely, 7, 113, 165, 166
territory, urban, 1, 5, 62, 71, 170, 181, 184
  families, 76
textile industry, 22, 29, 42, 47, 49, 77, 79, 87, 90, 137, 155, 168, 174, 201, 210, 226, 229, *see also* economy, urban
  baize, 43
  broadcloth, 36, 39, 203
  cloth, 20, 39, 43, 45, 47, 48, 49, 51, 78, 202
  clothiers, 49, 53, 54, 72, 78, 84, 87
  damask, 43, 203
  decline, 49
  drapery, 49
  drapiers, *see* textile industry:clothiers
  embroidery, *see* art
  fustian, 51, 203
  kerseys, 203
  light draperies, 203
  linen, 36, 39, 43, 51, 54, 78, 87, 210, 214
  quality, 36, 47, 49, 82, 84, 90, 174, 175, 210
  satin, 203
  say, 43, 49
  serge, 156
  silk, 40, 50, 51, 204, 210, 211, 212, 218
  silver or gold brocade, 203
  tapestry, *see* art
  textile, workers, 48
  velvet, 203, 210
  weaving, 87, 110, 112
  wool, 34, 36, 39, 47, 54, 203, 210
  woollen broadcloth, 45
  woollen cloth, 46
The Hague, 31, 178, 198, 211, 246, 258, 263
  De Blauwe Schaar, 198

Index

theatre, 146, 150, 159, 223, 262, *see also* chambers of rhetoric
  competition, 149, 152
  esbattementen, 148
  puys, 147
  sociétés joyeuses, 146
Theoduinus of Liège, 96
Thérouanne, 120, 131
Thierry of Alsace, 147, 166
Thuin, 102, 120
Tiel, 63, 165
Tielt, 36, 89, 145
Tienen, 9, 81, 107, 119, 178
Timback, Gerard, 85
time, urban, 181
  clockwork, 181
Tongeren, 117, 120, 131, 164, 174
Tournai, 180, 245, 249, 263
  art, 49, 50
  belfry, 162, 180, 182
  craft guilds, 117, 177
  elite, 64
  gateway, 131, 164, 165
  middling groups, 149
  municipal government, 63, 109
  population, 27
  princely interaction, 131, 182
  religion, 131, 132, 145, 155, 157, 261
  schools, 228
  textile industry, 43
  town accounts, 90, 97, 131
  urban network, 79, 181
  urban space, 162, 178, 179, 180, 184, 189, 196
Toussaert, Jacques, 142
town–countryside relationship, 22, 29, 31, 33–4, 46, 49, 54, 62, 65–6, 71–2, 74, 81, 156, 166, 183, 217, 257, *see also* agriculture
  cottage industry, 33
  exploitation, 31
  power relations, 31, 36
  proto-industrialisation, 43
  rural industry, 42–3, 72
  surplus extraction, 36
town hall, 18, 96, 100, 119, 121, 162, 175, 177–8, 180, 185, 261
trade, 35, 43, 44, 46, 57, 64, 68, 124, 126, 165, 166, 176, 212, *see also* economy, urban
  agents, 42, 48, 55
  commercial, institutions, 39
  commercial, transactions, 41
  company, commercial, 42
  share-holding, 43
  fair, 40, 42
  international, 44, 54, 56, 257
  interregional, 38–45
  merchant hall, 18, 164, 173–4, 177
  merchants, 14, 21, 38, 48, 54, 55, 59, 62, 64, 68, 69, 72, 83, 84–5, 87, 115, 118, 166, 181, 220, 231, 234, 264
    German Hanse, 40
    hanse, 63
  mother trade, 44
  network, 38
  rich trade, 44
  trading, techniques, 39
  wholesale, 73
trade, maritime, 39, 257, *see also* sea network, 26
transport, 13, 166, 257, *see also* sea; river
  gateway town, 14, 38, 39, 258, 260
  land route, 9, 39
  river, 9, 10, 13, 26–7, 28, 29–30, 31, 32, 34–5, 37, 38, 39, 43, 44, 46, 164, 165, 166, 168, 184, 191
  tolls, 10, 72, 164, 172, 186
  transportation, cost, 50, 257
  water, 174, 179
Trent, 144, 228
Trio, Paul, 144
Turnhout, 152

United Kingdom of the Netherlands, *see* Netherlands
United Provinces, *see* Republic
universities, 20, 30, 226, 232, 234, 240, 241, 243, 244–8, 250, 251, 258
  jurists, 247
  Trilingual College, 250
uprising, urban, *see* revolt, urban
urban history, 1–7
urbanisation, 6, 9, 17, 24, 28, 31, 45, 65, 131–5, 139, 165, 231, 245, 255, 256, 257
  de-urbanisation, 1, 44
  model of the Low Countries, 28, 29, 30, 31, 139, 256
  percentage, 22, 50, 139
  pre-urban nuclei, 169, 170
  process, 17, 22, 28, 30, 31, 32, 38, 45, 47, 57, 62, 65, 71, 79, 131, 139, 151, 169
  ratio, 1, 22, 26, 33, 35, 136
  resilience of the urban system, 9, 31, 81
  social consequences, 71
  suburbanisation, 1
  urban network, 1, 12, 22–31, 49, 60, 79, 149, 256, 258
    competition, 178
  urban potential, 27
  urbanisation ratio, 31

302　Index

Utrecht (prince-bishopric), 186
  art, 148
  religion, 132, 139
Utrecht (town), 144, 263
  Buurkerk, 143
  craft guilds, 56, 70
  Dom, 142
  gateway, 131, 165, 166
  market, 44, 47, 173
  middling groups, 152
  municipal government, 111, 246
  population, 45
  princely interaction, 11, 113, 131
  religion, 136, 146
  schools, 227
  town accounts, 96
  urban society, 142
  urban space, 120, 143, 196

Valenciennes, 28, 50
  art, 147
  belfry, 180
  elite, 73
  Grand Place, 180
  municipal government, 63
  population, 27
  princely interaction, 180
  religion, 137, 145, 155, 156, 157
  schools, 225
  textile industry, 43
  town accounts, 63, 96, 161
  urban space, 170, 180
values and norms, *see* ideology; urban
van Artevelde, Jacob, 113
van Boendale, Jan, 123, 125, 161, 204
van Borssele, family, 72
van Boschuysen, family, 72, 73
Van Bruaene, Anne-Laure, 95
van Buyten, Cornelis, 205
van Campene, Cornelis, 243
van Campene, Philips, 243
van Cotthem, Wein, 125
van Dalem, Andries Pieterszoon, 198
van der Elst, family, 76
van der Elst, Nicolaas, 154
van der Heyden (à Myrica), Gaspar, 250
van der Luere, Boudewijn, 159
van der Molen, family, 55
Van der Wee, Herman, 5, 47, 200
van der Weyden, Rogier, 249
van Deventer, Jacob, 184, 250
Van Dijck, Maarten, 105
van Dixhoorn, Arjan, 151
van Dixmude, Jan, 209
van Dommele, Hector, 227
van Ghistele, Gheeraard, 217

van Hoboken, family, 76
van Immerseel, family, 73
van Leeuwen, Jan, 123
van Leiden, Jan, 155
van Lemego, Johan, 161
van Leyden, Philips, 98
van Lichtervelde, Jacob, 102
van Maerlant, Jacob, 16, 122, 123
van Maldeghem, Arnold, 245
van Mansdale, family, 178
Van Melle, Jan, 119
van Orley, Bernard, 154
van Os, Peter, 160
van Pede, Hendrik, 180
van Poelgeest, family, 73
van Ruusbroec, Jan, 204
van Ruysbroek, Jan, 177
van Schoonbeke, Gilbert, 169
Van Uytven, Raymond, 5, 14
van Werveke, Hans, 5
van Wesele, family, 76, 250
van Zanden, Jan Luiten, 75, 233
van Zwieten, family, 73
vanden Coornhuuse, Gillis, 206
vanden Rake, Jan, 245
Vauchez, André, 128
Veere, 46, 72, 156, 167
Venice, 27, 28, 261
Vercauteren, Ferdinand, 5
Verhoeven, Gerrit, 151
vernacular
  administration, 16, 99–100
  etiquette books, 213, *see also* manners, urban
  handbooks, 237
  instruction books, 223
  literature, 150, 220, 238
  religious texts, 140–1, 153, 237
Verviers, 4
Vesalius, Andreas, 232, 250
Veurne, 29, 132, 172
  Our Lady and Saint Walpurga, Chapter of, 132
Vijd, Joos, 141
Villers, 224
Vilvoorde, 114, 137, 168
violence, 16, 112, 115, 116, 124, 213
Visé, 120
Vives, Juan Luis, 91, 226, 228, 242, 243
Vlissingen, 72, 167, 178
Voorne, 211
vroedschap, 67, 73, *see also* elite, urban

Waal (river), 29
Waas, Land van, 37
Walcheren, 167

Index

Walloon Flanders, 10, 147
Walraversijde, 37
war, 36, 79, 80, 81, 125, 167, 171, 259,
    see also infrastructure, urban:
    town walls; ramparts
  city militia, 59, 72, 100, 263
  factional conflict, 76
  plunder, 81
  siege warfare, 81, 184
  urban demolition, 5, 120
water management, 7, 33, 166, 168–9, 175
  canal house, 199
  canalisation, 33, 46, 164, 166, 167, 256
  drainage, 166
  dyke, 65
  sluice, 166–7
  source of energy, 168
waterway, *see* transport: river
Weber, Max, 4
Weert, 42, 43
weigh house, 18, 164, 171, 173
Wenceslas of Brabant, 112
Wesel, 250
Westkapelle, 72
Westphalia, 35
Willems, Wim, 6
William Clito, 107
William IV of Bavaria, 100
William of Normandy, 12
women, 63, 78–9, 103, 150, 189, 209, 215
  beguines, *see also* religion, urban
  discourse, 125
  education, 79, 242
  gender division, 77, 214
  gender equality, 77
  ideology, 15
  labour, 75, 77, 86
  legal status, 78
  marriage, 75
  patriarchy, 77–9
  servants, 32, 78, 214, 229
  widowhood, 103, 199, 215

Ypres, 123, 167, 168, 174
  art, 148
  belfry, 174
  cloth hall, 115, 162, 174, 176
  craft guilds, 52, 115
  gateway, 165
  market, 30, 37, 172, 174, 258
  middling groups, 210
  municipal government, 91, 106, 109, 174, 176
  population, 27, 80
  religion, 132, 136, 145
  textile industry, 45
  town accounts, 32, 99
  urban network, 10, 28, 29, 79, 113
  urban society, 71, 77
  urban space, 162

Zeeland, 7, 9, 12, 100
  art, 148, 151, 251
  economic development, 33, 34, 46, 57, 65
  elite, 72, 73
  market, 44, 72, 218
  middling groups, 251
  municipal government, 100
  population, 45
  princely interaction, 258, 261
  religion, 132, 135, 139, 150, 156, 158
  urban network, 30, 49, 167
  urban society, 255
Zenne (river), 32
Zierikzee, 46, 135, 138
Zottegem, 37
Zoutleeuw, 9, 90, 96, 107, 110, 119, 149, 174
Zuiderzee, 27, 28, 166
Zuilen, 211
Zutphen, 9, 81, 173
Zwin, 40
Zwolle, 27, 44, 136, 139, 152, 196, 242
  Grote School, 241